# Curriculum for a New Millennium

# Curriculum for a New Millennium

**Wilma S. Longstreet**
*University of New Orleans*

**Harold G. Shane**
*Indiana University*

Allyn and Bacon

Boston    London    Toronto    Sydney    Tokyo    Singapore

**Series Editor:** *Virginia Lanigan*
**Production Administrator:** *Susan McIntyre*
**Editorial-Production Service:** *Ruttle, Shaw & Wetherill, Inc.*
**Cover Administrator:** *Linda Dickinson*
**Cover Designer:** *Suzanne Harbison*
**Composition Buyer:** *Linda Cox*
**Manufacturing Buyer:** *Megan Cochran*

Copyright © 1993 by Allyn & Bacon
A Division of Simon & Schuster, Inc.
160 Gould Street
Needham Heights, MA 02194

**Library of Congress Cataloging-in-Publication Data**

Longstreet, Wilma S.
  Curriculum for a new millennium / Wilma S. Longstreet, Harold G.
Shane.
    p.    cm.
  Includes bibliographical references and index.
  ISBN 0–205–13966–3
  1. Curriculum planning—United States.   2. Curriculum change—
United States.   3. Education—United States—Curricula—History.
I. Shane, Harold Gray, 1914–   . II. Title.
  LB2806.15.L66   1992
  375′.00973—dc20                                          92–31356
                                                              CIP

Printed in the United States of America

10  9  8  7  6  5  4  3  2  1     96  95  94  93  92

# Contents

## II.  Anticipating Tomorrow

## 9  Futures Studies: Fathoming a New Millennium    159

**15    The Changing Language Arts and Foreign Language Curricula: Emerging Needs for Improved Communication Skills    289**

# Preface

Designing the school's curriculum requires both insight and foresight. We need to understand our past and the nature of its influence on our educational practice today; also we need to confront our current problems as well; but most important for our children and the quality of their adult lives, we need to be informed about probable futures even while understanding that the most certain phenomenon our children will face is uncertainty itself.

Allowing our children to remain essentially ignorant of the challenges ahead is the equivalent of allowing the haphazard course of technology and a still-accelerating explosion of knowledge to take over the directions of their future and lead them where they might not otherwise wish to go. The risk is loss of any control over the world of tomorrow.

In this context, all of us, students and professionals alike, must strive to develop an educational philosophy for the future as well as our own personal image of what we want that future to become. We owe our children the knowledge and skills necessary to shape their own lives in the decades ahead and a broad and substantial foundation for reflecting on the complex problems and judgments they will surely face and the decisions they will surely make in the midst of substantial uncertainty. Educators planning curricula need to incorporate more fully into their work the social, cultural, economic, political, and analogous trends, suggestions, and research likely to impact on the nature of the events of the next century.

We seek in this book to suggest a number of different approaches to curriculum design that would open up the possibilities of what is studied and how it is studied in the schools. In addition, we have looked at the realities of our current elementary and secondary curricula and prospects exist for new directions even within our traditional models of instruction.

We have examined periods of dramatic change in history as well as the cultural inertia that currently afflicts our schools. We have tried to explore those aspects of our lives today that have rendered our future uniquely different from any of the futures our ancestors of preceding centuries experienced. In this regard, we have dealt with such concepts as intragenerational disjunctures, experience compression, and hyperturbulence, all unique to our times and clearly making urgent future relevant curriculum planning. While we have sought to develop a background for those new to the field of curriculum, we have also tried to establish the bases for viewing the design and implementation of curriculum from nontraditional perspectives and in ways new to many professional educators.

We know we have barely scratched the surface. It is for the reader to extend what we have initiated.

In ending this preface, we wish to thank our spouses, Catherine McKenzie Shane and Shirley Engle, for their support and tireless efforts to improve this work. They read countless drafts, proofed our many pages, and showed patience and kindness as we devoted all of our spare time to completion of the manuscript.

We also wish to take this opportunity to thank our reviewers, Steven Thornton, Bonnie Handler, Don Reyes, James Sears, Richard Isaf, and Dan Riordan. They were insightful and constructive in their comments, and this work is the better for their efforts.

*Wilma S. Longstreet*
*Harold G. Shane*

# The Educational Past: Shaping the Present

## Introduction

Lamenting the state of education and asserting the need for change have become as ubiquitous in the media as talk of the weather. Still, education has remained remarkably unchanged throughout the twentieth century. Moreover, even though the U.S. Constitution places the responsibility for education squarely on the shoulders of individual state governments, the face of the curriculum is nearly the same in all fifty states. Most high school students take four years of English, two to three years of science, two to three years of mathematics, three years of social studies, and two years of a modern foreign language. Most elementary school curricula are dominated by the language arts and introductory arithmetic. Social studies, science, music, and art are typically present but are not central in the elementary program, and the amount of time devoted to these subjects often depends on the teacher's areas of interest.

The similarities among school programs extend to the actual studies pursued under each subject. Take biology as an example. Among the very first topics studied is the amoeba, followed by ____? (Can you remember?) The paramecium! Several generations of youngsters, including the present one, can recall drawing the weird "mouth" of the paramecium and the strange cilia around the perimeter. In English, Shakespeare's *Julius Caesar* or *Romeo and Juliet* may be studied as early as the ninth grade, whereas American literature, which offers a simpler form of language for youngsters, is delayed until the tenth or eleventh grade. Instruction in grammar typically begins in the fifth grade, while learning to read is introduced in kindergarten and even earlier.

It is really quite extraordinary that in a vast, pluralistic nation such as the United States, which has historically been without a national mandate for the conduct of education, the curriculum is essentially the same everywhere and has been so for most of the twentieth century. We have witnessed the most astounding progress in the history of humankind, from the invention of airplanes and walks on the moon to the genetic manipulation of life and the still immeasurable impact of television on how we relate to each other. Nevertheless, the curriculum is taught much as it was when the recommendations were made by the influential Committee of Ten in the 1890s.

The organization and administration of our public schools have also remained basically the same. For example, there are two tiers of grades: elementary and secondary. The junior high school (grades 7, 8, and 9) or the middle school (grades 4, 5, 6, and 7 or 5, 6, 7, and 8) may or may not be present in a system's organization. Each grade represents approximately 180 school days. The superintendent heads the school administration, which is hierarchical in nature; that is, the assistant superintendents report to the superintendent; the principals report to the assistant superintendents; the teachers report to the principals; and the students, who are at the lowest rung of the hierarchy, report to the teachers. It is an organization that reflects rather closely the way factories were organized during the heyday of mass production.

As we face a new millennium, changes in our way of life continue to accelerate. Knowledge continues its proverbial "explosion" unabated, and the decisions we must make about what is most important for children to learn have become increasingly complex. The generally static state of education and its curriculum is a continuing contradiction to the changes and growing uncertainty that surround us.

For the professional educator, the question is how to direct the activities of our schools and their curricula so that greater relevancy between what we do and what we hope to do, and the realities of our circumstances can be achieved. This book is designed to help the professional educator think about schooling and the crucial importance of taking command of the curriculum and its directions. First it serves as an introduction to the study of curriculum and its potential contributions to the future of our young. It pursues the significant disparities in goals, practices, and curriculum designs that separate our elementary from our secondary schools and our schooling from the future we hope to achieve. It seeks to build new conceptions of the curriculum and new ways of educating our young, even while taking into account the profound resistance to educational change long exhibited by the schools.

This work further explores the potential impact of futures research on the design, development, and implementation of the curriculum. We believe long-range planning for the education of the young will improve the quality and relevance of their education. However, our collective visions of what the future "will" or "should" be have hardly kept pace with the technological developments of the twentieth century. Futures that appeared to be science fiction only a few decades ago are today's realities. There is every reason to believe that the twenty-first century will be equally full of unimaginable realities. Bringing futures research and long-range planning into curriculum development is a way of coming to terms with a future our young must confront and we can hardly conceive.

First, however, we will start with the past and try to understand how we have come to be where we are now. There is much to be learned from our past in terms of both constructive insights and the mistakes that we hope to avoid as we build new educational futures.

## In the Beginning

To be educated is a natural human proclivity. To understand and to become more competent are goals that all of us experience throughout our lives. As we come together in our social groupings and share not only our interests but also our needs, a system of education tends to evolve—one that fosters our ability to respond and control the world around us.

In the simpler social groupings of prehistoric times, instruction was likely to be based on apprenticeships such as taking part in a hunt or preparing tools. More formal instruction, when it appeared thousands of years ago, revolved around the child's initiation into adulthood and into the group's religion. As in ancient Judea, this initiation involved a kind of knowledge that could not simply be observed; it required abstract insights about the community's beliefs as well as the community's approval of what was to be taught.

There are no historical records indicating how education was first provided to the young, so we can only imagine how it was. It is reasonable, however, to assume that as the social grouping became larger and more complex, instruction by apprenticeship and imitation became inadequate for the needs of society. The Sumerians, who had the first organized education system in recorded history, based their instruction on memorizing and copying in the cuneiform script. Reading, writing, surveying the land, farming, and tool making were among the first steps taken in ancient times toward the educational complexity we know today.

In early historic times when only a few individuals needed to acquire more advanced and abstract forms of knowledge, the vast majority learned by informal apprenticeship while only a small minority received formal schooling. The records show that instruction was based mostly on memorization, and motivation was induced by harsh, physical discipline. For example, archeologists found an ancient Egyptian clay tablet on which a child had written: "Thou didst beat me and knowledge entered my head." Religion, war, trade, and government were among the factors providing initial impetus for developing formal educational systems.

The Jews in early times were possibly the first group to insist that children, regardless of class, be educated so that they all could practice their religious beliefs with an understanding that would bring them closer to God. Girls were generally excluded from formal instruction, but they were taught to read by their parents presumedly so they could learn the laws of their religion. Synagogues were places for education as well as worship. The Jews established elementary schools for boys from ages six to thirteen, and if a young man chose to pursue his studies, he then became the disciple of a rabbi or "teacher."

## The European Roots

### The Hellenic and Roman Periods

In the ancient Greek city-states, the goal of education was to prepare children for citizenship. In Athens, this meant studying philosophy and the arts. In Sparta, military skills were deemed more important because the young were to become soldier-citizens. In fact, young boys were required to leave home for training under military officers. From age 7 to 18, they were subjected to rigorous physical training and were taught to endure pain. At 18, they became military cadets and were schooled in the art of war.

The question of whether women should be educated was debated in Athens during the lifetime of Socrates. It was his student, Plato, who felt that women of the ruling class should receive the same education as men. However, few Greek males supported Plato's views. For the most part, public education for women was a rarity in the Western world before the nineteeth century.

The Greeks, especially the Athenians, had a profound impact on Roman education, even though the Romans were the military conquerors of the Greeks. Originally, the Roman father taught his son how to read and about the law, history, and customs of his heritage. The art of oratory was considered especially important not only for government but also in the practice of commerce.

Schooling away from home and the introduction of books as a central element of instruction were changes shaped by the Greeks. Young Roman boys and girls were sent to the public elementary school regardless of their socioeconomic class, although a small payment was required from their parents. They studied reading, writing, and counting. Around the age of 12 or 13, youngsters from the upper classes would attend a "grammar" school, where they studied both Latin and Greek grammar and literature. Only the boys could expect to go beyond the primary grades. At 16, those wishing a career in public service would attend "rhetoric" school where most of the teachers were Greek.

Both the Romans and the Greeks believed that education would ultimately lead to good citizenship. The qualities they attributed to such an end differed significantly. For the Greeks, it meant preparing the well-rounded individual in such curricular realms as art, music, science, and gymnastics. For the Romans, it meant preparing youngsters to engage in commerce and public service, which led, educationally, to an emphasis on public speaking and literature. It should be noted that literature was studied primarily as a means to improve one's public speaking skills.

The emphasis on grammar and rhetoric that typified Roman education was to influence European education for centuries after the fall of the Roman Empire in 476 A.D. Indeed, Latin remained the language of commerce and scholarship throughout the Middle Ages. Nevertheless, had it not been for the Catholic clergy and their monasteries, what we now refer to as Western learning might never have survived the fifth century. Except for the cathedral, monastic, and palace schools, formal schooling for the populace-at-large all but disappeared in the early Middle Ages.

## The Medieval Period

Although grammar and rhetoric remained central to the medieval curriculum, the reasons for studying these subjects changed fundamentally. Students learned to read Latin so that they could contemplate the Scriptures and better prepare themselves for God's service and the afterlife; they studied simple mathematics so that they could calculate the dates of religious festivals; and they studied music so that they could take part in church services. On the other hand, physical education was repressed as a part of an unclean, earthly world that was ultimately to be left behind.

The rise of universities toward the end of the Middle Ages marked a significant turning point in the development of Western education. On the surface, the curriculum does not appear to be radically different from that of the early Medieval period. There was a two-tier division: the first level was the preparatory *trivium* comprised of grammar, rhetoric, and logic, and the more advanced level was the *quadrivium* including arithmetic, geometry, music, and astronomy. However, during the twelfth century, Latin translations of Aristotle's works became increasingly available and his analytical methods became widely known in the scholarly community. Unlike Plato, who had sought understanding and insight from an ideal world beyond the confines of the earth, Aristotle sought insight from the analytical study of this world. He also believed that rationality was the basis of all knowledge.

The very earliest foundations of experimental science were set forth with the rise of universities—the new academic centers of their day—which were quite different from the church-based monasteries where education had been lodged for centuries. Coherent systems of philosophy, theology and jurisprudence, known as scholasticism, were developed during the flowering of this period, between the tenth and fifteenth centuries. At the crux of scholasticism was understanding the nature of the relationship that presumedly needed to exist between faith and reason. The ascendency of Aristotelian thought represents the beginning of the movement away from otherworldly idealism to a concentration on the ways of this world. This was the age of chivalry when young men living at court learned poetry, manners, and dance and engaged in the development of their battle skills and physical prowess. It was also the age when craftsmen throughout Europe organized guilds to protect the pricing of their goods as well as to supervise the training of apprentices. The essence of the Renaissance is clearly apparent.

On the surface, the curriculum of the Renaissance does not appear to be very different. The seven subjects of the *trivium* and the *quadrivium* were supplemented by studies in history and physical education. However, what people expected as outcomes of their study modified radically. After nearly a thousand years of studying grammar as an end in itself, grammar began to be studied as a means of gaining access to literature; astronomy became clearly separated from astrology; and there was a growing emphasis on understanding nature and the human body.

## Developments after 1500 A.D.

The increasing worldliness of the Catholic Church, its wealth and continued sale of indulgences, were at the crux of Martin Luther's Ninety-Five Theses, posted on the door of the Castle Church in Wittenberg on October 31, 1517. It signaled in Europe the end of the dominance of the Catholic Church as well as the rise of a new political order based on powerful nation-states, whose power, notably, did not come from the Church. The Protestant Reformation rejected the priest as middleman between the believer and God, a development that led to the reconceptualization of the purposes of education. If the faithful were to interact directly with God, they needed a personally based understanding of the Scriptures. The Bible was translated from the traditional Latin and Greek into German by Luther and into English in the 1611 King James version. This, in turn, meant education had to be made available to rich and poor alike. It was in Luther's native Germany that the institutionalization of universal education first took hold.

As the ideal of universal education grew in the European's consciousness, it was inevitable that childhood and how children learn would take on a new importance in scholarly discourse. Throughout the Middle Ages, children were conceived to be "little adults." Seven-year-old children would do adult work as best they could. In the monastic schools of the day, a sixteen-year-old and a six-year-old were likely to be seated side by side in the same class. While it was not until the eighteenth century that childhood was recognized as a set of experiences distinct from adulthood, the effects of universal education on European educational thought were already apparent in the 1600s.

John Amos Comenius (1592–1670) was one of the first scholars to link the success of education to the unique qualities of childhood. Effective education for Comenius had to take the nature of the child into account. Education, he said, needed to begin with the actual experiences that children had rather than with the perception of children as miniature adults who could learn as adults do. The dreary methods of memorization and harsh discipline that had typified schooling for centuries led Comenius to characterize the schools as "the slaughter-houses of the mind." Instruction needed to begin with children observing either actual objects or models and pictures of them. In fact, Comenius published the first textbook in the history of Western education to have illustrations for children to look at. *Orbis Pictus* (translation, *The World in Pictures*) was at first ridiculed but was ultimately to be widely used by schools for two hundred years.

The English philosopher John Locke (1632–1704) focused the attention of the scholarly world on how learning occurs. The child's mind was likened to a blank tablet, lacking any innate knowledge but possessing a number of faculties for learning such as perceiving, discriminating, comparing, and recalling. For Locke, learning was the product of exercising these faculties on the raw material of sense impression derived from experiencing the objects of the real world. Otherworldly conceptions of education were clearly abandoned because Locke insisted on first-hand experience. The objects of the world were deemed crucial to what children learn.

In a sense, Jean Jacques Rousseau (1712–1778) was the spiritual descendent of Comenius for he, too, saw childhood as a set of unique experiences qualitatively different from those of adulthood. To treat a child as though he or she were an adult was to ignore the innate goodness of the child and the qualities unique to each individual learner. The potential for good living was already in the child, and education needed to allow this innate potential to develop. For Rousseau, the theory of "mental faculties" and the schools' efforts to develop these in all children in uniform fashion ignored the individuality of children and their innate potential. Indeed, Rousseau questioned the usefulness of formal schooling prior to the age of fifteen. Although his views have survived centuries of educational debate, they have never really been in the mainstream of educational development. Ironically, shortly after his death, Prussia established the first centrally controlled school system in the modern Western world.

While emphasis on religous learning had faded in importance, during the Renaissance the idea of universal education continued to gain prominence. There was, in this Age of Enlightenment, a deep belief that knowledge should be available to all and that the exercise of God-given reason would lead to the truth about the nature of man and his universe. Among scholars, there was a denial of miracles and revelation and a sincere effort to avoid the superstitions of antiquity. The spirit of scientific inquiry and a growing sense that one's own religion should not be forced on others permeated the thought if not the politics of the day, which evolved more slowly. Furthermore, a new continent had been discovered and waited to be settled.

## The Curriculum: The Captive of Cultural Mindsets

### Resistance to Change

In this abbreviated review of our European educational past, the impact of tradition, or what may also be called "cultural mindset," on the nature of the school's curriculum is evident. While the purposes of schooling changed fundamentally, the curriculum changed hardly at all. The Roman Empire fell and public speaking became, at best, irrelevant. Nevertheless, rhetoric and grammar, along with Latin, remained central in most curricula of the era. Of course, the rationale for studying such content was linked to the reading of the Scriptures. The Middle Ages saw the rise of scholasticism and a renewed concern with worldly issues. Although subjects were added to the curriculum, the mainstays of study remained Latin, rhetoric, and grammar. The purposes shifted somewhat to include classical studies, which were in no way related to Christian religious principles. By the end of the Middle Ages, Latin was no longer the dominant language of commerce. Nonetheless, throughout the Renaissance and the Age of Enlightenment and even during the notable rise of science and industry, the schools clung to Latin grammar and rhetoric in the curriculum.

To say that schools were for centuries stagnant and unable to become relevant to their times is to state the obvious. A like statement could be made of our own times in the United States. Today we are experiencing a similar kind of cultural inertia even though we have spent vast amounts of energy and resources to achieve change. The conundrum remains as to why the curriculum has been so unyielding to clearly needed changes. No certain answer exists but there is room for both analysis and speculation.

As societies pass their traditions on to the young, they embed deeply in the psyches of the young the expectations and behaviors of their culture. Furthermore, they do so long before the young are capable of evaluating rationally what they are learning. The traditions and the past on which these traditions rest are learned powerfully but hardly with consciousness. The educated elders of the Middle Ages as well as of the Renaissance and the Age of Enlightenment expected a curriculum based on Latin, rhetoric, and grammar. They found new educational purposes to support their expectations. In a sense, both the present and the future are captives of the past. This is not to say that nothing new develops, but rather that clear purposes and rational analyses do not appear sufficient to bring major change to long-standing societal institutions such as education represents.

## Vectors of Change

There are moments in history when the complex elements involved in change are so profound that the usually gradual course of cultural change is overwhelmed and a new cultural order, a sudden turning, or "vector," develops so swiftly that the traditional institutions no longer fulfill their functions. A great divide between the past and present arises in the form of a vast cultural gap. Certainly, the fall of the Roman Empire in 476 A.D. was one such period; the Reformation was possibly another. A vector of change represents such a marked departure of the present from the past as to be tantamount to a "system break," rendering many long-standing traditions ineffectual. This does not mean that the traditions disappear, but that they may continue to exist either without purpose or without meeting the purposes for which they were first developed.

## Forces Shaping American Education

The Colonial period in American history was characterized by a series of far-reaching cultural changes that are still in the process of unfolding at the end of the twentieth century. The magnitude of change that the American nation has witnessed in the past century has had no precedent in history. Imagine coming to a new land, metaphorically speaking, that is light-years away from the cities, towns, and countryside you had previously come to know. You left a homeland in the throes of Reformation, perhaps seeking the right to practice your religion, or to gain economic advantage, or quite possibly both. You came to a vast wilderness bringing your values and traditions which were already under stress and weakening in Europe.

Initially, it is likely that your group tried to establish institutions that resembled those of its past. Puritans, for instance, attempted to establish universal education because, as with many Protestant sects, education was seen as a means for coming closer to God. In fact, in 1642, Massachusetts, dominated by the Puritans, passed a law requiring that all children be taught to read so that they could gain knowledge of the Scriptures. Five years later, with the devil as its target, the "Old Deluder Satan Act" was passed requiring every town of 50 or more families to establish an elementary school. In addition, if there were at least 100 families, a grammar school had to be established. The colorful name of the Act reflected its purpose, namely, to defeat Satan's efforts to keep people from reading the Scriptures.

Although the attainment of moral purposes typified the goals of most colonial school curricula, it was not long before the realities of a new continent, along with the rise of individualism and the burgeoning commercialism that it engendered, reshaped the purposes and form of education. Practical content was soon a steady component of school study. Nonetheless, the tradition of the Latin grammar school curriculum persisted. Even the Academy, established by Benjamin Franklin in 1751 to offer more practical schooling, maintained the traditional Latin rhetoric and grammar as part of its offerings. However, the Academy did offer subjects such as history, geography, merchant accounts, modern languages, and surveying. The diversification of the curriculum introduced in the Academy and the efforts to meet practical needs were the first signs of a truly new curricular order.

The Revolutionary War and the period that followed were not supportive of public education, and, for the most part, the curriculum was still dominated by an increasingly irrelevant Latin grammar school curriculum. Then, in 1816, the British infant school was established in Boston. Its adoption marked a reawakening of public interest in education. It also marked the acceptance of the idea that primary education including reading, writing, singing, playing, and generally learning to get along with others was properly supported by public funds. The infant school eventually provided a foundation for the primary grades of our current elementary schools.

Academies, supported mostly by private funds, also grew substantially in numbers. Unfettered by state restrictions, these academies were able to offer their students new kinds of studies, and the 1800s was a period of significant curricular experimentation at the secondary level. Indeed, by the middle of the century, diversification of the curriculum characterized virtually all American secondary schools. Needless to say, the universities were distressed by the diversity in preparation of the students who were admitted to their courses.

The report of the National Education Association's Committee of Ten, issued in 1893, established college entrance requirements and effectively ended much of the curricular experimentation that had characterized most of the nineteenth century. While the introduction of the infant school brought curricular innovation to the primary grades, elementary education had changed little in this period. The "stabilizing" of the secondary curriculum ultimately had its impact on the elementary curriculum, especially in what are now grades 4 to 6, for these were the grades that were to prepare youngsters for the secondary schools. The domino effect on the elementary curriculum of college entrance requirements has increased steadily throughout the twentieth century. The introduction of different number bases in the study of elementary mathematics and the increasingly experimental approach to the study of science are illustrative of the impact that secondary and college level studies have had on the elementary curriculum. Admittedly, the influences have been somewhat haphazard and may have even aggravated our confusion over what we expect from the elementary schools.

### The Emergence of State-Supported Education and the Common School

The nineteenth century saw American education come into its own with the establishment of state-supported secular schools for all children. As a consequence, educators were faced with the challenge of developing an appropriate curriculum to serve youngsters of diverse socioeconomic backgrounds. Quite naturally, a central problem was determining what knowledge should be studied by all. The answer was hotly debated back in the 1830s even as it is today.

The common school movement gained impetus when Massachusetts established a Board of Education in 1837 under the leadership of Horace Mann (1796–1859). By the end of the century, the common-school system was firmly established throughout the United States, and there was growing support for state-financed higher education.

### Contributions from European Educators

During the common-school era, the professionals in American schools looked to Europe for guidance. Mann, for instance, studied the Prussian school organization and imported much of it to the Massachusetts school system. Before free schools for all were established, the monitorial system, largely devised by a British schoolmaster, John Lancaster, was introduced in the United States, and proved to be popular among the city school systems because 200 or more students could be taught by one teacher and several well-informed student "monitors." Oddly enough, at least from a twentieth century perspective, the monitorial system was thought to be well suited to the elementary schools since it was believed children learned best by memorizing in small groups organized according to ability, and student monitors were all that was necessary for such a simple activity.

Even though American educators often accepted the leadership of Europeans, the nineteenth century European elementary school still resembled the schools of the sixteenth, seventeenth, and eighteenth centuries. Beating, bullying, and ridiculing were the typical methods of maintaining control over children who had to be forced to memorize and recite. Widespread written reactions in Europe to the educational abuse of children affected American schooling. Charles Dickens's words eloquently describe the feelings of many toward the schools' methodologies: ". . . childhood with its beauty gone and only its helplessness remaining."[1]

Even though Mann had instituted the first teacher preparation program in the United States, how to instruct large numbers of children effectively within the context of free, universal education remained a major concern for American schools. To find ways of teaching more effectively and humanely was a source of scholarly discussion on both sides of the Atlantic. The schools and methods of

Swiss national Johann Heinrich Pestalozzi (1746–1827), very much in the vein of Comenius's writings a century and a half earlier, attracted thousands of visitors from Europe and the United States. They saw children who were excited about learning, involved in firsthand observations, preparing to learn how to read by playing with letter blocks, and generally enjoying themselves. For Pestalozzi, the teacher's job was to guide children through their natural development, helping them to direct their experiences toward the realm of ideas. The curricular emphasis was not on the memorization of subject matter, but on the selection of experiences that would foster the child's understanding and intellectual growth.

Among Pestalozzi's followers was Fredrich Wilhelm Froebel (1782–1852), who is best known as the founder of the kindergarten. Like Pestalozzi, with whom he studied, Froebel believed that learning occurred best through activities sustained by the interests of the child. The kindergarten was to provide an open environment with materials designed to encourage appropriate learning. Blocks of different shapes and sizes encouraged children to measure, count, compare, and contrast. To develop motor coordination, children engaged in drawing, coloring, modeling, and sewing.

Another of Pestalozzi's admirers was the German philosopher and psychologist Johann Friedrich Herbart (1776–1841). Unlike Froebel, he did not think learning was achieved through a natural unfolding of the mind. Nor did he believe, as Locke had proposed, that training preexisting faculties of the mind resulted in learning and an educated individual. Instead, he construed the subjects to be the building blocks of education and teachers were the builders. It was up to the teacher to form the child's mind. Presumably, this was to be done through the teaching of history, science, and mathematics, subjects that were assumed to be the products of the collective culture. The problem for Herbart was how to present knowledge to children so that it could be understood rather than memorized by rote. Teachers were expected to be professional and knowledgeable in developing effective instructional methodologies.

While the ideas of Comenius, Pestalozzi, and Froebel had a substantial impact on American educational thought, the rise of state-supported, universal schooling favored systematic lesson plans, record-keeping, and scope and sequence charts associated with Herbart's views, the nineteenth century Prussian school organization, and the legacy of the Lancasterian monitorial system. Pestalozzi emphasized the uniqueness and individuality of youngsters; Herbart, on the other hand, emphasized the commonality of cultural knowledge and urged that an intellectual milieu be created to facilitate and perpetuate this knowledge. Herbart's work held the promise that a systematic method of instruction could be developed—one that was the same for all youngsters. It was an approach that proved to be compatible with the growing bureaucracy of state-sponsored education.

The rise of the large city school district contributed to the increasing power of the educational bureaucracy. The explosive growth of the cities and the severity of inner-city problems have increased the complexity of instructional and curricular decision making, and tend to lead toward more dependence on organizational and bureaucratic leadership. Accelerating change was further exacerbated by the great migratory waves pouring into the United States from Eastern and Central Europe. If the new immigrants were to be suited for the factories that desperately needed their labor, they had to learn how to function under the typical system of factory operation. Faith in science and industry also supported the factory-like bureaucracy that has become the hallmark of most American school systems in the twentieth century.

## The Great Divide: Vectors of Change, 1890–1940

### The Impact of Change

The history of the twentieth century has involved sustained and far-reaching changes in social, political, economic, and moral traditions the world over. The present and the future have become linked in an ongoing surge of knowledge.

For most developed nations, the cultural upheavals associated with an industrial society started as early as the mid to late 1800s. Conversely, the great cultural divide is only now beginning to reach many Third World nations. The United States has struggled throughout this century to work out new kinds of social arrangements that would function appropriately with innovations in the realm of electronic media, industrial production, farming technology, and the conditions of daily living.

Public education has shared this struggle. Nowhere has the struggle been greater than in our efforts as educators to create a nurturing, albeit relevant, environment for the development of our young. The rise of curriculum as a professional field reflects this profound involvement of education in what may be called "the great divide," a change of such magnitude that it is unprecedented in recorded history.

### Changing Lifestyle: A Twentieth Century Phenomenon

To understand both the rate and the extent of the changes that took place in a single lifetime, as well as their impact on schooling, it is helpful to look back to the turn of the century. What was the United States like in 1900?

If you skimmed through a pictorial history of the era, you probably would be struck first by the use of muscle power rather than machines. This is reflected in the number of horses pictured in the act of pulling ice wagons, mail wagons, buggies, and farm equipment. It was a time in which perhaps no more than half of our population had ever seen an automobile! Only 13,824 cars were licensed in the America of 1900, and the first auto to cross the Mississippi didn't appear until 1899, when it was exhibited at a fair in Emporia, Kansas. Ironically, the auto was obliged to make the last of its journey aboard a train, which hauled it from Chicago to keep it from breaking down on the rough gravel and dirt roads of the era.

Social life, as described in contemporary accounts, was rigidly controlled. Young ladies led a sheltered existence and were chaperoned in urban centers or kept under parental surveillance on the farm. Bars and even the smoking cars on trains were off-limits, and "nice" girls, it was assumed, would help around the house until a suitor appeared. A stolen kiss was tantamount to a proposal, and many women entered marriage with no understanding of sex and occasionally even harbored the idea that physical relations with their husbands was a nasty necessity. The mores at the turn of the century also held divorce to be a catastrophe, and there were elderly couples who for years never exchanged a word—unfortunates living out a cobra-and-mongoose relationship in a state of shared hate, yet who never dreamed of separating, let alone seeking a divorce.

The vast majority of homes had no electricity, and hence had no refrigerators, washers, or similar appliances. Telephones were few and awkward to use. Indoor bathrooms were rare and, as the week progressed, many increasingly smelled of sweat and soil until the once-a-week, Saturday night bath in a claw-foot tub temporarily restored personal cleanliness. Because of primitive plumbing and poverty, supplies of hot water were limited. Children in some families took turns bathing in a single tubful, with a series of brownish rings appearing on the white enamel as one after another splashed about. The first movie to be produced was still some years off, radio would not appear for nearly twenty years, and no magazine had reached the million mark in circulation, so there was little to do but go to bed after that Saturday bath!

### City Size and Transportation

A glance at yesterday in retrospect also reminds us how small the cities were. In 1900 Los Angeles had just passed the 100,000 mark, and bustling Houston could claim no more than 45,000 residents. While New York City could boast of one building that soared past the 300-foot mark, it had yet to complete a subway and had just replaced steam engines with electric cars on its elevated railways.

Speaking of transportation, almost everyone sought to find a home within walking distance of a trolley stop, and neighborhoods were dotted with stores and shops to which women walked with wicker market baskets that could be filled to overflowing for no more than 50 cents. The contents of these baskets, by the way, would appall today's diet- and health-conscious American. Meat, potatoes, and bread were staples from October to April, an interval during which fresh vegetables and fruits were unavailable. In part, this was due to the transportation system, which, in combination with low wages, kept items such as citrus fruits in the luxury class during all seasons.

### Wages

The typical American earned less than $500 per year in 1900—roughly $2000 in purchasing power today, if we allow for the diminished value of the present dollar. But the most striking feature on the economic scene was the income differential between the very rich and the average worker. Social historian Frederick Lewis Allen calculated that Andrew Carnegie's personal income in 1900 "was . . . well over

23 million dollars—with no income taxes to pay." This would have been close to 100 million dollars in the late 1980s, again allowing for inflation, although Carnegie's net gain today would be subsequently reduced by taxes.

The past without modern media is a distant and strange past that survives mostly through oral and written history and through our imagination. How different from the past of the 1950s and 1960s, a past that we all can still experience in movies, television sitcoms, radio, and audio recordings. The past is much more a part of our present and our future than was ever possible before. This, too, is a fundamentally new phenomenon, for even while we are changing rapidly, because of technology, we are better able to view and experience the change. Indeed, rapid change itself has become a way of life.

## The Great Immigrations and Their Impact on American Life

Perhaps the most unique characteristic of this period—and one with important implications for the curriculum—was the continued immigration of Europeans to the United States. It has been estimated that some 60,000,000 immigrants came to North America between 1821 and 1932. At the turn of the century, immigration into the United States was at an annual peak of 1,500,000 persons. For the most part, the newcomers of this period were from Central and Southern Europe. Unlike earlier immigrants, they spoke little or no English and followed customs and traditions that were very different from those of the people already living in the United States. The poverty that many of the immigrants had known in Europe has few if any parallels in American history. For the most part, the newcomers were immediately better off on their arrival, although at the outset, they were almost all among America's "have-nots." They manned America's industries and took over the lowliest of service jobs. One of the most striking images of immigrants in 1900 was the outdoor marketplace, such as Bathegate Avenue in New York City, packed with pushcarts and stands, filled with poorly dressed European peasants shouting the prices of their wares to passersby.

The immigrants usually had numerous offspring and provided a vital source of labor for the phenomenal growth of American industries. While the changes brought about by technology were profound, those caused by the huge immigration of Europe's poor were no less influential. They contributed mightily to the sense of upheaval and loss of social direction that developed even while the gains of business and science became more visible and more impressive. The immigrants brought their labor, their enthusiasm and creativity, their cultural differences, and all of the problems likely to arise when large segments of the resident population are essentially displaced.

The cultural adjustments were many, and the schools were expected to help prepare the immigrants and their children for the "new life" they had chosen. This new life, however, was itself in the midst of readjustment, and directions were frequently unclear. In the face of all these difficulties, the need to plan new curricula grew in urgency and complexity.

For all citizens, whether immigrants or residents going back for generations, changes came fast and furiously. The values that had been inculcated during their childhood of the 1890s or the 1920s or even the 1940s functioned poorly in an environment that continued to be revolutionized. The great divide that technology had wrought between the eighteenth and nineteenth centuries on the American continent, in the twentieth century became a divide between the upbringing of one's childhood and the realities of one's adult life.

## Intragenerational Disjuncture

The human propensity for questioning and evaluation throughout history has led the younger generation to scrutinize the efforts of previous generations and to institute change. Customarily, the older generations have viewed such change with skepticism. However, there is a profound difference between the change of past centuries and that of the twentieth century. Up to the turn of this century, the accelerating pace of change appears to have been within limits that would allow for reasonable continuity between one's childhood and the adult world. By 1929, to use the words of Alfred North Whitehead, technology had brought us to "the first period in human history in which it could not be assumed that each generation will live in an environment substantially similar to that of the preceding generation."[2] Langer, Whitehead's student, expressed a sense of being ". . . swept along in a violent passage from a world we cannot salvage to one we cannot see,"[3] and in the 1970s, Lester R. Brown noted, ". . . we are making decisions on the basis of a world that existed at some time in the past."[4]

These observations are educationally significant. After all, parents and teachers can prepare children only for an environment they themselves understand. It is all well and good to teach a reasonable measure of flexibility to children. However, to teach flexibility when confronting unknown futures, including some that may be abhorent to adults, is beyond the realm of reason. Furthermore, the accumulated traditions and the imbedded cultural heritage of one's earliest childhood cannot be simply dismissed at will. What purposes can education serve under such circumstances? What are the implications for instruction and curriculum development in our schools?

Technology has changed so rapidly in the twentieth century that individuals who are adjusted to one set of beliefs and norms find themselves in a situation in which the norms are simply not organically related to their technologically changed environment. It is no longer merely the generation gap; it has become an *intra*generational disjuncture in which the cultural underpinnings of one's childhood upbringing become inoperative and even confusing to the decision-making processes of one's adulthood.

First we must clarify the significance of intragenerational disjuncture with a concrete example such as a cultural group's native language. Imagine that our native tongue is in a period of accelerating change and that we are native speakers who have learned our language well—as do virtually all children by the time they are four or five. So long as the changes occur gradually, we can assimilate them easily. Now suppose the rate of change continues to accelerate and reaches a pace with which we can no longer keep up. The language we learned as children no longer functions adequately in our adulthood. It is still our native language and deeply embedded in our way of thinking and being, but it is no longer the basic language of the culture. Furthermore, we discover that others are in the same predicament, and the steps they have taken to accommodate these new linguistic circumstances are different from the ones we have taken. So even our "flexibility" is not terribly helpful.

Thankfully, this extreme example is unrealistic and serves only to put into stark relief the effects that an accelerating pace of change could have on our heritage as that pace reaches a given threshold. Up to the turn of the century, the accelerating pace of change appears to have been within limits that allowed for reasonable continuity between one's childhood and the adult world. We appear now to have passed the point of reasonable continuity.

Again, let us offer a few concrete examples. Choices about when or whether we have children, about organ transplants, about genetic engineering and man-made bacteria are all choices that were unthinkable only a few decades ago. For many, certain alternatives are still unthinkable and constitute blasphemy. They are choices within our technological capacities but not within our cultural conceptions. The traditions of our not very distant past persist but all too frequently function inadequately. The curricula of the 1980s and 1990s have differed little from the curriculum of the 1920s. Our intragenerational disjunctures continue to exacerbate. Education, if it is to remain meaningful, cannot continue to ignore their gravity.

## QUESTIONS FOR DISCUSSION AND REFLECTION

1. In the context of this chapter, what is meant by a "vector of change"? Have we experienced such a vector of change in American education? When? What were the effects?

2. In what ways were Roman and Medieval education similar? How would you explain the similarities, given how very differently people lived? Are there any remaining signs of the trivium and quadrivium in current curricula?

3. What were the long-term educational results of Martin Luther's Ninety-Five Theses? In what ways can the influence of the Theses be observed functioning in education today?

4. What similarities and differences can you perceive in the views of education of John Amos Comenius and Johann Friedrich Herbart? Both have made important contributions to current practices in the field of education. Can you surmise from the discussion in this chapter what some of these are?

5. How were Jean Jacques Rousseau's and Johann Heinrich Pestalozzi's views of education similar? How were they different? Would you agree with the statement that Rousseau is better known for his work than Pestalozzi but has had less real effect on educational practices? Why or why not?

6. Consider the various changes within your own lifetime. What technological change causes you uneasiness? Examine your own intragenerational disjunctures and identify the ideas and ideals presented in your childhood that might cause this uneasiness.

7. Looking back at your own education:
   a. Make a list of some of the things you were taught that you think may hinder you as an adult.
   b. Identify activities or subjects that you think could be helpful to you in today's world.
   c. What things do you feel should have been included in your elementary and secondary education that were not?

8. Choose what you believe are the three most important purposes of modern education. What are some purposes currently pursued by the schools that you would eliminate? Why?

9. How resistant are you to changes in the school's curriculum? Do you think you are more open to new ideas than your elders? Why do you think so? What can we do to effect real change in the school's curriculum?

## NOTES

1. Dickens, C. (1868, corrected edition). *Nicholas Nickleby*. London: Hazell, Watson, and Viney, p. 142.
2. Whitehead, A.N. (1967). *The aims of education and other essays*. New York: The Free Press (original copyright 1929), pp. 18–19.
3. Langer, S. (1964). *Philosophical sketches*. New York: Mentor Books (original copyright 1962), p. 141.
4. Brown, L. R. (1973). *World without borders*. New York: Vintage Books (original copyright 1972), p. 349.

**2**

# Curriculum in Social and Historical Perspective

## Introduction

More than most fields, "curriculum is an historical accident. . . ,"[1] that is, it has not been deliberately developed to accomplish a clear set of purposes. Rather, it has evolved as a response to the increasing complexity of educational decision making. The explosion of knowledge, the intragenerational disjunctures afflicting many of us, and the ongoing upheavals in our system of values have all contributed to a growing cacophony of demands being made on our schools. The demands have been of every kind, from extending and improving vocational training to developing humanistic scholars familiar with the great philosophical questions; from socializing the young and making patriotic, obedient citizens to developing independent thinkers capable of evaluating and changing society. The school's curriculum and its purposes have been a matter of intense societal debate throughout the twentieth century. The field of curriculum grew up in the midst of the debate, and, to a considerable degree, was seen as the means of responding professionally to the multitude of dilemmas posed.

Chapter 2 explores and reviews the development of curriculum in the United States from its inception as a field around the turn of the twentieth century to the present. It pursues the establishment of today's elementary and secondary curricula, which occurred even as the field was being established as a professional endeavor. Finally, it briefly reviews the sets of beliefs that underlie the debates and, ultimately, the directions pursued.

## The Pre-Curriculum Era

The focus of education in times past was primarily on the teacher, and curricular choices were for the most part the results of whatever analyses teachers undertook.

Even as the emphasis shifted to the content of study, as it did with the rise of the universities in the late Middle Ages, what was to be studied in school was virtually a mirror-like reflection of a few existing disciplines such as rhetoric, theology, and physiology. Curricular decisions primarily dealt with how to simplify various disciplines so that they might be more effectively taught to young learners. It was up to the teacher to arrange the content and methodologies. Through the 1800s, the expansion of knowledge had taken place so slowly and society had changed so gradually that the educational needs and content could be inferred from the past. School teachers knew what was needed because they had gone through established, analogous instruction when they were in school.

### Curriculum: The Rise of the Field

Curriculum became a field as the growth of industrialized society gained momentum and as the immense benefits of the scientific method became more widely recognized. By the 1920s, the increasing complexities of societal life arising from industrialization had brought views of what the school's curriculum ought to be to a state of ferment as well as one of readiness. The readiness, however, was for the most part among avant garde school communities seeking to implement new curricular conceptions for an emerging new era.

The curriculum-maker's role developed along with a deep-seated belief that our schools could make a wholesome difference in American society as well as in the competence of the individual. Initially, the difference sought had been religious in nature. That is, education was designed, in cooperation with the church, to bring people closer to God. The difference became more political when, as our founding fathers saw it, education was deemed essential for the survival of a democracy. In the late 1800s, belief in the power of education was linked to fostering a planned, socially progressive society. Charles W. Eliot, president of Harvard, countered that only the rational development of human intellectual power could protect the people from misleading promises, specious oratory, and unwise social decisions.[2] The belief in the power of education to improve the quality of life has persisted despite a continual flow of negative criticism regarding the performance of American schools. Americans often have had widely differing ideas about educational goals and the precise kind of difference they want education to make, but few have ever doubted that it would make a difference in the lives of children.

In 1926, for example, Harold Rugg spoke of the transformation of American life from an essentially individualistic order to one contingent on the interdependence of large and quite complex societal systems.[3] Furthermore, in Rugg's opinion, neither the home, nor the church, nor the press,

> . . . could be expected to cope with the multitude of educational problems arising from continued technological advancement and industrialization: only the schools were equipped for such a task.[4]

The task had indeed become a major enterprise for educators during the early 1900s. It was in this era that proponents of the liberal Progressive Education

Association (founded in 1919) and their conservative opponents collided. The result was a series of curricular and instructional debates that have continued to this day. While the traditional disciplines were slowly giving way to such "newer" disciplines as chemistry and physics in the high schools, a debate raged about what was most important for young children to learn and what were the most acceptable and effective means of teaching subject matter.

The controversies dealt with such questions as: Should the curriculum be content-centered or based on the unique needs and interests of children? Should the content be problem-oriented or based on the discipline? Should memorization or reflective thinking and inquiry be the primary approach to teaching young children? Ultimately, the early years of elementary school became the period when children's individual differences and needs were cared for, while the high school focused on the teaching of content and remained, for the most part, dedicated to the preparation of adolescents for college.

## The Curriculum Era Emerges

### Significant National Committees of the Early Twentieth Century

The years around the turn of the century abounded with efforts to reform classroom instruction. This era saw the establishment of large accrediting organizations such as the North Central Association (1894) and the College Entrance Examination Board (1900). The Carnegie Foundation for the Advancement of Teaching was founded in this same period.

It was also the period when the educational ideas of the German philosopher Johann Friedrich Herbart (1776–1841) were at the peak of their influence in the United States. The Herbartians, as the philosopher's followers were called, emphasized a systematic approach to the organization and selection of content as well as to instructional delivery. Planning the nation's curriculum was at the turn of the century, as Kliebard put it, "a popular issue."[5] The field as we know it today was beginning to emerge.

The establishment of "blue ribbon," nationally based committees to work on improving the public school's curricula flowed naturally from the milieu of the times. Two of the most influential committees that helped to create the curriculum as we know it today were created in the last decade of the nineteenth century. These were the Committee of Ten, organized in 1893 by the National Education Association (NEA) to reform secondary education, and the Committee of Fifteen which reported in 1895. The Committee of Fifteen was organized by members of the NEA to counter what they perceived to be the radicalism of the Committee of Ten. The work of these two committees foreshadowed the dichotomy between elementary and secondary education that exists to this day. Their efforts eventually encompassed school organization, coordination of primary and grammar school curriculum, and teacher training.[6]

Even at the turn of the twentieth century, it was not a simple affair to select the content for study that was most important for young people to learn. The proverbial explosion of knowledge was already a reality, and the conundrums of an unknown future posed difficult problems for American education. The Spencerian question, "What knowledge is of most worth?" had become increasingly difficult to answer. The quantity of disciplinary knowledge was mind boggling even then. Which disciplines should be included as subjects of school study, which should be excluded, and why? Should school subjects reflect the structure of disciplines or should some other, perhaps more effective organizing principle be followed? Would social or vocational needs—at least for some learners—be more useful organizing principles on which to plan curriculum than the structure of the disciplines?

### Emerging Patterns of Curriculum Content

While analogous questions and doubts have continued to mount through the years, today's secondary curriculum continues to pursue, to a considerable degree, the patterns proposed by the Committee of Ten in the 1890's. Nine subject areas were recommended: (1) Latin, (2) Greek, (3) English, (4) modern languages, (5) mathematics, (6) physics, chemistry, and astronomy, (7) biology, (8) history, government, and political economy, and (9) geography.[7] Latin, Greek, and modern languages are indeed gone from college entrance requirements, but they remain in the minds of many as desirable, "hard" subjects that help to develop intellectual discipline. On the other hand, music, art, and such social sciences as anthropology, psychology, and economics are still thought by many to be high school "frills," because they are still not part of most colleges' entrance requirements.

Charles Eliot, president of Harvard and Chair of the Committee of Ten, did not limit his committee's deliberations to the secondary school curriculum. Presaging the concept that was later to be labeled the junior high school, the Committee recommended reducing the number of years allocated to the elementary school from ten to eight; it further recommended that the study of grammar be reduced, that the natural sciences be taught with emphasis on experimentation in the primary years, that introductory physics be taught in the upper elementary grades, and that algebra be substituted for mathematics in the seventh and eighth grades.[8]

Within a decade after the report had been issued, vocational education, neglected by the Committee of Ten, became a major issue. Literally millions of Europe's peasant poor, mostly from non-English speaking countries, had migrated to America, and, for the most part, their children needed to go to work long before the age of college entrance. What indeed were the purposes of American education when the vast majority of youngsters attending the public schools would not go on to college? Should not the curriculum be differentiated in a way that would meet the needs of non–college-bound students, helping them to adjust to the social and industrial realities of American life?

On the other hand, might such differentiation not become a means of keeping the children of migrants and of the poor in general in lower status jobs? In a democracy, the opportunity to go to college should belong to every intellectually capable individual. At least this was the ideal put forth by Eliot in defense of the Committee of Ten's Report and of its curricular design. The curriculum was similar for all students and was based on a limited selection of disciplines with an emphasis on the sciences.[9]

The Committee of Fifteen, headed by William T. Harris, continued to stand its ground in opposition to the Committee of Ten. While they accepted the shortening of the elementary period and the development of the junior high school, the Committee rejected extensive utilization of the scientific method and maintained that the traditional elementary school subjects of history, geography, grammar, literature, and arithmetic were more suitable to children who were not yet ready to engage properly in criticism but were rather at the stage of imitation.[10] Furthermore, the position of the Herbartians, who sought to unify the curriculum by correlating the various subjects through a core of either history or literature, also was rejected. Harris led the Committee of Fifteen to take the position in 1895 that the "five windows on the soul or basic divisions of knowledge [such as mathematics and grammar] were inviolate."[11]

Both committees were to have a profound, immediate, and long-term effect on the curricula of the secondary and elementary schools. The scientific and mathematical disciplines assumed a major role in the secondary curriculum, while the language arts remained the cornerstone of the elementary curriculum. To this day, the sciences are likely to be neglected by many elementary school teachers, and fractions, not readily grasped by young learners, may be taught over and over again through the eighth grade.

Another NEA committee, The Commission on the Reorganization of Secondary Education, needs to be recognized here, notwithstanding its obvious emphasis on the upper school grades. The commission issued its report in 1918. It was substantially a reaction, albeit a belated one, to the report of the Committee of Ten and the subject area specializations that it had fostered in the high schools.

The commission was strongly influenced by John Dewey when it set forth the proposition that education needed to reflect and support democratic ideals. The increase in specialization and in the study of the disciplines that had resulted with the circulation of the report of the Committee of Ten were countered by the commission with the presentation of seven goals or *Cardinal Principles of Secondary Education*. These were: health, command of fundamental processes (reading, writing, arithmetic, and oral and written expression), worthy home membership, vocation, citizenship, worthy use of leisure, and ethical character. They were presented in the report as goals that were closely related to each other and formed together the bases for the development of democratic social skills and values that would serve all the people in their roles as citizens of a democracy.

In setting forth goals that were clearly common to everyone, the commission believed it was opening secondary education to all rather than to the elite few that would go on to college. Only one of the goals, "command of fundamental processes," was related to college entrance requirements. As Tanner and Tanner note, "the *Cardinal Principles of Secondary Education* are generally regarded as a kind of Declaration of Independence by the high school from college domination."[12]

According to the commission, the content of the secondary education program should be based on an analysis of the needs of society, the nature and background of the learner, and the best knowledge of educational theory and practice available.[13] It is an approach to curriculum development that is respected and followed to this day.

Although the seven principles generally are incorporated in one form or another in most statements of goals developed today, the study of the disciplines as separate and distinct areas of knowledge continues to dominate the secondary school curriculum. The offering of electives and the inclusion of courses having vocational or recreational purposes can be attributed to the influence of the report. The ideas contained in the *Seven Cardinal Principles* have had greater impact on the elementary school where the disciplines have not held as strong a grip on the curriculum.

After World War I, the influence of John Dewey and the progressive movement's emphasis on education for individual growth and democratic citizenship gradually transformed the elementary school curriculum. The Progressive Education Association (PEA) was founded in 1919. The platform of the association included the scientific study of child development, the conception of the teacher as a facilitator (rather than as a disciplinarian and lecturer), child interest as a primary motivator of learning, and cooperation between the school and home in meeting the needs of the child.

Although the "three R's" remained a significant component of the curriculum, the elementary school became a place where learning occurred through a variety of activities from participating in plays and the writing of poetry to craft work and dancing. "Getting along well with others," "maintaining good work habits," and "cleanliness" were among the items to appear on children's report cards. These certainly were a significant change from the bullying and forced memorizations of a century earlier.

## John Dewey and the Genesis of Democratic Curriculum Practices

Although John Dewey was a foremost proponent of a science of education, his conception of science included inquiry into such subjective and elusive areas as morality and the problems of everyday living. Demonstrations of the kind achieved in the experimental school he directed at the University of Chicago in the late 1890s were considered "scientific" even though they probably could be neither replicated nor specifically verified. If science could not help us to improve our everyday living, then, for Dewey, it was not meaningful to humankind.

Dewey's conception of important learning, as it was expressed in 1920, was the development of skills that could be used throughout life to help citizens solve their personal problems as well as social ones. For Dewey, "acquisition of skill, possession of knowledge, attainment of culture" were not ends, but the means of continuing education.[14] While acknowledging the importance of scientific and technological knowledge, he believed the development of intellectual skills, when held solely within the confines of scientific disciplines and technological applications, overlooked the complex personal and social problems that technological advancement and growing industrialization had brought to the world. Dewey himself lived through the development of a great cultural divide, one that we have suggested had led in his lifetime to intragenerational disjuncture.

The Progressive Education Association sought to develop a child-centered curriculum, as this had been developed in the writings of Dewey. However, the social-problems orientation to the school's content, which had been equally a part of Dewey's philosophy, was, by neglect, relegated to a second order of importance. The social and political questions he would have used were generally replaced by questions of how to achieve the cultivation of self-expression and creativity — capabilities believed to coexist "naturally" within every child.

*The Child-Centered School*, written by Harold Rugg and Ann Schumaker in 1928, best represents this increased emphasis on the development of self and of self-expression with these words:

> *The pupil is placed in an atmosphere conducive to self-expression in every aspect. Some will create with words, others with light. Some will express themselves through the body in dance; others will model, carve, shape their ideas in plastic materials. . . . But whatever the route, the medium, the materials — each one has some capacity for expression.* [15]

In ignoring the social-problems orientation that Dewey would have given to the curriculum, Dewey's conception of the curriculum was skewed, possibly inadvertently, into a wholly child-centered orientation. What was ignored was that he always stressed a *balanced* integration of the needs of society and the needs of children as the basis for curriculum design. Dewey's child-centered/social-problems orientation to the curriculum is referred to in this book as the "child-in-society" curriculum.

## Dewey's Concept of the Child

Dewey saw the child as an intelligent, contributing member of society whose unique qualities were to be accepted and fostered. Together with the growing importance of the study of child development and G. Stanley Hall's proposition that each child's curriculum ought to be individualized to suit the child's development,[16] the challenge to the disciplines was powerful, though by no means overwhelming.

In essence, Dewey's position was a challenge *not* to the old traditional disciplines of the day (Latin, grammar, and the like) — they were already being displaced — but to the adoption, as school subjects, of such disciplines as chemistry and physics. His challenge to the disciplines came even while he supported the scientific mode of thinking. Skillful inquiry into personally felt social problems within a supportive community such as the school was the ideal presented by Dewey, and its appeal was widespread — its challenge to the primacy of the disciplines profound. Had it prevailed, it would have shifted the school's curriculum from a content-centered emphasis to a child-in-society one.

### The Elementary / Secondary Curriculum Dichotomy

What we have had developing in education is a curriculum dichotomy. The elementary schools have tended to adjust their programs to the individuality of children and to their physical, social, and intellectual diversity. On the other hand, secondary schools have been appreciably more content-oriented. The child-in-society orientation posed by Dewey (minus most controversial social problems) fits comfortably into the language arts / social studies curriculum fostered by the work of the Committee of Fifteen. Conversely, there was far less flexibility for such an orientation in the strict disciplinarian approach and strong scientific emphasis that came to typify American high schools in the first half of the twentieth century.

The Deweyan approach added a host of new curricular questions: If the disciplines were not to be used, on what basis was content to be chosen and who was to do the choosing? What sequence of study needed to be followed? Should the same social problems be dealt with by all? If so, in what fashion when the backgrounds of students ranged from inner city to prosperous suburban? What assurances could be had that the development of desired skills would actually be achieved when individuals varied so greatly? Were the inventories and questionnaires of experimental psychology really capable of assessing the child's development, as Hall suggested? If so, could these measures be effectively related to the programs of the public schools, which were seen as the proper socializing agent for improving society?

## Our Cultural Mindsets about Education

In the face of innumerable questions that have only partially been answered, the tendency in the United States generally has been to follow tradition and to accept one's cultural mindsets about the proper conduct of education. Historically, this has generated a great deal of discussion about innovations such as those that Dewey proposed. At the same time, innovations and changes in the classroom have sometimes been so slow that they have been virtually imperceptible, creating the impression that no change has occurred. Given the hectic rate of change in society as a whole, this is a rather surprising and worrisome state of affairs.

The academic versus social dichotomy in American schooling began to develop very early in the twentieth century. It has become more deeply embedded in the traditions of schooling as the years have passed. Indeed, we are hardly aware of the disparities that exist between our goals for the elementary school and what we expect from the high school.

From the perspective of many secondary school teachers, elementary school programs contain too many "frills" that fail to prepare students for the kinds of studies they will need to undertake in the high school. In their view, elementary school studies should be directed toward the preparation of youngsters for the more advanced studies that presumedly characterize the secondary curriculum. It may be all right, these educators feel, to be caring and humane, allowing children the freedom to explore, to be creative, and to reflect a measure of individuality in the primary grades. By the fourth grade, however, an understanding of academic content must begin to come first and "really serious" studies need to be pursued. This, at least, is the attitude that appears to have become a subliminal part of our cultural mindset regarding the proper conduct of education.

### The Tools of "Science" as Tools of Professional Curriculum-Making: Tests and Measurement

The development of objective intelligence and achievement tests in the first decades of the twentieth century was yet another element contributing to the growing belief that science could be applied effectively to education. By 1916, when Terman's influential revision of Binet's intelligence scale appeared, New York City and other large cities were using standardized tests to ascertain student achievement.

In 1917, America's entrance into World War I created an urgent need to develop large numbers of skilled workers for a variety of military and industrial purposes. The educational response was nothing short of revolutionary. Over a million young men of draft age were tested to quickly assess their learning capabilities. The jobs of skilled workers were analyzed according to the tasks that were to be accomplished. These tasks were then related to the specific knowledge and skills required. They were then successfully taught within a few weeks to young men who had been selected and grouped on the basis of test results.

It was an impressive performance that paralleled technological planning in American industry and also made excellent use of scientific methodologies. Tests and measurement of children's abilities and achievements became firmly entrenched in educational practice as tools involved in both curriculum making and curriculum evaluation. The impact on the educational thought of the day was considerable.

Edward L. Thorndike's scientific investigations into the value of traditional high school subjects such as Latin and Greek for the "general improvement of the mind" demonstrated powerfully that no one discipline was in and of itself superior to another for achieving "good thinkers." Thorndike said:

> When the good thinkers studied Greek and Latin, these studies seemed to make good thinking. Now that the good thinkers study Physics and Trigonometry, these seem to make good thinkers.[17]

Even more important than undoing the widely held belief that some subjects were productive beyond their content because of the mental discipline their study imparted, Thorndike's investigation involved the successful use of an objective test with 8,564 high school students. His work confirmed among professional educators the applicability of the scientific method for increasing understanding of the curriculum-making process.

## Testing and the School's Curriculum

At first, tests and measurements were used primarily to assess the performance of advanced high school students. However, in recent decades, the use of these instruments has increased appreciably not only in the number administered, but also in the age groups that are tested. For example, in Louisiana, as of 1988, kindergarten youngsters were being tested to assess their readiness for entrance into the first grade. Achievement batteries for elementary school children, such as the *California Achievement Tests*, the *Iowa Tests of Basic Skills*, and the *Metropolitan Achievement Tests*, are routinely administered throughout the nation. So-called social promotions have been eliminated in numerous states by requiring youngsters from the fourth grade on to pass "minimum competency" tests.

The progressive decline in students' test scores, which began in 1964 and leveled off in the late 1980s, has been a major factor in the accelerating use of nationally normed, standardized tests. Testing has become the instrument of choice for gauging the success of schooling, and, in turn, of teachers. Newspaper and magazine headlines have placed so much emphasis on the rise and fall of test scores that a sizable portion of the public has come to believe they are a complete and accurate reflection of the school experience. An obvious result of this belief is that testing has had a profound effect on the content and instructional methods employed in our schools. Rather than being a tool used by the curriculum worker to achieve scientifically based results, tests have become a form of curriculum guide. Whatever the original intent, the classroom teacher tends to teach for students' success on the test. Whatever is typically included in the test will take on special importance in the classroom, becoming the effective content of study. In a sense, it is the testing program "tail" wagging the curriculum "dog."

The significance of the increased stress on test scores for the elementary school lies in the renewed emphasis on learning and probably memorizing content regardless of children's needs, backgrounds, or personal creativity. Open-ended humanism including respect for individual differences is out of the question when all children in a class must take the same test at approximately the same time, without any consideration for their ethnic, social, or economic diversity. On the other hand, the testing phenomenon may contribute to an improved alignment of elementary school study with that of the secondary schools, possibly overcoming the curricular schism that has typified American education in this century. This, of course, assumes that a content-centered curricular design is to be preferred over other possible orientations.

## The Survey as a Tool of Curriculum-Making

In 1911, The Committee on Economy of Time was established by the National Education Association (NEA). Its purpose was to use the survey as a means of making the school's curriculum more efficient and, especially, less repetitive. The ultimate goal was to satisfy the public's demand that the schools either prove their benefits to society or start reducing their budgets.

The committee undertook to analyze the minimum essentials of education in terms of both content and methodology by surveying prevailing practices of daily living among adults. Subsequently, it sought to determine, again with the use of surveys, the activities engaged in by people who presumedly were leading well-adjusted lives. Curriculum change was to be based on the resulting analysis of successful, current practices. In effect, the survey became another of the tools adopted by the curriculum worker for the scientific planning of the curriculum. It was not long before a number of educators adopted this approach in their own curriculum work, the most prominent among them being Franklin Bobbitt.

Franklin Bobbitt, a professor of educational administration at the University of Chicago, was in the forefront of the drive to have public education improve its efficiency by following the example of industry and indicating clearly what its "products" were to be.[18] In 1918, he published a book entitled *The Curriculum*,[19] which is often referred to as the first significant work to have emerged from curriculum study as a modern field of professional endeavor. To make education's outcomes relevant to the needs of the times, Bobbitt proposed conducting surveys under the auspices of business to determine what activities of adult life needed to underlie the goals and content of the curriculum. The surveys were painstaking in their minute analyses of life activities, for, as Bobbitt conceived them, such surveys were to assist in achieving, ". . . for the first time a scientific curriculum for education worthy of our age of science."[20]

In terms of current curriculum planning, a survey of the fastest growing professions issued by the U.S. Department of Labor might be used as the basis for deciding what needs to be included or emphasized in the curriculum. Table 2.1 is the Labor Department's 1990–91 selection of the fastest growing jobs through the end of the decade. In keeping with Bobbitt's approach to curriculum planning, we would probably select studies that would prepare students for the positions listed.

Underlying Bobbitt's conception of how to build a curriculum was the assumption that the current activities of society comprised the most worthwhile content of schooling. Even in the early decades of the twentieth century, accelerating technological change had to make such an assumption a highly questionable one. It is worth noting that while the methodologies for curriculum development used in World War I and proposed by Bobbitt for public schooling are similar, the differences in purpose are fundamental. Training for the military or for industrial production is directed toward the fulfillment of very specific tasks in the immediate future, while schooling, even when it has a vocational orientation, is directed toward life-long purposes that inevitably involve ambiguity.

### Curriculum Engineering

In 1924, Bobbitt published another influential book, *How to Make a Curriculum*.[21] In its pages, he likened the curriculum maker to an engineer who needed to survey the existing terrain in order to determine what the "products" of engineering should be. Once the data from Bobbitt's detailed surveys were generally understood, the curriculum maker needed only to develop the specific activities that were to be taught in instructionally manageable units in the schools.

This approach to curriculum making might appear, at first glance, to involve

**TABLE 2.1**   *America's 50 Fastest-Growing Jobs, 1988–2000*

| Occupation | Number of New Jobs | Percentage Increase |
|---|---|---|
| 1. Paralegals | 62,000 | 75% |
| 2. Medical assistants | 104,000 | 70 |
| 3. Radiologic technologists | 87,000 | 66 |
| 4. Homemaker—home health aides | 207,000 | 63 |
| 5. Medical-record technicians | 28,000 | 60 |
| 6. Medical secretaries | 120,000 | 58 |
| 7. Physical therapists | 39,000 | 57 |
| 8. Surgical technologists | 20,000 | 56 |
| 9. Securities and financial-services representatives | 109,000 | 55 |
| 10. Operations-research analysis | 30,000 | 55 |
| 11. Travel agents | 77,000 | 54 |
| 12. Actuaries | 8,500 | 54 |
| 13. Computer-system analysts | 214,000 | 53 |
| 14. Physical- and corrective-therapy assistants | 21,000 | 52.5 |
| 15. Social welfare service aides | 47,000 | 51.5 |
| 16. EEG technologists | 3,200 | 50 |
| 17. Occupational therapists | 16,000 | 49 |
| 18. Computer programmers | 250,000 | 48 |
| 19. Service sales representatives | 216,000 | 45 |
| 20. Human-services workers | 53,000 | 45 |
| 21. Health-services managers | 75,000 | 42 |
| 22. Corrections officers | 76,000 | 41 |
| 23. Respiratory therapists | 23,000 | 41 |
| 24. Receptionists | 331,000 | 40 |
| 25. Electrical and electronics engineers | 176,000 | 40 |
| 26. Employment interviewers | 33,000 | 40 |
| 27. Registered nurses | 613,000 | 39 |
| 28. Flight attendants | 34,000 | 39 |
| 29. Licensed practical nurses | 229,000 | 37 |
| 30. Recreational therapists | 9,500 | 37 |
| 31. Management analysts and consultants | 46,000 | 35 |
| 32. Computer and office-machine repairers | 44,000 | 35 |
| 33. Podiatrists | 5,700 | 35 |
| 34. Information clerks | 441,000 | 34 |
| 35. Guards | 256,000 | 32 |
| 36. Engineering, science, and data-processing managers | 83,000 | 32 |
| 37. Nursing aides and psychiatric aides | 405,000 | 31 |
| 38. Aircraft pilots | 26,000 | 31 |
| 39. Dispensing opticians | 16,000 | 31 |
| 40. Lawyers and judges | 188,000 | 30 |
| 41. Childcare workers | 186,000 | 30 |
| 42. Actors, directors, and producers | 24,000 | 30 |
| 43. Nuclear-medicine technologists | 3,000 | 30 |
| 44. Meteorologists | 1,800 | 30 |

**TABLE 2.1**   *Continued*

| Occupation | Number of New Jobs | Percentage Increase |
|---|---|---|
| 45. Social workers | 110,000 | 29 |
| 46. Computer and peripheral equipment operators | 92,000 | 29 |
| 47. Underwriters | 30,000 | 29 |
| 48. Landscape architects | 5,500 | 29 |
| 49. Engineering technicians | 203,000 | 28 |
| 50. Physicians | 149,000 | 28 |

*Source: Job Outlook in Brief*, 1990–91, and *The Occupational Outlook Quarterly*, Spring 1990, both published by the U.S. Department of Labor.

aspects of both the child-in-society and the content-centered curricula. After all, the activities of successful, presumably happy members of society were fundamental to the premises of the surveys and were to comprise the content of the curriculum. However, since no studies were made to determine the source of happiness, or even what definition of "successful" was to be used, the results of the surveys failed to go beyond describing the prevailing activities engaged in by working people. In the context of schooling, as some educators saw it, these surveys could be used to determine what children needed to know to become productive members of society. Generally, the kind of curriculum that tended to develop Bobbitt's process was a societally oriented one. The assumptions underlying this line of thought are that children need to learn how to fit into society and that the schools are proper socializing agents.

What is quite striking in the foregoing discussion is the profound faith in the applicability of scientific management to such a complex social enterprise as education without any real attempt to adhere to the principles of science. "Activities" could range from simple, easily described tasks to elusive and purely qualitative goals such as "getting along well with others." "Engineering" was likened to "curriculum making" without important and necessary distinctions being made — an approach quite acceptable to the literary artist but certainly questionable for the scientific manager.

Educationally, the early decades of the 1900s represent more an expression of faith — *the ideology of scientism* — rather than the development of a scientific approach to curriculum making. Nevertheless, it was this ideology of scientism that led to the first major discussion of curriculum making as a process, namely, Bobbitt's books, *The Curriculum* and *How to Make a Curriculum*. Indeed, scientism as ideology continues to underlie much of what is done in curriculum making today.

### The 26th Yearbook of the NSSE

The rise of the field of curriculum making as a professional enterprise was probably most clearly underscored in the 1927 publication of the National Society for the

Study of Education's (NSSE) 26th Yearbook, *Curriculum Making: Past and Present*.[22] The work of curriculum committees, such as the Committee of Fifteen and the Committee of Ten, were labeled "piecemeal" efforts that tended to look at administrative requirements rather than the needs of people as a basis for curricular design.

In the *Yearbook*, the editor, Harold Rugg, presented a view of what curriculum work was about, a view that is now largely taken for granted (though perhaps not wisely). Three major tasks were seen as fundamental: (1) the determination of objectives underlying the curriculum as a whole, (2) the selection of appropriate materials and activities, and (3) the experimental determination of the most effective organization and sequencing of materials and activities.[23]

Implicit in these tasks was the idea that curriculum making should involve the holistic development of plans that were then to be studied scientifically to collect data about their actual functioning. Evaluation of curricular effectiveness became an important tool for curriculum development. Simply said, did the implementation of the curriculum actually do what the plan said it would do? What could be done to improve the effectiveness of the curriculum? As Tyler pointed out in his review of the 26th Yearbook, the emphasis had passed from "armchair reflection" to the use of "objective studies."[24] The curriculum maker needed to collect data so that plans could be developed and/or improved.

### The Popularity of Progressivism

Progressivism as an educational movement changed the way Americans thought about the education of children. As a set of ideas, it was immensely popular, even though its nationwide impact on how schooling was conducted was quite limited. It embodied an abiding belief in progress and in the goodness of change. Faith in the future and in humankind's ability to achieve better tomorrows brought the Eliots and the Deweys together. As Bernier and Williams note, it was largely "the compatibility with various political belief systems"[25] that made progressivism so immensely popular. Social Darwinism, which utilized Darwin's theory of evolution in the context of economic survival of a few over the many, had an affinity with progressivism. So too, did the Socialists such as Robert Owen and the more moderate reformers such as B. F. Skinner and John Dewey.[26]

Above all, progressivism embodied the belief in humankind's ability to plan in the light of empirical evidence and to continue improving planning by continuing to increase the evidence. This was universally accepted not just by scientists and industrialists but by social reformers as well. Obviously, the means for achieving evidence would need to change as the context changed; the socially oriented progressivists would continually assess the consequences of social action much as scientists would assess the results of their experiments.

Although the progressivists accepted scientific methodology, they tended to remain in vague ideological realms, with "change" and "progress" poorly defined but conveying a positive sense of something "good." Progressivism and scientism, together with a profound respect for the marvelous advances of science and industry, formed the ideological—albeit often intellectually unclear—context within which curriculum making grew and reacted to the events of the twenties and thirties from prosperity to depression.

Reconstructionism emerged from the progressive education movement as a reaction to (1) the social and economic crises of the depression and (2) the decade of the 1920s, during which some educational liberals had, in varying degrees, overemphasized individual creativity and self-expression. George Counts and Theodore Brameld led the return to the social problems orientation in curriculum, proposing that the schools become the major institutions for the planned restructuring of society. In *Dare the School Build a New Social Order?* published in 1932, Counts declared that education must:

> . . . *face squarely and courageously every social issue, come to grips with life in all of its stark reality, establish an organic relation with the community . . . fashion a compelling and challenging vision of human destiny, and become less frightened than it is today at the bogies of imposition and indoctrination.*[27]

The basic proposition of Counts and Brameld was that the school's curriculum should be designed to include an ideal vision of an equitable socioeconomic and democratic future. Children ought to be "indoctrinated" with the skills of better living and the vision of a better life than the one they had come to know if that better life were ever to be achieved.

There is a fundamental conflict for the curriculum developer to resolve with respect to the social viewpoints and strategies reviewed above. The conflict is rooted in: (1) responding to prevailing needs and practices of the times, as Bobbitt proposed be done, and (2) creating a better society for tomorrow, as Brameld recommended. The former conserves what already exists; the latter would move toward an essentially new order of societal arrangements, requiring the schools to take the burden of leadership. Neither would dwell at any length on the needs and concerns that individual children might bring with them to school. In sum, there are a variety of different conflicts that have arisen among those who would center the curriculum around the child's development, those who would make social problems (and possibly their remediation) the curricular core, those who would make the disciplines the bases of school subjects, and those who would concentrate on minimal, essential skills.

With World War II and the surge in scientific and technological advancement that followed (in part as a result of the war), the sense of urgency with respect to more effective planning of educational experiences continued to grow. Indeed, the questions seem not to have changed very much to this day. "Why can't Johnny Read?" Flesch asked in 1955.[28] Why are our schools failing? both Bestor and Rickover demanded to know.[29,30] The pressures on educational planning have continued to multiply throughout the twentieth century.

### Futures and the Curriculum

While belief that social problems can be "planned away" through education waned significantly during the 1970s and 1980s, exploring possible futures in education remains an important factor in curriculum making. The study of futures may be typified as education's effort to foresee tomorrow's realities so that the current educational preparation of the young will not become obsolete in their adulthood. In a sense, futures study in curriculum involves "anticipatory foresight," an ongoing search of the future to understand what is likely to happen, so that the curriculum may include the kinds of knowledge and skills necessary to the future well-being of all of humankind. From this perspective, educational futurism may also be thought of as an effort to help young people face a future of sustained intragenerational disjuncture. As the increasingly powerful explosions of knowledge become even more severe, futures study has taken on greater importance for the work of curriculum maker.

The view that education should enable the young to be capable of dealing with alternative futures is one that is widely held even among those who vehemently reject the ideas of Counts and Brameld, namely that the schools should be directly involved in the reconstruction of society. The concern today is not whether the curriculum should be future oriented, but how the future is to be treated in the course of study. Whether the curriculum maker is dealing with the present or the future, the basic questions about goals and content remain perplexing, and are examined in detail in subsequent chapters.

# The Widening Divide: 1940 to Date

### The Deepening of Intragenerational Disjuncture

Changes between 1900 and 1940 obviously were tremendous. Developments after 1940 were virtually unbelievable, and after the 1960s and 70s almost incredible — even to the people who lived through these decades. It is in this recent past that we find many of the roots of the problems and numerous crises that have plagued, and continue to plague, all of our institutions. Among our troubled institutions, of course, are the schools. Many of them have discipline-centered curricula that were not designed to cope with the present eruption of knowledge, let alone with the world of tomorrow.

In the years since 1940, scientific, technological, and biological developments have led to a host of deeply disturbing social and environmental changes. Even now, as we have begun to take these innovations for granted, we are not yet fully able to comprehend their effect on our lives. A roster of the factors causing upheavals in long-established lifestyles would certainly include nuclear power, a world population of over five billion, instantaneous communication via satellites, inexpensive transportation by jet plane, major organ transplants, the solid-circuit computer, reliable oral contraception, repeated moon landings, and unmanned space travel beyond the outermost planets. Our list also must include global pollution, hunger, genetic manipulations such as cloning, the mixed blessings of DNA research, tremendous gains in the speed and accuracy of data processing, and the evolution of sophisticated weaponry. By the mid 1960s the influence of accelerating change already had vastly impacted life in the United States, and by the 1970s the entire planet was reflecting them. It is not an exaggeration to say that in the years since 1920 there has been greater and more widespread change than in the previous fifty centuries!

### The Challenge of Tomorrow's World

The problems generated by years of unsettling transitions became more ominous in the middle and late 1960s. There was discontent, protest, and confrontation on campuses and violence and disaster in the ghettos. The unpopular Viet Nam war destroyed a president's credibility, and political hooliganism forced his successor to resign in disgrace. Most forms of authority, no matter how legally constituted, were questioned with vehemence, rancor, and sometimes physical force. Moral maps that churches had long provided seemed inadequate to guide us through the terrain we were crossing. Crime and personal violence climbed to a level of medieval intensity. The alienated among the young, and some not so young, sought authenticity by breaking with traditional behavioral patterns. Often, they tried to "find themselves" through protest movements, new religious experiences, or experiments with drugs, sex, and imaginative and sometimes bizarre personal grooming. Biophysicist John Platt felt justified in calling the situation "a crisis of crises."[31]

In America and overseas, terrorism increased, and in place after place a wide variety of individuals, often with homicidal fury, tried to punish the world for failing to conform to their social or political ideas. While only a small minority of the population participated in either confrontations or experiments involving unconventional lifestyles, virtually everyone felt their impact. The media contributed in large part to what has become an ever-present awareness of the dissidents in our midst. Americans were obliged, especially in the late 1970s and early 1980s, to reassess their views regarding an unprecedented environment that, in varying ways, either inspired and encouraged or alarmed and threatened them. Inevitably, the school's curriculum became a part of the self-examination process, which has reached new levels of concentration in recent years.

Significant in contributing to the turbulence of the present is that most of humankind—from the ignorant to the well-informed—is made instantly and repeatedly aware, by the media in general and TV in particular, of the unrest and disjunctures present in our social lives. Days passed before American and British troops at the Battle of New Orleans learned that they had fought some two weeks after a peace treaty had been signed. Today, for all practical purposes, we are "on the plane" with the hostages or in the war zone while bombs are dropped because of media coverage. We have become armchair participants, simultaneously involved in and helpless to change the course of events.

Perhaps the most important aspect of this crisis of so many crises is that there is a waning confidence in our ability to plan better tomorrows. Both scientism and progressivism shared the belief that the world could become more humane and rewarding to the earth's billions. Indeed, that tomorrow was going to be bigger and better than today was a sense of "manifest destiny" that most Americans shared regardless of their backgrounds and circumstances.

Unfortunately, somewhere in the crises of the 1960s and 1970s, with economic problems multiplying, with the social programs of the Kennedy–Johnson era faltering everywhere, with the diminishing availability of oil and other natural fuels, with the inability of some of America's largest industries, such as steel and automobiles, to compete sucessfully against foreign industries, a lack of confidence in our ability to plan for tomorrow began to pervade the American scene.

### Educating for a Better Tomorrow

In retrospect, the continuing crisis in public education through the 1970s, 1980s, and into the 1990s is not unlike the crisis in public education that occurred around the turn of the century. It was claimed then, as it was claimed in the 1970s and 1980s, that children were not learning the minimum essentials, that too much money was spent on administration, and that too little attention was given to the individual development of youngsters, and so forth. The fundamental difference between then and now lies in what we as a people believe about our ability to plan the educational programs of children.

It has been said that "curriculum is moribund." While the claim may be exaggerated, in most school districts it does reflect the crisis in curriculum making—a crisis in our beliefs about *how* and *what* we can plan. We have grown preoccupied with the limits to planning and less sure that we can plan in worthwhile ways. This is the crisis of crises for education.

At the very same time that our confidence in planning has waned, our ability to plan has increased immensely. So, too, has our need. In 1976, the microprocessor chip began to become widely available. In essence, these chips are the miniaturization of what was once considered powerful computers occupying large halls of space. By 1977, microprocessor computers were being sold to the public for $1,000—instruments that only ten years earlier would have cost half a million dollars. Microprocessor chips have already been used by the millions in cars, microwave ovens, refrigerators, and sewing machines. The potential is vast; the changes to come are perhaps among the most profound of this century.

As we educate learners of all ages for tomorrow's world, we must keep in mind that such technological developments as the microprocessor computer have already increased the need for educational planning. It is also one of the most powerful tools at the disposal of planners. Though our rather romantic belief in planning has been diminished by a pervasive sense of discouragement, now, more than ever, we need to engage in future planning. Perhaps planning with clear insights about the limits to planning will be even more productive educationally than ever was the case when the ideal of "scientific planning" was part of the American educational ideology.

## QUESTIONS FOR DISCUSSION AND REFLECTION

1. How did the Committee of Ten influence the American curriculum? Would some changes have occurred with or without the committee's work? Explain your response fully.

2. What influence did the Committee of Fifteen have on curriculum? Compare the work of the Committee of Ten with the work of the Committee of Fifteen. What differences are there in the school's curriculum today that can be traced back to the differences in the views of the committees?

3. What important differences existed between the views of the Committee of Ten and and those of the Commission on the Reorganization of Secondary Education? In what ways can the commission's work be observed in today's curriculum?

4. In what ways does the child-centered school reflect Dewey's ideas for progressive education? What in the child-centered movement might Dewey have disagreed with?

5. In what ways does standarized testing affect the curriculum? Would it be possible to modify the impact current tests have on the curriculum? What would you do, if anything, to change the nature of their influence?

6. How do you think Bobbitt's type of survey would work today as a tool for curriculum development? What would be its advantages and disadvantages?

7. Name and summarize the four different perspectives that one might take in analyzing the curriculum.

8. Do you believe the Committee of Ten and the Committee of Fifteen succeeded in defining what was needed by members of their society to be ready for their future? Why or why not? What else could have been done? What should not have been done?

9. List the personal and social problems you think the current generation of students will face as adults. Briefly describe what you think should be included in the development of a curriculum that would address the needs you have identified.

10. Would you use the list of the fifty fastest growing jobs included in this chapter as a basis for curriculum development? What are the reasons for your position?

## NOTES

1. MacDonald, J. B. (1971). Curriculum development in relation to social and intellectual systems. In: *The curriculum: Retrospect and prospect*, XVII (NSSE, 1971 Yearbook), p. 95.
2. Eliot, C. W. (December, 1892). Wherein popular education has failed. *The Forum*, 14, pp. 423–424.

3. Rugg, H. (1926). The school curriculum and the drama of American life. *Curriculum making: Past and present* (26th NSSE Yearbook, Part 1), Bloomington, IL: Public School Publishing Company, 1926, pp. 5–6.

4. *Ibid.*, p. 6.

5. Kliebard, H. M. (1968). The curriculum field in retrospect. In: Witt, P. F. (ed.), *Technology and the curriculum*. New York: Teachers College Press, p. 70.

6. National Education Association (1895). In *Addresses and Proceedings*. Washington, D.C.: The Association.

7. National Education Association (1894). *Report of the Committee of Ten on Secondary School Studies*. Chicago: The American Company.

8. National Education Association Committee of Ten on Secondary School Studies (1893). *Report*. Washington, D.C.: U.S. Printing Office.

9. Tanner, D. and Tanner, L. N. (1975). *Curriculum development*. New York: Macmillan Publishing, p. 186.

10. National Education Association Committee of Fifteen Report (1895). In *Addresses and proceedings*. Washington, D.C.: The Association.

11. Schubert, W. T. (1988). *Curriculum: Perspective, paradigm and possibility*. New York: Macmillan Publishing, p. 73.

12. *Op. cit.*, Tanner, D. and Tanner, L. N., p. 231.

13. Commission on the Reorganization of Secondary Education (1918). *Cardinal principles of secondary education*. Washington D.C.: U.S. Printing Office, p. 7.

14. Dewey, J. (1957). *Reconstruction in philosophy*. New York: Beacon Press, p. 186.

15. Rugg, H. and Shumaker, A. (1928). *The child-centered school*. New York: World Book, p. 63.

16. Hall, G. S. (1904). The contents of children's minds on entering school. *Pedagogical seminary*, Vol. 1, pp. 139–173. Also, Hall, G. S. (1904). *Adolescence*, New York: D. Appleton.

17. Thorndike, E. L. (1924). Mental discipline in high school studies. *Journal of Educational Psychology*, Vol. 15 (February), p. 98.

18. Bobbitt, F. (1912). Elimination of waste in education. *The Elementary School Teacher*, Vol. 12 (February), pp. 268–310.

19. Bobbitt, F. (1918). *The curriculum*. Boston: Houghton Mifflin.

20. Bobbitt, F. (1913). The supervision of city schools: Some general principles of management applied to the problems of city school systesm. Twelfth Yearbook (NSSE), Part 1, p. 11.

21. Bobbitt, F. (1924). *How to make a curriculum*. Chicago: Houghton Mifflin.

22. Rugg, H. O. (ed.). (1927). *Curriculum making: Past and present*. Twenty-sixth Yearbook of the National Society for the Study of Education (Part I). Bloomington, IL: Public School Publishing.

    Also quite influential in the establishment of the field was the companion volume: Rugg, H. O. (ed.). (1927). *The foundations of curriculum making*. Twenty-sixth Yearbook of the National Society for the Study of Education (Part II). Bloomington, IL: Public School Publishing.

23. *Ibid.*, (Part I), p. 51.

24. Tyler, R. W. (1971). Curriculum development in the twenties and thirties. In: *The curriculum: Retrospect and prospect*, pp. 26–44, McClure, R. M. (ed.). Chicago: University of Chicago Press.

25. Bernier, N. R. and Williams, J. E. (1973). *Beyond beliefs: Ideological foundations of American education*, Englewood Cliffs, NJ: Prentice-Hall, Inc., p. 293.

26. *Ibid.*, p. 294.
27. Counts, G. S. (original edition, 1932). Dare the school build a new social order? In: Rena L. Vassar, (ed.), *History of American education*, Vol. II. New York: Rand McNally, 1965, p. 277.
28. Flesch, R. (1955). *Why Johnny can't read*. New York: Harper and Bros.
29. Bestor, A. (1956). *The restoration of learning*. New York: Alfred A. Knopf.
30. Rickover, H. (1963). *American education — A national failure*. New York: E. P. Dutton.
31. Platt, J. (1981). The acceleration of evolution. *Futurist*, Vol. 15 (February), pp. 14–23.

# 3

# Curriculum Work: Concepts and Definitions

**Introduction: The Basic Questions**

At first glance, it does not appear difficult to define the job of curriculum making. A number of basic questions conceptually underlie all curriculum work. These include:

1. Who should be educated?
2. What should be the goals of education?
3. What should be the content of education?
4. Should the content be organized as child-centered, society-centered, subject-centered, or some variation such as child-in-society?
5. How should objectives be formulated and evaluated?
6. Should there be multiple organizations and alternative forms of school programs?
7. What systems and materials need to be developed to achieve successful and efficient experiences for children?
8. Who should be responsible for designing and developing the curriculum?
9. Who should be responsible for instructional methodology?
10. Who should be responsible for evaluation?

Each of these questions is a matter of intense debate. Together, they may be said to comprise the complex core of work called "curriculum making." The job of the curriculum maker is to achieve increased understanding of the issues involved in these questions, to assist others concerned with educational matters to arrive at the best possible responses, and to take a leadership role in the development of learning experiences consistent with the responses.

For both the elementary and secondary school specialist, there is also the question of how to relate to each other as well as to the junior high or middle school. Should the elementary schools prepare youngsters for what will be studied in the upper grades, in essence treating them as little adults, or should they accept children and how they learn as being fundamentally different and needing unique curricular arrangements? If the latter position is taken, then the curriculum of the upper grade levels would have to adjust to the curriculum of the lower grades; this assumes, of course, that coherent linkages between the elementary and secondary schools are educationally desirable. Such a "downward" adjustment is a position practically unheard of today, but it certainly could become part of a curriculum reform movement. Curriculum work involves planning how broadly held beliefs about the proper nature of education will be infused with content and linked to each other in a set of meaningful experiences.

## Curriculum and the Significance of Definition

There is, it should be noted, a measure of glibness in the preceding words as well as a tendency to ignore significant definitional problems that should not be ignored if what is done by the professional curriculum specialist is to make a truly professional contribution to schooling. As the brief list of questions above suggests, curriculum work is a multifaceted, complex undertaking that deals with questions nearly as broad as life itself. Without some delineation of the meaning of curriculum and its related terms, without some understanding of what should be included and, equally important, excluded in curriculum work, the professional is left in a wide-open and often directionless situation to which all kinds of educational needs can be attached according to the fad of the day.

### The Term "Instruction"

Let us take a fairly straightforward term such as "instruction." Is it or is it not part of the curriculum? If a teacher requires pupils to memorize the most salient facts of a unit, rather than treating the content as a set of problems needing resolution and the textbook as a reference to be used even during a test, is what students learn from the instructional methodology a part of the curriculum, or does it represent a set of learnings distinct from the curriculum?

The question is more important than may at first meet the eye. If we view instructional methodology as part of the curriculum, then a large portion of the curriculum maker's job lies in the selection, ordering, and possibly development of instructional methodologies. Such an interpretation leads to the "central office" administrator, who is in charge of curriculum, as well as being in charge of instructional methodology in the classroom.

With centralized control over instructional methodology, the professional decision making of teachers as we know it today might well be severely curtailed. While many administrators would not do this, it is possible (and has happened frequently in the last several decades) that teachers would be required to teach certain sections of the textbook according to central administration "deadlines" and to give a preestablished number of quizzes for each grading period. They could further be required to have students write a minimum number of compositions or to teach reading by the phonics method. This concern with instructional methodology on the part of some curriculum workers has at times been interpreted as "teacher-proofing" the curriculum, that is, not allowing "poor" or misguided judgment by teachers to divert the intent of the curriculum plan.

On the other hand, instructional methodology could be viewed as distinct from the curriculum. Under such an interpretation, the teacher would retain responsibility for deciding how the curriculum is to be taught and evaluated in the classroom. This is generally the current system, although increased standardized testing around the nation has made considerable inroads here.

## The Impact of Obscure Terms on Public Policy

Outside of textbooks such as this one, it is rare to discuss definition of terms and their potential impact on what we do in the schools. Notwithstanding the lack of discussion, in practice we do share a set of definitions; otherwise, we could not communicate with each other.

Our educational terminology, however, is full of nuances that are the products of very different perceptions about how education should be organized. We frequently do not communicate very clearly with each other. Allowing key terms to remain obscure or so full of connotations that no one is quite clear as to their meaning contributes, all too often, to our finding ourselves in educational situations we would not have been in had we understood the full significance of terms bandied about in public policy discussions.

For example, if a policy position has been taken that the curriculum should include specific performance objectives, students (and most likely teachers) will be evaluated on the bases of such very specific performances as students being able to supply the major dates of the Civil War as listed in Chapter 8 (or whatever) of the textbook. With a policy requiring the development and implementation of specific performance objectives, the teacher can do little individualization of instruction and will tend to avoid discussion of broad, humanistic questions unsuitable to the kinds of evaluation formats typically related to specific performance objectives. Requiring specific performance objectives as part of the curriculum plans undertaken may be a desirable policy, but it is certainly one whose implications should be fully understood. The nuances between such terms as "specific objectives" and "specific performance objectives" can make an enormous difference in the nature of the classroom experiences children have.

## The "Content" of the Curriculum

Before a clear definition of "curriculum" can be established, we need to achieve a fuller understanding of the possible interpretations of "content." The question of whether instructional methodology is part of the curriculum is really a question about whether what is learned through a particular methodology is part of the content. In any case, the relationship of "content" to the curriculum is somewhat problematic. Is the term "content" a synonym for the curriculum plan, that is, whatever is planned for the curriculum equals the content? Or, to the contrary, should we consider children's experiences outside of school part of the content? This would mean that content extends well beyond the curriculum plan. After all, children do not learn in a vacuum. Many studies have shown that content having roots in children's personal experiences is more readily learned than content foreign to their backgrounds. If the experiences that children bring with them to school are deemed to be, inevitably, part of the school's content, then the curriculum worker must devise ways of learning about the outside experiences of children.

What about experiences within the school's walls but outside the classroom? Are these part of content? For example, a fourth grade boy is standing on the lunchroom line waiting his turn when another older boy pushes ahead of him and grabs the last available piece of fruit. The younger boy tries to protest, but the older boy shoves him and moves away with the fruit on his tray. A great deal of learning has gone into that experience. Is it part of the elementary curriculum's content? Some would say it is because the school organization with its lunch periods and self-service operation caused the learning experience. On the other hand, many would consider all experiences outside the classroom as distinct from the curriculum and not part of its content.

The content of the curriculum may also be viewed from either a static or dynamic perspective. That is, the content may be conceived within well-delimited parameters meeting clearly established goals and objectives set prior to classroom instruction, or it may be conceived as being in a state of becoming; a set of learnings that can be fully known only when they have unfolded in the classroom. If the static view of content is taken, then it is most likely that the content and the curriculum are virtually synonymous. The curriculum *is* the plan for studying the content. It reflects a clear understanding of the goals and a precise translation of this into objectives.

On the other hand, if the position is taken that content is dynamic and can be fully known only when the curriculum has happened in the classroom and has encountered the diverse backgrounds, personalities, and abilities of students as well as teachers, then there is considerable difference between the curriculum plan and the content of the curriculum. While curriculum goals may be well understood, the learning objectives for the content need to be sufficiently open-ended so that what happens in the course of the plan's unfolding can ultimately be recognized as a part of the content that has been learned. The learning of processes, such as the experimental method, and of abstract skills, such as those involved in critical reading, are likely to be considered an important aspect of content, whereas the specific facts dealt with are relegated to lesser importance.

In a dynamic view of content, the teacher and, possibly, the students would have greater control over the objectives and ultimate outcomes of study than in the static view, which favors the prior establishment of specific objectives and outcomes as well as "central office" control. In most school districts today, content is perceived to be static, something that can be precisely delimited, taught with clear objectives in mind, and measured by tests to determine student achievement.

If the current interpretation of the content of curriculum was, instead, a dynamic one, curriculum practice could potentially return to the condition that existed for centuries in what we called at the beginning of this book "the precurriculum era." The curriculum maker and the teacher then were the same person, and almost no distinction was made between content and instructional methodology. The teacher, within the limits imposed by society, was in control of the curriculum. Both negatives and positives can be envisioned from this potential because "teacher control," as history reflects, has often led to very brutal and narrow-minded forms of education. No doubt, with a loving teacher or an intellectually brilliant one, curricular control by the teacher could become a vehicle of enlightenment. This was the case with Pestalozzi, Montessori, and Dewey.

Of course, when we speak of static or dynamic content, of being in or out of curricular control, we are speaking of extremes. The reality, especially in a democratic republic such as ours, is usually the result of a series of compromises. Often, the compromises satisfy no one, but they persist because no agreement about what actually is best has been achieved among the general public or even among the professional groups most directly involved.

The field of curriculum has developed through a series of compromises without ever having succeeded in establishing a foundational definition of its own nature on which to base its work. The confusion about content is especially problematic because contradictions abound with very little public or even professional awareness. In practice, content is treated as both including and excluding instructional methodologies. For example, teachers are encouraged to attend college courses and seminars to upgrade their own knowledge so they can introduce enrichment materials and new ways of dealing with the content, and then they are informed by the central administration about lists of specific performance objectives that must be taught within a given time frame and about minimum competency tests the youngsters will have to pass if the teachers expect to be considered "meritorious."

Another area of confusion involves content that emphasizes the learning of processes, a dynamic conception of content, while the achievement tests given children emphasize the static nature of the content studied. For example, historical methods of research may be emphasized during instruction but rather than being evaluated on the use of such methods, children are required to respond to specific questions such as the dates of the Civil War or of the fall of the Alamo. If the field of curriculum is "moribund,"[1] as has been suggested by the literature of the field, it is more out of confusion about what the content, scope, and purpose of its work need to be than out of a sense that it is not an important endeavor.

### The Many Uses of the Term "Curriculum"

In addition to a lack of agreement about the term "content" and its conceptual relationship to curriculum, the term, "curriculum," has been used in so many ways that one must suspect it represents several distinct, albeit subliminally held meanings. These different uses are no doubt important to people talking about their educational concerns. However, left in an embroilment of nuances, as has been the case, the many nuances have only added to the confusion regarding the nature of curriculum work.

We have, for example, heard a good deal about the "**concomitant** curriculum" that is, about those sets of out-of-school learnings derived from the home, church, government, industry, and so forth. The term "**phantom** curriculum" has been used to represent the kinds of learnings derived from television and other widespread public media. Among the most popular of these many variations on a theme is the "**hidden** curriculum," which refers to the kinds of learnings children derive from the very nature and organizational design of the public school, as well as from the behaviors and attitudes of teachers and administrators. Closely related to the hidden curriculum is the "**tacit** curriculum," which refers to the set of unwritten school policies and practices that influence children's learning. Another widely used variant is the "**latent** curriculum," which lies deep within each student as the sum of learning that has accumulated from the student's experiences and background. There is also the term "**para**curriculum," which refers to the resources for learning available outside the school walls, such as in museums, art institutions, and the like. In 1981, still another term involving curriculum was coined. This was the "**societal** curriculum," which, to quote its author, Carlos Cortes,

> . . . is that massive, ongoing, informal curriculum of family, peer groups, neighborhoods, churches, organizations, occupations, mass media, and other socializing forces that "educate" all of us throughout our lives.[2]

The predicament for the curriculum maker is obvious. Just exactly what would the job of the curriculum maker be in the "societal curriculum" or, more modestly, in the "hidden curriculum" or the "latent curriculum" or the "paracurriculum"? It is indeed mind-boggling, for what all these many usages of the term "curriculum" have in common is that they refer to phenomena that are not traditionally considered part of the school's content. In all of them, learning happens powerfully although well outside the school's planned activities for learning.

While both the hidden curriculum and the tacit curriculum are embedded in the fundamental operations of the schools, they are not part of any plan to lead students into learning, but are rather characteristics that would belong to any institution and would influence people's learning as they come in contact with the institution, regardless of the intent. Nevertheless, it must be recognized that students do learn a great deal from the functioning of the hidden and tacit curricula. Does this fact make them a true part of the school's curriculum?

The definitions of these many variations of curriculum do not involve the development of an educational design intended to guide, encourage, or improve learning. They simply reflect the fact that learning goes on inside or outside the school whether or not a plan exists. In a sense, by using the term in a context that would otherwise not be appropriate, these variations become statements about the importance of some kinds of learning to the school's curriculum. The tacit curriculum is sending the message that it is important to understand the impact of the school's policies on the planned curriculum. The paracurriculum could offer a vital set of resources to the school's curriculum if only there were recognition in the school's curriculum of this fact.

Notwithstanding the utility of these terms, they have served to deepen the ambiguity regarding what curriculum work is all about. It is important to note that whatever professional judgment might be involved in curriculum making is precluded in all of these many variations of the term. There is an implication in each of them that everyone is potentially a curriculum maker and that no special expertise is necessary. Learning happens because some set of circumstances exists without any intervention on the part of the curriculum maker. The curriculum, in sum, would be whatever is learned, whether it has been planned or not.

## The Definition of "Curriculum" Is in Reality a Continuum of Definitions

No single definition of curriculum is accepted among practitioners of the field. There is, instead, a wide-ranging continuum of interpretations with numerous intermediate positions. Table 3.1 presents a sampling of what has remained the persistent spread of opinion regarding the nature of curriculum among the top experts of the field since its inception in the early decades of the twentieth century.

All of the statements included in Table 3.1 fall along a definitional continuum of curriculum defined by the following two descriptions:

### 1. The Curriculum Is the Sum of Planned Content

The curriculum is the course of study designed for student instruction under the direction of the school. Content may be treated as either static or dynamic insofar as processes and skills may be included in the course of study. However, the perception of the curriculum as a clearly delimited set of plans is more compatible with a static interpretation of content, the specific outcomes of which may be described prior to class instruction and measured for the sake of evaluation following instruction. Instructional methodology may or may not be considered a part of the curriculum's content. Henry C. Morrison's 1940 description,[3] Hilda Taba's 1962 interpretation,[4] and Philip Phenix's 1962 definition,[5] all briefly summarized in Table 3.1, exemplify this narrow conceptualization of the curriculum. If what students learn or even if what teachers teach is not part of the specific plan for learning, then, regardless of the value of the experience, it is not part of the curriculum.

### 2. The Curriculum Is All the Experiences under the School's Direction that Lead to Learning

The curriculum is defined broadly as the sum of experiences leading to the learnings that occur under the auspices of the school whether or not these are part of the written content guide. Since learnings must occur under the school's direction, some form of organization planned by educators is a prerequisite for inclusion in the curriculum. Planning, however, can be quite indirect as in the case of the boy in the lunchroom, who was no doubt taught to wait his turn on the line.

TABLE 3.1 *Definitional and Descriptive Statements of Curriculum, 1916–1982*

| Name | Year | Definition |
| --- | --- | --- |
| John Dewey | 1916 | . . . education consists primarily in transmission through communication. . . . As societies become more complex in structure and resources, the need for formal or intentional teaching and learning increases. |
| William C. Bagley | 1907 | [The curriculum] . . . is a storehouse of organized race experience, conserved [until] needed in the constructive solution of new and untried problems.[10] |
| Frederick G. Bonser | 1920 | . . . experiences in which pupils are expected to engage in school, and the general . . . sequence in which these experiences are to come.[11] |
| Franklin Bobbitt | 1924 | . . . that series of things which children and youth must do and experience by way of developing abilities to do the things well that make up the affairs of adult life; and to be in all respects what adults should be. |
| Hollis L. Caswell and Doak S. Campbell | 1935 | . . . all of the experiences children have under the guidance of teachers. |
| Robert M. Hutchins | 1936 | The curriculum should include grammar, reading, rhetoric and logic, and mathematics, and in addition at the secondary level introduce the great books of the Western world. |
| Pickens E. Harris | 1937 | . . . real curriculum development is individual. It is also multiple in the sense that there are teachers and separate children. . . . There will be a curriculum for each child. |
| Henry C. Morrison | 1940 | . . . the content of instruction without reference to instructional ways or means. |
| Dorris Lee and Murray Lee | 1940 | . . . those experiences of the child which the school in any way utilizes or attempts to influence. |
| L. Thomas Hopkins | 1941 | The curriculum [is a design made] by all of those who are most intimately concerned with the activities of the life of the children while they are in school . . . a curriculum must be as flexible as life and living. It cannot be made beforehand and given to pupils and teachers to install. [Also, it] . . . represents those learnings each child selects, accepts, and incorporates into himself to act with, in, and upon in subsequent experiences. |
| H.H. Giles, S.P. McCutchen, and A.N. Zechiel | 1942 | . . . the curriculum is . . . the total experience with which the school deals in educating young people.[12] |
| Harold Rugg | 1947 | [The curriculum is] the . . . stream of guided activities that constitutes the life of young people and their elders. [In a much earlier book, Rugg disapprovingly spoke of the traditional curriculum as one ". . . passing on descriptions of earlier cultures and to perpetuating dead languages and abstract techniques which were useful to no more than a negligible fraction of our population."][13] |
| Ralph Tyler | 1949 | . . . learning takes place through the experiences the learner |

**TABLE 3.1**  *Continued*

| Name | Year | Definition |
| --- | --- | --- |
| | | has . . . "learning experience" is not the same as the content with which a course deals . . . [The curriculum consists of] . . . all of the learning of students which is planned by and directed by the school to attain its educational goals. |
| Edward A. Krug | 1950 | . . . all learning experiences under the direction of the school. |
| B. Othanel Smith, W.O. Stanley, and J. Harlan Shores | 1950 | . . . a sequence of potential experiences . . . set up in school for the purpose of disciplining children and youth in group ways of thinking and acting. |
| Roland B. Faunce and Nelson L. Bossing | 1951 | . . . those learning experiences that are fundamental for all learners because they derive from (1) our common, individual drives and needs, and (2) our civic and social needs as participating members of a democratic society. |
| Authur E. Bestor | 1953 | The economic, political, and spiritual health of a democratic state . . . requires of *every* man and woman a variety of complex skills which rest upon sound knowledge of science, history, economic, philosophy, and other fundamental disciplines. . . . The fundamental disciplines . . . have become, in the jargon of . . . educationists, "subject matter fields." But a discipline is by no means the same as a subject matter field. The one is a way of thinking, the other a mere aggregation of facts. |
| Harold Alberty | 1953 | All of the activities that are provided for students by the school constitutes its curriculum.[14] |
| George Beauchamp | 1956 | . . . the design of a social group for the educational experiences of their children in school. [Dr. Beauchamp reflects growing emphasis on group processes by the 1950s.][15] |
| Philip H. Phenix | 1962 | The curriculum should consist entirely of knowledge which comes from the disciplines [while] education should be conceived as guided recapitulation of the processes of inquiry which gave rise to the fruitful bodies of organized knowledge comprising the established disciplines. |
| Hilda Taba | 1962 | A curriculum is a plan for learning; therefore, what is known about the learning process and the development of the individual has bearing on the shaping of a curriculum. |
| John I. Goodlad | 1963 | A curriculum consists of all those learnings intended for a student or group of students.[16] |
| Harry S. Broudy, B. Othanel Smith, and Joe R. Burnett | 1964 | . . . modes of teaching are not, strictly speaking, a part of the curriculum [which] consists primarily of certain kinds of content organized into categories of instruction. |
| J. Galen Saylor and William M. Alexander | 1966 and 1974 | [the curriculum is] . . . all learning opportunities provided by the school. . . . a plan for providing sets of learning opportunities to achieve broad educational goals and related specific objectives for an identifiable population served by a single school center. |
| The Plowden Report | 1967 | The curriculum, in the narrow sense, [consisted of] the sub- |

*(continued)*

**TABLE 3.1**   *Continued*

| Name | Year | Definition |
|------|------|------------|
| (British) | | jects studied. . . in the period 1898 to 1944. . . .[17] |
| Mauritz Johnson, Jr. | 1967 | . . . a structured series of intended learning outcomes.[18] |
| W. J. Popham and Eva L. Baker | 1970 | . . . all planned learning outcomes for which the school is responsible.[19] |
| Daniel Tanner and Laurel Tanner | 1975 | . . . the planned and guided learning experiences and intended learning outcomes, formulated through the systematic reconstruction of knowledge and experiences under the auspices of the school, for the learner's continuous and willful growth in personal–social competence.[20] |
| Donald E. Orlosky and B. Othanel Smith | 1978 | Curriculum is the substance of the school program. It is the content pupils are expected to learn.[21] |
| Peter F. Oliva | 1982 | Curriculum [is] the plan or program for all experiences which the learner encounters under the direction of the school. |

Both static and dynamic content may be considered part of the experiences of schooling. That is, a plan for some specific learnings may be established in typical, static fashion, but content may also be conceived as emerging from the unplanned experiences of schooling. In fact, the use of the term "experience" tends to emphasize the dynamic qualities of the curriculum, which, of course increases the curriculum's compatibility with dynamic content such as would be included in the teaching of how to do research or application of logical analyses to a number of different fields. Under this definition, the full curriculum can be known only after it has happened. This conception of the curriculum is most succinctly expressed in Caswell and Campbell's 1935 book *Curriculum Development*.[6] It was also championed by Lee and Lee in their 1940 book,[7] by Edward Krug in 1950,[8] and by Saylor and Alexander in 1966.[9] (It is interesting to note the significant difference in the latter's 1974 definition.)

Within the context of this broad definition, the "hidden curriculum" would be one kind of content in the school's curriculum. There is no allowance for the concept of the hidden curriculum in the narrower definition. Such experiences as having equal amounts of time for every subject, the ringing of bells for class changes, dress codes, and study halls, all under the direction of the school, are part of most students' school experiences, and they are certainly among the means utilized by the schools to prepare youngsters for acceptable modes of behavior especially in the context of business and industry.

### Democracy and the Definition of Curriculum

Defining the term "curriculum" is necessary to the delineation of the professional curriculum maker's functions. But we are not simply seeking a dictionary-like definition that would take no position on what ought to be the nature of the field. The definition that we ultimately accept to guide our work as curriculum makers must also be consistent with the political philosophy that our society holds about its educational institutions. As the educational philosopher Boyd Bode[22] noted over fifty years ago, education in a democracy must be qualitatively different from the forms of education that have arisen under autocracies and elitism. Similarly, the definition of curriculum must be consistent with the democratic principles of public education and equal oportunity for all.

A democracy must respect the individual's right to independent judgment and personal expression; it also requires that citizens live productively and respectfully with other members of society. The definition of curriculum must somehow balance these contradictory extremes that are, nonetheless, at the very heart of American democracy. Furthermore, the definition of curriculum cannot ignore the effect of each child's experience on the plan for learning. Children bring personal experiences with them, and curriculum making owes to our democratic principles recognition of these experiences. On the other hand, there must be a point of interaction and relationship between each child's unique requirements and societal needs as represented in the planned content of the curriculum.

A definition of curriculum needs to form the basis for an educational framework compatible with democracy. While the specific routes to be taken are often not clear, they do need to fall within a democratically based conception of governance. The curriculum can neither ignore the individual nor so fully embrace the needs of the individual as to ignore society. In a democracy, the individual and society are always in the act of balancing one another. How that balance is achieved is a major political activity. Even when societal good is deemed to be at the acme of importance and an emphasis on individual benefit is equated with selfishness, concern for how individuals behave is always present. Obviously, if only the individual is believed to be of significance in human life, anarchy is the result. If neither of these extremes is considered desirable, then an eclectic, perhaps dynamic compromise is necessary. In other words, societal needs and individual needs must be, somehow, balanced in the curriculum.

Accepting the tenets of democracy as fundamental to curriculum work still leaves many questions unresolved. For instance, how open shall the curriculum be to the development of such processes as the critical evaluation of American political institutions or the exercise of consumer rights? Shall youngsters be made to follow curriculum plans to the letter and taught that following instructions is the primary way of receiving rewards in society, or shall they be encouraged to work and think independently, and to even be willing to stand alone when their beliefs require such a position? Of course, no definition will completely "fix" the values built into the curriculum. Rather, it will offer a framework of compatibility for one or another set of curricular values.

### Eclecticism and Democracy

At its best, eclecticism represents a school of thought that would seek to bring together and integrate the most promising ideas put forth by competing schools of thought. This is the definition of what we would call *reflective eclecticism*. In practice, eclecticism is at the very heart of American democracy. We are in a constant state of compromising among competing conceptions of what our goals ought to be and the best ways to accomplish them. In the second half of the twentieth century, we have consistently voted for a Republican to be president while electing predominantly democratic congresses; we are deeply and humanely concerned about the health of the people, while simultaneously making judgments about national health expenditures based on cost effectiveness; and we have certainly straddled the line of ambiguity as well as compromise in our attitudes toward the governmental regulation of big business.

Of course, one can scrutinize forms of governance and present sharp ideological contrasts such as exist between communism and democracy, especially when presented in their most doctrinaire forms. From such a perspective, one would be hard pressed to relate the conception of democracy to eclecticism because that might appear to be "giving in" to communism or some other "-ism." In such extreme argumentative terminology, education in a democracy becomes a statement of beliefs bordering on propaganda. However, the real world practice of American democracy with its respect for individual rights, its pluralism of creeds and ethnicities, and its openness to progress and change make eclecticism, reflective or otherwise, peculiar to it and, quite possibly, crucial to its success.

The more eye-catching aspects of eclecticism may be experienced on seeing a restaurant sign advertising kosher pizza or Greek soul food. More seriously, it is reflected in what has been called "secular humanism." As Americans avoid making judgments about the beliefs and creeds of diverse groups, they seek to garner those ideas from each that support a humane and kindly way of dealing with each other that may be pursued by all groups in a common public arena—hence, "secular" humanism.

## An Eclectic Definition of Curriculum

For the authors of this text, the definition of curriculum needs to balance specific outcomes with emerging experiences. The needs of the child-in-society, that is, of an individual who ultimately must take stands and engage in decision making as an active citizen of a democracy, should be supported in our basic conception of curriculum making. In other words, the definition needs to lie somewhere in the center of the continuum. This compromise between educational extremes may be thought of as *educational eclecticism* and the authors of this text as *educational eclectics*.

We also think of ourselves as ardent proponents of democracy who recognize that, in a pluralistic nation such as our own, the carefully analyzed, well-constructed integration of ideas is at the very crux of our governance. The pursuit of reflective eclecticism is necessary to the development of an education uniquely suited to an American form of democracy.

The curriculum should include a written plan or curriculum guide dealing with the content selected for school study. The curriculum, however, is more than the curriculum plan. The plan is not only for the use of teachers and the school administration. It should also be designed for circulation and discussion among the public at large. Curriculum makers have a responsibility to the public to explain what they believe the curriculum will accomplish and how they think the plan will relate to the unfolding of the curriculum.

Our eclectic definition of curriculum is as follows:

*Curriculum is the result of the interaction of objectively developed plans for school study with the backgrounds, personalities, and capacities of students in a transactional environment created by teachers for the benefit of students as well as for the better implementation of the plan.*[23]

This is a definition that neither insists that all outcomes be known in advance nor that all planning await an analysis of the students' needs and/or personalities. It is also a definition that allows for continual variations in how the plans and students interact not only because of differences that students exhibit but also because of modifications to the planned learning environment brought about by the teacher.

The experiences youngsters have in school while following the curriculum will themselves be influential on how remaining curriculum is interpreted and learned. If the same students were to follow the same curriculum twice, it is safe to say that what would be learned and achieved the second time through would differ from the results of the first pass.

Similarly, instructional activities that interface with the plans for learning would necessarily become a part of the curriculum. The influence of instructional methodology is too powerful to be ignored. This, however, would not have to mean that all instructional planning would be overseen by the curriculum developer. Because the unique backgrounds, personalities, and capabilities of teachers and students inevitably have an important influence on the curriculum, the everyday observations that teachers can make and the individualized decisions they can make would serve as bridges between planning at the district level (or even the state level) and real world circumstances. From an eclectic's perspective, instructional methodologies are the teacher's efforts to mold the learning plan to fit the educational situation at hand. While the curriculum plan can establish in broad outline what should be studied, the curriculum can be fully known only when it has finally come into being.

Under our eclectic definition, the following composite of statements about the nature of curriculum would be appropriate:

1. The curriculum contains a written document that suggests the educational content and other experiences to be pursued by students for whom the school accepts responsibility. It may include objectives, suggested materials, and recommended methods.
2. The curriculum should represent a societal consensus concerning the breadth and general sequence of what is to be learned. In this context, the development of the curriculum should involve participatory planning or consultation with community groups and agencies as well as teachers and students.

3. The curriculum should have the capacity to allow for and even encourage diversity among children. Children are neither perfect reflections of society nor autonomous beings living apart from the structures of society. The curriculum needs to strike a balance between the requirements of society and the independent, unique development of each child.

4. The exact curriculum can be fully known only as the curriculum plan is encountered by individual students. A distinction is made here between the written document, which is the curriculum plan, often referred to as the curriculum guide, and the curriculum, which is what is learned by youngsters when the interaction of the plan and their backgrounds actually unfold as experiences in the classroom. This represents a dynamic conception of content.

5. The success of the curriculum is largely dependent on the instructional decisions made by teachers. While curriculum and instruction are conceived as separate entities, the relationship is really one of integration, with the curriculum plan impacting on instruction and instruction impacting on the resulting curriculum.[24]

6. Assessment for evaluation of desired academic, personal, and social changes, or the absence thereof, is desirable and necessary. However, standardized tests are rarely appropriate because they exclude both the curriculum maker and the teacher from the evaluation process. If our curriculum and instruction are to improve, feedback must come in forms relevant to the actual curriculum and not as a quantified summary of performance (e.g., a standard test score), which is usually based on a static conception of content.

## QUESTIONS FOR DISCUSSION AND REFLECTION

1. Table 3.1 on page 000, presents a series of differing definitions for the term "curriculum," as proposed by a number of scholars in the field.
   Which of the definitions may be clearly classified as belonging under the following categories:
   a. Curriculum as "planned content."
   b. Curriculum as "all learning occurring on the school premises."
   c. Curriculum as the "dynamic interaction of a plan, students' backgrounds and personalities, and the teacher."
   d. The definition does not fit any of the above. (Please explain.)

2. Which definitions in Table 3.1 would be:
   a. static
   b. dynamic
   c. both static and dynamic

3. What are the differences between an eclectic definition of curriculum and:
   a. a definition that considers curriculum as being only the written plan.
   b. a definition that considers curriculum as all the learning experiences students have in school.

4. From your personal point of view, which definition of curriculum would you support and why?

5. Given today's circumstances and America's likely short-term future, which definition of curriculum from Table 3.1 would be most appropriate for current educational realities and why?

6. What rational linkages may be made between the eclectic definition of curriculum and democracy as a form of government? Is the eclectic view of curriculum necessary in a democracy, or does the definition of curriculum make no political difference? Explain your viewpoint and, if necessary, the disagreements you may have with the authors of this work.

7. Under the eclectic definition of curriculum, six generalizations about curriculum were presented. Can you recall these and state them in your own words? Would you add to the generalizations, perhaps taking ideas from your own experiences as an educator?

8. It was suggested in this chapter that instruction significantly affects the nature of the curriculum. What definition of curriculum is implicit in this statement? Can you give several specific examples of how instruction might impact on the curriculum?

9. Seven variations on the term "curriculum" have been presented in this chapter. Can you identify and explain the meaning of each? In your opinion, why have so many variations come into use? Does the increased usage of the term "curriculum" help or hinder our understanding of the field? Explain your opinions.

10. At the very beginning of this chapter, a set of ten basic questions was presented to the reader. How would you personally respond to each? You may need to think about your answers while reading the remainder of Part I.

## NOTES

1. MacDonald, J. B. (1971). Curriculum development in relation to social and intellectual systems. In: *The curriculum: Retrospect and prospect*, XVII NSSE Yearbook.
2. Cortes, C. E. (1981). The societal curriculum: Implications for multiethnic education. In: Banks, J. A. (ed.), *Education in the 80's: Multiethnic education*. National Education Association, 1981, p. 24.
3. Morrison, H. C. (1940). *The curriculum of the common school.* Chicago: University of Chicago Press.
4. Taba, H. (1962). *Curriculum development: Theory and practice.* New York: Harcourt Brace Jovanovich.
5. Phenix, P. H. (1962). The uses of the disciplines of curriculum content. *Educational Forum* 26(3), pp. 273–280.
6. Caswell, H. L. and Campbell, D. S. (1935). *Curriculum development.* New York: American Book Company.
7. Lee, J. M. and Lee, D. W. (1940). *The child and his curriculum.* New York: Appleton-Century.
8. Krug, E. (1950). *Curriculum planning.* New York: Harper & Row.

9. Saylor, J. G. and Alexander, W. M. (1966). *Curriculum planning for better teaching and learning*. New York: Holt, Rinehart and Winston.

In the same context, we have also referred to the 1974 revised version of this work.

10. Bagley, W. C. (1907). *Classroom management*. New York: Macmillan.

11. Bonser, F. G. (1920). *The elementary curriculum*. New York: Macmillan.

12. Giles, H. H., McCutchen, S. P. and Zechiel, A. N. (1942). *Exploring the curriculum*. New York: Harper & Brothers.

13. Rugg, H. (1947). *Foundations for American education*. New York: World Book.

14. Alberty, H. (1953). *Reorganizing the high school curriculum* (revised edition). New York: Macmillan.

15. Beauchamp, G. A. (1956). *Planning the elementary curriculum*. Boston: Allyn and Bacon.

16. Goodlad, J. et al. (1963). *Planning and organizing for teaching*. Washington, D.C.: National Education Association.

17. Report of the Central Advisory Council for Education (1967). *Children and their primary schools*. London: Her Majesty's Stationery Office.

18. Johnson, M., Jr. (1967). Definitions and models in curriculum theory. *Educational Theory*, Vol. 17 (April).

19. Popham, W. J. and Baker, E. I. (1970). *Systematic instruction*. Englewood Cliffs, NJ: Prentice-Hall.

20. Tanner, D. and Tanner, L. (1975). *Curriculum development*. New York: Macmillan.

21. Orlosky, D. E. and Smith, B. O. (1978). *Curriculum development: issues and insights*. Chicago: Rand McNally.

22. Bode, B. H. (1938). *Progressive education at the crossroads*. New York: Newson.

23. The kernel of this definition was utilized by Shirley H. Engle in his curriculum classes at Indiana University in the mid 1970s.

24. Peter F. Oliva notes that curriculum and instruction have "a continuing circular relationship." Oliva, P. F. (1982). *Developing the curriculum*. Boston: Little, Brown, p. 13.

# 4

# Curriculum Design: Principles, Issues and Caveats

### Introduction

Curriculum design is the outcome of a process by which the purposes of education are linked to the selection and organization of content. Content may be conceived as being in either a dynamic or static state. It may include a broad range of experiences under the direction of the schools; it may include the selection and development of instructional methodologies. Depending on the interpretation of the term "content," curriculum design may also include the evaluation of curricular outcomes.

## Designing the Curriculum

### Control

The discussion about the definition of "curriculum" turns out to be a discussion as well about the nature and extent of the control to be exerted over the curriculum by parties other than the teacher. The more control to be exercised over the specific outcomes of a plan, say by the central administration, the more closed the classroom curriculum is likely to be. A curriculum design based on a very precise selection of the content to be studied, including specific instructional guidelines and evaluation of outcomes based on measurable student performance, leads to a closed curriculum that is easily controlled from outside the classroom.

To the degree that one or more of the preceding characteristics is given more flexibility, the design itself becomes more open. If outcomes are conceived in more general terms—say, "children shall be familiar with the plants of the region" instead of "children shall identify at least three of the following five plants. . . ."— then the exact outcomes must be determined by the teacher and evaluation will depend to a considerable degree on the teacher's input. This makes the design more open to variation by placing it under the control of individual teachers.

### Responsibility

The more closed the curriculum design is, the more narrow is the responsibility accepted by the schools. Limiting the school's curriculum to the learning of the selected content diminishes the school's responsibility for other kinds of learnings that occur under its auspices whether or not they are part of the official curriculum. For example, American elementary schools often include on children's report cards such items as "gets along well with others" and "works well independently." The only way to get at the content of such items is to observe them as processes that become concrete through the children's experiences. As items in a continuous state of unfolding, they are dynamic content well-suited to an open conception of curriculum. They also represent acceptance by the schools of responsibility for children's social behavior that goes well beyond any planned content that the curriculum could present or any specific behaviors that the design could describe as outcomes prior to the actual implementation of the curriculum.

### Purposes, Aims, Goals and Objectives

Logically, the purposes of schooling form the bases for curriculum design. Whenever education is organized into formal schooling by society, the undertaking is purposeful. Purposes represent the values as well as the needs of society, and thus give direction to schooling. When educational purposes are expressed systematically but quite broadly, they are called aims. "Preparing the young to be productive members of society" is a purpose that may support aims of vocational training, self-realization, citizenship, and intellectual development. The aims are the translation of society's purpose into a set of open-ended categories[1] indicating where the schools are to give their emphases.

Statements of goals turn aims into general outcomes that the schools can accomplish. Goals define in broad terms the policies that, if implemented well, are expected to fulfill the aims held by society for the curriculum. Logically, it may be said that goals underlie the selection and treatment of content and are at the very heart of curriculum design. Several examples of curricular goals follow:

- Students should develop skills in mathematics.

- The well-educated person is knowledgeable about health and is able to protect his or her own health.

- Students shall learn to read and write effectively.

- Successful education will develop in the young appreciation of the arts.

- Skills necessary to the effective practice of citizenship in a democracy shall be acquired by all students.

Objectives represent the analyses and transformation of goals into actions believed to support the achievement of the goals. The development of objectives is important in determining the content of the curriculum and how it is to be dealt with. It is crucial to the processes of curriculum design. It is also an exceedingly difficult undertaking. What exactly are those skills that support the effective practice of citizenship? How can appreciation of the arts be developed? Of the many mathematical skills students might acquire, which ought to be taught and why? Questions such as these must be answered if the objectives translating the broad generalizations of goals into practice are to be successfully achieved.

Objectives may be classified into one of three groups: *broad objectives*, *specific objectives*, and *specific performance objectives*. A major but certainly not the only difference among the three groups entails the degree of specificity required in describing the expected outcomes of schooling. Again, we are involved in the question of control imposed from outside the classroom.

As the name implies, broad objectives are the least restrictive and most often address higher order learning such as that involved in analyzing the multiple layers of meaning in great literary works, or affective learning such as fostering a love and appreciation for classical music. Any number of learning activities and resulting behaviors on the part of students may be interpreted as contributing to the achievement of the broad objective. The responsibility of the teacher is considerably greater when the curriculum design uses only broad objectives than is the case when the other types of objectives are used. There is also greater flexibility and openness as to the conduct and outcomes of the curriculum. It is not unusual, however, to find that the broad objective is used in the curriculum design as a form of bridge between the goals and the more specific objectives.

Both specific objectives and specific performance objectives specify the nature of the learning activities to be undertaken. However, the specific performance objective requires that the description of outcomes be made in terms of observable and measurable behaviors and that the measures themselves be included as part of the objective. Specific objectives also clearly delineate the content to be learned but without indicating what the measures of instructional success are to be.

To contrast the difference between these two types, a specific objective in music might be: "Students will be able to distinguish between the music of Bach, Mozart, and Beethoven," while a comparable, specific performance objective would be: "Students will be able to identify three compositions by each of the composers Bach, Mozart and Beethoven after having listened to performances of the included list of compositions and having read the accompanying explanatory notes."

It is important to realize that both kinds of objectives are explicit in their expression. The specific performance objective describes its outcomes in terms of observable and measurable behaviors, while the specific objective delineates the learning to be achieved but remains open to an array of behavioral outcomes depending on the instructional methodologies pursued by the teacher. The specific performance objective tells teachers exactly what is expected of them and their students. In the process, classroom flexibility is given up and the professional contributions that teachers could make to the curriculum are severely limited. The broad objective, in contrast to both of these, might refer to such nebulous content as understanding and appreciating Elizabethan literature. It would not indicate the learning activities to be undertaken or the mode of evaluation to be pursued, leaving those decisions to the judgment of each teacher.

### Logic, Cultural Mindsets, and the Goals of Education

The discerning reader may have noticed our frequent use of such terms as "logically" and "rationally" in our discussion of purposes, aims, goals, and objectives. There is, however, a considerable distance between what our reason would have us do in the design and implementation of curriculum and what we actually do.

Curriculum is not merely a rational enterprise, although rationality is fundamental in most of our current efforts to improve schooling. Together with the gathering of evidence and a willingness to look at the evidence objectively in order to achieve universal propositions about curriculum, systematic and logical planning are perceived to be at the very heart of curriculum work. However, establishing a set of basic questions for curriculum work, as we did in the preceding chapter, developing responses to them that reflect our needs and values as well as the precepts of a democracy, turning these responses into goals and objectives that will guide learning activities, and even the recognition that what we do in the schools is often not consistent with the policies we have thus developed are all rational steps that will *not* alone lead to any significant change in what we have children study in the schools.

Education is part of the cultural fabric of society. The rational analyses performed by curriculum professionals may make the difference if the cultural circumstances are right—if, for instance, a major vector of change undoes the existing cultural organization and society has no choice but to reshape its structures. To prescribe, however, in the curriculum that children shall study, say, statistics in junior high instead of geometry because current circumstances have made statistics very important to our decision-making processes would encounter opposition from a wide range of sources and would not alone make much difference. Professionals in the realm of mathematics would probably be concerned about communicating the basic nature of mathematics to young children. This would require geometry rather than statistics. The adoption of statistics in place of geometry would probably lead to considerable unrest among parents, especially those concerned about their children meeting college admission requirements, which might well not be satisfied by a course in statistics. The more theoretically inclined, looking toward a future of unknowns, might feel that statistics is an ephemeral kind of knowledge that would not yield long-term benefits for either children or society. Every change in curriculum is a societal debate touching our basic cultural fabric but often without changing the texture of the fabric at all.

### Designing Curriculum and Cultural Mindset

The "ideal" approach to designing a curriculum, as typically described in textbooks such as this one, follows a systematic and logically based framework. The purposes and aims of schooling become stated goals. These, in turn, become the guiding forces undergirding the development of objectives and content selection. The goals and objectives represent the rational, analytical approach to schooling. That is, we know as a society what we want from schooling, and our goals express our purposes in ways that support the appropriate selection of content. As described, it is all a very rational process. Descriptions of curriculum design based on systematic frameworks such as the one we have alluded to can be found in Saylor and Alexander's 1974 work,[2] Ralph Tyler's still widely used 1949 model,[3] and Francis Hunkin's 1980 effort.[4]

In our overview of the history of education in chapter 1, we noted that the Latin grammar school curriculum design remained the dominant form of curriculum from the fall of the Roman Empire until well into the nineteenth century. Across this long period of history, the purposes of schooling changed significantly, while the basic curriculum design remained unchanged. From the dominant role of commerce in Roman times to the domination of religion and then of science, the Latin grammar school curriculum design remained essentially intact. Maintaining this design required a great deal of rationalization that hardly makes sense as we, in the wisdom of hindsight, look at our curricular past as though it were a mindless aberration of not very advanced societies.

Closer to the truth is that we absorb almost by osmosis the traditions of our society and are hardly aware of all the preconceived notions thus embedded in us from generation to generation. The power of tradition in education, along with the expectations about education built into our cultural mindsets at the earliest stages of our development, undermine the best of our logical analyses.

Since World War II, every decade has witnessed a significant movement calling for educational reform. While a few area studies here and there have changed, the basic curriculum designs of both the elementary and secondary schools continue to reflect the work of two national committees organized in the 1890s, the Committee of Ten and the Committee of Fifteen, along with their fundamentally different views of the purposes of schooling.

All of us have experienced as youngsters the curriculum designs fostered at the turn of the century; all of us have experienced a similar grading system, a similar way of organizing the schools, and a very similar content. For example, around the seventh grade, most of us memorized the capitals of the forty-eight contiguous states, filling them in on a blank map of the United States along with the names of major rivers and mountain ranges. In the fifth grade, most of us learned about the Boston Tea Party and Paul Revere's ride as though they were of equal importance to the American Revolution. All too many of us struggled with fractions from grades four through eight either completely mystified at their workings or bored to tears with the repetition.

Buried deep within our cultural mindsets is the system of schooling and the curriculum designs of our youth. Through the inevitable enculturation of our youth, we become "hooked" on the past. Reform movements that appeal to our reason and that depend on logical, systematic planning to accomplish their visions of a more effective curriculum are not enough to change ways of behaving and believing learned before we could even evaluate the quality of what we were involved in.

If Americans are asked about the quality of American schooling in general, they describe it as mediocre at best, assigning a "C" to its performance. On the other hand, if they are asked about their own personal educational experiences, the vast majority think their own experiences were good, either an "A" or "B." Obviously, there is a significant contradiction between the views we hold about American education in general and the views we hold about our own personal educational experiences.

Logic and systematic planning about curriculum are not sufficient. Reasoned analyses of our current circumstances lead us toward reform. We know our schools' curricula have lost much of their relevance for the lives we must lead. Furthermore, achievement tests in recent years tell us that we are not doing well in such traditional subject areas as mathematics and reading. Logically, we are ready for reform, and yet very little change has taken place. Our childhood memories of bygone school days and the set of perceptions about "good" education, learned so early and buried so deeply in our subliminal mindsets we hardly know they exist, nonetheless interfere with the enactment of our reforms.

Our conceptions about schooling are so firmly fixed in our minds that new approaches to curriculum coping with new expectations, even ones we would agree with in light of the evidence and our own rational analyses, are often rejected as being impractical and unsuited to the "real world." For example, the "New Math" of the late 1950s and 1960s was a reconceptualization of the elementary school mathematics curriculum. Rather than persisting with the traditional drill and practice of addition, subtraction, multiplication, and division, it introduced elementary school children to number bases and set theory, both exceedingly important for a good understanding of computer operations.

The need for the new curriculum was widely accepted until parents and teachers realized that children were no longer practicing the basic arithmetic skills of addition and subtraction. Instead, they were involved in exercises that they, the adults, often did not fully understand. The goal of the "New Math" curriculum was to teach underlying mathematics concepts rather than the memorization of a few basic algorithms. Even now, as we move into the 1990s, and are witnessing a phenomenal increase in the power and uses of computers, the "New Math" is found only rarely in the elementary schools. The traditional arithmetic curriculum that most of us experienced as children prevails.

Similarly, in the social studies, a sixth grader who can discuss presidential campaign tactics but cannot give the correct dates for the Civil War is usually viewed as having been inadequately educated.[5] Certainly, the question about the Civil War is likely to be on an achievement exam, while the ability to analyze current political problems in an objective and logical fashion is just as likely to be ignored. Our achievement tests, like our traditional curriculum, reflect cultural mindsets in education that evolved at the turn of the century.

## Curriculum Designs and the Patterns Followed

### Four Conceptions

In the course of our discussion reviewing various definitions of curriculum, its history and purposes, we have at different times, either directly or indirectly, referred to four distinct conceptions of curriculum design related to the selection of content. Each represents a set of values about what is important in education. Taken together, they are generally representative of the thinking of the field. They are as follows:

1. The society-oriented curriculum,
2. The child-centered curriculum,
3. The knowledge-centered curriculum, and
4. The eclectic curriculum.

Each of these categories involves a different set of purposes underlying the selection of content. If the purposes of the curriculum revolve around meeting the needs of the social group as a whole, then the curriculum maker, pursuing a logical format, asks questions and seeks content that are relevant to those needs. In this context, a goal of schooling might be to prepare children to understand the problems confronting society and to enable them to participate in the solutions. In searching for appropriate content, the curriculum maker might ask, *"What are the major concerns of society that children will need to know about in their future?"* The responses to this question would lead to the development of goals and objectives and, of course, to the selection of content, which might include topics such as pollution and unemployment.

If the purposes of schooling are conceived as being the maximization of each child's abilities and talents, then curriculum design reflects a dynamic content that can only be determined with the individualized analysis of each child's potential. In such an instance, the curriculum designer and the teacher are likely to be one and the same.

In the case where the purposes of school study are linked to the children's acquisition of objective or disciplined-based knowledge, the curriculum designer seeks to determine the kinds of knowledge that establish a foundation for children so that as adults they will be able to use their knowledge to live better, fuller lives. A humanistic interpretation of this purpose could lead to Shakespeare's plays being selected as content because of their insights into the human mind, the beauty of their expression, and the perennial quality of the problems treated. On the other hand, a more utilitarian view could lead to the selection of scientific disciplines and modern languages.

Even when experts agree on the basic approach to curriculum, they may diverge significantly from each other. For example, the fact that "in their future" was included in the question posed above dealing with the major concerns of society holds real significance for the selection of content. Current needs of society are certainly a reasonable basis for choosing content without turning to the future. The fact that the future was brought into consideration could be a source of debate. Indeed, what do we know about the future needs of society that would be important to utilize as a basis for curriculum design? Many would say we don't know enough about the future to make it a source of content. Curricular experts who may otherwise agree on the conceptual bases of schooling may nevertheless disagree on the approach to take. In designing the curriculum, purposes are filtered through a series of questions that represent the curriculum worker's own views about what needs to be considered in the process of linking goals to content. It is thus not unusual for underlying conceptions of curriculum design to evolve along different lines even though there may be agreement about the basic purposes of schooling.

The following discussion takes each curriculum design category and explores its purposes and structures in greater depth. In particular, each category will be viewed from several perspectives.

### The Society-Oriented Curriculum

This conception of curriculum design is based on the view that the purpose of schooling is to serve the needs of society. Society and its perceived needs form the bases for content selection.

Examples of this approach to curriculum design may be found in statements from Smith, Stanley, and Shores in their 1950 work, *Fundamentals of Curriculum Development*,[6] and in Beauchamp's several editions of *Curriculum Theory* (latest published in 1981),[7] in which the curriculum is defined as the design of a social group for the in-school experiences of children. Faunce and Bossing's 1951 statement is the most explicit of the three sources listed here in its support of the societal needs of curriculum.[8] It is their view that the curriculum is an instrument of society that is designed to influence children and youth in ways prescribed by their culture.

The society-oriented curriculum design can be interpreted from a number of fundamentally different perspectives, each of which affects the kind of content that will be selected. Those that we will deal with here are:

1. The status quo perspective,
2. The reformist perspective, and
3. The futurist perspective.

*The status quo perspective* seeks to perpetuate the existing social order. The curriculum is the plan for passing on the knowledge and skills that children will need as adults to fit into the current social order and to perpetuate it essentially unchanged. The curriculum is based on the most important aspects of society as assessed by the designers. Early in this century, Franklin Bobbitt surveyed the content of the major magazines of his day in order to discover by scientific methods what most preoccupied the thinking and activities of society.[9] The areas of study developed for the curriculum were based on his analysis of the findings. In other words, the "realities" of the times were to be the direct source for the design and content of curriculum. More recently, as Glatthorn suggests,[10] the career education movement of the 1970s based its curricular designs on analyses of the types of work that prevailed in society. In Ohio, a K–12 curriculum design for career education following this approach was adopted.

*The reformist perspective* has many more proposals and proponents than implementations. These designs have in common the intent to reform the curriculum in major ways as a means of improving society. As we noted earlier, a cultural resistance to fundamental curricular revision exists that is not overcome by the mere presentation of a new design, however well developed and apropros of the times. While several reformist designs have received considerable publicity and have on occasion been implemented, none has been seriously tried on a large scale in the United States. The reformist perspective bridges a gamut from those who would prepare the young to reconstruct society in a more perfect, democratic image, to those who would deschool society and education, distributing the educational process among the members of the community.

Counts is most often credited with initiating the movement in education toward social reconstructionism with his 1932 book *Dare the Schools Build a New Social Order?*[11] in which he challenged the schools to devise a curriculum that would have as its goals a more just society. In the 1950s and 1960s, Theodore Brameld[12] presented a reconstructionist curriculum design based on the major problems confronting society. War, crime, and poverty in the midst of wealth, political oppression, and racial conflict were among the problems that students, representative of the population at large, were to confront and be prepared *collectively* to bring under a more just and democratic control. Students were to become the skillful planners of society. Schools were not merely to follow the existing ways of society, but were to lead society toward greater equity and justice. More recently, Henry Giroux[13] wrote forcefully in support of social reconstructionism and the advocacy role of the schools.

The idea of "deschooling" society and allowing the curriculum to arise from the populace as a function of their needs is most frequently associated with Ivan Illich and his book *Deschooling Society*.[14] Members of society would respond to each other's needs and become each other's instructors. Education would become an organic response to the developing needs of society as opposed to being a fully organized institution of government with a preestablished curriculum plan. In a similar vein is the work of Paolo Freire,[15] the Brazilian educator who has had a significant impact on the thinking of left-oriented and neo-Marxist, American educators. For Freire, the purposes of education are to enlighten the masses about the inequities that their social order has inflicted upon them and to empower them to acquire their freedom. Whatever is learned is learned as a function of these purposes. Thus, reading is taught *not* to prepare people for a job or for the sake of coming to know great literature, but so that they may become aware of the oppression that characterizes their lives.

*The futurist perspective* is sometimes linked to the reconstructionists,[16] and reconstructionists are often thought of as futurists. However, the futurist perspective generally lacks the ardor of reform and has no specific agenda for society other than helping the present society to be aware of and prepared for the consequences of accelerating technological progress. There are tremendous choices to be made, and they cannot be made well by an unprepared society.

The educational futurist Harold Shane, one of the authors of this work, notes in his 1981 book, *Educating for a New Millennium*, that "we may be on the threshold of major changes in industrial society that . . . can rearrange the world we have known with spectacular suddenness." He goes on to say that "revolutionary changes" in education could so disrupt the system as to end in educational anarchy.[17]

Shane continues with a description of an "evolutionary curriculum change paradigm," based on Thomas Kuhn's structure of scientific revolutions.[18] This paradigm for scientific change starts from an existing tradition, then a set of anomalies related to the functioning of the tradition arises leading to a crisis and the proposal of a new paradigm to replace the traditional one. A battle of conflicting ideas ensues with the new paradigm becoming accepted and identified with tradition. It is Shane's view that such a paradigm could be incorporated into the curriculum planning process to make curriculum change evolutionary. Figures 4.1 and 4.2 model the two paradigms.

**FIGURE 4.1**   *The structure of scientific revolutions*

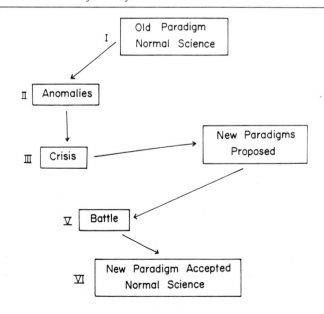

**FIGURE 4.2**   *A paradigm illustrating the structure of evolutionary curriculum change. (Designed by Harold G. Shane. Graphics by Kevin Wah.)*

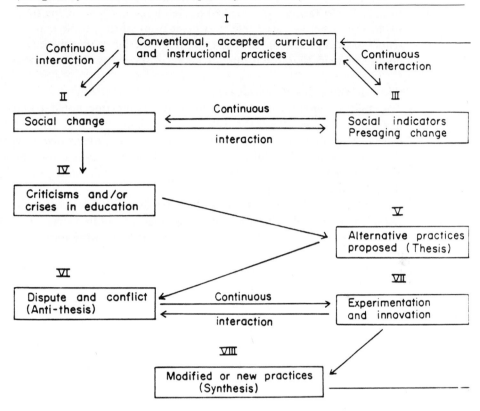

To pursue Shane's curricular approach, both our cultural heritage and indicators of probable futures would need to become a part of the curriculum planning processes. The cultural heritage would function as the base of departure (i.e., the traditional paradigm), while the social indicators of change conceptually parallel anomalies. Moving toward new and societally desired "new" traditions would complete the parallel with the Kuhnian paradigm. Designing learning experiences that contribute to productive transitions between our contemporary realities and our likely futures would lead to an evolutionary curriculum for the future. Thus, designing curriculum for the future would involve an anticipatory approach to learning derived from scholars' concepts of tomorrow, the study of both present and future real world problems, and an ongoing examination of values, especially of those in transition.

Futurists are more bound to the processes of anticipating and acting upon their images of probable futures than they are to achieving a specific set of goals. Of course, futurists do vary, but generally their purpose is to help society to be prepared to deal effectively with the extraordinary changes and their consequences that experts believe are likely to occur. Their vision of the future is that of a society in control, but one that can move in a number of directions, as it sees fit. As the futurist David Livingston expressed it, we ought not look at the future prescriptively, but rather as a series of alternatives from which people may choose.[19] The school's role is to develop skills and useful knowledge so that the members of society can participate in the future directions of society as decision makers.

### The Child-Centered Curriculum

The child-centered curriculum represents an array of educational designs that have in common the belief that the child is the crucial source of all curriculum. Given this as a fundamental premise, all child-centered curricula involve a dynamic conception of content. The curriculum can only be fully known as it unfolds. If plans are developed, they must be sufficiently open to allow the qualities of children to dominate the curriculum.

The child-centered curriculum may be viewed from several distinct perspectives. These are related to the qualities ascribed to children that are given special importance. We shall discuss in greater depth the following four:

1. the Rousseauian perspective,
2. the existentialist perspective,
3. the child-in-society perspective, and
4. the psychological curriculum perspective.

Under the *Rousseauian perspective* of childhood, innate goodness is ascribed to the child. Children are to be protected from the vice and errors of adults. The philosophical writings of Jean Jacques Rousseau, in particular his 1762 work, *Emile*,[20] form the foundation of this perspective. Rousseau's position is that it is the meddling of adults that undermines the goodness God has given children.

In their earliest years, children should be allowed free play in natural settings with their mothers, and as apart from adult society as possible. Between the ages of five and twelve, sensory and concrete experiences should dominate their learning, and such abstract subjects as history and geography should be abolished from the curriculum. Only after their twelfth year would children be introduced to abstract learning. The purpose of early education for Rousseau is to allow children's innate goodness to develop. Only when children are nearing adulthood should adults other than the parents be allowed a truly active role in their education.

The *existentialist perspective* is another, very different conception of childhood that has had significant impact on the child-centered curriculum. As its name implies, its origins lie in existentialism. This twentieth century philosophy establishes existence as the primary property of humankind. At birth, all that can be said is that we exist. As each of us lives and makes choices, we achieve our identity and, possibly, goodness. All of life is an act of becoming in which the individual is responsible for the quality of life ultimately achieved.[21]

An existentialist perspective of childhood is fundamentally different from the Rousseauian perspective. Under the latter, children already embody God's goodness. The purpose of education is to protect children from the degenerations of adulthood. Under the former, children must not only find their own way toward a meaningful life, but must also define the parameters of a quality life in the highly individualistic terms of the "self." The purpose of education is to foster knowledge of self, the ability and sensitivity to express one's innermost consciousness, and personal skills of valuing and choice making.

Within the Rousseauian context, children may or may not be very different from each other. Differences are not particularly important since all children represent at birth the perfection of God's making. On the other hand, the existentialist perspective premises very individualistic outcomes of varying quality, based on each child's personal characteristics, abilities, and sense of moral responsibility in making choices.

The arts, drama, and music, as vehicles of self-expression and development, along with sensitivity training are likely components of a child-centered curriculum of the existential variety.[22] Discussion sessions focused on each individual's search for inner meaning comprise another likely component. Both subjective and objective knowledge are considered important if the individual is to ultimately take responsibility for the definition of self. However, because every individual is a unique entity, the objective knowledge studied must be chosen by the individual.

A. S. Neill's school, Summerhill, founded in 1921 in Suffolk, England, embodied much of the existential philosophy.[23] Classes were held at Summerhill, but student attendance was optional. If children were interested enough to learn, then they would go to class and would learn. No special teaching methods were considered necessary because if children wanted to learn, it was thought, they most certainly would learn. For Neill, the aim of life is to find happiness, and the purpose of education should be to prepare for life.[24] Love and approval need to play essential roles in education, but before parents and teachers can approve of children as individuals, they need first to approve of themselves as individuals. Education must include emotional and artistic development if intellectual growth is to be meaningful.[25] Children need to get along in the world through their own self-development; they must not allow themselves to be dominated by society.

These two very disparate conceptions of childhood and the purposes of schooling, the Rousseauian and the existentialist, are rarely distinguished in curriculum literature. This may be because the difference in observable classroom organization is hardly discernible. Under the existential conception, the teacher follows a set of very broad goals that on the whole encourage children to develop in their own way, while under the Rousseauian conception, the teacher is to provide opportunities for learning, but the child is to learn without benefit of the teacher's direct intervention. Under one, the "goodness" of life must be built by each individual; under the other, the younger children are, the closer they are to God's goodness and the teacher must not interfere with the natural unfolding of that goodness. In an actual classroom situation, children under both conceptions appear to be doing "their own thing."

*The child-in-society perspective* is most closely associated with the works of Francis Parker[26] and John Dewey.[27-31] Parker, superintendent of schools in Quincy,

Massachusetts, from 1875 to 1883, was deeply influenced by the works of Pesta-lozzi and Froebel. Like them, he believed in the active involvement of children in real world experiences as the means of learning. Parker crusaded against "unnatu-ral" teaching methods and isolated subject matter. Learning was to follow the way knowledge is experienced in life and the way children learn as their lives unfold out in the world. For example, geography was to be learned through field trips or by sketching different kinds of landscapes, rather than by reading and memorizing a textbook. Instead of emphasizing the study of grammar, writing and conversation about children's everyday activities were to be the primary vehicles for language instruction. Artificial divisions among the subjects were to be ignored for the sake of natural learning and experience.

The curriculum, as Parker saw it, was to start with what children already had experienced — their family, their physical and social environment, the simple forms of life around them. The content of the curriculum was to be whatever was central to the lives of children. The traditional subjects would lose their artificial divisions and knowledge would be unified as it is in the experiences of life. Self-realization was to come through the learning of what was naturally interesting to the child, which for Parker (and Dewey as well) was the life and society that the child experi-enced every day.

Parker's interpretation of the child-centered curriculum is quite different from either the Rousseauian or the existentialist perspective. In particular, partici-pation in society is considered a natural part of the child's development. Self-expression means talking or writing about one's life in society. Children are inter-ested in knowing more about the experiences they are having, and they want to improve their performances as members of society. The schools need to emphasize how children learn and what they are interested in learning to become more effec-tive in their instruction. Such an emphasis, however, is not antithetical to the de-velopment of a curriculum plan that organizes studies considered important to society because they will also be important to children who are, to use Parker's terminology, "naturally" a part of society and very really interested in their own participation. As with the existentialist perspective, children are in a state of be-coming, but they are not each alone in defining the self; their ongoing interaction with society is necessary to their own identity as well as to the continued develop-ment of society.

John Dewey, who was strongly influenced by Parker, noted in his 1916 work, *Democracy and Education*,[30] that in any society, no matter how primitive, educa-tion is fundamental to its reproduction and survival. Children learn by interacting with elders, and they learn to act in acceptable and even praiseworthy ways because they naturally seek approval. As societies grow more complex, children need more formal education to master the complexities of living.

Education brings meaning to the experiences children have in society. Edu-cation, to quote Dewey, "is that reconstruction or reorganization of experience which adds to the meaning of experience, and which increases ability to direct the course of subsequent experience."[32] Children's first experiences are impulsive, disconnected, and relatively void of meaning. As they make connections among their experiences, they gain greater control over their environment. Thus, these connections take on intrinsic worth.

Basic to Dewey's conception of the curriculum is the idea of finding what is of intrinsic worth to students. Students will be motivated to learn only that which they can relate to their own experience, for that has value to them in helping them to understand their environment. Self-motivation is the Deweyian key to effective education.

In 1896, Dewey was able to establish a laboratory school at the University of Chicago. The curriculum was to be based on life itself, on such fundamental human characteristics as socializing, constructing, inquiring, and creating. The school tried to replicate a miniature society including occupational activities typically found in the real world. In the elementary grades, beginning activities were always familiar ones that were to be subsequently linked to broader, more generalizable activities. For example, six year olds would first study household occupations and then occupations that generally supported the well-being of households in America. Groups of young children would prepare their own luncheon on a weekly basis, taking into account receiving guests, setting the table, and serving the meal. Subsequently, food classification and the physiology of digestion would be studied.[33]

Dewey's school was organized as a democratic social community in which teachers were representatives of the adult culture. It was the teachers' responsibility to harmonize adult ends and values with the individuality of each child. Discipline was an acknowledged necessity, but to the degree possible, children were involved in the development of the rules, and teachers were to capitalize on children's "natural" social interests to maintain order.

This child-in-society perspective has often *not* been distinguished clearly from the other perspectives. This was true even in Dewey's day. Tanner and Tanner note, for example, that Kilpatrick, a progressivist and admirer of John Dewey, proposed the project method, which was based on a definition of "project" as any activity that was " 'purposed' by the child and done 'whole-heartedly.' "[34] The curriculum, according to Kilpatrick, would be comprised of a series of projects. As the Tanners see it, this was no more than a policy of allowing children to follow their immediate interests.

We would add that Kilpatrick's project method, widely publicized in a 1918 work of the same name,[35] was more consistent with the Rousseauian perspective of the child-centered curriculum than it was with the Deweyian child-in-society perspective, for teachers were to take a minor role in guiding children's learnings, which were to unfold through projects that responded to the children's own purposes. Even though Kilpatrick perceived individual and group projects as necessarily involving the social environment, there is little else in his proposal to reflect the Deweyian view of education as a social process through which the individual becomes a more responsible and effective citizen of society.

Dewey bemoaned the misinterpretation and trivialization of his conception of the child-centered curriculum in his 1938 work, *Experience and Education*.[36] Child interest had come to be the dominant consideration in the selection of content. To quote Dewey:

> *It is a ground for legitimate criticism . . . when the ongoing movement of progressive education fails to recognize that the problem of selection and organization of subject-matter for study is fundamental. Improvisation that takes advantage of special occasions prevents teaching and learning from being stereotyped and dead. But the basic material of study cannot be picked up in a cursory manner.*[37]

As Dewey saw it, adults were renouncing their obligation to cultivate those interests of children that were both individually and socially beneficial. Liberating the curriculum from inflexibly conceived subject matter and meeting the child's interests and capacities whatever they may be is a position significantly different from one allowing the ephemeral interests of children to take over curriculum development.

The core curriculum concept, which reached its peak of popularity in the period between the two World Wars, reflects the child-in-society perspective fairly well. The separate disciplines (as represented by school subjects) are unified in the curriculum through the study of persistent social problems. The disciplines are to serve as sources of expert knowledge and skills. The social problems, to be selected by teachers and students in collaboration with each other, need to be sufficiently important to be of concern to all members of society, and of personal relevance to each student as well. Whatever the social problems selected may be, all students, regardless of their ability or background, are expected to study them. This active involvement of students in the investigations and analyses of persistent social problems premises that young people will ultimately and democratically be involved in their resolution.

Teachers are to provide for individual differences as they arise. Indeed, teachers are also to develop resource materials when necessary. As the Tanners note, this requires enormous resourcefulness on the part of teachers, as well as a dedication in time and effort rarely provided for in school budgets. It is the Tanners' view that this lack of support was one of the major reasons why the core curriculum never achieved widespread acceptance.[38] They also note that the educational background of the teachers was in the subject-based curriculum and teachers were not really accustomed to a social-problems orientation, especially one that often involved controversy. We would say the cultural mindset of the teachers actively interfered with the establishment of an integrated curriculum based on social problems of personal relevance.

The *psychological curriculum perspective* is not often identified in curriculum textbooks. There is, however, a body of literature presenting the provocative idea that the *true* curriculum is an unwritten one that consists primarily of what learners internalize from their in-school experiences rather than what has been planned for them to learn about subjects. The curriculum is whatever has been added to or otherwise modifed in children's ways of thinking and behaving because of schooling. In our review of the various uses of the term "curriculum," we discussed at length the "hidden curriculum," which, to a degree, is similar to this perspective. What children experience in school and the interpretations they make of their experiences within themselves comprise the real curriculum.

Essentially, this means that the psychological curriculum can be a product of any set of experiences organized by the school. As Shane and McSwain noted in their 1958 discussion of the psychological curriculum, "The real question is 'What *kind* of experiences will most adequately help to make the child's inner or psychological curriculum the best possible one for *him?*' "[38a] Harris[39] in 1937, and Hopkins[40] a few years later, were, perhaps the first to write of the inner or "under-the-skin" curriculum as the product of a learner's personalized transactions with his school environment.

Weinstein and Fantini's curricular model, first published in their 1970 book, *Toward Humanistic Education: A Curriculum of Affect*,[41] is seemingly a response to the Shane and McSwain question. Their curriculum design includes a "diagnostic" step that would analyze the societal forces acting on the learner as well as identify learners' awareness skills in terms of their feelings. Teaching procedures, included as part of the authors' conception of "curriculum," would emphasize the close matching of instructional methodology and the learning styles of students. "Organizing" ideas for the content would be based on the concerns of the learners.

Weinstein and Fantini make a clear distinction between interests and concerns, with the former indicating activities attractive to students and the latter representing their basic psychological, physiological and sociological drives. Subject content is considered important, but, to be learned well, they believe, the content must become a part of the child's personal affect.

The psychological curriculum in the 1970s, as represented in the Weinstein and Fantini work, has come to be known as the "confluent" curriculum. As Ornstein and Hunkins note, the confluent curriculum stresses the "integration of thinking, feeling, and acting."[42] The emphasis on individual development that typifies the confluent curriculum has led us to include this type of design with the child-centered group. However, the integration of the cognitive, affective, and psychomotor domains along with the attention given to socialization make it a curriculum in which the teacher acts as an orchestrator, rather than a facilitator or guide, of student experiences so that they are brought together within the student to make a profound, under-the-skin difference. The teacher is in charge of students' experiences in a manner hardly typical of most child-centered curricula designs, which generally posit children take leadership roles in the structuring of their own learning experiences.

However, like all the child-centered curricula, it is virtually impossible to know what the confluent curriculum is to be until it has unfolded. Moreover, given that the curriculum must be judged on what children have internalized, its results are even more difficult to assess than the typical child-centered curriculum.

*The Child-Centered Movements of the 1960s and 70s.*    Several movements developed in the late 1960s and 1970s based on child-centered curriculum ideas. A radical reform movement, sometimes referred to as the "neoprogressives,"[43] was given considerable media coverage. The linkage that has often been made, however, with progressivism and, by association, with the Parker-Dewey views of child-centered education, was quite misleading. For example, Paul Goodman, one of this group's leading authors, fervently believed that the attempt "to channel the process of growing up according to a preconceived curriculum" was wasteful of our natural human powers.[44] According to Goodman, the educational system is harmful to the development of a vast majority of children, who would be better off if there were no system.[45] Throughout Goodman's works is the theme of children's innate potential being undermined by the educational establishment. Though the religious overtones of the Rousseauian perspective are not present here, Goodman's view of children and their relationship to education is very much like Rousseau's.

John Holt held similar views, although his works are grounded less in abstract analysis and more in the practice of educating, as the titles of some of his better known works clearly indicate: *How Children Fail* (1964),[46] *The Underachieving School* (1969),[47] *What Do I Do Monday?* (1970),[48] *Freedom and Beyond* (1972),[49] and *Teach Your Own* (1981).[50] Learning, for Holt, is part of the growth process, a natural and holistic moving and expanding of children into the world around them. Holt attributes children's failures to adults, their inane questions, and foolish reward systems. His quest is to find ways to educate children so that the great potential that we know is in every child can be fostered rather than interfered with. For Holt, it is important to achieve a love of learning rather than a set of studies for a future we cannot know.[51] Thus, curriculum planning as it is usually practiced in the schools is not, for him, a very useful undertaking.

Goodman's and Holt's views are quite consistent with the Rousseauian perspective of child-centered education. The idea of "deschooling society" was attractive to both, although their purposes, unlike those of Illich and Freire, were almost entirely within the context of individual growth and development. They are significantly different from the child-in-society perspective supported by Dewey, Parker, and many progressivists such as Boyd Bode and William Bagley. In Holt's 1972 work, *Freedom and Beyond*,[52] there is some movement in the direction of Dewey as Holt recognizes structure as a fundamental characteristic of freedom and the basic desire of children to know what their limits are. Ultimately, however, he blames adults for intervening in children's learning, leaving children with less time to find and develop their own ways of meeting their needs, which only they can truly know.

"Open education," a child-centered curriculum movement that reached its peak of popularity in the 1970s, has contributed considerably to the public's current confusion regarding child-centered curricula. All three perspectives were involved in the movement and were treated as one monolithic whole by the popular press.

Holt, for example, was supportive of the movement, pointing out that the structure of open classrooms needed to be very complex if they were to accommodate the needs and abilities of the children as well as of the teachers.[53] Affective education emphasizing self-actualization very much in the existentialist vein received considerable visibility in the open education movement. A. S. Neill's *Summerhill*, an existentialist approach to children's education, also received a great deal of publicity as an example of open education.

Several child-in-society programs were based on the British infant school model. This movement tended to ignore subject divisions in favor of what was called the "integrated day." Although the curriculum was to be fitted to each child's individual characteristics, individualizing was limited for the most part to sequence and pacing.[54] Although children could select from different collections of study materials, called learning centers, the content was established in its broad outlines by some combination of school board members, administrators, and teachers. Teachers had major responsibility for creating a rich, interactive learning environment for each center. Children were to be encouraged, guided, and helped in their learning. While there was great flexibilty in how children were to pursue their studies, the broad outline and direction was built into the curriculum. These are characteristics quite distinct from either the Rousseauian or the existential perspectives. Nevertheless, in the popular literature of the day, distinctions were rarely made.

In the public's understanding or *mis*understanding of the child-centered curriculum, one can find strange combinations of ideas. For instance, children following a child-centered curriculum may or may not study the materials contained in a selected learning center, depending on how they feel. The materials in learning centers tend to be boring, usually no more than collections of worksheets that would be better presented in a book, and which, in any case, the children complete in half the time allocated, often wasting the rest of their time in disorderly conduct. Another odd combination of ideas about the child-centered curriculum involves traditional grading. That is, teachers are not supposed to discourage students no matter what the students have decided to study, and so they assign "As" to all their students, even the ones who can't pass the achievement tests. Youngsters who have learned almost nothing are promoted anyway!

No matter that these are intellectually "foggy" combinations of ideas! They have entered our cultural lore through quite different perspectives of the child-centered curriculum design. We have come to think of the child-centered curriculum as an innovative curriculum design supported by fuzzy-thinking radicals with little practical understanding of the realities of life. The fact is that there have been efforts to implement some form of the design in this country for at least a century. Several of this century's most significant thinkers, including John Dewey and Bertrand Russell, worked at the development of an intellectual and practical base for its implementation. That they did not succeed in changing our traditional curriculum design is really not surprising. History, after all, shows us the incredible resilience of the Latin grammar school curriculum through hundreds of years of social change and radically different needs. What we have called the "cultural mindset" is a powerful force that plays a major role in our cohesiveness as a nation, in our being able to identify ourselves with each other as Americans, and in the slowing of change so that cultural identity will not be lost, even when our reason may tell us we must change. Continued rational analysis and widespread debate are tools in the process of overcoming cultural mindset.

### The Knowledge-Centered Curriculum Design

The knowledge-centered curriculum design would position objectively based knowledge at the heart of the curriculum. Proponents believe the needs of society as well as of the individual will be best served if the content of the curriculum is comprised of knowledge that is generalizable to groups or classes of situations, as opposed to knowledge uniquely suited to children's learning styles or otherwise unique needs. The purpose of the knowledge-centered curriculum design is to transmit to the younger generation that knowledge which is most "important" to all of humankind.

The selection of knowledge, the forms it shall take, and the relative importance of different forms of knowledge to the long-term well-being of society are topics of endless discussions among curriculum makers. School subjects represent an array of different knowledge structures from chemistry and physics to art and urban studies. For the most part, they are still treated as distinct entities needing equal time, even though there have been numerous calls for the integration of knowledge in the school's curriculum.

***The school subject: a metastructure.***    Most of us share a conception of knowledge that has been communicated to us by the traditional school subject. Chemistry, for example, is a school subject based on the discipline of chemistry; English is a school subject based on a collection of contents and activities related to each other by the use of the English language; and business is a school subject based on the functioning of businesses in real world settings. We tend to identify the organization of school subjects with their real world counterparts. Whether the way these subjects are structured and related to each other is the most effective way to design the school's curriculum is an important aspect of the debate.

The school subject is, in a sense, a *meta*structure; that is, it is a pedagogical structure about other structures related to our worldly conception of knowledge. The school subject of chemistry is about the discipline of chemistry; it is not actually the discipline. Sometimes, the subject or metastructure is a close replica of a knowledge structure out in the real world, and sometimes it is not, being obsolete or overly static or no more than a set of responses to urgently felt, real world needs.

It has been a matter of considerable debate whether subjects should closely resemble the disciplines, being no more than a minor rearrangement of their content for instructional purposes, as Phenix[55] and Schwab[56] suggested in the early 1960s, or whether they should represent structures unique to schooling for the educational purposes of society. Would it not be reasonable, for example, to ignore the disciplines altogether and deal with the fundamental concepts of science underlying all scientific disciplines? Would it not be beneficial to have a subject based on the active involvement of students in governmental activities emulating the involvement we hope they will have as adults? Curriculum makers debate such questions all the time. But if we are honest, in the real world of the public schools, one can hardly discern any debate at all. As we have already noted, the curriculum designs established at the turn of the century remain essentially intact.

The cultural mindsets many of us harbor about the structures of knowledge, with which we became familiar as youngsters through our own schooling, often blind us to the potential control that we as individuals and that humankind in general have over these structures. Structures of knowledge are cultural artefacts and relatively arbitrary. That is, there can be multiple ways of organizing the study of a substantive area. For example, psychology and neurology overlap a good deal in their substantive areas of study. However, psychology has as basic to its structure the concept of the *mind*, while neurology studies the *brain*. The term "mind" is quite distinct from "brain," even though both refer to the same physical entity. The system developed under each will organize its knowledge differently in no small part because of the difference in meaning of these two concepts.

The selection of school subjects is based on people's judgments about what is important for children to learn and how it should be conveyed. In concrete terms, should students study the brain or the mind, respecting the structures of the disciplines from which these concepts come, or should they study both together, possibly ignoring the structures of the disciplines and inventing a structure serving the school's purposes?

Since the 1930s, the number of subjects that are offered in the public schools has increased dramatically. For example, at the junior high school level, one can find Black studies, consumer economics, and ecology; at the elementary level, there is visual literacy and career education. Nevertheless, the subjects we consider really important and that we assign status to in our interactions with students have not changed very much in the past sixty years. Electives have indeed been added to the high school curriculum, but such subjects as mathematics, biology, chemistry, and English remain steadfastly among our basic requirements and receive the overwhelming attention of politicians and the public alike.

This tendency toward a static curriculum concerns many professional educators who otherwise support the knowledge-centered curriculum design for the public schools. Not only are new areas of knowledge developing at a rapid pace, but also existing structures of knowledge are in a dynamic state of change. Genetics, for example, is in a constant state of restructuring itself with each new major discovery, while semiotics and information theory are relatively new fields of knowledge. The restructuring and multiplication of knowledge pose significant problems for the curriculum designer. How many new disciplines can be reasonably added to the curriculum? Furthermore, if real world knowledge is still in a state of ongoing change, as has been the case throughout this century, should the schools be teaching the disciplines as subjects full of content needing to be memorized?

Would it not be wiser to present students with the questions and problems that experts are actually involved with in real world practice? The content of disciplines is continually being updated while the content of their corresponding school subjects changes much more slowly. Why have youngsters memorize content that is likely to be significantly modified by their adult years? The question

Herbert Spencer posed in 1860 is still unanswered and with us: "What knowledge is of most worth?"[57]

Instead of pursuing existing structures of knowledge (usually the disciplines) and developing school subjects that are *meta*structures, why not create new kinds of structures of knowledge for the curriculum—school subjects that are not based on the disciplines, and that could have greater affinity with the purposes of education. Let us suppose, for example, that a purpose of education is to familiarize students with modern research techniques. Students could study four or five separate school subjects each of which is a metastructure of a research discipline, as is now often the case. Students study introductions to biology, chemistry, physics, calculus, geometry, history, and so forth. It would be possible, instead, to develop a sequence of courses organizing the great research techniques of the sciences and humanities into one holistic structure, independent of the existing structures of the disciplines but possibly more useful to adults of the twenty-first century, and surely more responsive to the educational purpose. At least, the study of research techniques could go beyond the introductory level.

We shall pursue, in greater depth, four distinct perspectives from which the knowledge-centered curriculum may be viewed. Each of these perspectives conceptualizes the sources of knowledge differently as well as the purposes of education. They are:

1. the great knowledge perspective,
2. the great research disciplines perspective,
3. the integrated knowledge perspective, and
4. the process-as-content perspective.

*The great knowledge perspective* is best represented by a quote from one of its foremost proponents, Robert Hutchins: "Knowledge is truth. The truth is everywhere the same."[58] The selection of content is guided by conceptions of what is important to human intellectual development across centuries and nations.

Robert Hutchins states the case as one of finding eternal and absolute truths. He sees this as being accomplished through the study of those works revealing humankind's intuitive and deductive reason. He would make grammar, rhetoric, and logic the heart of the school's curriculum.[59] Grammar would not be our current, rather narrow study, but would return to the days of the Latin grammar school and would include reading the great works of the past. Through the study and preservation of these great works, Hutchins believes we can move toward the discovery of "first" principles underlying all knowledge. Once all these principles are found and ordered, the school's curriculum would consist of this knowledge. The humanities, in particular philosophy, literature, and history, would be the primary sources of knowledge to be studied in the schools.

Proponents of the great knowledge perspective suggest that schooling should pertain to helping people transcend specific facts and experiences so that they may reach this consistent body of absolute truth. In a 1981 work, Mortimer Adler[60] proposes for inclusion in the curriculum the study of enduring ideas such as truth, beauty, justice, and liberty, along with the study of great works. Allan Bloom, a professor at the University of Chicago (where Hutchins served as president some fifty years earlier), in a 1987 work decrying the failure of the American university to deal with significant knowledge, states:

> *The humanities are the specialty that now exclusively possess the books that are not specialized, that insist upon asking the questions about the whole that are excluded from the rest of the university, which is dominated by real specialties, as resistant to self-examination as they were in Socrates' day. . . . The kinds of questions children ask: Is there a God? Is there freedom? Is there punishment for evil deeds? Is there certain knowledge? What is a good society? were once also the questions addressed by science and philosophy. But now the grownups are too busy at work, and the children are left in a day-care center called the humanities, in which the discussions have no echo in the adult world.*[61]

From his own vantage point, Bloom, like Adler and Hutchins, is proposing the study of eternal truths, which, interestingly, he sees young children still engaged in doing. The humanities, as opposed to the sciences and other "specialty" subjects, are seen as repositories of the great thought of humankind.

*The great research disciplines perspective* is the most pervasive conception of the knowledge-centered curriculum design in American education today. Its origins harken back to the report of the Committee of Ten and its recommendation that physics, astronomy, chemistry, biology including botany, zoology and physiology, physical geography, geology, meteorology, and political economy all be made part of the high school curriculum and that their study be prerequisite to college entrance. However, the case certainly can be made that its roots return to the days when Latin, Greek, and theology were the great research disciplines for research then was about religion.

Under the great research disciplines perspective, the most important knowledge to communicate to students is the systematically developed and deductively proven or empirically verified knowledge developed by the scientific and mathematical disciplines. The Committee of Ten also included modern and ancient languages as well as history. While these disciplines are usually placed among the humanities, languages could certainly be considered important tool subjects in the study of the scientific disciplines, and history, at the time the committee was deliberating, aspired to join the sciences. Scholars of the day frequently spoke of "scientific history," for economics and sociology were still largely functioning within history. Smith, Stanley, and Shores in discussing the great research disciplines in their 1957 work included history to the degree that it represents scientific (as opposed to humanistic) scholarship.[62]

In 1958, the Russians were first to place a missile in orbit around the earth. This turned the United States' attention to what were considered the inadequacies of the schools, especially in the sciences and mathematics. The School Mathematics Study Group (SMSG), the Physical Science Study Committee (PSSC), and the

Biological Science Curriculum Study (BSCS), among others, received substantial support from the federal government to develop updated materials for the schools. The question of how to reflect the structures of scientific and mathematical disciplines more effectively in school subjects was at center stage with both scholars and the popular press. Even when federal funding was extended to include the social sciences and English, the emphasis remained on replicating the structure of the scientific and mathematical disciplines. This was true even at the elementary school level.

It must be recognized that in this period the study of the scientific disciplines was given far greater importance by the federal government than the study of the humanities. Even though there was recognition, at least among educators, that the structure of the school subject was not necessarily linked to the structure of the disciplines[63] and that the schools needed to have a more balanced curriculum, the structure of school subjects became, even more so than previously, a reflection of the scientific and mathematical disciplines.

There is a very real tension between those who support the great research disciplines perspective of the knowledge-centered curriculum design and those who support the great knowledge perspective. Allan Bloom has expressed the tensions with considerable clarity in his work *The Closing of the American Mind*:

> *The natural sciences are able to assert that they are pursuing the important truth, and the humanities are not able to make any such assertion. That is the critical point. Without this, no study can remain alive. Vague insistence that without the humanities we will no longer be civilized rings very hollow when no one can say what "civilized" means, when there are said to be many civilizations that are all equal.*[64]

Bloom goes on to point out how the big questions of life have become inadmissible, while the specialty areas with their minute and, by inference, trivial questions dominate secondary and university study.

It is worth recalling in this context that the Committee of Fifteen resisted the scientific thrust of the Committee of Ten and succeeded in maintaining a humanistic underpinning for elementary education. As we indicated earlier, Bloom finds the elementary school child seemingly the only one left asking significant questions. In 1965, the National Endowment for the Humanities was established to give the humanities the kind of support the National Science Foundation had given the sciences, and while it can hardly be called a success story, the Endowment has contributed to the continued role of the humanities in American education.

The separation of the sciences and humanities remains a fact of American education, with science holding the dominant position. This means, specifically, that valuing and the philosophical analyses underlying valuing have remained separate from the sciences, often to the point of neglect. In the popular mind, as Dewey noted in 1903, and it is no less true today, "scientific judgments depend on reason, while moral valuations proceed from a separate faculty, conscience, having its own criteria and methods not amenable to intellectual supervision."[65] Generally, as C. P. Snow[66] and Dewey[67] before him both recognized, the humanities such as music, art, drama, philosophy, and literature have been separated from the sciences and mathematics as though there were two distinct cultures inhabited by separate groups of scholars—the scientists and the humanists. It is a separation that Dewey found unreasonable because both are necessarily grounded in human experience and both are about improving human experience. In experience they are integrated, and that is how they must function to be of any real significance for human life. Experience, for Dewey, was the bridge between logical-scientific abstractions and the enlightened individual confronting the complex problems of life. Integration among the knowledge-centered group would rest not on experience but on how curriculum designs reflect the structures of knowledge.

*The integrative knowledge perspective* is generally an effort to overcome the divisions of knowledge among school subjects as well as diminish the distance that increasingly separates the humanities and sciences. Proponents of this perspective do not question the centrality of knowledge for achieving the purposes of education. However, they see merit and benefit in bringing different kinds of knowledge together in a more holistic conception of what needs to be studied.

As we have noted several times, a vast increase in knowledge already confronted educators at the turn of the century. An integrative approach to knowledge was seen as a way of avoiding an unreasonable multiplication of the subjects students had to study. The American followers of the German philosopher Johann Friedrich Herbart were especially keen to achieve a unity of knowledge that could stave off what appeared to be the inevitable fragmentation of the curriculum. Furthermore, for the Herbartians, virtue was founded on knowledge, which was to be inculcated by good instruction. Moral development was, for them, the primary purpose of education, and it was best achieved through a knowledge-centered curriculum. It was up to the teacher, through proper instructional methodology, to develop in children the interest necessary for a successful learning experience.[68]

Throughout the twentieth century, as the reader has no doubt come to expect, there have been vigorous disagreements concerning (1) whether curriculum should approach knowledge as an integrated whole and (2) if integration is desirable, by what principle(s) it should be achieved. Francis Parker, coming very much from the child-in-society perspective of curriculum design, would have unified knowledge into what he called "central subjects," the initial structure for which was to be founded in the experiences of children in their first years of life. In other words, knowledge as naturally encountered by the child in daily life would serve as the basis for integration.[69] Given Herbart's view of knowledge as something communicated to children to activate ideas in them and to make them capable of virtuous behavior, it stands to reason that Herbartians would not agree with a unification of knowledge based on the ways children experience knowledge in their earliest years.

In fact, Charles De Garmo, one of the founders, in 1892, of the National Herbart Society, resisted the loss of identity of the separate subjects implicit in Parker's proposal. De Garmo saw the uniqueness in the structures of the separate disciplines as important to the integrity of knowledge.[70] As Tanner and Tanner point out, however, De Garmo proceeded to suggest that geography could be a unifying subject of the curriculum. In making this suggestion, he undermined his own argument about the necessity to maintain the separate identities of the subjects.[71] As we see it, De Garmo's position was consistent with Herbartian thought that conceived of the child's mind and soul as a *tabula rasa* ("blank tablet") awaiting ideas and organizing experiences from without. To allow the disparate experiences of early childhood to be the unifier of knowledge would be for the Herbartians like allowing the blind to lead the sighted through the woods. In any case, the Herbartians were, for the most part, integrationists within the knowledge-centered curriculum design.

Two major variations of the subject curriculum have been directed toward an integrative study of knowledge within the context of the knowledge-centered curriculum design: the correlated curriculum and the broad-fields curriculum. The correlated curriculum would leave the traditional subjects intact but would articulate their contents to emphasize a set of commonalities. For instance, the study of the physical geography of the American Far West might be linked to the westward movement in American History, and Mark Twain's accounts of the Nevada silver rush to literature. The purpose of this approach is to decrease the fragmentation of learning that arises from compartmentalized subjects. However, it should be remembered that the subjects are not modified in any way; they are simply arranged so that linkages become obvious. The divisions between the sciences and the humanities is hardly touched at all.

The broad-fields curriculum is based on survey courses that encompass several related but specialized subjects. For example, a course in general science can draw its materials from geology, physics, chemistry, botany, and zoology. Early broad-fields courses tended to maintain the structures of the disciplines from which they drew their content,[72] making them a conglomeration of "mini" meta-structures and quite antithetical to the purpose of presenting an integrated view of knowledge. Gradually, there was the realization that some principle of structuring other than reproducing the structures of the disciplines would be necessary. For example, a synthesis of knowledge could be achieved by establishing topics or themes to be studied using several disciplines as resources for the study. "The Increasing Interdependence of Humankind" or "The Migrant Person—Ever on the Move" are two examples of themes that could serve as organizing structures. Another approach could involve history as the organizing thread as, for instance, with a history of great inventions.

Broad-fields courses were initially developed at the university level, where they are most often referred to as "survey" or "general" courses and are directed toward those students who do not intend to continue in an area of study. With time, the broad-fields concept "trickled" down to the high schools and the elementary schools.[73] Currently, the middle and later grades of the elementary and junior high schools are the most likely places to find examples of the broad-fields curriculum. Emphasis on learning the specialized disciplines increased throughout the 1980s, diminishing the attractiveness of survey courses especially in the high schools.

*The process-as-content perspective* is an offshoot of the great research disciplines perspective insofar as the study of the scientific disciplines is considered central to the purposes of the school's curriculum. However, the curriculum design, rather than being a static reflection of the state of the disciplines at a given point in time, is a dynamic representation of how scholars actually engage in their inquiry activities. The student focuses not on learning a series of facts, but on basic concepts and principles that are to be used as scientists would use them in the processes of discovery. The real content of the curriculum are broad conceptual insights and the related processes of inquiry.

Although knowledge-centered, the sense of science-in-the-making that characterizes this perspective resonates well with the child-in-society perspective, which would engage youngsters in the active resolution of personal and societal problems much as citizens outside of school would be engaged. The active involvement of students in the development of the knowledge they are learning is present in both conceptions of curriculum design. The understanding of the kind of knowledge that is most important for youngsters to learn, however, is fundamentally different.

The process-as-content perspective was especially popular in the 1960s and early 1970s, shortly after the Russians' successful launch of the first missile in orbit. Jerome S. Bruner, a cognitive psychologist from Harvard University, chaired a conference of scientists, mathematicians, and psychologists at Woods Hole, Massachusetts. The conference was sponsored by the National Academy of Sciences with the purpose of finding ways to improve the elementary and secondary science curricula. A report of the Conference was issued in 1960, written by Bruner, entitled *The Process of Education*.[74] It captured the educational imagination of the decade perhaps because it proposed an approach to science instruction that reflected qualities typically associated with the child-centered curriculum design, while remaining clearly within the knowledge-centered curriculum. It took on qualities of humanism as this often-repeated quote clearly shows:

> *Intellectual activity anywhere is the same, whether at the frontier of knowledge or in a third-grade classroom. What a scientist does at his desk, or in the laboratory, what a literary critic does in reading a poem are of the same order as what anybody else does when he is engaged in like activities—if he is to achieve understanding. The difference is in degree, not in kind. The schoolboy learning physics* is *a physicist. . . .*[75]

The idea of discovery learning involving the processes of inquiry had widespread appeal. Parker and Rubin, for example, identified in their 1966 work a set of basic processes that the school's curriculum needed to provide to students, such as the basic processes "through which one acquires information."[76] The social science projects funded by the federal government in the mid 1960s all reflected the influence of the Brunerian conception of inquiry. Louise Berman in her 1968 textbook on curriculum dedicated an entire chapter to the organization of "broad areas within the curriculum so that children and youth have the opportunity to become process-oriented persons. . . ."[77]

The discovery approach appeared to be open to the integration of the scientific disciplines especially in the very earliest grades, by introducing youngsters first to "the most fundamental understanding that can be achieved of the underlying principles that give structure to that subject."[78] Although recognizing the need for further research, Bruner was clearly suggesting that the teaching of ideas underlying several sciences would be a beneficial approach to the study of the sciences in the early grades:

> *Indeed, it may well be that there are certain general attitudes or approaches toward science or literature that can be taught in the earlier grades that would have considerable relevance for later learning. The attitude that things are connected and not isolated is a case in point. One can indeed imagine kindergarten games designed to make children more actively alert to how things affect or are connected with each other—a kind of introduction to the idea of multiple determination of events in the physical and the social world.*[79]

The process-as-content approach appealed not only to many knowledge-centered proponents of the curriculum, but also to many with progressivist leanings (as, for example, Berman, 1968), who saw the active involvement of children in learning and the integration of knowledge through the thought processes of children as steps in the right direction for the school's curriculum. Bruner conceptualized children as little adults who could emulate adult scientists in some valid way if the proper instructional techniques were adopted. On the other hand, Dewey had conceived of children as individuals who learned and worked quite differently from adults. This difference was hardly noticed in the heyday of the process-as-content approach. Nor did there seem to be much awareness of the different kinds of content that were being proposed by the two disparate groups until Bruner joined the Education Development Laboratory in Newton, Massachusetts, to create a set of social science materials entitled, *Man: A Course of Study* (MACOS), which received $2,166,900 from the National Science Foundation. The materials were designed to introduce students to anthropology and cross-cultural studies as social scientists would approach them. They were very vivid materials describing the harsh environmental circumstances of Eskimo life and their cultural adaptations to the realities of their existence. Presentations of the materials were instructionally effective but essentially without a value base.

There was a congressional uproar. Congressmen complained that young children were being exposed to wife-swapping, sexual promiscuity, infanticide, and murder.[80] The materials were widely criticized for being too "humanistic" and "progressive,"[81] which, from an analytical perspective, they were not. The progressivists would have been most unlikely to present materials of Eskimo family life to be studied by youngsters as scientists would in as value-free a context as possible. First of all, the youngsters would have had to perceive and develop the parameters of the problem(s), and they would have sought solutions within a value base as citizens of a democracy and not for the sake of scientific investigation.

The post-MACOS period, which we would say begins after the 1975 congressional sessions devoted to the materials, saw a steep decline in the popularity of both the child-centered and process-as-content curriculum designs. The back-to-basics movement took hold and more or less proposed a return to the "reading, writing and 'rithmetic" tradition that dominated most of our memories of schooling, as it still does.

### The Eclectic Curriculum

This conception of curriculum design most closely reflects the reality of the traditional curriculum design in America's public schools. "Eclecticism" in curriculum refers to the selection of content based on different sets of principles or doctrines. It implies a conscious decision, which may often not be the case in the real world of the schools.

In curriculum work, the effects of both reflective and mindless eclecticism may be observed. As stated earlier, much of what we do in the schools is under the influence of the cultural mindsets of our youth that support a multitude of contradictory behaviors. For example, we encourage children to do the best they can do, but then we grade their performance on a bell curve, which, of course, compares their performances to those of others. We believe in treating children as unique individuals, even while the administration of standardized achievement tests multiplies by leaps and bounds. We want our elementary schools to be humanistic both in what is studied and how children are treated, while we expect high schools to emphasize the sciences and mathematics, and judge our children with appropriate objectivity. At times, it appears as though we implement both open and closed curricula simultaneously.

We have in the traditional subject curriculum a potpourri of contents covering the array of designs discussed here. Language arts in the elementary school and English in the secondary school usually represent the humanistic thrust of the great knowledge perspective; the typing and driver's education courses represent the thrust toward vocational education that is often found in the child-in-society curriculum design; the social studies in its efforts to prepare children for citizenship in a democratic society reflect the child-in-society thrust as well; and the study of the scientific and mathematical disciplines through the school subjects represents a partial implementation of the great research disciplines perspective. However, underlying these designs are different educational philosophies that are often in direct contradiction to each other.

In the vein of compromise and eclecticism so characteristic of American democracy and its educational thinking, we often avoid, even in the midst of very cogent, logical analyses, making clear-cut decisions about our purposes for schooling. We opt, both consciously and unconsciously, for an eclectic approach. That is, we try to bring very disparate purposes together in what we hope will be a functional amalgam. Society is viewed pluralistically, knowledge is seen as a rapidly changing panoply, and schools are to be molded to the needs of society. Objectives are broadened to allow for a diversity of behaviors and outcomes. Although there are likely to be a few fundamental principles of education guiding curriculum development, the curriculum design process is characterized by preferred conditionals rather than absolutes.

Eclecticism draws from a wide range of conceptual sources. No one view of education is clearly preferred over others. Rather, there is a range of conditions conducive to learning from which to draw. The reflective eclectic works at devising a curricular design capable of incorporating what may be very disparate preferences. For example, followers of John Dewey believe education must start by "taking children wherever they may be" and tailoring the curriculum to their needs. A great many eclectics, not really followers of Dewey, would agree with this view of instruction. As true eclectics, however, they may also agree that all children should study certain core subjects and activities, recognizing that children must fit into society and meet society's requirements. Accepting children both as unique individuals and as individuals who must give up some of their uniqueness in order to fit into society is the kind of problem that comprises the eclectic's challenge.

Eclecticism may be a wise compromise among competing views and a necessary enterprise for public education under a democratic system of governance. It may also be a mindless conglomeration of poorly understood ideas. In this latter context, eclecticism probably reflects a hodgepodge of rationally derived positions and cultural mindsets that all too frequently dominates the reality of curriculum design.

The effects of the quickening technological revolution, which we have summarized with the term "*intra*generational disjunctures," have increased in severity with each passing decade, rendering our personal satisfaction with our own education a little less believable even to ourselves. The need to reconceptualize the school's curriculum is becoming more obvious and grass-roots rebellions against public education more numerous. Cultural mindsets and the rosy memories of our distant youth notwithstanding, a major vector of change for education is in the making. We expect education in the twenty-first century and the curriculum designs that underlie its directions to be a significant departure from what we know today. Of course, we would prefer to be in logical control of the educational directions to be taken in the future. Cultural mindsets that change haphazardly and without an understanding of what the changes are really about do not promise a successful educational future. It does make a difference whether we shall be reflective or mindless eclectics.

## Confronting Cultural Mindsets and the Curriculum Environment

As reasonable people, we ask how education can best serve society. What is it that we want from the schools for children? These two simple questions contain significant choices about the purposes of schooling that can be approached logically. Should the school's curriculum serve the needs of society, or reflect the characteristics of each child, developing the individual potential to its zenith whatever and wherever that may be, or should it ignore both by being a disseminator of objective, formal knowledge for its own sake?

Certainly, the choices would be anything but trivial if we were actually making them. We have been, instead, accepting our existing curriculum designs as though they were cultural givens. There have been numerous, minor changes in the specific content, but we have done very little to modify the designs themselves. What is to be done? Should we give up our logical analyses and systematic planning?

The last question is posed tongue-in-cheek for it seems obvious that in delivering educational services to millions of youngsters, a logically based system of some sort is indispensible. It does appear, however, that we have tended to narrow the object of our analyses to the basic structures of the curriculum, such as goals and specific performance objectives, while ignoring the cultural environment within which current conceptions of curriculum have developed.

The cultural environment of the curriculum may be viewed from at least two perspectives: external and internal. The environment of the curriculum is external insofar as the social order in general establishes the milieu within which the schools operate; it is internal insofar as each of us carries around in our mind's eye models of how the schools should function and what the curriculum should be. The external environment is full of disparate but overt conceptions about what the schools should be doing. The internal environment is a multiplicity of largely unconscious and often distorted views of our educational realities for, as individuals, we are caught by our own cultural mindsets about what should be, rather than by a recognition of our swiftly changing, current realities.[82] The external environment can be thought of as the sociopolitical embodiment of our many disparate beliefs, which, over the years, have come together to form the bases of our educational traditions. As our history grows more dense with experience, the origins of what we do tend to be forgotten and new rationales are assigned. The internal environment can be thought of as the sociopsychological development that each of us experiences educationally well before we are capable of evaluating the quality of what is taking place.

Little has been done to bring the impact of cultural mindset on education into the conscious, logical realm of analysis. The tremendous contradictions about education that each of us seems capable of carrying about in our mind's eye are virtually ignored in our popular discussions of education and even in the professional literature on curriculum. For example, most of us as individuals and as a society believe all children should have an opportunity to go on to college. Carried to a logical conclusion, as it was by Charles Eliot at the turn of the century, all children through high school should be prepared by the same, college-oriented curriculum. On the other hand, the vast majority of us also believe that the school's curriculum should be relevant to the capabilities and talents of children and to the needs of society. Taken to a logical conclusion, as John Dewey did, vocational education is a perfectly reasonable direction for the curriculum to follow. The point here is not that these two gentleman disagreed, but that we as individuals have grown up with both positions buried unconsciously in our cultural mindsets, and we move back and forth between them depending on the contexts of our discussions. The instant expertise of journalists and politicians has fostered these culturally embedded contradictions for the positions they take almost always represent a single set of beliefs with little analyses about the multiple meanings of terms and the deeply held contradictions they often represent. In tomorrow's newspaper, another headline is likely to appear representing a quite different position but sounding very much as though it were in keeping with the preceding article.

We are suggesting that the rational analyses of our internal and external cultural mindsets need to become a part of curriculum work. While it is necessary to work systematically and logically with the curriculum, its various elements, and its design, that is not sufficient. Curricular analyses must also deal with the cultural environments of the curriculum. In particular, the subliminal, often contradictory, cultural mindsets that all of us have buried within us need to be made overt and subject to discussion and analyses. The failure to do this in the past has, in our view, undermined our ability to change the curriculum significantly. We have no doubt but that, in light of *intra*generational disjuncture and the continuing acceleration of technological invention, the curriculum will change with or without the professional contributions of educators. However, it is also our belief that a well-planned set of changes dealing consciously with the existing cultural environments of the curriculum will lead to a more effective curriculum for the future and in the future.

## QUESTIONS FOR DISCUSSION AND REFLECTION

1. As discussed in this chapter, what is the difference between a purpose and an aim? Why should we bother to make any distinction at all? Some purposes can lead to very different curricular designs. Can you think of several examples?

2. How are goals and objectives different? When is it difficult to distinguish between them?

3. Write down a purpose that you believe is important in education and then:
   a. Write one related aim;
   b. Write a goal that is related to the aim;
   c. Write a broad objective that addresses the goal;
   d. Write a specific objective that addresses the goal; and
   e. Write a specific performance objective that addresses the goal.

4. Four distinct conceptions of curriculum, each with several variations, have been presented in this chapter. As a review, list these, explaining each in your own words. Review the aim, goal, and objectives you have written for question 3 and decide under which conception you would place your work. Please explain your choice.

5. From your experience, is the following statement true: American elementary and secondary education are in a dichotomous relationship.

6. In a society-oriented curriculum, how do the reformist and futurist perspectives differ?

7. What do the child-in-society and the Rousseauian perspectives have in common? Discuss their very important differences as well.

8. In what ways are the existentialist and child-in-society perspectives alike? What are their important differences?

9. What factors in American schooling today would make a psychological curriculum difficult to implement?

10. Explain the concept of *meta*structure and the idea that a school subject may be considered a *meta*structure. Use specific examples.

11. Could/should the schools develop structures of knowledge unique to their instructional goals? Should, for example, political science and history be studied as a way of developing citizenship, or should there be a specially designed subject based on an organized collection of facts, concepts, and generalizations based on citizenship?

12. In what important ways does the process-as-content perspective differ from the child-in-society perspective? Do you see the possibility of overlap between these two curricular perspectives?

13. In your opinion, would we be more willing to adopt the New Math curriculum today than we were in the 1960s? Explain your views fully.

14. Explain how control of the educational experience is related to the kind of curriculum design followed.

15. What do you think is the most influential force on curriculum development and implementation? Explain your answer.

16. What groups in a community do you think would have to come to an agreement in order for a curriculum based on the great knowledge perspective to be instituted? What individuals or groups might oppose the implementation of such a curriculum?

17. We are a multicultural society in which many elements are viewed differently. Different groups internalize different ideals and practices. How do you think this affects curriculum design?

18. In what ways might cultural mindsets inhibit the adoption of curriculum designs that would address intragenerational disjunctures?

19. Which responsibilities for educating children should the schools accept in their curricula, and which should they leave to others? Why?

20. Choose a specific type of curriculum and perspective to investigate further. Explore the professional literature, starting your search with the works of people we have referred to in this chapter. From this search, you should be able to find additional references. Find specific examples of its implementation and determine, when possible, whether it was a success.

## NOTES

1. For a more extensive discussion of this idea, see: Ornstein, A. C. and Hunkins, F. P. (1988). *Curriculum: Foundations, principles, and issues.* Englewood Cliffs, NJ: Prentice Hall, pp. 146–149.
2. Saylor, J. G. and Alexander, W. M. (1974). *Planning curriculum for schools.* New York: Holt, Rinehart and Winston.
3. Tyler, R. (1949). *Basic principles of curriculum and instruction.* Chicago: University of Chicago Press.
4. Hunkins, F. P. (1980). *Curriculum development program improvement.* Columbus, OH: Merrill.
5. Bennett, W. J. (1988). *American education: Making it work.* Washington DC: Government Printing Office.
6. Smith, B. O., Stanley, W. O., and Shores, J. H. (1950). *Fundamentals of curriculum development.* New York: Harcourt, Brace and World.
7. Beauchamp, G. A. (1981). *Curriculum theory.* Itasca, IL: F. E. Peacock. (revised edition, previous editions published in 1961, 1968, and 1975 by Kagg Press, Wilmette, IL).
8. Faunce, R. and Bossing, N. (1951). *Developing the core curriculum.* New York: Prentice-Hall.
9. Bobbitt, F. (1924). *How to make a curriculum.* Boston: Houghton Mifflin.
10. Glatthorn, A. A. (1987). *Curriculum leadership.* Glenview, IL: Scott, Foresman.
11. Counts, G. S. (1932). *Dare the schools build a new social order?* New York: John Day.
12. Brameld, T. (1956). *Toward a reconstructed philosophy of education.* New York: Holt, Rinehart and Winston.
13. Giroux, H. A. (1983). *Ideology, culture, and the process of schooling.* Philadelphia: Temple University Press.
14. Ilich, I. (1971). *Deschooling society.* New York: Harper & Rowe.
15. Freire, P. (1970). *Pedagogy of the oppressed.* New Yorker: Herder and Herder.
16. Ornstein, A. C. and Hunkins, F. P. *Op. cit.*, p. 187.
17. Shane, H. G. with Tabler, M. B. (1981). *Educating for a new millennium.* Bloomington, IN: Phi Delta Kappa Educational Foundation, p. 73.
18. Kuhn, T. S. (1970). *The structure of scientific revolutions.* 2nd ed. Chicago: University of Chicago Press.
19. Livingston, D. W. (1983). *Class ideologies and educational futures.* Sussex, England: Falmer Press, pp. 215–216.
20. Rousseau, J. J. (1762). *Emile.* This edition 1979 (trans. Bloom A.). New York: Basic Books.
21. Morris, V. C. (1961). *Philosophy and the American school.* Boston: Houghton Mifflin.
22. Zais, R. S. (1976). *Curriculum: Principles and foundations.* New York: Thomas Y. Crowell, p. 154.
23. Neill, A. S. (1960). *Sumerhill.* New York: Hart Publishing.
24. *Ibid.*, p. 24.
25. *Ibid.*, p. 117.
26. Parker, F. W. (1894). *Talks on pedagogics.* New York: John Day (1937 original publication date).
27. Dewey, J. (1897). My pedagogic creed. *The School Journal*, 54(3), pp. 77–80.

28. Dewey, J. (1900). *The school and society*. Chicago: University of Chicago Press.

29. Dewey, J. (1902). *The child and the curriculum*. Chicago: University of Chicago Press.

30. Dewey, J. (1916). *Democracy and education*. New York: Macmillan.

31. Dewey, J. (1931). *The way out of educational confusion*. Cambridge, MA: Harvard University Press.

32. *Op. cit.*, Dewey, J. *Democracy and Education*, p. 76.

33. For an account of the curriculum and work of Dewey's Laboratory School, see: Mayhew, K. C. and Edwards, A. C. (1936). *The Dewey school: The laboratory school of the University of Chicago, 1896–1903*. New York: D. Appleton-Century.

34. Tanner, D. and Tanner, L. N. (1975). *Curriculum development: Theory into practice*. New York: Macmillan, p. 301.

35. Kilpatrick, W. H. (1918). *The project method*. Bulletin, 10th Series, No. 3. New York: Teachers College Press.

36. Dewey, J. (1938). *Experience and education*. The Kappa Delta Pi Lecture Series. New York: Collier Books.

37. *Ibid.*, pp. 78–79.

38. *Op. cit.*, Tanner, D. and Tanner, L. N., p. 493.

38a. Shane, H. G. and McSwain, E. T. (1958). *Evaluation and the elementary curriculum*. New York: Holt, Rinehart and Winston.

39. Harris, P. E. (1937). *The curriculum and cultural change*. New York: D. Appleton-Century.

40. Hopkins, L. T. (1941). *Interaction: The democratic process*. Boston: D. C. Heath.

41. Weinstein, G. and Fantini, M. D. (1970). *Toward humanistic education: A curriculum of affect*. New York: Praeger.

42. *Op. cit.*, Ornstein and Hunkins, p. 182.

43. *Op. cit.*, Ornsteine and Hunkins, p. 40.

44. Goodman, P. (1970). *New reformation*. New York: Random House, p. 86.

45. Goodman, P. (1964). *Compulsory mis-education*. New York: Horizon Press, p. 39.

46. Holt, J. (1964). *How children fail*. New York: Pitman.

47. Holt, J. (1969). *The underachieving school*. New York: Pitman.

48. Holt, J. (1970). *What do I do Monday?* New York: E. P. Dutton.

49. Holt, J. (1972). *Freedom and beyond*. New York: Delta.

50. Holt, J. (1981). *Teach your own*. New York: Dell.

51. John Holt set out his views in his early work, *How Children Fail* (*op. cit.*). In works such as *What Do I Do Monday?*, he expands on his early ideas. While taken by the possibility of "deschooling society," he has little expectation of that happening and only in his later work, *Teach Your Own*, are his efforts fully directed toward undoing the existing compulsory system.

52. *Op. cit.*, Holt, J., 1972.

53. *Ibid.*

54. Weber, L. (1971). *The English infant school and informal education*. Englewood Cliffs, NJ: Prentice-Hall, p. 169.

55. Phenix, P. H. (1962). The disciplines as curriculum content. In: Passow, A. H. (ed.). *Curriculum crossroads*. New York: Teachers College Press.

56. Schwab, J. J. (1962). The concept of the structure of a discipline. *The Educational Record*, 43, July.

57. Spencer, H. (1860). *Education: Intellectual, moral, and physical*. New York: D. Appleton. Note: the first chapter of this work had this question as its title.

58. Hutchins, R. M. (1936). *The higher learning in America*. New Haven: Yale University Press, p. 66.

59. *Ibid.*, pp. 59–87.

60. Adler, M. J. (1981). *Six great ideas*. New York: Macmillan.

61. Bloom, A. (1987). *The closing of the American Mind*. New York: Simon and Schuster, p. 372.

62. Smith, B. O., Stanley, W. O., and Shores, J. H. (1957). *Fundamentals of curriculum development*. (rev. ed.). New York: Harcourt, Brace & World, p. 604.

63. Schwab, J. J. (1970). *The practical: A language for curriculum*. Washington, DC: National Education Association.

64. *Op. cit.*, Bloom, A., pp. 373–374.

65. Dewey, J. (1903). *Logical conditions of a scientific treatment of morality*. First published as a pamphlet; this version appears in *John Dewey on education*, Archambault, R. D. (ed.), 1974. Chicago: University of Chicago Press, p. 26.

66. Snow, C. P. (1959). *The two cultures and the scientific revolution*. New York: Cambridge University Press.

67. Dewey, J. (1922). *Human nature and conduct*. New York: Henry Holt.

68. Herbart, J. F. (1895). *The science of education: Its general principles deduced from its aims*, (trans. Felkin, H. M. and Felkin, E.). Boston: D. C. Heath.

69. *Op. cit.*, Parker, F. W., p. 23.

70. De Garmo, C. (1895). Most pressing problems concerning the elementary course of study. In: McMurry, C. A. (ed.) *First year book of the National Herbart Society for the Scientific Study of Teaching*. 2nd ed., published 1907. Chicago: University of Chicago Press, p. 26.

71. *Op. cit.*, Tanner, D. and Tanner, L. N. pp. 204–205.

72. *Op. cit.*, Smith, B. O., Stanley, W. O., and Shores, J. H., (Rev. ed.) p. 258.

73. *Ibid.*, p. 256–257.

74. Bruner, J. S. (1960). *The process of education*. New York: Vintage Books.

75. *Ibid.*, p. 20.

76. Parker, J. C. and Rubin, L. J. (1966). *Process as content: Curriculum design and the application of knowledge*. Chicago: Rand McNally, pp. 11–12.

77. Berman, L. M. (1968). *New priorities in the curriculum*. Columbus, OH: Charles E. Merrill, Chapter 11.

78. *Ibid.*, p. 31.

79. *Ibid.*, p. 27.

80. Spring, J. (1978). *American education: An introduction to social and political aspects*. New York: Longman, p. 150.

81. *Op. cit.*, Beane, J. A., Toepfer, C. F., Jr., and Alessi, S. J., p. 224.

82. For a curriculum-based discussion of Royce's concept of "encapsulation," which we have persistently referred to as "cultural mindset," see: Zais, R. S. (1976). *Curriculum: Principle and foundations*. New York: Thomas Y. Cromwell, pp. 218–229.

# 5

# The Politics of Curriculum

### Introduction

Notwithstanding the intellectual bases necessary for curriculum work, the implementation, evaluation, and revision of the curriculum design—that is, what is usually referred to as curriculum development—cannot be well understood from a strictly analytical perspective. Implementing a curriculum design is a complex cultural undertaking involving major political, psychological, and cultural considerations. Politics of every sort and at every level of society affect the curriculum implementation process, complicating many times over what may appear at first glance to be no more than a simple process of translating the overall curriculum design into a practical plan for student learning.

Ralph Tyler's very brief book, entitled *Basic Principles of Curriculum and Instruction*,[1] captures this expectation for simplicity and straightforward operations quite well. This may explain why it has remained a best seller among education books for well over forty years. In Tyler's words, his book was an effort to present "a rationale for viewing, analyzing and interpreting the curriculum and instructional program of an educational institution."[2] The entire work is based on pursuing four fundamental questions:

1. What educational purposes should the school seek to attain?
2. What educational experiences are likely to attain these purposes?
3. How can these educational experiences be effectively organized?
4. How can we determine whether these purposes are being attained?

Tyler recognizes that multiple sources must be consulted in responding to each of these questions. He believes that after due consideration, difficulties and conflicts from these multiple sources can probably be worked out. For example, in Tyler's view, objectives developed to support educational purposes should be based on the nature, needs, and interests of both children and society.[3] An additional source is studies of contemporary life outside of school.[4] The frequent, often strident conflicts between the individual and society are largely ignored in this discussion of sources. Indeed, although Tyler proceeds to acknowledge "the problems involved in formulating objectives in a way that they can serve as useful guides,"[5] he essentially infers that we can achieve a "satisfactory formulation of objectives" if enough time and care are given to the job.[6] The countless contradictions and conflicts arising between the demands ("needs") of society and those of the young are thus tamed within a linear approach in which the curriculum developer first deals with purpose, then with experiences that could represent the purposes well, then with the selection of appropriate instructional methodologies, and finally, logically, with the evaluation of the curriculum.

In Tyler's pat description of curriculum development, an underlying assumption is that we, the American public, as well as professional educators, know what we want from the curriculum. Certainly, in the latter part of the twentieth century nothing could be further from the truth. While the number of electives offered and allowed for high school credit have expanded in near mind boggling fashion,[7] the traditional high school curriculum that helps students enter college and is accorded "status" by parents and politicians alike still reigns supreme. It is the curriculum that harkens back to the 1893 proposals of the Committee of Ten. On the one hand, the public clamors for courses relevant to their needs, courses in the prevention of drug addiction, AIDS, driver's education, sex education, consumer education, typing, and so forth; on the other hand, these are the very courses seen as "dumbing" the curriculum and undermining the quality of curriculum that our youth are asked to pursue. Tyler's approach to curriculum development could hardly deal with this "wanting it all" and "wanting it the way it was."

## The Political Perspective

### Curriculum Development

The political and intellectual power of any professional field is largely related to that field's ability to clarify the range and nature of its research and to produce knowledge therefrom that is useful in real world settings. Medicine is a successful professional field both politically and intellectually because the area of its investigation and the objectives established for its work are well delineated and have clear applications in the real world. We have a fair understanding of the kind of decisions that will be made by medical doctors. Curriculum development, on the other hand, is beleaguered by ambiguities.

We have already discussed the various interpretations of such key terms as "curriculum" and "content." An entire chapter is devoted to the presentation of an array of curricular designs that have been tried in one place or another during this century and/or have been the subject of extended study and discussion. When we reach the curriculum development phase, the ineffectiveness of curriculum work becomes apparent. Curriculum development involves the processes of determining how a curriculum design shall be prepared for classroom implementation, who shall participate in this preparation, and how the actual classroom implementation will occur. Curriculum development is fundamentally a political undertaking.

Cultural mindsets about schooling and the curriculum, developed at the turn of the century, are only minimally affected by the rationally based discourses of curriculum experts. Mindless eclecticism and inconsistencies in what the public expects from the schools abound while the work of curriculum specialists has hardly moved beyond keeping teachers "up to date" in subjects traditionally accorded status by virtue of their being required for college entrance.

## Curriculum Decision Making in the Real World of the Public Schools

The dismal view of curriculum development expressed above does not diminish the need for the field of curriculum. The field is, after all, a relatively young one charged with confronting questions that go to the very heart of what our society is about, and for which, as a society, we have no clear answers. For example: (1) What is important for us all to know? For only some of us to know? (2) What should we exclude from the education of the young and why? (3) How can we best communicate our values to the young? (4) Are we sure we know what our values are? (5) Should the structure of disciplines continue to underlie the curriculum design of the schools, or should other possible structures be adopted that might be more useful to the development and exercise of democratic citizenship?

Our questions go to the core of what we believe not only about education, but also about the nature of our humanness and the society we belong to. For many of us, the complexity of today's world and the continued rapidity of change have left our beliefs in a state of ambiguity. The future is an unpleasant enigma we can hardly bear to look at even though education of the young must inevitably reflect some view of the future. In this context, we need to remember that expecting life to be as it has been in the past is also a view of the future.

All of us in our cultural lives wear different hats: we are parents, we are workers, we are voters. As we move from one role to another, our answers to the hard questions facing us are affected. As parents, we are likely to want children to have a well-rounded education that will help them to lead fuller lives even into old age. As workers who know how important technological knowledge and an advanced degree are for getting ahead, we are likely to want children to have a solid foundation in scientific and technological studies, even though the achievement of such a foundation would consume a major portion of their program. Indeed, if we are business people as well, we would probably add the study of economics and such subjects as accounting and typing. Now the parent in us rises again! Should we just go on ignoring the moral education of our young? And shouldn't children come to appreciate the great works of our civilization—the pleasure of Mozart, the insightfulness of Shakespeare, the vision of Leonardo de Vinci? Those of us concerned with the political health of our democracy would add still more subjects—not only reading literacy but visual literacy as well, especially video literacy and how to "read" the packaging of political candidates. Back to our hats as parents! What about the physical well-being of our children and the sports that help them to develop those positive character traits of perseverance and cooperation that will serve them well for a lifetime? And so it goes. The demands made on the schools seem to have no end.

With the proverbial multiplication of disciplines and of knowledge in general has come an increasing divisiveness among the public, and even within each of us as individuals who wear many hats. Curriculum professionals are asked to make decisions that most of us succeed in avoiding and apparently prefer to leave in a state of ambiguity.

In the real world of the public schools, curriculum decision making has become the act of balancing an array of reasonable, but often contradictory views about what is important educationally. The professional must work against a backdrop of vacillating public support and a nearly permanent state of ambivalence. Decision making has become primarily an effort directed toward pleasing as many of us as possible, rather than the intellectual act of fashioning a logically defensible, workable framework for the school's curriculum. Instead of framing and clarifying the choices confronting the public and taking a leadership role in the educational decision-making process, curriculum specialists have allowed decisions for our future directions to drift inconclusively while the traditions of the past continue to dominate the curriculum.

In such a state, education and the curriculum have become easy foci of political rhetoric at both the national and local levels. In the last few decades of the twentieth century, a series of reform movements have had their impetus primarily from national political leaders. In the 1960s, largely as a consequence of the Soviet Union's success in space, millions of federal dollars were directed toward discovery learning and the updating of school content in the sciences and, subsequently, the social sciences and English. In the 1970s, Sidney Marland, as director of the Office of Education, initiated the career education movement and fostered the cry for "back to basics." In the 1980s, the National Commission on Excellence in Education urged the strengthening of high school graduation requirements to include three years each of mathematics and the social studies, four years of English, two years of a foreign language, and a half year of computer science.[8]

The states and many local school districts were eager to follow the recommendations, but even though resources were increased they fell far short of the needs. The performance of American students on standardized tests, especially when compared with students of other developed nations, remained poor and so, in the 1990s, President Bush called a summit meeting of the nation's governors to establish "clear national performance goals that will make us internationally competitive."[9]

Six goals to be attained by the year 2000 were developed as a result of this meeting between the President and the governors. These have been widely disseminated. On the whole, they reflect significant problems confronting the schools. Nevertheless, the professional educator tends to have a "yes, but how?" reaction to them. The list of six national education goals follows:[10]

GOAL 1: By the year 2000, all children in America will start ready to learn.

GOAL 2: By the year 2000, the high school graduation rate will increase to at least 90 percent.

GOAL 3: By the year 2000, American students will leave grades four, eight, and twelve having demonstrated competency in challenging subject matter including English, mathematics, science, history, and geography; and every school in America will ensure that all students learn to use their minds well, so they may be prepared for responsible citizenship, further learning, and productive employment in our modern economy.

GOAL 4: By the year 2000, United States students will be first in the world in science and mathematics achievement.

GOAL 5: By the year 2000, every adult American will be literate and will possess the knowledge and skills necessary to compete in a global economy and exercise the rights and responsibilities of citizenship.

GOAL 6: By the year 2000, every school in America will be free of drugs and violence and will offer a disciplined environment conducive to learning.

There is a good deal of political rhetoric and educational naiveté contained in this set of six goals. Indeed, the set appears to be a wish list that is not quite related to reality but with which hardly anyone could disagree. The conference of governors and the national political attention paid to the schools are no doubt heartening to many educators who believe that such attention will bring new resources and a new willingness to achieve reform.

## The Politics of Curricular Decision Making

The real world of the public schools is primarily a political one. That is, it is factional, argumentative, and bureaucratic. The bureaucracy not only has our educational traditions embedded in its organizational structure, it has the objective of its own survival as well. This means that any significant change is often viewed as disruptive and undesirable. Curriculum specialists working for school districts are members of the bureaucratic corps—taking the leadership role referred to above may be the equivalent of asking them to put their jobs on the line. Why should they, rather than the superintendent or the principals or even the members of the school board, take the risk? Shouldn't all educational experts be involved in achieving significant curricular changes? The response must be, "Of course, they all need to be involved." Nevertheless, if the professional field of curriculum is to serve any purpose at all, it must assume both the intellectual and political leadership for the future of the school's curriculum.

All too frequently, important discussions about the directions school studies need to take are sidetracked by issues that capture the passions of the moment but have very limited impact on the major goals of schooling. Curricular arguments in the real world of the public schools tend to revolve around questions that have little to do with the basic design of the curriculum or the philosophies that underlie it. "Should we have sex education in the school?" is a typical question. The question implicitly accepts the traditional subject design. The various factions debating the question are no doubt discussing whether the topic of sex is a fitting content for school study and what constitutes appropriate methodologies for its instruction. These are intellectual and philosophical questions of considerable import, but the breadth and depth of their debate is held to a minor corner of the curriculum that in no way threatens the place of the existing curriculum design based on the disciplines or on its related administrative structures.

Control of the schools both internally and externally is a source of power. Debates frequently seem to be more about control than about the curriculum and the goals we hope to achieve. For instance, if more foreign language studies are required by the schools, then some other subject will have to relinquish time. Which will it be, and to what extent will the status of other subjects in the curriculum be threatened? Whose job will be abolished?

Political debates related to the curriculum abound at all levels from the federal government to the principal's office. The factions and the debates seem to balance each other out. Viewed from nearly a century of curriculum work, curriculum development has meant for all practical purposes the maintainance of the 1893 status quo. Whether sex education is taught in the schools or not ultimately has very little impact on the way the schools function, on the national norms set forth to measure youngsters' achievement, or even on what makes us think a school is a good one. The "good" high schools do a "good" job preparing students for college!

## The Real World of Political Cacophony

In the real world of public schooling, curriculum decision makers confront a continual cacophony of complaints. A book used by a teacher may be deemed offensive. The content of the curriculum is not "hard" enough. The curriculum is too concerned with "slow" children and not sufficiently concerned with gifted children's intellectual development, or vice versa. Pressure is exerted by parents, the local government, the federal government, business associations, and religious groups, among others. In such a milieu, curriculum decision making is a political process that may involve philosophical and logical analyses, but only on occasion and hardly ever with the consistency necessary to achieve a wholly cogent curriculum. Allowing the cultural mindsets of society to set the course is the path of least resistance and often the most attractive among a number of difficult choices for the beleaguered curriculum worker. In such an environment, the textbook descriptions of curriculum development border on the telling of fairy tales.

The textbook descriptions are orderly and sequential. First, the story goes, aims are established representative of the desires of society at large. One way this step may be accomplished is through legislative resolution at the state level; another way is through the appropriation of federal funds.

Some form of commission or steering group is then organized, typically with teachers, administrators, students, school board members, and local business people. This group, possibly with the assistance of the school superintendent, organizes a set of educational goals applicable to the school district as a whole. What philosophical analyses occur during the deliberations are typically short-lived and sketchy because members of this group are usually new to thinking about curriculum. They often believe that their "gut-level" understandings about what is needed to improve education are superior to jargon-filled and seemingly endless discussions about what directions education needs to take. A usual *modus operandus* is to review sets of goals established by similar committees developed for other school districts. From this basic departure point, the group assesses what it would like to add, delete, or otherwise change. This way of operating assures continuity and consistency in American education throughout the country even though there is no federal legislative authority over the operations of education, except for federally supported programs. It is also a method that may reinforce the status quo even in the most reform-minded of periods.

Typically, the group's work ends with a series of goals broad enough to satisfy a wide range of diverse public opinions. For example: *Students will acquire the knowledge and skills necessary to participate effectively in their own democratic governance*. Even if this group holds public hearings, it is not likely to encounter any significant opposition. Few of us would disagree with participating effectively in our own democratic governance.

The next stage involves linking theory and practice, that is, developing a series of broad instructional objectives that transform the idealistic statements of educational direction into general activities the schools can pursue. At this point, there are often significant gaps of logic between the statement of goals and the broad objectives. For example, given the above goal regarding democratic governance, a series of objectives might be developed requiring the learning of basic skills, such as reading, writing, and mathematics; knowledge about the physical geography of the states; knowledge about the history of the founding of America's democracy; and development of attitudes necessary to funtion well under our American system of government. Knowledge of the states and their capitals would appear to be a very emotional objective; any suggestion that its accomplishment would consume more time than its contribution to the goal is worth often leads to indignation. If it is suggested that mathematics may only contribute peripherally to effective democratic citizenship, the uproar may come from mathematics teachers, who, of course, will do all in their power to demonstrate otherwise. At times, the curriculum specialist invites teachers to develop suitable specific objectives. More often, the list of specific objectives is developed in the central office, incorporated into the curriculum guide, and shipped to teachers for implementation. Sometimes, a group of teachers is appointed to work with the specialist on the list.

In any case, the curriculum worker is continually involved in public relations and damage control. Even at the point of developing specific objectives, achieving consensus and support for what is usually no more than a set of minor revisions is of the utmost importance for the "stability" of the specialist's position within the school district. By the time reform is implemented, it is often without the strength of a rational base or widespread professional support. Numerous groups will have important reservations, and all sorts of special interests will have been satisfied.

### The Political Role of Evaluation

After the new curricula have become part of classroom instruction, an evaluation component is usually developed. Often this will involve *formative evaluation*, that is, ongoing feedback to the teacher about how students are doing during implementation so that adjustments to the curriculum may be made. However, *summative evaluation,* or a final summary of how well students have learned what the objectives have set forth for learning, is usually given far greater importance. This is the culminating activity of the curriculum development process.

Although summative evaluations are often thought of as looping back to the processes of developing objectives so that revisions may be made, most often they are highly publicized and widely disseminated, and they communicate a message of success or failure to the public. The worry here is that the tests used for summative evaluation frequently come from national sources that may conceptualize curricular objectives quite differently from those used in the actual curriculum.

These national standardized tests are often imposed by state board or state legislative fiat for purposes of school accountability with little awareness or concern about the work of numerous committees, local curriculum specialists, and even the teachers who are professionally prepared to deal with children of disparate backgrounds and learning styles. They have become a de facto means of external control over the functioning of the school's curriculum. Thus, any reform that may develop at the grass-roots level from within school systems is subject to the control of summative evaluation instruments that have been designed for the most part by commercial companies.

### The Political Role of the Curriculum Developer

We have considered at length the definition and nature of the curriculum, its purposes, designs, and relationship to instruction. All too frequently in curriculum textbooks, that is where the discussion ends. It is somehow assumed that once these elements of curriculum work have been presented as an idealized system, curriculum work in the real world is self-explanatory. Political pressures of all kinds are adroitly ignored with the apolitical description of the field through objective flow charts and outlines.

The impression left is that curriculum work is primarily a task for educational philosophers or possibly for social scientists. On the one hand is the expert, erudite about the nature of knowledge and its relationship to our values and our perceptions of reality, "designing" a cogent and logically defensible approach to the content of education. On the other hand is the social scientist involved in studying the community, its needs, and its relationships to the schools, so that whatever is developed for school study is consonant with the nature and needs of the community.

However, neither the social sciences nor philosophical analyses offer a sufficient basis for the adequate functioning of the curriculum worker. Nor, for that matter, could the curriculum worker do justice to either of these endeavors. There is no clear delineation of the curriculum worker's territory, no clear set of functions, no viable research system for coming to know about curricular things. In such an amorphous state, there can be no accumulation of knowledge on which to base curricular decisions. Anyone and everyone thinks he or she is expert in curriculum. Under such circumstances, the political power of the field is almost nil.

The real world of public schooling can hardly wait for the rational development and diffusion of more adequate curricular designs. Children grow up and no decision becomes a decision. Nor can curriculum workers aspire to achieve objective analyses and/or conclusions about curriculum as though they were social scientists or philosophers. Public education as a whole, and curriculum work in particular, is a value-ladened, culture-bound, and fundamentally political enterprise. To utilize social scientific objectivity in one or another scholastic instance may be perfectly reasonable, but to expect it to be the rule of operation for curriculum development is to deny the real nature of schooling. To act as though the complexities of public education can be reduced to scientifically controllable situations is to ignore the heterogeneity, the myriad inconsistencies, the deeply imbedded mindsets about how school ought to be, and the increasing flux of the educational scene. The stipulation of terms, the isolation of questions or problems from each other so that the resulting simplification will allow more thorough study of the isolated part, and even the possibility of taking no action at all are behaviors representative of social science work and even of philosophical reflection, but they are behaviors poorly suited to the educational scene and to the work of curriculum specialists.

Perhaps curriculum development can best be conceived as a series of political operations with a necessary underpinning of intellectual analysis. The curriculum worker is not an analytical political scientist reflecting on the processes of development but rather a problem-laden person dealing with a wide variety of political situations subject to external control, compromise, conflicting values, and a host of unpredictable events. The curriculum specialist must bring coherence, viability, and vision to what is studied in the schools. On the one hand is the underlying philosophy of the curriculum and its overall design; on the other hand is the understanding of how children learn and the relationship of knowledge to learning; in the middle lie the many wants and demands of a democratic society somewhat uncertain what it really expects from education.

The real work of the specialist is about balancing the quite rational processes of curriculum design with a multitude of fundamentally political, even irrational, situations of schools and school districts. The curriculum developer's job is to be both an intellectual and political leader. This is often a discouraging undertaking that makes a mockery of our idealistic views of curriculum making. This is not to say the ideals are without worth. The ideals push us to discuss our aims and goals when we develop our written curricular plans. To the degree that we are forced to reflect on our educational beliefs, they are useful even in a period when a state of inertia dominates educational thinking.

The specialist must be a public relations expert, possibly contributing to changing the direction of education but only insofar as the people being served are able and willing to go. The curriculum developer must somehow take the multifarious environments of education into account if she or he is to be effective. This means involving various special interest groups at every level and stage of the development process; it means interpreting the aims and purposes of society; it means selecting and linking together what shall be the contents of education; it means understanding the backgrounds, abilities, and needs of learners; and it means helping teachers to teach the curriculum well.

This is not the stuff of revolutions. Just as revolutions in the work of a community of scientists, to paraphrase Thomas Kuhn,[11] come from outside their established paradigms, revolutions in curriculum will need to come from without. Revolutions in the field of curriculum are both conceivable and desirable. Nevertheless, the curriculum worker is the least likely individual to be involved in leading curricular revolutions. That is for others coming from other fields and other perspectives. It should be noted in this context that John Dewey was primarily a philosopher, that Harold Rugg was trained as an engineer, and that Jerome Bruner was a cognitive psychologist.

Curriculum workers are necessarily part of the mainstream. They need to be in a state of intellectual readiness, able to recognize the significant trends of the future and to bring these into the curriculum in viable and coherent ways. They stand on the edge between what is currently viable and what is necessary to the future. By the very nature of institutional work in a democracy, and all public education in America fits that description, the curriculum worker is a political eclectic, trying to put all the pieces together in a form that is viable for the cultural milieu as well as respectful of the views and needs of the many diverse groups comprising the community.

## Reflective Eclecticism and Curriculum Work

In curriculum work, eclecticism functions in widely disparate ways. It can epitomize the activities of the nondoctrinaire specialist, touching all bases and pleasing as many factions as possible, often without regard for the numerous inconsistencies of purpose inherent among the activities pursued. This is an example of mindless eclecticism. A certain amount of rationality is always present in educational planning, but its presence too often remains piecemeal and noncontributing to the coherence of the overall enterprise. Standardized testing often falls into this mold. That is, in and of itself, standardized testing is a quite rational effort. However, when it is placed together with goals of developing critical thinking while its objectives remain at the lowest levels of recall and memorization, and it is utilized by schools as the major way of determining instructional success, it becomes a significant contributor to mindless eclecticism. Educational eclecticism can also engage the best of our rational and reflective powers and lead toward carefully synthesized, well-rounded curricular plans based on the best ideas proposed by an array of interest groups.

Educational eclecticism has all too frequently been mindless, often no more than a knee-jerk reaction to the political passions of the moment. In recent years, we have added to the school's curriculum, among others: career education, AIDS education, foreign language requirements, computer education, law education, and family studies. "Concern for the health of the nation," "a response to the swift rise in teenage pregnancy," "a return to the basics of schooling of times gone by," and "a recognition of growing technological needs" are among the numerous reasons that have moved us to make curricular changes. Taken together, they form a grab bag of remedies without any underlying structure. Naturally, they add themselves as well as possible to the existing subject-based curriculum design.

Reflective eclecticism is of quite another kind. It is a careful, rational process that brings complex and multifarious conceptions together in new and sometimes groundbreaking arrangements. Above all, it pays attention to the overall coherence of the various parts. Significant examples of reflective eclecticism can be found in American history, for instance with the development of the United States Constitution. The three separate branches of government, the difference in how the states were represented in the two Houses of Congress, and the attachment of the Bill of Rights to the Constitution as a set of amendments all reflect the painstaking efforts of this nation's founders to achieve a plan for democracy that would cover many bases and meet the legitimate concerns of many disparate groups. The rights of property owners were to be protected, but so were the individual rights of all people no matter how poor. Populous states were to have their greater size represented proportionally in the House of Representatives, but small states were protected by equal representation in the Senate. The President was to be popularly elected but only indirectly through the electoral college. No such comprehensive examples of reflective eclecticism can be found in the development of curriculum.

While examples of curricular eclecticism abound in today's schools, they tend to be a product of cultural mindsets, trends of the moment, and knee-jerk responses to immediately felt needs. In sum, they are products of mindless eclecticism. For instance, the study of consumer economics was added to many high school social studies curricula in the 1960s and 1970s and has often been accepted in partial fulfillment of the social studies requirement, a requirement that has as one of its major goals the development of good citizenship. Presumedly, being a wise spender makes one a good citizen—certainly a questionable proposition but clearly a compromise between those who would have more practical content studied in the schools and those who would make the preparation of good and wise citizens a major purpose of schooling. Other instances include "Touring the United States" as an alternative course to one in geography, and the reading of a collection of short stories in current magazines as a substitute for the more traditional course in American literature. Nothing is especially "wrong" with any of these newer courses. It is, rather, that the goals they fulfill are so diverse from those of the courses they are to substitute that one has to wonder whether, as a society, we really understand what our educational eclecticism is doing to our goals.

### The Usefulness of Noneclectic Curriculum Designs

Describing curriculum designs in their ideal forms, that is, as noneclectic conceptions, as we tried to do in Chapter 4, helps us to view more clearly the kinds of choices that the curriculum specialist must confront. However, it is equally important to remember that just because choices can be expressed in their ideal and therefore often extreme form, does not mean that we must make our choices only among the extremes, that the decision-making situation must be necessarily an either/or case, that we must have either a child-centered curriculum or a knowledge-centered one, and so forth.

In the preceding chapter, we presented the concept of the eclectic curriculum along with curriculum designs more typically included in such lists because the concept of eclecticism lays a foundation for making choices that are thoughtful compromises among the extremes. Eclecticism does not represent a singular design but rather compromises from among several designs. The configurations these compromises may take are of all kinds. Eclectic designs may have nothing in common other than the effort to compromise and to forge a more effective plan from the compromises achieved.

Granted, eclecticism as we know it in the schools today is mindless—a crazy quilt of fads sewn together to satisfy various special interest groups and not making too much sense for the overall meaning of the curriculum. In particular, there is the tendency in many school districts to bring various curriculum designs together without any strict analysis of the goals and objectives involved in each design, as though essentially different premises could be fused by simply adding them together. What is often ignored is the fact that goals underlying diverse designs represent significant differences among the public's values and beliefs about education. So long as these differences are ignored while the designs are treated as though they could, by some eclectic magic, be added together in a brew that will satisfy the public as a whole, the traditional curriculum will continue to dominate our cultural mindsets because the results of our eclectic efforts have little intellectual power of their own.

To offer a concrete example, if the Arabic numeral "20" is added together with the Roman numeral "II," the sum might conceivably be "20II." This takes us no further than we were before the addition. In fact, the results achieved are less useful than either of the numerals taken alone. Unless steps are taken to relate "20" and "II" within the design adopted to achieve the sum, the addition is actually counterproductive. Of course, such a difficult undertaking would be pursued only if clear advantages were perceived in bringing the two systems together.

In similar fashion, the purposes of the knowledge-centered and child-centered designs cannot be simultaneously pursued by simply adding them together in a single curricular effort. That is, taking a couple of class periods for open-ended, expressive activities and adding several hours of "solid" mathematical and scientific studies is an eclectic hodgepodge likely to lead to the denigration of one and an overemphasis on the other. Translated into the circumstances of our own times, the open-ended, expressive activities would probably be assigned a very low status since they are not of much use in meeting college entrance requirements. Politically, mathematics and science would receive the greatest support not only financially but also in terms of praise and attention.

If a seamless integration between the two were undertaken, questions of status could certainly be overcome. However, we would need to recognize first that the tensions arising from the encounter of two very different conceptions of curriculum design require a design of their own, with characteristics that may not be found in either of them alone. An essentially different design with its own set of premises and linkages between goals and content would need to be established. Indeed, the very idea of eclecticism is founded on a set of philosophical premises about the nature of humankind, of knowledge, and of the ultimate goals of life that is distinct from those of other philosophies underlying curriculum designs. As we have already noted, the practice of democracy would not be possible without the reflective operations of eclecticism.

## Compromise, Democracy, and the Art of Eclecticism

If there is anything certain among the myriad of complexities confronting us as a nation, it is our uncertainty. Many of us experience relief when a clear and definite decision can be made or when someone else will finally make it for us. Nevertheless, the survival of our form of democracy necessarily entails ongoing debate about our uncertainties and a willingness to entertain new ways of dealing with our problems. It entails our reaching a consensus from disparate views and gaining the general support of the public for the directions education takes. It is possible to derive an effective set of curricular compromises by carefully integrating aspects of what might on the surface appear to be competing concepts. Indeed, an eclectic curriculum might well be the only kind that is workable in a pluralistic democracy such as ours.

In everyday life, the juggling of choices, the plucking of the best from each, and the compromise that satisfies the broadest array of needs are typical activities. This is, in a sense, the kind of decision making that the curriculum expert needs to undertake. The professional must, of course, exercise skill in negotiation and leadership as well, which we think of as the art of eclecticism. The conduct of education in a democracy is an eclectic enterprise.

## A Guiding Philosophy

One of the fundamental differences between reflective eclecticism and mindless eclecticism lies in the awareness of the philosophical positions being pursued in the curriculum. Awareness is the key to a guiding philosophy. As Tanner and Tanner note: "In the absence of a guiding philosophy, the curriculum tends to be a product of *ad hoc* decisions—typically stemming from a combination of traditional practices and more immediate expediencies."[12]

## QUESTIONS FOR DISCUSSION AND REFLECTION

1. A large school district decides to develop a new curriculum. The superintendent decides to design the K–12 curriculum with a small group of assistants. She consults with local university professors, who all think the design is an excellent one, and has presented her proposal to the school board. Do you think the plan will be adopted? What scenario do you think is likely at the school board meeting? If the plan is not accepted, what are the next steps the superintendent needs to take?

2. In the situation described in question 1, how should the purposes of society and its aims for education be determined? Would you be satisfied if the school board worked on this part of the curriculum? Should others from the community be included? Should the federal government have more than a consultative role? In sum, how should we go about laying the groundwork for the curriculum's aims, goals, and objectives?

3. What would your reaction as a parent be if you were confronted with a controversial new curriculum, say, "Man: A Course of Study" or the New Math? What if your role were, instead, the teacher? the student? the curriculum supervisor? the principal? the taxpayer?

4. Develop a set of generalizations describing the range of political constraints often encountered in curriculum development. Relate your set to Ralph Tyler's question-steps for curriculum development.

5. If the school board were to adopt a curriculum that departs significantly from the cultural mindsets of society, what actions might be taken by the board to gain acceptance for the new curriculum before its full implementation?

6. How does formative evaluation affect the acceptance of a new curriculum?

7. How does summative evaluation affect the acceptance of a new curriculum?

8. How is reflective eclecticism different from what tends to occur in our current efforts at curriculum development?

9. Where or by whom do you think significant curricular change will be initiated?

10. Let us suppose you are a member of a school board and you receive a copy of the six goals developed by the conference of governors convened by President Bush. Would you look on a set of national goals with favor? What actions, if any, would you want the school board to take to pursue the recommended goals? Do you consider the list of goals "eclectic," and, if so, in what sense(s)

would you assign the label? If you could rewrite the list of goals, what revisions would you make?

## NOTES

1. Tyler, R. W. (1949). *Basic principles of curriculum and instruction*. Chicago: The University of Chicago Press.
2. *Ibid.*, p. 1.
3. *Ibid.*, pp. 9–13.
4. *Ibid.*, pp. 17–18.
5. *Ibid.*, p. 62.
6. *Ibid.*
7. To pursue the question of multiplying electives, see: Goodlad, J. I. (1984). *A place called school*. New York: McGraw-Hill; Boyer, E. (1983). *High School*. New York: Harper.
8. Commission on Excellence in Education (1983). *A nation at risk*. Washington, D.C.: U.S. Government Printing Office, p. 24.
9. U.S. Department of Education (July, 1990). *National goals for education*. Washington, D.C.: Department of Education, p. 1.
10. *Ibid.*, pp. 4–10.
11. Kuhn, T. S. (1962). *The structure of scientific revolutions*, 2nd ed. enlarged. Chicago: University of Chicago Press, p. 208.

    In a postscript, Kuhn acknowledges the application of his theses far beyond the sciences: "To the extent that the book portrays scientific development as a succession of tradition — bound periods punctuated by noncumulative breaks — its theses are undoubtedly of wide applicability. But they should be, for they are borrowed from other fields. Historians of literature, of music, of the arts, of political development, and of many other human activities have long described their subjects in the same way. Periodization in terms of revolutionary breaks in style, taste and institutional structure have been among their standard tools. If I have been original with respect to concepts like these, it has mainly been in applying them to the sciences, fields which have been widely thought to develop in a different way."
12. Tanner, D. and Tanner, L. N. (1975). *Curriculum development: Theory into practice*. New York: Macmillan, p. 63.

# 6

# The Philosophical Bases for Curriculum Decision Making

### Introduction: The Practicality of Philosophical Talk

Part of the difficulty in understanding what the curriculum specialist needs to do lies in the vastly different philosophies underlying the public's beliefs about education. Often the public carries in its figurative mind's eye incompatible conceptions of "good" education without much awareness of the fundamental incompatibilities among them. There are many, for example, who would demand that we return to the "basics," meaning reading, writing, and arithmetic, while simultaneously demanding that the curriculum become more relevant to the technological revolution of our times, which would mean including the newer forms of communication, such as television and computing. They are often the very same people who would have the schools develop the unique abilities and talents of children while teaching the great works of Western civilization. The incompatibility of positions often espoused by the same individuals, sometimes even on the same occasion, reflects a public that is philosophically naive and basically not ready to participate effectively in the curricular decision making of the schools.

Any effort to talk philosophy with the public or even in graduate education classes tends to meet with resistance and protests on the grounds that such talk is impractical. We believe that nothing could be *more* practical. The mindless mixing and compromising of values characterizing much of the politics in American education has us going around in circles. The curriculum should meet the needs of the individual child, of society, of business, of the arts—and, of course, we must all be well-versed in the sciences! So long as the philosophical questions remain couched in political rhetoric and obscurity, it is unlikely that curriculum planning will become effective planning for the future. We need to be a lot clearer about what we believe. We all have beliefs and we all philosophize about them. Educators along with the public at large tend to do so, however, unsystematically and without the persistence needed to achieve clarity.

The current, confused state of education is, in part, a reflection of our cultural laxness toward the systematic analysis of our beliefs. As education becomes increasingly more important vis-à-vis the technological revolution and the intragenerational disjunctures that we have all come to know, educational philosophy grows in importance as well. The next several sections review the spectrum of philosophical positions that have influenced the educational scene and curriculum work.

## The Taxonomies of Educational Philosophies

### Multiple Taxonomies

For a number of years, efforts have been made to develop a taxonomic system by which to classify the various philosophical positions and accompanying values affecting educational decision making. We base our taxonomy on a classification system used by Theodore Brameld in the 1950s and 1960s. In addition, we expand the system to meet philosophical developments that have become important to education in more recent times.

Certainly, multiple systems could be used to classify our many disparate educational belief systems. There are, for instance, Zais's other-worldly/earth-centered/man-centered schema,[1] which organizes philosophical thought about education into three categories depending on where the main locus of authority for educational decision making is placed, and Schubert's more traditional schools of thought as represented by Idealism, Realism, Neo-Thomism, Naturalism, Pragmatism, Existentialism, and Phenomenology.[2] Each offers a different way of viewing the spectrum of philosophical positions and values about education. Each yields some additional insight into the meaning of these for curriculum makers.

We choose to pursue Brameld's system because its salient characteristics are derived from a consideration of the problems of education and how the discipline of philosophy may be utilized in helping us to clarify our thoughts about these problems.[3] Furthermore, Brameld, in organizing his system, was keenly aware of the cultural context within which philosophy functions, noting, at one point, that philosophy and education are both "cultural experiences":

> *They [philosophy and education] spring from the culture; they develop and mature within it; they react upon it; they cannot be understood without it.*[4]

Brameld saw the cultural crises of this century much as we have discussed it earlier in this work, stating that philosophy and education "permeate every fiber of our crisis-culture."[5] He goes on to say:

*Philosophy does so, because every culture, including the American, has a pattern of basic beliefs, which provides those who accept that culture with greater or lesser articulation and significance. Education does so, because every culture provides formal or informal symbols and trainings, which aim to translate its philosophy into habits and skills by showing its members how to serve it most fruitfully. If philosophy expresses the beliefs of a culture, education helps to carry them out and, in so doing, builds additional habits and skills useful to that expression.*[6]

Brameld's system, more than the others, is an *educational* philosophy system. Its emphasis is on the field of education rather than on the schools of philosophy, which, admittedly, have had an important impact on our educational beliefs but have often largely ignored our significant albeit real world educational problems.

Whatever taxonomic system may be used, each of the categories deals with three fundamental, philosophical concerns: the nature of reality, of knowledge, and of values. Philosophers are continually probing the nature of reality in a branch of their study called *ontology*; they are involved in exploring the essential qualities of knowledge in a branch of their study called *epistemology*; and they are engaged in inquiry about the nature of values and the ultimate good in a branch of their study called *axiology*. Thus, in Zais's system, under the category of "other-worldly" philosophies, absolute reality is derived from a supernatural world, knowledge is achieved by revelation or other mystical means, and God or some perfect "ideal" is the source of goodness.[7]

**Brameld's Patterns**

In 1950, Theodore Brameld completed work on *Patterns of Educational Philosophy*,[8] in which he presented a taxonomic system of four categories, each of which characterized a particular philosophical view of education and the appropriate conduct of schooling. The categories form a continuum of the educational choices before us from the reactionary to the conservative to the liberal and, finally, to the radical. The following is a brief explanation of each of Brameld's four categories.[9]

*Perennialism*

As characterized by Brameld, perennialism is a reactionary educational philosophy that would return the content of education to its very earliest roots. Knowledge of the everlasting principles of truth, goodness, and beauty, rather than of the cultural heritage and its social implications, would be at the core of educational studies. True knowledge is universal and, when clearly understood, is eternal in its form. It is not bound to a specific time or place.

According to this philosophy, there is only one reality and it is absolute. It is up to us to discover its salient qualities. The great works of humankind—from the works of Plato to those of Shakespeare and Milton—help us to see this reality more clearly. Human beings share a common nature and, therefore, everyone can benefit equally from studying these absolute truths and should do so.

Absolute reality is, of course, ideal reality. Coming as near to understanding the ideal as possible is a highly desirable goal and, if achieved, would bring us closer to the supreme good. Perennialism is consistent with religious conceptions of divine control over life and of a form of knowledge that is external to the human being and to this world. However, religious conviction is not a necessary characteristic. For example, Plato's view of perfect knowledge as external to the human mind was not grounded in religious conviction.

There is in perennialism, however, the conviction that truth and good are self-evident and that, by logical analysis, their "first principles" can be discovered and their nature fixed in our knowledge for all time. In this context, there is a certain antidemocratic undercurrent in perennialism since the wisdom to determine what is "perennial" in knowledge resides in only a few intellectual leaders to whom the populace needs to look for guidance.

The schools have the function of awakening the latent rationality residing in all human beings. Learning, as Brameld points out, is not doing, but rather reasoning.[10] The curriculum ought not reflect the diversity of children's interests, for knowledge that is important to know is the same everywhere for everyone. All children should become familiar with and sensitive to the great works, although only a few are likely to become intellectual leaders.

### Essentialism

This philosophy of education emphasizes our cultural heritage and the need to pass on to the young the skills and knowledge essential to the continued functioning of our society. Mathematics, the sciences, and other stores of basic knowledge are the foundations of learning. While essentialism does not conceive of knowledge as absolute, it does give great importance to time-tested content that has proved its worth to society.

From this perspective, education has the function of cultural conservation and the responsibility to pass along those principles and standards that can serve as the basis for moving forward.[11] As Brameld points out, this is a conservative philosophy of education that is not opposed to change, but rather expects change to come in an orderly and disciplined fashion along pathways that have already been laid. Established beliefs and institutions are not only an important part of reality, they are also intrinsically good. War and poverty usually arise as a result of mistakes in human judgment rather than as evils inherent in the nature of things.

Schools, then, become the means of maintaining rather than altering the cultural structures of society.[12] These structures and the underlying beliefs supporting them offer a foundation of stability based on this world, and it is up to the schools to develop in the young the certainty and trust necessary to sustain the culture and society. The world and all of life follow a predetermined order that is good. Education should contribute to discovering the inviolate dictates—the laws—of worldly existence. It should help humankind to adjust to these laws and the society that has developed within their context.

### Progressivism

While perennialism may be most closely associated with the ancient and medieval philosophers and essentialism with the more earth-bound philosophies of the Renaissance and the Enlightenment, progressivism has its roots in the pragmatism of the late nineteenth and early twentieth centuries. Both progressivism and pragmatism are reflections, as Brameld puts it, of *"technological, experimental, this-worldly habits and accomplishments that have so powerfully shaped our modern culture."*[13]

Pragmatism, as posed by William James and Charles S. Peirce, suggests that ideas are meaningless until they become a part of human experience. For them, an idea that is never experienced and never makes a difference in human life is of little worth.[14] The theoretical is of value only when it has practical significance. John Dewey would carry this conception one step further by suggesting that ideas are instruments for action, that is, for achieving desirable consequences:

> *The thinker, like the carpenter, is at once stimulated and checked in every stage of his procedure by the particular situation which confronts him.*
>
> *Logical theory will get along as well as does the practice of knowing when it sticks close by and observes the directions and checks inherent in each successive phase of the evolution of the cycle of experience. The problem in general of validity of the thinking process as distinct from the validity of this or that process arises only when thinking is isolated from its historic position and its material content.*[15]

While essentialism is characterized by its emphasis on a set of rationally based, universal laws that govern the functioning of this world, progressivism is characterized by an open-minded, flexible attitude that views all knowledge about the world in a state of flux. Peirce proposed and James accepted a conception of the universe that had an important element of chance inherent in its nature.[16] For the pragmatists and, subsequently, the progressivists, the universe is in a continuing state of development with new experiences integrating into the existing mass of prior experiences. Instead of the scientist in search of a singular, preexisting, grand framework governing all of life, as conceived by the essentialists, scientists and citizens generally are in a continuing state of questioning and challenging the structure and state of knowledge. Since the nature of the universe is self-modifying, human knowledge needs to be continually "reworked" so that it is a more adequate reflection of the current mass of real world experience. While each individual must be responsible for engaging in the decision-making processes of his or her social group, human beings are, by their very nature, willing members of social groupings.

In this sense, progressivism represents the quintessential philosophy of education for a democratic society. There is an underlying belief in each individual's ability to deal with the great questions of the world and to be an active participant in solving the problems confronting society. Thus, education should meet each individual's capabilities, wherever they may lie, and develop them so that greater involvement with the decision-making processes of society is possible for everyone.

Progressivism (and the liberalism it embodies) is also a philosophy that builds the seeds of revolutionary change into its very texture without suggesting what the change shall be. It neither posits an overarching, grand framework that gives order to all of existence, nor sets forth the outcomes it deems most desirable. For the critics of progressivism, this lack of an ultimate vision is its fundamental flaw. Faith in the individual capabilities of people and in the very processes of developing knowledge is at the heart of the progressivists' vision. Basic to the progressive view is the idea that if the quality of the processes pursued is "good," then the quality of the outcomes will follow.

John Dewey, in his 1917 work, *Essays in Experimental Logic*,[17] expresses quite clearly his belief that humankind can significantly improve its social environment by applying a system of logical analysis, experimental inquiry, and practical judgment to worldly experience. Experience is the key term and its continual reconstruction the key process. Experience includes chance, novelty, uncertainty, and the unforeseen as well as the expected. Ongoing, thoughtful reflection is the "glue" that brings all this together in sets of actions that are continually adapting to new circumstances. The willingness to sustain a state of doubt as a stimulus to inquiry, considered by Dewey crucial to reflective thought,[18] is a central precept of his philosophy of education.

Dewey, the pragmatist–progressivist, sees education as preparing people to engage, in effective and desirable ways, in the decision-making activities of the community. He would have the schools reflect community life and engage children in experiences that are important to them and about which they can make real decisions. The reflective pursuit of the processes of democracy and not specific outcomes ought to be, as he made abundantly clear in *Democracy and Education*,[19] the ultimate goal of education.

Schools should start with interests and problems close to children and gradually guide them toward achieving greater "instrumental" control of abstract knowledge. Knowledge is social as well as individual. It is above all a product of activity.

In such a conception of education, the traditional, expository method of instruction gives way to an inquiry or problem-solving approach in which students take on major responsibility for the direction of their study. Schooling becomes experience-centered. This means that it is to be dynamic, specific to real world matters, and pluralistic in the sense of dealing with multiple kinds of relations from the spiritual to the intellectual and the emotional. Experience means involving "the whole child," his body and mind, his feelings and emotions. The curriculum is not child-centered, but rather child-in-society oriented.

### Reconstructionism

In many respects, reconstructionism is a further elaboration of progressive ideas with one significant difference: "a passionate concern for the *future* of civilization,"[20] to use Brameld's words. For the reconstructionists, the established institutions of society, even those of liberal origin, are no longer sufficient to deal with the problems of our times.

From the perspective of the reconstructionists, the progressivists do not pay enough attention to the institutions undergirding social reality. In their view, emphasizing the needs of individuals, as the progressivists have done, is a positive step forward, and they are quite willing to acknowledge this contribution made by the progressivists to educational thought. However, in their view, not enough attention has been paid to the organization and behavior of groups. Nor has sufficient attention been given to the seeking of social consensus and the institutions that enable consensus-seeking behaviors. For the reconstructionist, it is of the utmost importance that humankind become conscious of its role in culture not only as a product but also as the producer.

Reconstructionists hold a utopian vision of a just society in which all the members contribute to the benefit of the group and thus to each other. As they see it, we need and can achieve "a planned democratic order" able to put our resources to better use than is currently the case.[21] The future should receive at least as much scrutiny as our past, for the present is a function not only of the past but of the future as well. Having a conception of what the future should be like informs our decision making in the present.

Brameld, one of the foremost reconstructionists of the twentieth century, was only minimally interested in future forecasting. What is important for him is having a vision of what ought to be the future:

> *The reconstructionist does not hold that by analyzing future trends it is possible to answer in advance the question of whither mankind is inevitably bound; he does not presume that the groove of the future is already mysteriously cut. He does hold that to know what the future* should *be like is essential to knowing what it* could *be like and that if we implement our choices with power and strategy, we can determine what it* will *be like.*[22]

Reconstructionism is very much a human-centered philosophy, as is progressivism. However, it would conceive of a grand social design that would guide the activities of society toward a better life, while progressivism would allow the future to unfold, hopefully toward the better, as a result of the improved decision-making powers of people confronting the unique and unpredictable problems of their own times. Reconstructionism is a future-looking philosophy, and, as such, is distinct from perennialism and essentialism, which are oriented toward the past, as well as from progressivism, which is predominantly oriented toward the present, notwithstanding its emphasis on processes and a state of becoming.[23]

The reconstructionists would ask: "Problem-solving for what? Doing for what? Critical thinking for what?"[24] The emphasis on *outcomes* rather than *processes* is what clearly separates progressivism and reconstructionism. Schooling for the reconstructionists is to be used to achieve a planned set of outcomes for a better life. The schools are to be instrumental in fulfilling the utopian vision of a new and better social order. They are to serve as the medium for instilling those "cooperative methods and objectives by which the widest possible majority of the people, young and old, actively unite in behalf of the domestic and world order they can agree upon."[25]

Subject matter, within this normative framework of a better social order, would be placed in one of four "categories of knowledge-experience": social reality, proposals for social reconstruction, means to achievement, and goal-seeking interests. The latter category would respond to the question of where we want our society to go in the future.

Although a certain propagandistic tendency is inevitable, especially in establishing goals for the future, reconstructionists would subordinate this tendency to an open, "cooperative quest of individuals and groups for goal-governed structures and strategies."[26] Students would learn from the evidence of their own direct experiences, from free and open communication with each other, from the processes involved in achieving majority agreement as well as in the related group dynamics.

## Philosophical Continua

The four educational philosophies discussed above form a continuum extending from a reactionary or regressive posture at one end of the spectrum to a future-looking stance at the other. That is, perennialism with its view of knowledge as eternal would bring the study of the great works of the past to center stage; essentialism would emphasize the knowledge that is well established and functioning in the present world—knowledge, it should be pointed out, developed usually in a relatively recent (as opposed to ancient) past; progressivism would pursue knowledge of the processes contributing to the effective decision making of people confronting the problems of the present; and reconstructionism would develop knowledge of what the future should be and the means for reconstructing society so that development toward a desirable future might be achieved.

A continuum based on the past, present, and future is not the only one that can be used in characterizing these four educational philosophies. A continuum based on the locus of important knowledge offers another way of viewing the four. Important knowledge, of course, must be linked to what is held to be most valuable in human life. If life is conceived to be a process of preparation for an afterlife, then knowledge related to this afterlife—other-worldly knowledge—is of the utmost importance. If the perfectability of life is seen as a process of coming to know the nature and structure of this world, then obviously earth-centered knowledge is of the utmost importance. If the achievement of a better life in this world is seen as directly related to how well people devise their social and economic structures, then their individual experiences and ability to make decisions within their social grouping—that is, human-centered knowledge—is assigned the greatest importance.

To relate this discussion to the four educational philosophies presented above, consider the following points: (1) *Perennialism* would interpret important knowledge as being external to this world and would assign little value to knowledge acquired from the pursuit of our everyday activities. (2) *Essentialism* would place the locus of important knowledge within the structure and organization of this world and would see this knowledge as broader and more significant than that which can be derived from the exigencies and experiences of daily life. Both (3) *progressivism* and (4) *reconstructionism* would conceive of important knowledge as coming from the experiences of people, and, given the flux of experience, as being in an ongoing state of reconstruction. Progressivism and reconstructionism also would agree on the subjective and constantly changing nature of knowledge. Experience means including not only cognition but also action and emotions as forms of important knowledge.

On Zais's three-point continuum extending from other-worldly through earth-centered to human-centered knowledge,[27] both progressivism and reconstructionism would be classified as human-centered. However, both conceptualize human nature as essentially social, so that we really have a child-in-society approach to knowledge. Between these two philosophies, there would be much discussion concerning *not* the conception of the individual, whose very essence derives from membership in society, but rather the extent to which emphasis should be placed on the individual or on society. The interactive relationship of the individual in society is basic to both. There would also be considerable discussion about whether processes for improving decision-making activities or engagement in consensus activities for democratically determining future social structures should comprise the most important kind of knowledge to be included in the curriculum.

Linear continua are hardly complete reflections of our philosophical beliefs about education. They are reductionistic tools that allow us to view quite complex ideas from a singular perspective. This method can be very useful in helping us ascertain whether a set of categories covers the complete range of ideas relevant to a topic, in this case education.

What the continuum based on the locus of important knowledge shows quite clearly is that a category that accepts the individual as the primary source of knowledge (i. e., independently of any belonging to a society or relationship with others) is lacking if the continuum is to cover the complete range of possibilities inherent even in its simple structure. One important philosophical position posits that the potential for the perfectability of human life is contained within all individuals and their struggle to find the meaning of life. From this view, known as *existentialism*, it is entirely possible that the world is meaningless, that is, there is no prior reason for human existence. It is up to individuals to achieve meaning for their lives. This is a view of the human being as standing alone, drawing primarily from the inner self for knowledge of life. It is the extreme position of human-centeredness.

## Existentialism and Education

We would develop a category utilizing the existing nomenclature of "existentialism." However, this term in our educational context would include phenomenological as well as existential perspectives of the individual as a primary source of knowledge. While the phenomenologists believe knowledge must be derived as a result of individual human experience, they would reject introspection as being an unreliable way of obtaining knowledge about reality.[28] For phenomenologists, describing and reporting the data of individual consciousness *without* subjective bias would be the primary means of achieving knowledge. Knowledge begins with immediate phenomena experienced by individuals and exclusive of any transcendental conceptions we may have.

The existentialists also believe individual human consciousness is central to the development of knowledge. However, they give considerable attention to knowledge about the transcendental self. They do not think of the "transcendental" as being outside the "course of natural existence," as did Dewey, and believe they can arrive at a conception of transcendental that is contained within the limits of human existence.[29] The phenomenological/existentialist position vis-à-vis the primary locus of important knowledge revolves around such questions as "How do I live in the world?" and "How do I live time?" Dewey would ask, instead, "What is experience?" and ultimately he would follow the objective, natural science model which asks how people live in this world.[30]

"Educational existentialism," as we are using the term, places its emphasis on the self as a primary source of knowledge about life and its meaning. To achieve understanding about life, one must first achieve understanding about the self. Whether this is achieved subjectively or objectively is a matter for debate both philosophically and educationally. The debate, however, does not change the essential locus for the derivation of knowledge, which is the self.

Interestingly, existentialism as a philosophy does not exclude religious faith. Kierkegaard, an early philosopher of the existential movement and a theologian, asserts the subjectivity of truth. Existence means the separation of the objective and the subjective, but this does not mean for Kierkegaard that "existence is thoughtless."[31] Rather, "it [existence] has brought about, and brings about, a separation between subject and object, thought and being."[32] Individuals strive for a more complete understanding of their subjectivity. In objectivity, the truth of Christianity remains necessarily uncertain and "absurd." Objective certainty makes subjective faith possible. Faith is achieved through the subjective strivings of each individual seeking, in freedom and essential independence, the continuity of subjectivity.[33]

In developing this fifth category, educational existentialism, as an extension of Brameld's four categories, we are making provision for an educational emphasis that would perceive the individual child as the primary source of knowledge, independently of any social grouping to which she or he may belong, and without specific reference to other-worldly or earth-centered authority. The human condition is what each of us can know. The achievement of Christian faith, when it occurs, is the result of human-centered, inward strivings to achieve better understanding of the self.

### The Linkages between Educational Philosophies and Curriculum Designs

In the best of all logical worlds, each curriculum design would be a clear reflection of a philosophical perspective. In fact, in Chapter 4, we presented a set of curriculum designs that can be classified according to the five educational philosophy categories, although not without some reorganizing and discussion of numerous caveats.

For example, in Chapter 4, the child-centered curriculum was viewed from three quite different perspectives: Rousseauian, existentialist, and child-in-society. As we review the philosophies of education, it seems quite clear that both progressivism and reconstructionism conceive of important knowledge as arising from the experiences of individuals, who are, however, by the very nature of humanness, members of society. That is, their position is a child-in-society one. Education needs to be about improving the decision-making skills of people working to ameliorate the social order.

Because Dewey is often thought of as a proponent of child-centered education, and there can be little doubt but that his writings, suggesting that educators accept children as unique in their own right, have had a powerful influence on educational thinking to this day, we included the child-in-society curriculum under the general rubric of child-centered curriculum designs. The reality is that while the child-in-society curriculum design reflects both progressivism and reconstructionism well, it is out of sync with educational existentialism. The Rousseauian, existentialist, and psychological curriculum designs, notwithstanding the differences among them, are clearly child-centered designs. In other words, the child is the source of important knowledge and the curriculum design would reflect the thoughts and decisions of each child. Educational existentialism requires curriculum designs that are wholly child-centered. Eclecticism of the sort represented by the child-in-society designs are simply not valid representations of this philosophical position.

Generally, but cautiously, it may be said that society-oriented curricular designs are essentialist in their orientation but in a very eclectic way. That is, the passing along of time-tested principles and content is perceived as important to the continuity of the culture and to society itself. The knowledge studied is important to society and, therefore, presumably, to individuals. People need to adjust to society, which is seen to be greater than the sum of the individual members belonging to society. However, essentialism does accept change in the social order, provided the change is based on the existing structures and organization of society. There is respect for flexibility and the capacity to adjust to new circumstances quite similar to attitudes held by the progressivists and reconstructionists. While opting clearly for conservation and stability, there is an underlying quality of eclecticism in essentialism, one that would accept the flexibility and decision making emphasized by the progressivists, albeit with constraint and significant reservations.

The knowledge-centered curriculum design adds to our eclectic confusion. Again, cautiously, it may be said that essentialism responds most closely to curriculum designs based on objective knowledge that has proved its worth to society. The current emphasis on the study of the scientific disciplines is an essentialist approach to education that we have called "the great research disciplines design." Vocational studies, which are more suited to the progressivist, child-in-society approach to curriculum, would hardly be considered "real" knowledge by the essentialists. This is because they think of vocational preparation as very short-sighted, limited education. On the other hand, the process-as-content design, which is an offshoot of the great research disciplines perspective, resonates well with the progressive conception of education because of its emphasis on students experiencing science as working scientists do and confronting, as well, the problems that scientists confront.

The essentialists would opt for enduring knowledge. However, they would not agree with the perennialists that there is a core of eternal, unchanging knowledge that should always be taught regardless of current events. While essentialists are eager to come to terms with changing industrial–scientific circumstances,[34] the perennialists stand firm in their belief that important knowledge transcends the specifics of human life and is timeless and spaceless. The perennialists therefore support a knowledge-oriented curriculum design based not only on enduring knowledge, but also on knowledge that is eternal and beyond the needs and requirements of any one society. They would scoff at the idea that knowledge is changing, as are the needs of society, and that a certain amount of flexibility is needed to accommodate society's newer exigencies.

The perennialists, like the educational existentialists, stand firm against an eclectic perspective. Nevertheless, in the real world of educational politics, the perennialists and the essentialists will often stand together in their pursuit of "enduring" studies. The study of foreign languages, for example, satisfies both their views, as does the study of history.

In essentialism, progressivism, and reconstructionism is an underlying eclecticism. None of the three would exclude studies relevant to and, possibly, supportive of societal structures. None of the three would completely ignore individual capabilities and interests. The differences among them involve a question of degree. For the essentialist, the individual's best interests are served by preparing people to live well within their society. For the progressivists, individual best interests are served by meeting the unique background and capability of each individual and empowering each to deal with the significant problems of society. For the reconstructionists, individual best interests are served when people are prepared to lead society toward a new social order based on a democratic vision of equity and justice.

It is very difficult to state categorically that all society-oriented designs are clearly linked to essentialism. The reformist and futurist perspectives discussed earlier as forms of the society-oriented curriculum could both be construed as linked to reconstructionism rather than essentialism. This gray area of the linkages between philosophical positions and curriculum design may be the underlying reason why American education has been afflicted by so much "mindless" eclecticism. From essentialism to progressivism and reconstructionism, numerous points of agreement exist despite the very real differences among these philosophies.

We seem to want a society-oriented curriculum of the essentialist kind, as well as a curriculum that emphasizes individual development of the kind pursued by the progressives *simultaneously* without making the necessarily conscious adjustments between the two philosophies. And, of course, most middle and upper class parents want their children to study the great classics and have the literary background that will serve them well throughout life, especially when they confront eternity and the meaning of their being. But, as the existentialists note, and many of us who are not existentialists would agree, each of us must confront our eternity alone and with the tools that we have developed within ourselves.

Since these different positions are often discussed in public forums but not necessarily in contrast to each other, the logic of each generally remains unchallenged and quite convincing. The positions become a part of our way of thinking about education despite their obvious inconsistencies with each other. For example, all children should be treated equally, given the same exams, graded objectively, and made to live up to the same set of criteria. However, the unique backgrounds and capabilities of children should be considered in instruction, grading should take into account the real progress each child has made, and all children should have an opportunity to experience success. This "back-and-forth switching" of philosophical positions reflects the "mindless" eclecticism beleaguering the schools today.

## Making the Linkages

Figure 6.1 attempts to present an overview of the linkages between curriculum designs and the various educational philosophies. Its purpose is to summarize in a straightforward fashion the preceding discussions. In reducing complexity, however, many caveats are ignored.

**FIGURE 6.1**    *Educational philosophies and types of curriculum designs.*

| Design Types | Perennialism | Essentialism | Progressivism | Reconstructionism | Existentialism |
|---|---|---|---|---|---|
| *Society-Oriented Designs* | | ← Status → | | | |
| | | ← quo → | | | |
| | | | ← ——————— Reformist → | | |
| | | ← ———— Futurist ———————— → | | | |
| *Child-Centered Designs* | | | | | ← Rousseauian → |
| | | | | | ← —— Inner- —— → |
| | | | | | ← Oriented → |
| | | ← ———— Child-in-Society ———————— → | | | |
| | | ← ————————————————— Psychological → | | | |
| *Knowledge-Centered Designs* | ← — Great —→ | | | | |
| | ←Knowledge→ | | | | |
| | | ← ———————— Great ————→ | | | |
| | | ← ———————— Research ————→ | | | |
| | | ← ———————— Disciplines → | | | |
| | | ← ———————— Integrative —→ | | | |
| | | ← ———————— Process-as-Content ——→ | | | |
| *Eclectic Designs* | | ← ———————— Eclectic Zone ————————→ | | | |
| | | ← ———————— Compromise ————————→ | | | |
| | | ← ——— Reflective Eclecticism ————→ | | | |

As Figure 6.1 attempts to summarize graphically, most curricular designs tend to represent a philosophical position, but also bear important characteristics that would be supported by other philosophical positions. This has led to an "eclectic zone" in philosophical positions extending roughly from essentialism to reconstructionism. This zone has entered into our cultural mindsets about education in subliminal fashion — that is, without much consciousness regarding the diversity of philosophical positions that our curricular designs encompass. Indeed, to the degree that a curriculum design is developed without an awareness of its philosophical positions, it may be said to be a result of "mindless eclecticism"; in parallel fashion, to the degree that a curriculum design is developed *with* an awareness of its philosophical positions, it may be said to be a result of "reflective eclecticism."

## QUESTIONS FOR DISCUSSION AND REFLECTION

1. Are there any practical reasons for having a stated philosophy of education? Can you state your own philosophy of education?

2. What are some objections that might arise if a perennialist curriculum were designed and implemented? For example, a curriculum based primarily on the reading and analyses of great works would comprise a perennialist curriculum. Where might support for such a curriculum come from?

3. Assuming an education based on essentialism, would intragenerational disjunctures be considered important enough to become a part of the curriculum's objectives? Which of the educational philosophies discussed would be most likely to deal with a psycho-socio phenomenon such as intragenerational disjunctures and why?

4. What groups in society (business, religious, parent, etc.) might object to a curriculum based on progressivism and why?

5. How do you think topics like ecology and business would be treated in a reconstructionist curriculum? Would existentialists support such topics in their curriculum?

6. What objections to an existential curriculum would you expect from the average school person? Would you agree with them? Why?

7. Place the five educational philosophies discussed in this chapter on a political continuum from the extreme right to the extreme left. What characteristics does each philosophy exhibit that influences your judgment about where it should be located on the continuum?

## NOTES

1. Zais, R. S. (1976). *Curriculum: Principles and foundations.* New York: Thomas Y. Crowell, Chapter 5.
2. Schubert, W. H. (1986). *Curriculum: Perspective, paradigm, and possibility.* New York: Macmillan, pp. 127–131.

3. Brameld, T. (1956). *Toward a reconstructed philosophy of education*. New York: Holt, Rinehart and Winston.

4. *Ibid.*, p. 59.

5. *Ibid.*, p. 73.

6. *Ibid.*

7. *Op. cit.*, Zais, R. S.

8. Brameld, T. (1950). *Patterns of educational philosophy*. Yonkers, New York: World Book.

    A substantial revision of this work was published in 1971 by Holt, Rinehart and Winston, Inc. (New York).

9. *Ibid.*, Chapter 3.

10. *Ibid.*, p. 384.

11. *Ibid.*, p. 210.

12. *Ibid.*, p. 212.

13. *Ibid.*, p. 96.

14. See "The Fixation of Belief" and "How to Make Our Ideas Clear," both by Peirce. In: Buchler, J., editor, (1940). *The philosophy of Peirce — Selected writings*. London: Routledge and Kegan Paul, pp. 5–22 and 23–41, respectively. Also important to this discussion is: James, W. (1907). *Pragmatism: A new name for some old ways of thinking*. Boston: Longmans, Green and Company.

15. Dewey, J. (1917). *Essays in experimental logic*. Chicago: University of Chicago Press, pp. 13–14.

16. This philosophical position proposed by Peirce is known as "tychism."

17. *Op. cit.*, J. Dewey (1917).

18. Dewey, J. (1910). *How we think*. Boston: D. C. Heath (revised edition, 1933).

19. Dewey, J. (1916). *Democracy and education*. New York: Macmillan.

20. *Op. cit.*, Brameld, T. (1950), p. 407.

21. *Ibid.*, pp. 408–409. It should be noted that Brameld was referring in particular to the Great Depression of 1929 and the two World Wars. However, his discussion is clearly applicable to conditions today.

22. *Ibid.*, p. 435.

23. *Ibid.*, p. 523.

24. *Ibid.*, adaptation of questions posed by Brameld on p. 553.

25. *Ibid.*, pp. 523–524.

26. *Ibid.*, pp. 567–568.

27. There is an extensive discussion of this continuum in Zais, R. S., (1976). *Curriculum: Principles and foundations*. New York: Thomas Y. Crowell, Chapter 6.

28. See, for example, this early work of the phenomenology movement: Brentano, F. (1874). *Psychology from an empirical standpoint*. Also, and more important for the phenomenological movement: Husserl, E. (1913). *General introduction to pure phenomenology*. The Hague: Martinus Nijhoff.

29. Troutner, J. F. (1974). John Dewey and the existential phenomenologist. In: Denton, D. E. (ed.), *Existentialism and phenomenology*. New York: Teachers College Press, pp. 20–21.

30. *Ibid.*, pp. 24–25.

31. Kierkegaard, S. (1944). *Concluding unscientific postscript* (Swenson, P., trans.). Princeton, NJ: Princeton University Press, p. 112.

32. *Ibid.*

33. *Ibid.*, p. 84.

34. *Op. cit.*, Brameld, p. 291.

# 7

# On Learning
# and Learners

**Introduction**

The processes of curriculum development involve linking what society believes is important for children to learn with how children learn and in what ways learning can be fostered. Even in precurriculum days, the teacher held a view, however unconsciously, of how children learn. The ancient Egyptian teacher who beat his student so that knowledge would enter his head had an image in his mind's eye of how learning occurred. We all carry models in our head about how children learn—however inaccurate the models may be—and they guide our judgment about how and when we should teach the curriculum and even what the content of the curriculum should be.

What learning is, how learning actually takes place, and the characteristics of children that impact on learning are major considerations in the design and implementation of the curriculum. Our conception of "learning," however, is far from settled. We are still debating the nature of learning. The debate ranges from those who define learning in terms of observable changes in behavior[1] to those who include in the definition changes in thoughts, feelings, and dispositions not ascribable to growth and usually not amenable to direct observation or objective measurement.[2]

Much of the disagreement is related to the philosophical conception of human nature brought by each learning theorist to the debate. As Allport noted, "Every learning theorist is a philosopher. . . ."[3] Indeed, one of the greatest educational philosophers, John Dewey, is also considered one of the important early psychologists. It is only as we progress into the twentieth century that the two fields, philosophy and psychology, go their separate ways, the former remaining a humanity, the latter becoming a science. Nevertheless, even in a science, the interpretation of data remains a value-laden, philosophical enterprise.

Our scientific knowledge of learning, while greatly increased in the twentieth century, is full of conundrums and lacuna. Limited knowledge, however, has not stopped us from theorizing about how learning takes place. Even in the long historical period before the emergence of the scientific study of human behavior, conceptions of how people learn had their impact on education. In an earlier section of this work, we referred to the views of Comenius and Pestalozzi, noting how very different their conceptions of the ways children learned were from those of their contemporaries. Certainly, Rousseau's conception of learning, which involved letting the inborn perfection of children develop unimpeded by adult instruction, was profoundly different from John Locke's view of the young mind as a "blank slate" awaiting the input of the adult world.

## Pre-scientific Theories of Learning

Philosophers have always been involved with the nature of knowing. Even in pre-scientific days, their views of learning influenced education and the curriculum in significant ways. For example, John Locke's view that learning was the process of exercising the mind's faculties imbued educational practice well into the twentieth century.[4] In what has come to be known as "faculty psychology," the child's mind was seen as being molded by the teacher, its faculties just waiting for development. Drill, practice, lecture, and discipline were widely accepted as appropriate instructional means, and the study of Latin and rhetoric were the preferred vehicles of intellectual development. To "train" the memory, poetry, Latin declensions, and the like were objects of constant drill. Geometry and algebra were studied to develop the powers of reasoning. The traditional subjects, such as Latin and Greek, were seen as being especially valuable for developing the child's mind.

Even though this conception of learning was shown to be scientifically unacceptable by Thorndike in the early 1900s,[5] there are many politicians, parents, and others who still subscribe to the theory. At present, instead of Latin, computer science studies are likely to be considered exceptionally useful in developing children's powers of reasoning. In the early grades, multiplication tables are still drilled into students' memories, while hand calculators are only allowed when thorough memorization has taken place.

Another philosopher whose "prescientific" analyses of learning had considerable educational impact was David Hume (1711–1776), who was a participant in what has been called the Scottish Enlightenment. He viewed learning as a product of association. The human mind was a collector of minute percepts, ideas, and feelings linked to each other by patterns of past and present experiences or associations. Associations, according to Hume, were fostered by such situational characteristics as resemblance, temporal/spatial contiguity, and causal relationship. For Hume, learning involved using associations to understand and express ideas.

Herbart's view of knowledge[6] as something communicated to children to activate ideas in them is directly related to Hume's prescientific conception of association. Herbart viewed sensations as being converted into ideas or "percepts" that were then linked in the unconscious mind to similar ideas in clusters or "apperceptive masses" to use Herbert's terminology. Building knowledge for Herbart meant presenting ideas to children that could be linked to their existing apperceptive masses.

Herbart's followers developed a systematic approach to instruction based on his views of learning. The teacher was to recall the pupils' prior learning, then present the new materials, followed by the development of an association between the old and the new through some form of comparison. Subsequently, generalizations based on the new learning were given meaning by applying them to specific instances.

### Contemporary Learning Theories: Overview

Contemporary learning theories, like their prescientific predecessors, reflect an underlying view of human nature; unlike their predecessors, they seek objective ways to gather evidence demonstrating their positions about how learning occurs. Two clusters of learning theories have dominated twentieth century research: behavioral theories and field theories. Of these two, the most influential for curriculum development has been behavioral learning theories.

Somewhat akin to field theory is humanistic psychology, which came to prominence at mid-century especially in the United States. A basic principle of this approach to psychology is the study of the whole being. People feel, love, hope, and think, and if we are really to understand human nature we must approach its study holistically. Beyond its clear opposition to behaviorism, humanistic psychology stands more as a reaction to the increasingly scientific nature of psychological research that occurred in the early part of the twentieth century than as a unified school of thought.

Also related to field theories of learning are the cognitive psychologists. These psychologists use scientific methodologies in their efforts to discern the differences in learning and problem solving between young and adult learners. They also pursue questions related to how the young learner becomes an adult learner. In the early part of this century, cognitive theorists were primarily European, although some of John Dewey's work could certainly be placed in this category.

## Behavioral Learning Theories

Behavioral learning theories are based on the view of the human mind as beginning somewhat like a "blank slate." As Langer notes, in behaviorism children are born devoid of "coherently organized content" and come to reflect the nature of their surrounding environment through the stimuli produced by it.[7] The effects of the environment and of experience determine what is learned and why people do what they do. It is not what they think or feel that leads to doing, but what they do that leads to thinking and feeling. If learning is to be understood, what people do must be studied.

### Classical Conditioning

Within the category of behavioral theories, classical conditioning and operant conditioning have been among the most influential. In classical conditioning, behaviors elicited directly by specific stimuli are called *respondents*. This conception of learning based on direct connections between stimulus and response (S–R) has had a major impact in this century not only on cognitive psychology but also on curriculum development.

In 1913, a young behaviorist, John B. Watson, published a kind of manifesto for the scientific study of human behavior, entitled "Psychology as the Behaviorists View It."[8] In this work, Watson argued that the study of such internal processes as perceiving, knowing, aspiring, and the like were not leading toward a science of human behavior. Most of the psychologists of the period were studying the mental phenomena of human consciousness, and Watson's position was a strong reaction against the mainstream psychology of the day. For Watson, studies based on introspective analysis precluded scientific objectivity and measurement. His position was that human behavior is triggered externally and needs to be researched scientifically from that perspective. His behaviorism was greatly influenced by the work of the Russian Ivan Pavlov who, in essence, laid the foundation for what we now call classical conditioning.

In a carefully controlled set of experiments, Pavlov taught a dog to salivate at the sound of a bell even when food was not presented to it. During the conditioning or teaching phase, food, considered the unconditioned stimulus, was presented repeatedly along with the conditioning stimulus of the sounding of a bell. When the dog salivated to the food alone, this was its unconditioned response; when the dog learned to salivate at the sound of the bell alone, this was considered its conditioned or learned response.

Watson sought to extend Pavlov's work by investigating the power of conditioning in human beings in the area of emotional learning. In a well-known experiment,[9] he and an associate conditioned an 11-month-old baby to be afraid of its pet white rat by striking a steel bar while simultaneously presenting the child its pet. The child soon became frightened at the very sight of the rat even when the loud noise was not made. On the other hand, the child's fear was quickly overcome or extinguished by simply giving the child the pet rat without striking the steel bar. Watson saw instructional applications of conditioning far beyond anything justified by his experiments. In a famous and often ridiculed statement, he said:

> *Give me a dozen healthy infants, well formed, and my own special world to bring them up in, and I'll guarantee to take anyone at random and train him to become any type of specialist I might select — doctor, lawyer, merchant, chief and, yes, even beggar and thief, regardless of talents, penchants, tendencies, abilities, vocations, and race of his ancestry.*[10]

Certainly more influential than Watson for American education was a contemporary, Edward Thorndike, who developed a theory of learning based wholly on trial and error behavior. The individual responds to a stimulus in a problem situation and if the response is successful it is reinforced by a sense of satisfaction. Adapting learned behaviors to changes in the environment is simply a question of strengthening or weakening of stimulus–response bonds.

How this strengthening or weakening occurs was a crucial question in Thorndike's research. He systematized the results of his efforts with the formulation of three "laws of learning."[11] These were:

1. The *law of readiness*, which refers to an attitudinal willingness to respond to a stimulus (rather than a maturational ability as intended in a term such as "reading readiness"). Response to the stimulus brings satisfaction, and not responding leads to frustration.

2. The *law of exercise*, which refers to the strengthening of S–R connections in proportion to the number of times, the intensity, and the duration reinforcement occurs.

3. The *law of effect*, which refers to the effects that follow response. To the degree that such effects are satisfying, the connection is strengthened; to the degree that effects are annoying, the connection is weakened. In the 1930s, Thorndike found that annoying effects had less impact on extinguishing behavior than he had previously believed, which led to a revision of this law based solely on the importance of rewarding consequences for learning.

Thorndike viewed learning as habit formation. Habits were the building blocks on which an increasingly complex structure of behavior was based. Learning could be sustained or weakened by varying reinforcement and satisfaction. Practice in the form of drill, exercise, and review, which had been basic to instruction for centuries, found support in Thorndike's law of exercise. Developing attractive and motivational ways of presenting learning to students found support in the law of readiness. The use of rewards and punishment found similar support in the law of effect. It was important to design and control instructional experiences or stimuli so that they would build in an integrated fashion toward more complex structures of learning.

Thorndike's theory leads to a conception of curriculum design based on discrete and relatively small components of learning that are laid upon each other much as a wall of bricks would be laid. It is an additive process as well as one that is strenthened from cumulative consistency and integration. Sequencing of the components of learning is extremely important to the successful teaching of more advanced content.

## Operant Conditioning

While Skinner was a behaviorist and, like all behaviorists, insisted that only observable behavior is suited for scientific study, he distanced himself from Watson's conception of behaviorism. In Skinner's view, early behaviorism was the product of limited knowledge and "hasty interpretations of complex behavior" based on one kind of learning, that is, reflexes and conditioned reflexes.[12]

According to Skinner, stimulus–response learning based on reflexes is primarily involuntary and accounts for only a small portion of human learning; a very different kind of learning occurs when the individual must deal effectively with new and complex environments because this involves voluntary behavior and the making of choices. That is, the individual feels the need to do something and chooses in random fashion from among previously learned behaviors and/or innate responses.

Skinner likens the individual's behavior in a new situation to evolutionary adaptations that arise in response to the changing circumstances of nature. A number of contingent behaviors are available from one's past learning experiences, and these may be chosen separately or in some combination. There is an element of chance in the selection of behaviors. The persistence of the behaviors selected, called *operants*, is related to the degree of success achieved. Skinner's theory of operant conditioning is based on the idea that if the operant behavior is followed by a reinforcing stimulus, it will be strengthened.[13] Thus, only after the behavior has occurred can it be reinforced by conditioning, a sequence distinctly different from the S–R connectionism of Watson and Thorndike.

In discussing thinking and its relationship to behaviorism, Skinner undertook to exemplify his understanding of thinking by discussing the work conducted by the field theorist Wolfgang Kohler with chimpanzees. Kohler was considered the father of classical gestalt theory and an arch opponent of behaviorism.

> In one classical account, a chimpanzee seemed to have fitted two sticks together in order to rake in a banana which was otherwise out of reach through the bars of his cage. To say that the chimpanzee showed "intelligent behavior based on a perception of what was required to solve the problem: some way of overcoming the distance barrier" is to make it almost impossible to discover what happened. To solve such a problem a chimpanzee must have learned at least the following: to stop reaching for a banana out of reach; to stop reaching with short sticks; to discriminate between long and short sticks, as by using long sticks to rake in bananas successfully; to pick up two sticks in separate hands; and to thrust sticks into holes. With this preparation, it is not impossible that in that rare (but poorly authenticated) instance the chimpanzee stuck one stick into the hole at the end of another and used the resulting long stick to rake in the banana.[14]

Skinner thus makes the case that instead of "insight" underlying the chimpanzee's behavior, an explanation favored by Kohler, the chances of the chimpanzee engaging in the appropriate behavior were more likely made by the skills and behaviors already learned. Shortly following this passage, in a discussion of creative behavior, Skinner suggests that "creative thinking is largely concerned with the production of 'mutations,' " which, he notes, are random in genetic and evolutionary theory.[15]

Skinnerian learning theory is sufficiently complex to allow for the variability and creativity of human behavior. It supports the idea that a carefully sequenced set of experiences can be used to shape and deepen students' learning. It also supports both positive and negative reinforcers but emphasizes the greater effectiveness of rewarding experiences over punishment.

All of this has proved quite appealing to educators, especially since the discrete, relatively small components of observable learning, which typifies curriculum design influenced by classical S–R conditioning, are still supported by the theory. Specific performance objectives, pacing, and the careful arrangement of selected experiences are familiar tools in curriculum development that are strongly supported by Skinnerian theory. Programmed learning, based on a sequenced, small-step approach to learning with immediate and numerous positive reinforcements and provisions for contingencies, best represents the practical implementation of Skinnerian theory.

### Field Learning Theories

The basic premise of all cognitive field theories is that human beings are innately interactive. As we behave in the environment, we and the environment are both changed. Even when a change in the environment is not observable by others, its meaning for the person that has interacted with the environment has been modified. Observing the physical interaction between the individual and the environment is relatively insignificant; what has developed psychologically within the individual is of major importance. Thus, while the behaviorists give little attention to the nature of the learner, assuming in essence a blank slate, the field theorists emphasize learner variables as having a significant impact on how stimuli are processed and the kind of responses possible. Rather than insisting on scientific observability, they seek ways of understanding what is going on internally when the learner interacts with the environment.

### Gestalt Learning Theory

Early field theorists were called "gestaltists," which is German for "pattern" or "configuration." The gestaltists viewed perception and learning as holistic experiences based on the grasping of patterns and configurations. The individual, for example, does not hear individual tones of music but rather the melody or pattern of tones; nor does the individual read letter by letter but rather by the configuration of groups of words. When the components of a "gestalt" are analyzed some increased understanding of the whole may occur.

In the view of the gestaltists, the whole is greater than the sum of its parts and real understanding of learning comes only at that level. Rather than the building block approach to instruction taken by the behaviorists, the gestaltists would develop a broad overview first and then deal with the structural components. Thus, for example, young music students would be taught to play complete songs and melodies before they would study the separate notes; foreign language students would engage in conversations before they would study the parts of speech.

Furthermore, Kohler[16] believed it was extremely important to distinguish among living species; all animals were not merely blank slates but genetically endowed with different perceptual and learning capabilities that impact directly on how they behave and undertake new learning. Because they displayed greater signs of intelligence, Kohler used chimpanzees in his experiments, instead of the cats and rats that had typified so many of the behaviorists' experiments. Putting cats in puzzle-box experiments as Thorndike did, and requiring them to manipulate levers rather than claw or scratch was abnormal and would yield misleading results according to Kohler. From his experiments with chimpanzees, Kohler claimed that the animal had shown an ability to grasp relationships not immediately evident from its perceptual field and was apparently capable of insight. The ambiguity of the term "insight" led to discussions from the behaviorists such as the one by Skinner cited above. Nevertheless, insight or understanding of the organization and relationships comprising the whole have been shown to increase long-term memory in humans and the transfer of learning to new environments.[17]

A contemporary of Kohler's and a founder of gestalt learning theory as well, Max Wertheimer, published a work in 1925 dealing with the perception of movement. He used the many illusions of movement arising from the various manipulations of lights as a way of supporting his position that the analysis of the whole into component parts was a futile undertaking.[18] Karl Koffka, in a work published about a decade later, suggested that several of the laws of perception developed by Wertheimer should be taken to be laws of learning as well. These gestalt laws of learning are listed and briefly discussed below. Comparison with Thorndike's laws of learning listed earlier in this section could be very useful in understanding how differently the behaviorists and the field theorist interpret the learning process.

1. The *law of similarity* refers to the achievement of gestalts based on components linked by their similarity. The pattern or relationship among the components is created by their similarity. For example, a mixed collection of circles and lines is likely to be viewed as a group of circles and a group of lines. Kohler was able to show the usefulness of the law for understanding learning by demonstrating that pairs of items were learned more easily if the members of the pairs were similar than if they were dissimilar.[19]

2. The *law of proximity* refers to the groupings that arise in our understanding of the environment because of spatial and temporal arrangements. That is, items that are closer to each other in space, or, as in music, in time, are grouped together in unitary gestalts. International Morse code is possible because of such groupings.

3. The *law of closure* refers perceptually to enclosed areas that form holistic units more readily than do areas delineated in open fashion. For example, two parallel lines do not create as complete a gestalt as a set of lines arranged so as to suggest a box. In Koffka's analogy to learning, the learner derives a sense of satisfaction when closure is reached in the resolution of problems — that is, when a complete, unitary understanding of the problem is achieved.

In a sense, closure serves the same function as rewards do in behaviorism. As Hill notes, there is some question whether the law of closure in perception is really the same as the law of closure in learning.[20]

4. The *law of good continuation* is most closely related to the law of closure for it refers to the perceptual and logical completion of incomplete patterns. An asterisk that is drawn incompletely will be completed by the observer; a sentence left "hanging" will often be completed by the listener. Thus, in instruction, giving learners a coherent overview of some pattern helps them to fit in components that complete the pattern.

As must be evident, perception and learning are nearly indistinguishable for gestalt theorists. Learning, rather than being additive as the behaviorists believe, is the organizing of perceptions and existing gestalts into new gestalts. It involves the rearranging of thought patterns and often occurs when people gain new insights into old ideas. As Bruner[21] noted, the emphasis is on the active involvement of the learner in the reorganizing processes, and not on the shaping or controlling of the learner through rewards and punishment.

### Humanistic Psychology

In the 1940s and 1950s, a new trend emerged in psychology, one that was to have a distinct impact on American education. The humanistic psychologists are not exactly a cohesive group, but they do share a number of rather important, unifying characteristics. Their disagreement with the behaviorists, who have dominated educational thinking throughout the twentieth century, is fundamental. The scientific approach to the study of human behavior is rejected; the human being is unique and distinct from all other species; complex traits such as "feelings," "attitudes," and "hopes" are considered essential to the understanding of humanness; and the study of human beings is best undertaken in terms of problem-centered wholeness involving internal and external influences.

The approach of the humanistic psychologists is reasonably consistent with field learning theory, but its attention to learning theory is at best indirect. For humanistic psychologists, it is not enough to study people in terms of perception or cognition; people need to be viewed outside the laboratory in all of the complexity of their lives and daily environments.

Abraham Maslow, a major contributor to humanistic psychology, developed a theory of human motivation based on this holistic view of humanness and the conception of ongoing interaction with the environment. Maslow identified basic human needs and arranged these into a hierarchy of prepotency. That is, before a higher order need can be satisfied, the preceding, lower order need must be satisfied. It is really a question of "paying attention to. . . ." For example, before one can pay attention to concerns about safety, physiological needs such as hunger must be fulfilled.

The basic needs, presented according to Maslow's hierarchy, are: (1) physiological needs, (2) safety or security needs, (3) love and belonging needs, (4) esteem needs, (5) self-actualization needs, (6) the need to know and understand, and (7) aesthetic needs.[22] These needs are largely unconscious, unchanging and genetic in origin. When they remain unfilled, the individual's behavior is dominated by a drive to satisfy them; Maslow called this "deficiency motivation." If the circumstances do not permit the fulfillment of needs, psychopathology occurs and the individual will become starved for food, safety, or esteem, as the case may be.

Once a more basic need is satisfied, then the next stage of need will take hold. Each individual determines for himself or herself how a need will be satisfied. In Maslow's terminology, human beings are their own determinants,[23] certainly an idea in distinct contrast to the behaviorists' conception of external stimuli shaping the individual. Psychologically healthy people, that is, people whose basic needs have been satisfied, are motivated, according to Maslow, "by trends to self-actualization."[24] In other words, they want to fulfill their own capacities and talents, and they will be self-motivated toward the acceptance and empowerment of their intrinsic nature.

Maslow's view of behavioral learning theories[25] is that they deal with a very small body of knowledge almost entirely derived from deficit-motivation. Learning derived from such contexts is no more than a set of habits or ideas tacked on externally to the person and quickly lost once the context or deficit-motivation is modified. Learning based on inner or "growth" motivation involves increased understanding and insight and, often, a deepening of personal meaning. The growth-motivated (as opposed to the deficiency-motivated) individual, because he or she is free of basic needs, can perceive reality with all of its contradictions, polarities, and incompatibilities more completely and with greater accuracy.

The open education movement of the 1960s and early 1970s was deeply influenced by Maslow's work. Maslow's hypotheses regarding motivation and learning were supportive of a child-centered approach to curriculum and a diversity of individual outcomes. The traditional set of specific objectives could be replaced by such holistic goals as the achievement of self-actualization for every child.

## Cognitive/Developmental Psychology

The work of the cognitive/developmental psychologists has continued throughout the 1900s figuratively developing along its own track; it has clear linkages to the field theorists. In particular, they share with field theorists the interactionist view. That is, cognitive development is a product of the interaction of the environment with the intellectual potential and activities of the individual. The child is not a machine predetermined by identifiable, external factors; nor is the child's intellectual development completely determined by some genetically established program of maturation. As Wadsworth notes, "The child is a 'scientist,' an explorer, an inquirer, critically instrumental in constructing and organizing the world and his own development."[26] In this vein, John Dewey was certainly a cognitive/developmental psychologist.

Most famous among recent cognitive/developmental psychologists was Jean Piaget.[27] His work involving long-term observation of children's cognitive development began in 1919 and ended in 1980 with his death. Piaget was especially interested in comprehending the *schemata* or patterns of perceptions, understanding and thinking about the world pursued by children as they matured.

The questions Piaget posed in his investigations related primarily to children's cognitive development: what patterns of reasoning do they follow in thinking about quantities, physical changes, causal relationships, moral issues, and so forth? He held a theory of cognitive change akin to the field theorists' conception of learning. When children become aware of inconsistencies between their schemata and their experience, the schemata are likely to be modified in a process called *accommodation*. Often, however, instead of the child changing a particular schema in light of disconfirming experience, the interpretation of the experience is influenced by the schema and made to fit. In other words, what children know and believe influence their perception and interpretation of reality. Piaget labeled this process *assimilation*. A state of *equilibrium* exists when existing schemata can assimilate new experience; a state of disequilibrium exists when new experience cannot be assimilated. Children strive for equilibrium and so they seek new schemata accommodating to the new circumstances.

In Piaget's conception of cognition, schemata develop in ongoing interaction with the environment but only if the child is developmentally able to deal with the change. Piaget posits a series of cognitive stages through which the child passes and that impact on the schemata he or she holds. As the child matures cognitively toward more advanced stages of cognition, the schemata become more complex and capable of handling abstractions.

Piaget conceptualizes the cognitive stages as being in a hierarchical arrangement to each other. That is, the order of maturation is fixed with the child necessarily progressing from "lower" stages to more advanced or "higher" stages of development. According to Piaget, it is not possible to reach more advanced stages of thought without having first passed through all of the preceding lower stages. His hierarchy is based on four developmental stages: (1) *sensory-motor*, covering the period from birth to age 2; (2) *preoperational*, covering the period from age 2 to 7; (3) *concrete operations*, covering the period from age 7 to 11; and (4) *formal operations*, covering the period from 11 to 16 and possibly beyond. It is important to note that the actual onset of each stage in the individual child may vary widely, as may the time needed to move from one stage to the next. What is invariant according to Piaget is the sequence of the stages.

Each stage is characterized by the advent of certain abilities that modify children's capacity to assimilate or accommodate new experiences. During the sensory-motor stage, children build their earliest schemata of the material world through their direct perceptual experience. They learn, for example, to relate certain objects and sounds; to expect objects that have disappeared to reappear; to differentiate among tastes, associating some with pleasurable sensations; and so forth. The preoperational stage coincides with the development of language and the ability to represent objects and events symbolically. Children begin to understand the representation of quantities such as the equivalency of "two" in "two apples" and "two houses." During the concrete operations stage, children develop the ability to classify and manipulate classifications, comparing, contrasting, and recombining classes of objects into new groupings. They no longer need to engage in actual experience to solve a problem but can carry out trial-and-error experiences in their heads. The formal operations stage is the stage of full, cognitive maturation when children can deal logically with complex abstractions. Terms such as "love" or "peace" can be explored and understood in all their implications and nuances. Intricate social behaviors can be evaluated and assessed for their desirability or importance.

As Glatthorn[28] notes, Piaget's hierarchical system of cognitive stages has often been taken as the foundational basis for structuring the curriculum in several respects:

1. that the content of the curriculum should reflect the cognitive stages of development;
2. that children should not be asked to perform at certain cognitive levels prematurely; and
3. that once children have entered a cognitive stage, experiential enrichment contributes to increasing the abilities associated with the stage.

To some degree, the question of children's intellectual readiness for learning has long been a consideration in curriculum development. Some critics of curriculum based on a presumed intellectual hierarchy are concerned that the curriculum itself becomes a self-fulfilling prophecy in which children do not perform beyond the expectations built into the curriculum, expectations that may well be less than youngsters' actual potential.

However, Piagetian principles are really not about the content or goals of the curriculum but rather about the methods adopted in pursuing the goals. This is not to say that Piaget did not hold educational goals that clearly aligned him with the educational progressives. Wadsworth cites Piaget as saying, "the principal goal of education is to create men who are capable of doing new things . . . men who are creative, inventive, and discoverers."[29] Effective teaching for Piaget needs to be based on the activity of the learner[30] and on truly understanding the child's cognitive development level. Duckworth[31] emphasizes that Piaget never took the position that the timing of stages was inviolate, but rather that what happened in school instruction was usually ineffectual for increasing the pace of development. Enriched experiences that meet children's cognitive needs and engage them actively will encourage learning and increase the pace of development.

In a memorandum prepared for a 1959 meeting of scientists, scholars, and educators supported by the National Academy of Sciences, Professor Barbel Inhelder, a longtime associate of Piaget, suggested ways that children "could be moved along faster through the various stages of intellectual development in mathematics and physics."[32] It was Inhelder's opinion that instructional methods could be devised to teach basic mathematical and scientific ideas to children at a younger age if children's "natural thought processes" were taken into account.[33] For both Piaget and Inhelder, the sequence of children's cognitive development was of crucial importance in developing a curricular sequence. Inhelder suggests, for example, that children can grasp the basic concept of probability long before they are able to learn the techniques of the calculus of probabilities.[34]

Jerome Bruner, secretary of this 1959 conference and a noted cognitive psychologist, hypothesized that any subject could "be taught effectively in some intellectually honest form to any child at any stage of development."[35] That is, major ideas can be translated into forms suited to the cognitive stages of development. According to Bruner:

> *What is most important for teaching basic concepts is that the child be helped to pass progressively from concrete thinking to the utilization of more conceptually adequate thought. But it is futile to attempt this by presenting formal explanations based on a logic that is distant from the child's manner of thinking and sterile in its implications for him. Much teaching in mathematics is of this sort. The child learns not to understand mathematical order but rather to apply certain devices or recipes without understanding their significance and connectedness.*[36]

While, at first glance, there would appear to be little disagreement with Piaget's analysis of intellectual development and its relationship to curriculum and instruction, Bruner departs from Piaget's strict, hierarchical interpretation of the stages quite significantly if not wholeheartedly. In Bruner's words:

> *. . . the intellectual development of the child is no clockwork sequence of events; it also responds to influences from the environment, notably the school environment. Thus instruction in scientific ideas, even at the elementary level, need not follow slavishly the natural course in cognitive development in the child. It can also lead intellectual development by providing challenging but usable opportunities for the child to forge ahead in his development.*[37]

The implication appears to be that not only can the pace of development be speeded up but also that the sequence of the stages need not be "slavishly" followed. Interestingly, Bruner devotes an entire chapter to a discussion of intuitive thinking without relating intuition to the cognitive stages of development.[38] Rather he states there is "little systematic knowledge available about the nature of intuitive thinking" and suggests that research in this area would provide information useful to the improvement of curriculum in general.[39]

Pursuing the hypothesis that any subject may be taught to children in some conceptually honest form, Bruner suggests the adoption of the "spiral curriculum," which would introduce an idea in some simple form and then continue to build on the idea in later grades, deepening and expanding on the original content of learning. As a curricular conception, it approximates the expanding environment curriculum pursued by progressivists for elementary social studies. In the early grades, children would study the home and neighborhood. Subsequently, expanding on the concepts acquired, they would study the city, state, region, and nation. Assuming that his hypothesis is true and that what is studied in school regardless of grade level ought to be worthwhile knowing in adult life, then, according to Bruner, it follows that the curriculum "ought to be built around the great issues, principles, and values" considered important by society.[40] This is an odd position to take in the middle of a report directed toward the improvement of teaching the scientific and mathematical disciplines in the schools. It is why earlier in this work it was noted that Bruner appeared to straddle the essentialist and progressive views of education.

## Educational Philosophies and Psychological Learning Theories

### Psychological/Philosophical Compatibility

We have reviewed several theories of human learning that have affected and shaped the development of curriculum. In particular, we have discussed behavioral theories, field theories, humanistic psychology, and cognitive learning theories. Each is more compatible with one category of educational philosophy than with the others.

Behavioral theories are most compatible with essentialism for they espouse a scientifically based understanding of human learning. Behaviorists are convinced that what is important to understand about learning can be studied empirically. Knowledge can be represented in small components subject to some form of measurement. This is a fairly mechanistic conception of intellectual operations that is quite consonant with the essentialist's world view.

Field theories posit that learning and environment are fundamentally interactive. This means that concepts related to learning are difficult to define, at least with the precision required by science, because they are involved in dynamic, ongoing change. Cognitive psychology, as represented by Piaget and Bruner, shares the interactionist approach of field theories. To the degree possible, both undertake empirical studies but neither is restricted in its analysis to only what can be measured. In general, both field theorists and cognitive psychologists hold positions compatible with a progressivist's or a reconstructionist's perspective.

Humanistic psychologists view people holistically in the complexity of their daily lives. Human motivation as a meaningful part of each individual's life is a crucial aspect of learning and must be understood before learning can be understood. Their perspective on learning is most compatible with an existentialist view of education.

Although we have tried to relate educational philosophies to perspectives on learning, it is important to remember that in the real world of education such consistency is often not a consideration. Indeed, we have referred to Jerome Bruner's position at length because, on the one hand, we have an essentialist involved in updating the scientific and mathematical disciplines as school subjects and in better formulating the structures of the disciplines for instructional purposes, and, on the other hand, we have a progressivist who refers to the processes of discovery and intuition independently of any given area of content. In our schools, we are increasingly administering standardized tests grounded in behavioral learning theory, while we continue to talk about meeting the needs of children. Often in the very next breath, we speak of eliminating the "fluff" content and having children study subjects that will serve as a basis for solid intellectual development throughout their lives.

These inconsistencies are a fundamental part of our political and cultural milieu. What they will lead to as American education works at reforming itself is not only a source of perplexity but of major concern as well. The doubts and hopes of the twenty-first century and a new millenium are upon us.

## QUESTIONS FOR DISCUSSION AND REFLECTION

1. Historically, Thorndike and Herbart fall into quite different periods in the investigation and study of how humans learn. There are, therefore, important differences in their work. Identify these differences; then indicate in what ways they might still be similar and supportive of each other.

2. Review Thorndike's "laws of learning" indicating how each might impact on the planning and development of curriculum.

3. Although Skinner was a behaviorist, he disagreed with what he considered the partial and oversimple theories of behaviorism. Review his position fully, explaining how operant conditioning is different from S–R learning.

4. In what fundamental ways are field learning theories different from behaviorist learning theories?

5. How would a curriculum developed on the bases of gestalt principles differ from one based on behavoristic principles?

6. Summarize the laws of learning as proposed by Wertheimer. What effect might accepting these have on the design and implementation of the curriculum.

7. What is the difference between "deficiency motivation" and "growth motivation"?

8. What are accommodation, assimilation, and equilibrium?

9. What are Piaget's developmental stages? How would they affect curriculum development?

10. What does Bruner mean by discovery learning? How would you relate this idea to the concept of the spiral curriculum?

11. How do educational philosophies and learning theories interact? What are the consequences for curriculum development?

## NOTES

1. See, for example, Skinner, B. F. (1953). *Science and human behavior*. New York: Macmillan.
2. See, for example: Gagne, R. M. (1970). *The conditions of learning*. New York: Holt, Rinehart and Winston.
3. Allport, G. (1961). *Patterns and growth in personality*. New York: Holt, Rinehart and Winston, p. 84.
4. See, for example: Locke, J. (1690). *An essay concerning human understanding*. New York: Dover Publications (edition published in 1959).
5. Thorndike, E. L. (1924). Mental Discipline in High School Studies. *Journal of Educational Psychology*, *15*, 98.
6. Herbart, J. F. (1904). *An introduction to Herbart's science and practice of education*, H. M. Feldman and E. Feldman (trans.). Boston: D. C. Heath.
7. Langer, J. (1969). *Theories of development*. New York: Holt, Rinehart and Winston, p. 51.
8. Watson, J. B. (1913). Psychology as the behaviorist views it. *Psychological Review*, *20*, 158–177. See, also: Watson, J. B. (1919). *Psychology from the standpoint of the behaviorist*. Philadelphia: J. B. Lippincott.
9. Watson, J. B. and Raynor, R. (1920). Conditioned emotional reactions. *Journal of Experimental Psychology*, *3*: 1–14.
10. Watson, J. B. (1925). *Behaviorism*. New York: Norton, p. 82.
11. Thorndike, E. L. (1913). *Psychology of learning* (3 vols.). New York: Teachers College Press.
12. Skinner, B. F. (1974). *About Behaviorism*. New York: Vintage Books, pp. 6–7.
13. Skinner, B. F. (1938). *The behavior of organisms: An experimental analysis*. New York: Appleton-Century-Crofts.
14. *Op. cit.*, Skinner, B. F. (1974), pp. 125–126.
15. *Ibid.*, p. 127.
16. Kohler, W. (1925). *The mentality of apes* (trans. E. Winter). New York: Harcourt Brace Jovanovich.
17. Hill, W. F. (1985). *Learning: A survey of psychological interpretations* (4th ed.). New York: Harper & Rowe, p. 91.
18. *Ibid.*, p. 89.
19. Zais, R. S. (1967). *Curriculum: Principles and foundations*. New York: Thomas Y. Crowell. p. 279.
20. *Op. cit.*, Hill, W. F., p. 93.
21. Bruner, J. S. (1966). *Toward a theory of instruction*. Cambridge, MA: Harvard University Press.
22. Maslow, A. H. (1962). *Toward a psychology of being*. New York: Van Nostrand.
23. *Ibid.*, p. 22.
24. *Ibid.*, p. 23.
25. *Ibid.*, pp. 36–38.
26. Wadsworth, B. J. (1978). *Piaget for the classroom teacher*. New York: Longman, pp. 10–11.
27. Piaget, J. (1926). *The language and thought of the child* (Trans. M. Worden). New York: Harcourt Brace Jovanovich. Piaget, J. (1968). *The psychology of intelligence* (Trans. M. Piercy and D. E. Berlyne). Totowa, NJ: Littlefield, Adams. (First published in English by Routledge and Kegan Paul, 1950.)
28. Glatthorn, A. (1987). *The Curriculum*. Glenview, IL: Scott, Foresman. pp. 57–58.

29. Wadsworth, B. J. (1978). *Piaget for the classroom teacher*. New York: Longman, p. 99.
30. *Ibid.*, p. 102.
31. Duckworth, E. (1964). In: R. Ripple and O. Rockcastle (eds.), *Piaget rediscovered*. Ithaca, NY: Cornell University Press, p. 20.
32. Bruner, J. (1977). *The process of education*. Cambridge, MA: Harvard University Press. pp. 40–41.
33. *Ibid.*, p. 42.
34. *Ibid.*, p. 45.
35. *Ibid.*, p. 33.
36. *Ibid.*, pp. 38–39.
37. *Ibid.*, p. 39.
38. *Ibid.*, pp. 55–68.
39. *Ibid.*, p. 57.
40. *Ibid.*, p. 52.

# 8

# Evaluating the
# Curriculum

## Introduction

Evaluation is judging the success and merit of an undertaking. Educational evaluation is judging the success and merit of educational programs.[1] It is usually included in the curriculum planning stage. That is, once the goals have been set, a design put forth, and learning activities selected, a set of procedures is established to assess how well the curriculum and its implementation have succeeded in helping students achieve the goals.

Strictly speaking, curriculum evaluation is concerned with the success and merit of the curriculum and its design, planned content, and implementation. If, however, one takes a broad view of the definition of curriculum as being all the experiences under the school's direction that lead to learning (see chapter 3), then there is little difference between educational evaluation in general and curriculum evaluation. In this broad conception, curriculum evaluation would include assessments of goals and purposes, curriculum design, content selection, curriculum implementation, classroom processes, student learning, counseling, supplies, equipment, and physical plant facilities. What is included as appropriate to curriculum evaluation is largely dependent on one's definition of curriculum.

In education a number of different interpretations are associated with the term "evaluation." At least five of these seem especially relevant to our discussion of curriculum. These are:

1. It is a synonym for the school's testing program.
2. It is a tool for determining the instructional skills and intellectual power of teachers.
3. It embodies society's values and makes it possible to apply these values in finding and remedying the problems important to society.

4. It is a means for studying changes in student behavior and diagnosing student needs.
5. It assesses the merit of educational practices and the appropriateness of the resources consumed.

The ambiguity of the term is hardly surprising. In the 1970s and 1980s, it became the object of newspaper stories seeking sensationalism based on poorly understood standardized scores and a favorite topic of politicians seeking favor from the lay public. In the midst of all this ambiguity, the uses of testing changed significantly from individual diagnosis and placement, which had typified the 1950s and 1960s, to comparative assessments of success among the nation's schools and even among the schools of different nations (including our own). Past and present meanings have comingled in a potpourri of obscurity.

Given the increasing emphasis on evaluation that has characterized the last decades of the twentieth century, understanding clearly the purposes and functioning of evaluation in relationship to schooling and the curriculum is especially important. This chapter is an overview and clarification of the evaluative process as it relates to curriculum. Standardized tests and their uses, along with a brief discussion of the politics of evaluation, will also be presented. Finally, evaluating for the future will be discussed.

## Dimensions and Purposes of Evaluation

### Dimensions of Curriculum Evaluation

Curriculum evaluation may be designed to assess various dimensions of the curriculum. A "dimension," as used in this discussion, refers to a set of activities contributing to an aspect of curriculum work believed to be central to the success of education. Three dimensions are typically pursued in curriculum evaluation: inputs, process, and outputs.[2] Logically, the particular dimension being examined impacts on how a study will be undertaken and data collected. An evaluation of the curriculum may concentrate on the dimension of inputs giving support to the curriculum. The activities selected as inputs may include the facilities; the home environment and its enrichment potential; the professional preparation of teachers and administrators; the scholastic, socioeconomic, and ethnic characteristics of students; and the quality of the curriculum design itself, among others. Depending on the particular nature of inputs selected, observation, objective description, case studies, and qualitative standards may need to be employed, along with such quantitative data as the number of books in a library or students' average family income.

A second dimension in curriculum evaluation may concentrate on the processes of implementation. The process dimension may include the instructional methodologies and the kinds of feedback used, the attitudes exhibited toward students, the kinds of responsibilities assigned to students, and so forth. Teaching style and technique are especially important in an evaluation of this dimension. While objective data such as the number of different instructional methodologies used in a given time period may be utilized in a process study, qualitative analyses related to attitude and style are absolutely essential.

Neither input nor process evaluation are widely followed by the nation's press. Possibly, this is due in the former case to the low level of resources assigned to the schools and the dim prospects of achieving significant improvements. In the latter instance, the kind of qualitative analyses required are daunting in their complexity, onerous of time and effort, and rarely conclusive. In lieu of these more difficult-to-conduct evaluations, state governments often opt for results on standardized tests.

The third dimension in curriculum evaluation is the one most widely pursued for it is based on output, which has been interpreted primarily in terms of student achievement in such subjects as science, mathematics, and history. The parameters of output evaluation may include the progress made by individual students, changes in student attitudes, improvement in reflective thought processes, and increased creativity, but these are not often among the parameters selected for output evaluation. Instead, standardized tests are typically used to assess the skills students have acquired and the level of knowledge attained from the intended experiences of the curriculum.

### The Formative / Summative Aspects of Curriculum Evaluation

Output evaluation may be used to give students and teachers feedback about how effectively a curricular unit is being taught and learned. This is known as formative evaluation, which is used during the delivery phase of a curriculum. Typically, student performance is assessed to determine those aspects needing improvement and in what ways the curriculum may need to be adjusted. Teachers sometimes use classroom quizzes as a means of offering formative feedback, but they also engage in numerous qualitative, albeit informal activities, such as classroom observations, student diaries, and small-group discussions. Formative evaluation does not currently attract a great deal of attention from the public.

Most typically in the 1980s and early 1990s, output evaluation has been used as a summative tool, that is, as the final results of a curricular / instructional effort, rather than for formative purposes. Summative evaluations of student performance have often, indefensibly, been used as measures of teacher accountability. The student in this case is likened to a product and the teacher to a manager who can be held accountable for output much like a foreman is held accountable for a factory's productivity. Student achievement is compared nationally or on a statewide basis, and teachers are judged by the scores of their students. Quantitative modes of data collection are very important in this context because objectivity and widely applicable generalizations are necessary to any national or statewide evaluation of school success.

Formative evaluation may also be found within the input and process dimensions, especially when a new program is being piloted or an existing one is under revision. In such contexts, qualitative approaches to evaluation are particularly important since the evaluator needs to appraise the success of the curricular design in achieving the goals and objectives of the curriculum while in the midst of putting the curriculum in place.[3] Evaluation in such instances must be capable of coping with a curricular situation that is in a state of becoming. Unexpected events are likely to arise and may even become new problems while anticipated difficulties dissipate. Somehow, in the midst of flux, the evaluator must determine, for example, whether students are acquiring the skills anticipated when the curricular content or activities were selected. How effective is the curriculum design? Are students, say, achieving the broad, conceptual grasp that had been expected from the reading of this or that work? Or, have more desirable attitudes been achieved?

The evaluator's report is usually a written document of what has happened. Models may be developed that represent the actual functioning of the curricular design. Crucial issues may be identified, interviews conducted, observations undertaken following preestablished protocols, and profiles of key figures generated. The clear and succinct results of formally structured, quantitative research, however, is virtually impossible to achieve in the formative stages of curriculum evaluation.

### Criteria and Standards

In undertaking the assessment of a program's output, planning must involve three basic components, no matter which definition of curriculum is operational. These are: criteria, standards, and instruments. Although the term "criteria" is often used in everyday parlance as a synonym for standards, in the context of evaluation, we use it to indicate the categories in which performance is to be assessed. *Reading*, *knowledge of literature*, and *science* are broad categories or criteria, while "skills in phonics," "knowledge of Elizabethan plays," and "experimental methods" are the respective subcategories or associated criteria.

In a sense, criteria are the assessment equivalent of goals and objectives. They may be based on specific performance objectives or on broadly understood, open-ended objectives. Criteria must not be confused with standards. It is typical in today's educational world, largely dominated by standardized tests, to cite rising test scores as evidence that we have improved the curriculum when very little change in the curriculum design has actually occurred. The goals and objectives—the bases for our assessment criteria—have remained essentially unchanged. By setting higher standards, we have decided to increase attainment within a given category of study but have otherwise changed very little.

### Evaluation as De Facto Curriculum Making

The reform movement of the 1980s and 1990s has paid relatively little attention to criteria while emphasizing standards. The criteria of the tests have tended to remain unchanged and have had a significant bearing on classroom teaching. Although obviously not the way we believe curriculum should be driven, tests have become a major influence on the unchanging nature of the school's programs.

College entrance examinations have been especially significant in creating this largely static state of the curriculum. For example, toward the end of 1990, the College Board announced that it would extensively revise the Scholastic Aptitude Test. Among the major revisions to be undertaken are: (1) increased emphasis on critical reading and reasoning, (2) increased length of reading passages, (3) increased emphasis on applied mathematics and interpretation of data, (4) students will be allowed to use handheld calculators in answering questions from the mathematics section, and (5) students will be required to respond in writing to at least 20 percent of questions (which are currently nearly all multiple choice). In addition to these revisions, new tests are to be developed in Asian languages, English-language proficiency for non-native speakers, basic English, and basic mathematics. A listening component will be added to several of the language tests. As the reader can readily note, the College Board is engaging in a great deal of tinkering with "sub-sub" criteria but is otherwise not suggesting any real changes to the school's curriculum design.

Of course, the design of the curriculum should not be driven by standardized examinations. We cannot, however, close our eyes to their de facto status as guides for curriculum development that standardized examinations have become. In September 1989, a joint statement was issued by the nation's governors and President George Bush at the end of a conference they referred to as an "education summit." In the statement, they declare their intention to "establish clear measures of performance and then issue annual report cards on the progress of students, schools, the states, and the federal government."[4] Along with President Bush, a number of groups have expressed interest in establishing a national testing system including the National Center on Education and the Economy, the American Federation of Teachers, the Congress, and numerous private funding agencies such as the John D. and Catherine T. MacArthur Foundation and the Pew Charitable Trusts. What is perhaps not well understood by our political leadership is that by merely raising standards without reassessing the criteria, that is, the subjects that are being tested, the curriculum is made even less susceptible to real change and less flexible to the needs of the future.

Standardized evaluation must also be seen from the perspective of control. To the extent that school districts select nationally normed, published tests to evaluate student performance, especially if selected after the curriculum has been planned, the districts give up control over the goals and objectives of their curriculum. Indeed, the de facto curricular effect of tests may even confound the more important purposes held for a curriculum if districts use them to achieve standards for criteria not well related to the districts' goals and objectives. It should be noted that many published tests do contain lists of objectives so that comparisons with the district's objectives may be made.[5] The selection of appropriate measurement instruments based on the consistency between district and test objectives is indeed a possibility in a good many cases. However, test-based lists of objectives are useful primarily when a school district has a set of clearly expressed specific objectives involving low-level cognitive processes. More advanced cognitive processes and broadly-oriented objectives are difficult to compare with such lists.

While standards may be quantified and set higher or lower, criteria represent our values and must be understood in all of their qualitative complexity if the standards are to make any sense. Although the public appears to overwhelmingly support (81%) the establishment of a national system of tests,[6] the wisdom of doing this is questionable so long as the design of the curriculum itself is in need of basic reevaluation. Would we want to "fix" nationally a curriculum that is widely believed to be inadequate? Do we want tests intended for evaluation to become the instruments of curriculum design and development as well? How shall our values be represented in our curriculum? Should the federal government acquire control over the curricula of the nation when the United States Constitution excludes such control? Where is the proper locus of curriculum control?

### The Important Differences between Research and Evaluation

Conducting an evaluation means engaging in research to gather the data necessary for making judgments. It is therefore understandable that people often think of educational research and educational evaluation as one and the same enterprise. Certainly there is considerable overlap, but as Borg and Gall point out, there are three important differences:

1. Educational evaluation is initiated in response to a need to make decisions and take action concerning curriculum, instruction, overall school/district policy, management, political strategy, or possibly all of the above. The impetus for educational research, on the other hand, is to seek relationships among two or more variables.

2. Data associated with educational evaluation is usually limited to a specific site and unique set of conditions, whereas data collected in educational research is likely to support widely applicable generalizations.

3. Results in educational evaluation are often expressed in subjective terms of worth such as "better" and "more successful," terms consistent with an enterprise that is judgmental. Results in educational research are, on the other hand, expressed in objective terms that transcend specific situations. For example, "the variable X appears to be a determinant of variable Y."[7]

Notwithstanding these differences, data collection and analyses in evaluation and research are often in appearance similar[8] to each other, for quantitative methodologies and the scientific paradigm have dominated both. Two distinct but equally important problems arise in practice because the differences between evaluation and research are paid scant attention.

First is the tendency to think of evaluation as though it were an objective research enterprise. However, evaluation involves determining merit and superior worth, an activity that is essentially subjective and qualitative. Quantitative methodologies are often inadequate or even inappropriate for the summative evaluation of student performance. If a curriculum design is planned to achieve increased creativity and reflective thought among students, a standardized test quantifying the recall of factual knowledge or presenting a set of multiple choice questions is hardly capable of collecting relevant or appropriate data for an evaluation.

In recent years, applications of qualitative methodologies in the form of ethnographic research strategies have grown dramatically among evaluation researchers,[9] while dissatisfaction with the scientific paradigm not only for evaluation but also for education in general has increased steadily among professionals.[10] In any case, among administrators, politicians, and the public at large, the popularity of quantitative methodologies is unabated. Indeed, quantitative measures of program output appear destined to dominate curriculum evaluation for years to come.

The second problem is that evaluation, which so closely parallels the quantitative methods and scientific paradigms of research, is itself sorely in need of well-conducted research. A great many claims have been made on behalf of evaluation based on standardized testing for which there is little supporting evidence. In particular, little evidence exists that the administration of standardized testing accomplishes the purposes currently ascribed to it. We are told, for example, that if youngsters improve their performance on science and mathematics tests, we will become, as a nation, more economically competitive. There are, however, numerous developed nations (e.g., Italy, Great Britain) whose students perform better on such tests than do ours, but their economy is arguably not more competitive than ours. We have also been led to believe that tests motivate students to study more, that teachers will improve their teaching abilities because the tests make them accountable for student performance, and that the tests can measure performance with fairness among culturally different populations. The claims made for our current forms of evaluation are value-laden and often emotional, but they are not supported by the results of objective research. If we are to have a national testing system, obtaining research and objective knowledge about the effects of such a system is of the utmost importance.

### Additional, Sometimes Inappropriate, Uses of Evaluation

Evaluation is, at times, used to keep people out of an academic program especially if, for whatever reason, there is a scarcity of student openings. In such instances, the performances of students are compared on some objective, usually quantitative scale that allows for discrete judgments to be made. Student A has achieved a higher score in mathematics than Student B and should therefore be admitted into the program. A prior evaluation that ought to be undertaken, however, before this point is ever reached involves an analysis of the pertinence of the criterion, mathematics, to success in the program. The validity of the criterion used in an evaluation, especially one whose purpose is to limit participation, is too often overlooked.

Evaluation may be used to assess or "diagnose" students' readiness for a particular kind or level of study to determine the specific content or curricular sequence where instruction should begin. The validity of criteria is equally important but a qualitative, humanistic approach is more frequently pursued because decisions based on comparisons with the performances of other students are not necessary to accomplish the purpose.

### Instruments for Quantitative Evaluation

Nationally normed, standardized tests are currently the primary means for determining (1) how well the schools are accomplishing the goals and objectives of the curriculum and (2) what areas of the curriculum need improvement.[11] Measurable student performance is the basis for making such judgments. Instruments developed by the Princeton-based Educational Testing Service, the California Achievement Test, the Iowa Test of Basic Skills, and the Metropolitan Achievement Test, are currently utilized from coast to coast in a rather uncoordinated effort to reach for each student's performance a representative number or indicator that will allow performances of all students to be compared with each other or, possibly, with their prior performances.

There are tests that report student performance relative to other members of a group that may be described according to age, sex, or other stipulated characteristics are called norm-referenced tests. Those tests reporting raw scores per item are called criterion-referenced tests. These are tests designed, as Popham notes, "to ascertain an individual's status with respect to a defined behavioral domain."[12] Nationally normed tests belong to the former while locally devised tests usually belong to the latter.

There are many, among them Albert Shanker, president of the American Federation of Teachers, who feel this unbridled embrace of nationally normed specific performance measures is premature.[13] Although standardized tests have greatly improved since their inception in the early part of the twentieth century, they remain inaccurate and overly narrow. What is assessed must somehow be made to fit a discrete response that can be both easily selected by the examinee and easily checked by the examiner.

Typically, test scores are used to measure the achievement of youngsters in reading, English and American literature, mathematics, history, science, and possibly government (civics) and geography. From time to time, newspaper headlines tell us of some startling deficits revealed by the tests, for example, a majority of high school students have failed to identify the hero who said "Give me liberty or give me death"; or students have performed so poorly in mathematics that their average score falls well below the averages of numerous other industrialized nations of the world; or a considerable percentage of adults cannot locate Afghanistan or Korea on a global map; and so forth.

Each time, the public is shocked and there is a new wave of demands for greater accountability. Discussions tend to revolve around the professional preparation of teachers and how instructional delivery can be improved so that students will be better able to deal with the multiple-choice, factually based questions that comprise most standardized tests. In other words, Johnny or Jeanne should know what Patrick Henry said or the formula for determining the size of a cone. Not knowing these or similar items is considered evidence that the schools have not succeeded in delivering the curriculum and the result is an inadequate output (i.e., student performance).

It is important to note, however, that this fairly usual, summative approach to evaluation is primarily involved with determining the efficacy of instruction through measurable student performance rather than the adequacy of the curriculum design, its content, or its implementation. This approach is an excessively limited perspective for those who would pursue a broad definition of curriculum and misses the point altogether for those who would pursue a more restrictive conception of curriculum. Measuring student performance really tells us very little about the quality of the curriculum. Evaluating the assumptions, goals, and design of the curriculum should occur before an evaluation of how well students have learned the content of the curriculum. What use is superior learning if the curriculum has misdirected children in what they learn?

### Intrinsic Evaluation and the Qualitative Approach

Certainly, concerns regarding the success of instruction are important and need to be pursued. However, questions relevant to the nature and effectiveness of the curriculum design and its content and mode of implementation are at least as crucial and would logically require attention before the assessment of students' cognitive achievement. Is the particular arrangement of content adequate to the goals established? Do the goals continue to be relevant to the changing cultural, political, economic, and social circumstances of the times? More specifically, are the competencies organized in mathematical or science studies those most essential for the future lives of our students?

These are questions that concern the *validity* of the curriculum design. One of the virtues of a superior teacher is that of contributing, in a significant way, to the ultimate nature and quality of the curricular outcomes. Objectives that require students to study content inappropriate to the basic goals of education are detrimental to the success of the curriculum, even if students do perform well on the relevant, nationally normed tests. For example, if the goals related to the teaching of mathematics emphasize the practical use of mathematical skills in daily life, then courses in advanced calculus hardly seem appropriate even for the precollegiate high school student. It may be appreciated by the public that students receive a high test score in calculus. This does not change the fact that such useful skills as simple bookkeeping for household and small-business budgeting have been ignored and would probably respond more adequately to the basic purpose of mathematical studies in the curriculum than does a course in advanced calculus.

Rarely, as we have noted previously, do we undertake to judge the educational merit of the curriculum itself. Scriven[14] refers to this kind of evaluation as *intrinsic*. As Ornstein and Hunkins put it, intrinsic evaluators ask, "How good is the curriculum?" before they ask "How well does the course or curriculum achieve its goals?"[15]

Intrinsic evaluators typically employ an open-ended, qualitative approach to their research because the questions they pursue are primarily of the humanistic variety. They may study, for example, the coherence of the curriculum between its philosophical assumptions, its goals, and its outcomes,[16] a study that can only be pursued logically. They may undertake to describe the characteristics of an educated person for that is ultimately what the curriculum is about.[17] They may deal with the sufficiency of the content selected to fulfill the requirements of the curriculum design, or analyze the appropriateness of the design with respect not only to intended outcomes but to unintended ones as well. They may explore the adequacy of the scope and sequence for the overall curriculum design or review the types of materials selected for validity and appropriateness in the context of the curriculum goals. They may also look into the implementation process, assessing how well teachers and the community have been prepared for accepting and working with the curriculum.

Whatever the case, intrinsic evaluators follow broad and often indefinite guidelines as they pursue qualitative questions quite intractable to quantitative analysis. The worth of a program, its curriculum design, and content selection are not amenable to precision-oriented, objective measures. Judgment depends largely on the subjective values and perceptions of the evaluators or, at least, on those who hold a stake in the evaluation.[18]

Eliot Eisner's Educational Connoisseurship and Educational Criticism Model[19] embodies the characteristics of inquiry necessary to intrinsic evaluations of the curriculum. As the name implies, the special appreciation of an expert educator, very much like that of an expert art critic, is used in a metaphor-filled, descriptive process intended to communicate what has actually happened in the curriculum. Educational criticism is the process of interpreting and appraising what has happened.[20] The quality of the criticism depends on the expertise of the critic and the willingness of the audience to be helped by the criticism, which of course depends on the skill with which it is offered.

## The Real World of Evaluation

### The Benefits and Wastes of Evaluation

There appears to be widespread agreement that accountability is desirable, that schools should stand behind their work and accept responsibility for the results, and that evaluations of school programs should be conducted both nationally and with regularity. There is also a view of evaluation among the top leadership (recall the education summit referred to earlier) that it is helpful to the conduct of education even without additional resources. What is more, a multi-billion dollar industry has evolved based on the development of nationally normed, standardized tests. Against this backdrop, state and national evaluations of student, teacher, and school performance have mushroomed beyond anyone's imagination only a few decades ago. There is an impression among educators that everyone involved in education is either about to be evaluated, going through evaluation, or just finishing up an evaluation.

The myriads of carefully compiled evaluation reports stored on shelves around the country but infrequently utilized are a discouraging reality.[21] The prevailing view among educators has been that "evaluations seldom influence program decision-makers."[22] The evidence is mounting, however, that evaluation does influence decision making, although in indirect and often gradual ways.[23] Evaluation reports have an informal impact on the professionals concerned. Rather than a direct, linear relationship, there is a delayed and rather amorphous reaction to an evaluation report, which, over time, impacts on the behaviors of those involved.

The ideal is a rational and clear linkage between the results of an evaluation and subsequent decision making. The reality is that the complex interaction of local personalities and circumstances affect in unpredictable ways the level and manner that a report will be used. Evaluative feedback is received through the formal report and informally through conversations, experience with the evaluators, and development of various documents required by the evaluators. An evaluation report may be employed months after it has been stored on the back shelf to apply pressure for increased funding in an area found deficient by the report. Or a department recognized for its quality may be allowed to establish a new course of study months after the report has been filed as a result of its favorable feedback. Students may be supported by school administrators to attend, say, a competition in Washington, D.C., as a result of recommendations to broaden the base of experiences available to students. There is a wide array of responsive actions that may be taken, but many of these are indirect and unpredictable.

## The Classroom Teacher and Qualitative Evaluation

It may be that the long-standing, widespread use of short-answer and multiple-choice tests by classroom teachers has given support to the vastly increased use of standardized tests that has occurred nationally. Certainly, at the secondary level, a teacher with 150 to 180 students in her classes has little choice but to use testing formats that can be corrected quickly and efficiently.

The situation has reached an extreme and many teachers are seeking ways to assess students' capabilities in dealing with complex questions that require critical analysis and reflective problem solving. This is especially true in the humanities and the social studies, which, above all, are intended to deal with the quality of human life. How open to new ideas, how critical of tradition, how logical in analyses, how able to assess difficult situations have students become because of the experiences of the intended curriculum? These kinds of questions do not ordinarily find answers in the multiple-choice, classroom-based tests that most teachers find necessary to administer frequently during a semester. If ways were found to pursue qualitative evaluation in the classroom, perhaps increased national efforts at qualitative outcome evaluation could be supported. The New Standards Project, sponsored by the MacArthur Foundation and the Pew Charitable Trust, has drafted a set of questions and tasks that are more relevant to youngsters' experiences and more open to creative responses. An example of the project's effort follows:

*The new Ninja Turtle cereal is offering a collector's set of four Teenage Mutant Ninja Turtle figures. Each specially marked box has only one figure: Donatello, Leonardo, Michelangelo, or Raphael. In order to get all four figures, you can collect one from each box of cereal, or you can send in one box top and $15.*

*If each box of cereal costs $2.39, what would be the cheapest way to collect all four figures? A. Send one box top and $15, or B. Purchase boxes of cereal until you have a completed set.*

*Design an experiment to determine how many boxes of cereal you must buy to get a complete set of four different figures. Did your test support your predictions?[24]*

Years ago, one of the authors participated in an effort to develop qualitative evaluation for the classroom that would take into account the large number of students assigned to high school teachers, as well as the need to exercise some objective control over the subjectivity inherent in us all that clouds our ability to judge fairly.[25] Instead of giving up the multiple-choice question, which offers teachers a quick and efficient format for grading purposes, a way of opening this approach to more personalized and qualitative responses was sought. Typically, multiple-choice items have four possible responses, only one of which is correct. Students were, instead, presented with items with a varying number of possible responses, several of which could be correct. Provision was also made for students to briefly defend a choice if they felt the need to do so. An example of one of the modified multiple choice questions used follows:

*The Mayor's victory in 1963 swept his ticket into office. For a while, the city council operated as a team, but then the team began to fall apart. What happened?*

*a. The members of the city council began to fight each other for political gain.*

*b. The increase in the number of council members and the defeat of two of the Mayor's close collaborators diminished the cohesiveness of the city council.*

*c. The city council members who supported the Mayor disagreed about major aspects of the Mayor's program.*

*d. The council chairman was not a supporter of the Mayor, even though he belonged to the same political party.*

*e. The Mayor's supporters were disillusioned when he was indicted by the grand jury.*

*f. The financial questions split the team.*

*g. Other possible answers. _____*

_____

_____

In this sample question, responses *b* and *d* were clearly correct. Response *f* is somewhat dubious because it is not clear which financial questions are being referred to. The teacher could assume that the answer was incorrect unless some comments were added about its ambiguity. If no one brought the point up, the teacher could do so when reviewing the test.

In addition to seeking new question formats, an approach to grading students' qualitative efforts was also devised. Evaluative questions about a student's performance were viewed from three perspectives: according to the teacher's own personal norms; according to the achievement of the class as a whole; and according to the student's initial abilities. The purpose of establishing three levels of teacher analysis was to help the teacher achieve greater objectivity over his or her subjective responses to students' qualitative performances. If, for example, the objectives being evaluated involve students' capacity to engage in critical evaluation, a series of questions concerning critical evaluation would be analyzed from the three perspectives. Have students increased their capacity to discern potential problems according to the teachers own norms, according to overall class performance, according to each student's initial capacity level?

Of course, simply devising more defensible ways of evaluating students' qualitative output will not alone overcome cultural mindsets decades in the making nor economic interests that have reached the level of a major, multi-billion dollar industry. Nor will the glib headlines of newspapers or the demogogic talk of politicians abate. Nevertheless, if a movement toward qualitative assessment is to take on strength, practical ways to implement such evaluations, especially in the classroom, are an apriori necessity.

## The Social/Political Reality

Discussions about school and program evaluation can be calmly pursued, as we have done in this chapter, when the discussants or their work are not being evaluated. The actual execution of evaluation is burdened with a host of significant problems that can lead to extreme tension.

Babbie[27] suggests that there are three major, socio-political problem areas whenever evaluation is conducted. First, vested interests include people's livelihoods as well as their pride in their work and in what they have produced. Often a subliminal fear exists that the evaluator will not really understand what a particular program is supposed to do or how it is being implemented and that a report unsupportive of the program's continuation may be developed. Even when such extremes are not probable, a certain tension and distrust may be found among those being evaluated.

A second problem involves people's beliefs about what a good program is. They have, in essence, mentally conducted their own evaluation of the program, and they are not about to change their minds no matter what a so-called expert reports!

A third problem has to do with the evaluator's ability to be understood clearly in his conversations with those participating in the evaluation and in his report. Data collection can be a very technical enterprise full of jargon not easily understood by the average educator. There is also the question of understanding how people going through an evaluation feel and communicating with them with a sensitivity that will somehow enjoin their cooperation. Achieving sincere cooperation and a willingness to consider the evaluator's work is a hurdle of major proportions that is often not overcome.

The real world of evaluation is hardly a "pure" one. Evaluations cost time and resources that may be very unwillingly given, especially by educators whose resources are abysmally inadequate. Past evaluations may have been used inappropriately, for example, to make newspaper headlines informing the public about the district's worst school. Imagine how students feel after being informed that their school or school district is among the worst in the state or the nation. Politicians have often used evaluations to make headlines of their own for their own ends. Instead of taking responsibility for the many difficulties facing education today, evaluations are used as a reason for not giving support, for finger-pointing, for thinking, "We'll look at you again at the next evaluation when perhaps we'll have more time."

## Evaluation for the Future

Evaluation is essentially an undertaking that looks at where we have been and how well we have done what we set out to do. The data it develops, however, are most useful to the decisions we must make for the future. But the future must be understood in a broad, long-term context. There is the future interpreted as what shall we do with the programs we have now. That is the short-term future. Then there is the future that presents an array of challenges and conundrums for which we must evaluate the potentials that lie before us and invent the programs of tomorrow. This is our long-term future, and it merits our most careful consideration.

Evaluation can be forward-looking. In the 1960s, the RAND Corporation developed the Delphi technique to help decision makers in business and industry make decisions about the future.[28] The method involves developing multiple panels of experts, soliciting their predictions for the future in their area of expertise, and then each expert independently appraising the predictions made by the others. The technique has been used from time to time in education but never with the persistence nor with the widespread involvement that it merits. We need to look much more carefully at the future than we have ever done before.

### QUESTIONS FOR DISCUSSION AND REFLECTION

1. The term "evaluation" has numerous referents often rendering it quite ambiguous. Choose those referents that you believe are most important, giving the rationale for your selection.

2. Three dimensions of curriculum evaluation may be pursued separately or as

an integrated whole. Identify these dimensions, explaining fully the meaning of each in terms of schooling. Can you think of other dimensions that might be used in evaluating the curriculum? The study of roles and their interactions in the pursuit of the curriculum might be a productive dimension to follow.

3. Distinguish between criteria and standards. What is the importance of this distinction?

4. Explain in your own words the statement: Standardized tests often function as de facto curriculum makers. Does this state of affairs concern you? Explain your position.

5. In one sense, evaluation is closely related to educational research; in another, it is quite distinct. Explain the contradiction and its significance for educators.

6. What significance may be attributed to the changes the College Board intends to make to the Scholastic Aptitude Test?

7. Distinguish between norm-referenced and criterion-referenced tests. What is important about the distinction?

8. Can you suggest additional ways that teachers can measure the qualitative outputs of the curriculum?

9. What are the major sociopolitical areas that must be confronted whenever evaluation of a school's curriculum is undertaken? Explain each area fully.

10. In your opinion, will the establishment of a national testing system change American education and the curriculum? Explain your position fully.

# NOTES

1. Borg, W. R. and Gall, M. D. (1989). *Educational research: An introduction*. New York: Longman, p. 743.
2. Tuckman, B. W. (1979). *Evaluating instructional programs*. Boston: Allyn and Bacon, p. 14.
3. Ornstein, A. C. and Hunkins, F. P. (1988). *Curriculum: Foundations, principles, and issues*. Englewood Cliffs, NJ: Prentice Hall, p. 255.
4. As cited by: Rothman, R. (1989). States Turn to Student Performance as New Measure of School Quality. *Education Week, IX*, 10, pp. 1, 12, 13.
5. *Ibid.*, p. 6.
6. Elam, S. M., Rose, L. C., and Gallup, A. M. (1991). The 23rd annual Gallup poll of the public's attitudes toward the schools. *Phi Delta Kappan*, 73, 1, p. 42.
7. *Ibid.*, pp. 743–744.
8. *Ibid.*, p. 752.
9. LeCompte, M. D. and Goetz, J. P. (1984). Ethnographic data collection in evaluation research. In: D. M. Fetterman (ed.). *Ethnography in educational evaluation*. Beverly Hills: Sage, p. 37.
10. Longstreet, W. S. (1982). Action research: A paradigm. *Educational Forum, XLVI*, 2, 135–158.

Eisner, E. W. (1979). The use of qualitative forms of evaluation for improving educational practice. *Educational Evaluation and Policy Analysis*, *1*, 6, 11–19.

House, E. R. (1979). The objectivity, fairness, and justice of federal evaluation policy as reflected in the follow through evaluation. *Educational Evaluation and Policy Analysis*, *1*, 6, 28–42.

11. Glasman, N. S. (1984). Student achievement and the school principal. *Educational Evaluation and Policy Analysis*, 6, 3, pp. 283–296.

12. Popham, W. J. (1988). *Educational evaluation* (2nd ed.). Englewood Cliffs, NJ: Prentice Hall, p. 132.

13. *Ibid*.

14. Scriven, M. (1978). The methodology of evaluation. In: J. R. Gress and D. E. Purpel (eds). *Curriculum: An introduction to the field*. Berkeley, CA: McCutchan, pp. 337–408.

15. *Op. cit.*, p. 254. Ornstein, A. C. and Hunkins, F. P. (1988).

16. *Ibid.*, pp. 385–388.

17. Zais, R. S. (1976). *Curriculum: Principles and foundations*. New York: Thomas Y. Crowell, p. 382.

18. *Op. cit.*, Borg and Gall, p. 770.

19. Eisner, E. W. (1979). *The educational imagination: On the design and evaluation of school programs*. New York: Macmillan.

20. Eisner, E. W. (1970). Using professional judgment. In: R. Brandt (ed.). *Applied strategies for curriculum evaluation*. Alexandria, VA: Association for Supervision and Curriculum Development, p. 46.

21. King, J. A. and Pechman, E. M. (1982). *The process of evaluation use in local school settings* (Final Report, NIE grant 81-0900), ERIC Document No. ED 233 037.

22. Alkin, M. C., Daillak, R. H., and White, P. (1979). *Using evaluations: Does evaluation make a difference?* Beverly Hills, CA: Sage.

23. Braskamp, L. A. and Brown, R. D. (1980). *Utilization of evaluative information*. San Francisco: Jossey-Bass.

24. Sample tasks to measure "new standards" in math, literacy (1991). *Education Week*. XI, *1*, p. 16.

25. Engle, S. H. and Longstreet, W. S. (1972). *A design for social education in the open classroom*. New York: Harper & Row, Chapter 10.

26. *Ibid.*, p. 175.

27. Babbie, E. R. (1979). *The practice of social research*. 2nd ed. Belmont, CA: Wadsworth.

28. Gordon, T. and Helmer O. (1966). Report on a long-range study. In *Social technology* (O. Helmer with Bernice Brown and Theodore Gordon). New York: Basic Books.

*9*

# Futures Studies: Fathoming a New Millennium

## Introduction

In the mid-1970s, as part of a study exploring attitudes toward the future,[1] a group of college freshmen were asked to imagine what the continued development of technology might mean to their lives in the year 2000. The compositions they wrote were pervaded by a sense of dread and inevitability. Fingers would be reduced to one on each hand for that is all that would be necessary to push the buttons on the electronic machines controlling human life on earth; the traditional family unit consisting of a wedded couple and their children would disintegrate; the Great Lakes would succumb to pollution and be dead; and atomic war would bring on a worldwide epidemic of cancer.

Now that we are nearly upon the year 2000, their predictions appear to be gross exaggerations, excesses of a generation that had "discovered" the negative side of technology and had overreacted. Nevertheless, those sad compositions were not written by some aberrant group of young men and women; they were the products of students admitted to one of the highly ranked universities in the nation — students whose future by all measures appeared to be full of bright prospects.

To a considerable extent, the way they felt then is still with us today. The pervasive sense of impending doom caused by technologies gone wild has become a part of our world view, our *weltanshauung*. With each new technology, the doubts have multiplied: When does human life really begin? When should the ill be allowed, or even "encouraged," to die? How can terrorism be stopped while maintaining a free and open society, or must society give up freedom for safety? How much power should the media be allowed in the elections of government

159

officials? Can we define a pollution-free environment, and do we really want to achieve such an environment? The need to deal with so many decisions fundamental to our values and conceptions of good living has grown more urgent with the passing years.

Our intragenerational disjunctures have become increasingly severe, while our willingness to think our problems through in quiet reflection for the long term has declined. We have grown accustomed to high levels of stimuli and quick changes of scenarios from one great, albeit brief, drama to another à la television. Even war, such as the ones we fought in Panama at the end of 1989 and in the Persian Gulf in 1991, has become a brief, televised event to be applauded or heckled as it unfolds—nearly indistinguishable from our sitcoms. Rather than participants, we have become the audience with our lives directed by a nameless, proverbial "they."

In this prolonged period of upheaval and uncertainty, what have the schools been doing to help youngsters participate in the complex decisions that will surely characterize their future adulthood? Indeed, is it within their power to make a difference? We cannot take it for granted that the schools or any other social institution can validly prepare children for the kinds of befuddling futures that have come to typify the twentieth century. The way we interpret "preparation for the future" can, however, vary greatly and, depending on the perspective taken, influence the "how" and "what" of education. If, for example, we perceive of the "what" of education in terms of processes for reflection and analyses, a greater potential clearly exists for making a significant difference on the future abilities of children to deal with unknowns than if the "what" remains memorized factual knowledge and translations into each child's own words.

Our views of education for the future are still in the making. While reconstructionists have linked their view of education to the remaking of society for a more democratic and better future, it remains unclear how existentialists or perennialists would face, say, the increasing crises of intragenerational disjunctures. As the future tumbles ever more quickly in on us, what visions of the future would essentialists or progressivists ultimately embrace? How would their vision affect the school's curriculum and its goals?

Furthermore, as the power of educational media grows and its availability increases, what will the impact of media be on how we pursue the goals of the curriculum? Will the video disk and computer-based instruction revolutionize teaching? Will children learn differently once they are in full command of the computer medium, or will computers be merely surrogate teachers pursuing traditional instructional methodologies? Will the future hold new conceptions of learning as yet difficult to envision?

This section explores our growing need to develop educated foresight with respect to probable futures and the ways that the curriculum can respond to an array of challenges. In this chapter, the discipline of futures studies will be viewed both historically and from the perspective of researching the future. The potential contributions to curriculum development that such research can make are discussed and several of today's critical trends are presented in terms of their likely impact on the future of education.

# The Emerging Need for Educated Foresight

### Preparing Children for the Future

Efforts to prepare children for their future lives as adults have been basic to education since the beginnings of recorded history. The first century historian, Flavius Josephus, wrote about education in the Middle East, indicating that some countries had established schools for all 6 to 13 year olds. The schools taught primarily reading, writing, and elementary mathematics, thought to prepare youngsters for the practical realities of life. In the ninth century, Charlemagne established schools in the monasteries and cathedrals to instruct the children of the common people and in his own palace at Aix-la-Chapelle to educate those of the nobility. Each group was to be prepared to assume its respective roles, roles essentially similar to those of preceding generations. On a more grandiose scale, Napoleon organized a state-controlled system of education from the primary grades through college. In this instance, too, education was designed to prepare the young for the life their parents were living, not for life continually involved in change and upheaval.

As recently as 1893, the Committee of Ten, whose work is discussed at length in Chapter 2, made recommendations for education suited to the world as it existed then, rather than for a world expecting rapid social and technological change. Among the committee's recommendations were stress on mental discipline; the omission of art, music, and physical education because these subjects were considered to be without disciplinary value;[2] and the equal weighting of the nine subjects[3] that had been included, which resulted in an equal allocation of time for each and the adoption of virtually indistinguishable instructional methodologies regardless of the subject taught.[4]

To prepare the young for their future, the Committee of Ten fostered a curriculum design that reflected the production, operations, and organization of the factory economy dominant in their day. At the time, it was a system of life that had yet to reach its peak. In less than a century, we have witnessed the decline of the factory economy and are already deeply involved in the so-called postindustrial revolution based on electronic microchips and a society where the production of goods is secondary to the offering of services. Indeed, in the United States, there is today an excess of labor. Machines and electronic robots have increased our manufacturing capabilities, freeing us up for other activities and rendering our traditional work ethic somewhat obsolete. This entire century has been an experience in significant, ongoing change.

How people were to deal with the numerous, often unforeseen cultural upheavals, which were already a part of the American experience in the latter years of the nineteenth century, was not considered by the Committee of Ten to be an appropriate concern for public education. College preparation and a view of knowledge as objective and generalized, rather than caught in the particulars of each passing event, permeated their efforts and the curriculum they produced. The intragenerational disjunctures that have come to typify twentieth century life were hardly a glimmer in the consciousness of educational planners then and, even now, are given little heed in the process of developing curriculum. There are, however, the beginnings of education oriented to the future and designed to prepare learners who, as one scholar put it, are "exposed to more information in a year than their grandparents were in a lifetime."[5]

## Cultural Inertia and Change

Much of what we do and believe is embedded deep within us as a part of growing up. Often, our attitudes and beliefs, acquired in the early stages of cultural development, are held at a subliminal level of consciousness. We are largely unaware of the numerous, culturally formed qualities that characterize our behavior. In this state of encapsulation,[6] in which we hardly see beyond our own cultural circumstances, we are prone to inertia and to following the traditions we have grown up with. While our minds may understand and even approve far-reaching technological change, the impact on how we live is ignored. All of us know someone who avoids computers as though they were the source of the plague even while acknowledging the power and benefits of computers. There is an intuitive resistance to the changes wrought, an unwillingness or, perhaps, incapacity to cope with new ways of working.

Cultural encapsulation and intragenerational disjunctures render us persistently unprepared to deal with future events. That is, the learning of our early years embeds powerfully into our cultural mindsets expectations about our lives that simply do not function with sufficient relevance in our adult world. Along with this, there is a widespread sense of resignation, even among teenagers, that it is "all" inevitable, that individual members of a society can exercise little influence over the directions of society.

Following tradition is, under today's circumstances, an expression of cultural inertia. The school's curriculum has exhibited extraordinary cultural inertia across the centuries, as we noted in our historical overview. Today's curriculum resists change while a veritable explosion of innovations characterizes our lives, and there is no sign of abatement.

## The Uniqueness of Change as We Experience It Today

Change is hardly a new phenomenon: the printing press increased access to knowledge; the Renaissance invigorated human minds and opened vast new areas of thought in architecture, music, painting, and science; and the Industrial Revolution extended the capacities and versatility of people by supplementing or replacing human energy with increasingly more powerful machinery. Even so, major innovations took decades and even centuries for their full impact to be felt. To illustrate, when Columbus crossed the Atlantic and opened a route to the New World in 1492, it was an historically significant occasion. However, his voyage and discoveries created neither significant nor immediate changes in the social orders of the day, in family living, or in the expansion or the applications of technology. For most people, modifications in their lifestyles arising from Columbus's discovery were nearly imperceptible.

Now, however, as biophysicist John Platt phrased it, ". . .the convergence of today's technological forces has produced a roaring waterfall of change."[7] If a group of Americans born in 1770 could have been transported to the United States in 1895, they would have found relatively little in the way of change. Farming was essentially a horse and human power affair; wells were still the chief source of water; medicine was improved but hardly the technological wonder of today. Aircraft, automobiles, electricity in the home, television, computers, nuclear energy, and in vitro fertilization are but a few of the innovations that have rocked the stability and inertia of our lives in the twentieth century. Kenneth Boulding, who was born in 1910, aptly described what has happened when he stated that his birth occurred in the middle of the world's history! He went on to say that ". . . our country represents the Great Median Strip running down the center of human history."[8] In his way, Boulding is describing the intragenerational disjunctures that have arisen as change and the acquisition of information accelerated during his lifetime. What efforts have been made to gain educated foresight have hardly kept pace with the explosion of new challenges that confronted one such as Boulding in the twentieth century. Our young are as unprepared today for their rapidly changing futures as they were in the days of Boulding's youth. What education for the twenty-first century may need most of all is a fundamental reconceptualization of its curricular and instructional paradigms so that confronting future uncertainty may be fully incorporated into the goals of education and the activities of schooling. At the very least, we need to help people acquire the tools to study the future.

## The Qualitative Aspects of Change

In addition to the continuing acceleration in the rate of change, the very nature of change itself has undergone major, qualitative differences. For example, wars were once experienced directly only by the combatants; civilians received second-hand, often censored reports days after the battles actually took place. As the televised medium has gained in picture and sound quality while simultaneously improving in mobility, war has been brought into the livingroom. Civilians experience "nearly firsthand" the realities of war along with an ongoing series of commentaries by news reporters of every ilk. The very way war is experienced has changed with the continued development of television.

Modern life has been imbued by changes that have reached deep within our mind's eye, modifying the very nature of our conceptions of life. In-the-womb surgery, surrogate motherhood, ova transplants, and major organ transplants have become commonplace, shaking the very foundations of our understanding of human life and when it begins. The fact that the average life span has increased from

47.3 years in 1900 to more than 75 years in 1986 has meant a fundamental change in how we view old age and aging.

Our understanding of place and of what it means to really be somewhere, as well as the significance we attach to distance, has been conceptually transformed in just a few short decades. Aircraft now on our drawing board could carry passengers from Europe to America in less than an hour. Already, millions of people have traveled thousands of miles to other continents. Their planes land in cities from Singapore to Budapest, and sometimes their stays are no more than a few short hours in an airport. Under such circumstances, have they really experienced Singapore or Budapest? Were they really there? The very idea that criteria might need to be established for determining whether an appearance in a place qualifies as a "stay" in that place points to what technological advances have done to some of our basic conceptions about living in this world. Furthermore, moon landings and unmanned satellites exploring outer space have forged for us new conceptions not only of our place in the universe, but the place of our universe among universes!

Hardison, in his work *Disappearing Through the Skylight: Culture and Technology in the Twentieth Century*,[9] suggests that a trend is developing that involves the disappearance of concepts once taken for granted—for example, nature, reality, and even humanity. Certainly, nature in terms of quarks, lightning speeds, and surrealistic visions of earth from outer space is a profoundly different "nature" from the one extolled by Rousseau in the 1700s or Wordsworth in the 1800s. The uniqueness that we have ascribed to our humanity in the universe continues to slip away as our expectations for finding extraterrestrial, intelligent beings grow. And reality no longer needs the confirmation of our senses for acceptance as reality.

## Experience Compression

As the number of innovations in communications, transportation, manufacturing, and data management have mounted, the phenomenon of experience compression[10] has become more apparent in our every day lives. Experience compression is the detachment of events from their existential context owing to the advances of technology. Temporal sequence, geographic contiguity, and cause and effect are among the rational bases that have traditionally linked events within a real world context and that have now been superseded by advances in technology. Many of our experiences today seem to be disassociated from reasonable relationships; it is as though they had been isolated and haphazardly placed in a collage of disparate events.

Experience compression challenges rationality by undermining the balanced interplay of our senses, our abilities to engage in inductive analyses based on the evidence of our senses, and our established systems of beliefs about how the world functions. It is one of numerous kinds of uncertainty confronting us all. Consider the incongruity of traveling at nearly 600 miles an hour 39,000 feet above the ground enjoying a hot meal not unlike one served in a restaurant near home while a storm rages miles below. Consider the abridgement of geographic space as televised newscasts bring into our livingrooms a series of unrelated events from famine in Ethiopia to a crushed revolution in China, from a terrorist's bomb threat in Columbia to the fall of the Berlin Wall. Consider observing hundreds, possibly thousands, of such events all treated with equal importance and superficiality. Consider the amassing of so much information that individuals cannot cope with it all and tend to reject its use as a basis for reaching decisions. Each of these examples, in its own way, is a form of experience compression. Each abridges our sensory data; each undermines in some way our abilities to engage in inductive analyses; and each throws our perceptions of the world around us into a state of uncertainty.

There have been and continue to be countless events of experience compression. They have contributed significantly to the intragenerational disjunctures that increasingly characterize people of the twentieth century. The roots of what Alvin Toffler called "future shock"[11] are deeply embedded in experiences that seemingly defy our traditional understanding of reality.

Sadly, we appear to be no better prepared to deal with the future today than we were in 1970 when Toffler coined the term. The cultural inertia exhibited by the schools, especially in the curricula followed, may not be surprising, but it is troublesome as people face a future of nonlinear, complex, and often incongruous events. Whether one is a technological determinist who believes that whatever will be will be or one is committed to the belief that humankind can and must be in control of technological developments, a curriculum that does not take the future seriously into account is destined to become quickly irrelevant.

## Educated Foresight for an Era of Hyperturbulence

In view of the continuing proliferation of technosocial, global developments, it has become increasingly important for educators to extend and to supplement their grasp of the future and its significance for the school's curriculum today. While historical hindsight, that is, a knowledge of our educational past, provides a helpful basis for curriculum development, it is even more critical today to acquire what we have labeled "educated foresight."[12] This term refers to the ability to understand the future significance of rapidly germinating developments in the technosocial milieu of our times.

Not only are we in the midst of numerous intragenerational disjunctures sustained by experience compression and a veritable explosion of knowledge, we are confronted by hyperturbulence as well. "Hyperturbulence" is defined by Selsky and McCann as "the condition that results when available resources and institutions prove inadequate to deal with the speed and diversity of change."[13] Nowhere is hyperturbulence felt more deeply than in our schools and among our educators. It is not simply a case of not having enough up-to-date technology available in the schools, although that is the situation even among more affluent school districts; there is also the question of not having adequate training for the competent use of technology and, importantly, of having a curriculum that makes little provision for its substantive use. There is among us a pervasive sense of losing control over the course of technological development while the schools seem hardly able to stay afloat.

### Futures Studies for Curriculum Planning

We see futures studies from a twofold perspective. First, we view it as an important area of study for students, one seriously neglected in today's curriculum. How to incorporate futures research methodologies and their results into school study ought to be a major issue for curricular experts. Instead, it has been ignored.

Secondly, we view futures studies as the bases for acquiring a set of tools particularly important to the development of educated foresight and, thus, to the competence of curriculum workers in the twenty-first century. The achievement of a relevant, more effective curriculum is, to a considerable extent, dependent on having administrators, supervisors, and classroom personnel who are both able to engage in futures research and willing to use the results in educational decision making. We need to recognize now that in the new millenium, the curriculum worker's approach to the future, however adequate or inadequate it may be, will have a significant impact on the quality of curriculum developed.

Preparing for the future means developing intellectual and social capabilities that will lead to greater control over the course of technology. It means for both students and experts alike learning to cope with uncertainty. It also means being as knowledgeable as possible about future directions while recognizing how much is yet to be learned.

The curriculum represents our joint decisions about how we should prepare our children not only for their own possible futures but also for the maximum benefit to society. Futures studies, and the research procedures that they support, have the potential to sensitize professional educators to alternative futures. It is up to educators, and of course the public, to determine how the curriculum can best contribute to the achievement of a better future. To be knowledgeable about the future, however uncertain, is an exceedingly important characteristic in educational planning and decision making, but it is one that has long been neglected.

## Researching the Future

### Futures Studies as a Developing Discipline

The study of alternative futures—and how to achieve the best possible tomorrows—is a relatively new discipline, although writers and philosophers have speculated about the future in centuries past. Futures studies and related research constitute a discipline concerned with the development of knowledge about the future. Its purpose is to lay a foundation for improved decision making in various realms of human endeavor, including government, education, and industry. Of course, the values we hold and the directions we believe most productive for humankind are bound to affect the nature of the decisions we make. Nevertheless, the organized study of and projected knowledge about the future can contribute significantly to our choosing wisely among alternatives.

### Premises Underlying Futures Studies

Professional scholars who probe trends and their probable implications and outcomes use the term *futures* rather than *future* studies or research. The plural form is favored by these scholars because what humans decide to do and how they follow through on their decisions determine which of various alternative or possible futures come into being.

The study of the future is concerned with neither reforming the past nor minimizing the flaws that disrupt the present. The basic ideas involved in futures studies and related research differ from those associated with conventional planning in a number of ways. The following is a set of premises underlying futures studies:

1. The future is not predetermined; we create it by what we do.

2. As a corollary of the preceding point, futures planning is governed by our values and beliefs.

3. The future emerges from the present; hence, the present is an important basis for futures studies.

4. Futures planning is not undertaken to reform the present; its focus is on the possibilities and consequences involved in our plans for better tomorrows.

5. In addition to statistical analyses and projections per se, futures research includes the rational study of anticipated developments, their likely results, and determining how desirable developments can be devised.

6. Humankind is currently capable of developing criteria for establishing the meaning of "better" for the future.

In fine, the study of the future focuses on creating better physical, social, and mental environments for humans.

### Early Background

Although the disciplined study of alternate futures is primarily a twentieth century phenomenon, there is substantial evidence as to the beginnings of and interest in futures studies. A number of examples exist from ancient and medieval times in the writings, commentaries, and auguries of seers, astrologers, and religious leaders.

A dramatist, philosopher–historian, poet, and satirist who personified early interest in tomorrow was Francois Marie Arouet (1694–1778), better known under the pen name of Voltaire. A study of his early writings indicates that he may have been the first person to have conceived of the concept of alternative futures. Voltaire proposed the use of the word "prevoyance" to describe futures research or speculation.

A man with whom Voltaire had some conspicuous arguments, Pierre-Louis Maupertius, was also a pioneer in the field. He wrote in his *Lettres* that for foreseeing the future, "The first means that presents itself is to derive from the present state the most probable consequences for the future."[14] His comment has such a contemporary quality that it might well have been made by one of today's futures research scholars.

A man widely recognized and respected for his knowledge of eighteenth century foreign policy, J.L. Favier (1711–1784) was perhaps the first person actually to engage in the study of the future. He was commissioned by Louis XV to apply his conjectures regarding coming events to the diverse futures that might be expected to confront the French monarchy. His treatise, completed in 1773, was interesting and comprehensive. It did, however, have a major shortcoming: Favier failed to foresee the imminent French Revolution!

A final individual meriting attention in this brief overview of early beginnings is H.G. Wells (1866–1946). His extensive writings, often in the form of science fiction such as *The War of the Worlds* and *The Time Machine*, forecast with surprising accuracy the shape of things to come in technology and society. Among his provocative statements: "Every disastrous thing that has happened in the past twenty years was clearly foretold by a galaxy of writers and thinkers twenty years ago."[15] Shortly before he died, a note of dispair crept into his thinking. In *Mind at the End of Its Tether* (1946), he noted that man's scientific advances were fatally contradicting his social and intellectual maturity.

### Current Developments in Futures Studies

Since the 1940s, futures studies have begun to reach the status of a respected and widely cited discipline. As a specialized form of inquiry, its early objectives involved the planning of wartime operations such as amphibious landings, bombing raids, and the probable consequences of dropping atomic bombs. Industry as well as the military and the government began to rely on tools modeling the future such as those discussed below.

By 1967, a thoughtful and futures-oriented scholar, Olaf Helmer, concluded that a wholly new attitude toward our futures has become apparent among policy planners. He went on to state that ". . .intuitive gambles are being replaced by a systematic analysis of the opportunities the future has to offer."[16] Helmer's views were reflected in the programs of many "think tanks" of the era, including the RAND Corporation which had begun to draw attention to "futures think" as early as the 1940s. This was the period when the Systems Development Corporation came into being. Only a short while later, in 1961, Herman Kahn created the Hudson Institute. Other centers such as The Institute for the Future began to appear.

In this brief overview of recent developments in futures study, the RAND "Report on a Long-Range Forecasting Study"[17] conducted between 1963 and 1964 by Theodore Gordon and Olaf Helmer merits special attention. It is a fascinating work in retrospect because the authors anticipated 130 scientific achievements due to be made along with a number of items that have already become reality. Among their predictions were moon landings and heart transplants.

In the last several decades, a number of American business organizations have begun to delve into futures research. To stitch together the complex webs of policy decisions, the Bell Telephone Company developed the "systems approach." The Singer Company, General Electric, Westinghouse, and various automobile companies developed in-house agencies that employed so-called policy research advisers. By the mid 1970s, methodical speculation about the future had become widespread both in the United States and overseas. The Club of Rome published *The Limits to Growth*.[18] The Futuribles Center was opened in Paris, and teams of scholars were at work in Britain, Germany, and elsewhere in Europe. Magazines such as *The Futurist* and the British journal *Futures*[19] also made their debut.

## Tools, Tactics and Definitions for Futures Research

A variety of tools and tactics for analyzing likely future developments have been perfected in the post–World War II period. Different approaches to *trends analysis* have been especially important in futures studies. It is necessary, however to lay a common basis for discussions about futures studies. We shall therefore first clarify what is meant by such terms as "trend," "fad," "issue," and "event."

An *event* is a discrete and confirmable occurrence in the past, the present, or the future. Conceptually, an event occurs in static time; that is, it does not continue or repeat or even transform itself over time but begins and ends within a relatively brief period.

A *trend* is the movement over time of a related series of events. Trends are dynamic in time relative to events, which are considered static. Because trends depend on the overlapping and interrelatedness of events, their parameters may be obscure and fuzzy rather than discrete.

In futures discussions, trends are usually identified with regard to social, technological, economic, or political characteristics. In some works, biological and psychological trends are included as well. However, most researchers tend to include biological developments with technological progress and consider psychological characteristics as a subset of social trends. These categories are a way of organizing those trends having substantial impact on the course of human behavior and on events that are linked to human behavior. Trends are expected to have long-term durability, which, importantly, distinguishes them from fads.

*Fads* may be mistaken for trends, but a "true" trend will significantly and permanently change some notable characteristics of human behavior, whereas fads are of an impermanent nature. A fad may capture one's fancy and create a furor but it has no lasting impact.

In the context of the preceding discussion, it should be noted that a singular series of events, that is, a series of events that occur rarely or in temporal isolation, may have a significant impact on the characteristics of human behavior. They do not, however, occur in dynamic time; they will not persist or repeat or transform themselves over an extended period. A devastating tornado occurring in an eastern city such as New York is an example of a singular series of events. Such a series of events may not occur again for decades or even centuries but will nevertheless have a significant impact on the social, political, and economic futures of New Yorkers.

An *issue* is a controversy arising from an event or a series of events. The importance of the issue is, of course, directly related to the events from which it arises.

Notwithstanding the effort here to distinguish among events, fads, and trends, the determination of each depends ultimately on the structures and objectives established when seeking trends and is thus always somewhat subjective. Although research in trends analysis is weighted toward measurable data, the overarching structures for organizing information and ascertaining trends are heuristic in nature. The types of categories for which information is sought and the relative importance given to different kinds of information may have some reasonable bases, but other bases would work as well. Often, it is the subjective judgment of a group of experts that determines how and why a trends analysis is structured in the way that it is.

The following diagram is an effort to partially summarize the preceding definitional discussion.

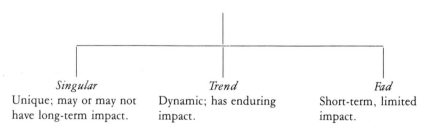

A related series of events may be:

| *Singular* | *Trend* | *Fad* |
| --- | --- | --- |
| Unique; may or may not have long-term impact. | Dynamic; has enduring impact. | Short-term, limited impact. |

*Trends analysis* refers to the set of procedures applied to a series of events to determine whether they comprise a trend and, if they do, the nature and direction of that trend. In futures studies, "critical" trends are those trends identified as likely to have a significant impact on the directions of a major institution. Critical trends often serve as categories of activities to be watched closely for any important changes in direction. In this sense, critical trends provide the underlying structure of a trends analysis.

When feasible, objective and measurable data are used in trends analysis. A distinction must be made between "forecasting" and "predicting." "Forecasting" involves specific calculations used to determine the directions of a trend. Measurable inputs are necessary to engage in forecasting. "Predicting" is a broader term that includes such vague conceptions of seeing into the future as "presage," "augury," and "prophecy." The prediction that everyone will own a personal computer by the year 2000 is partly based on an intelligent person's reaction to the growing importance and power of computers and partly on some wishful thinking about what an ideal future might look like. A forecast would, instead, determine the number of computers purchased annually over, say, the last five years, and the annual increase in the rate of purchase and then project the proportion of the population likely to own a personal computer by the year 2000 given the measurable data.

Trends analysis is directed primarily toward forecasting. However, the research tools now available are often incapable of producing measurable data about critical trends. For example, the drive toward a vaguely understood "democracy" that continues to sweep Eastern Europe in the early 1990s is certainly a critical trend but one contemplated beforehand by very few experts. It remains a poorly defined, but critical trend resistant to forecasts. The emotions of crowds demanding reform from their governments do not offer the stability, clear evidential parameters, or relevant quantifiable data needed for reliable forecasting. The qualitative prediction is often a necessary aspect of trends analysis.

### Linear or Classic Projection

One of the more straightforward and simplistic tools used in trends analysis is the linear or classic projection. The first stage of the linear projection is planning. This involves collecting descriptive data about current circumstances. For example, if a middle school is to be constructed, the number of youngsters attending elementary school would be obtained. Or, if a state is attempting to maintain a level of teacher certification equal to future needs, statistics relevant to the current birth rate would be collected.

The second stage in the linear projection approach involves making decisions and implementation. In this stage, allowances for lag time are made. That is, certain changes in the first-stage description are expected to occur in the time needed for implementation, and these are factored into the analysis.

The third stage or implemented plan is the future. Thus, if 400 children attended three elementary schools and there were a normal attrition rate of ten percent a year but an expected increase in the overall enrollment of five percent per year and three years were necessary to complete the project, the expected population for the middle school would be based on a linear analysis of these facts.

### Alternative Futures Projection

This approach provides for multiple possible futures. It is clearly more open-ended and complex than the linear projection. The data collected from the present are perceived as being capable of supporting multiple futures. Of course, in hindsight, there will be only one future but, from the perspective of the present, multiple directions are possible. Dynamic and creative involvement in the development of a complex future is basic to this approach. Linear projection often lends itself to the supine acceptance of some future plan as though it were inevitable; alternative projection involves the idea that we can direct or control to some considerable degree the shape of things to come.

## Cross-Impact Analysis

By the early 1970s, cross-impact analysis had come into general use. This involves a more comprehensive approach to the analysis of the future than a mere examination of possible alternative developments. It is based on the idea that significant interrelationships exist among our various future projections. For example, a future plan based on the widespread use of solar energy would necessarily affect the importation and pricing of oil, which in turn would affect our economic future. In its more technical applications, cross-impact analysis may employ quadratic equations to probe possible interrelationships among events likely to take place in the future.

## Bibliographic Analysis

As a research tool, bibliographic analysis involves implementing a system for collecting materials appearing in certain preselected journals or magazines. The purpose of such a system is to discern trends on the basis of entries found in relevant written materials. Bibliographic analysis is typically used in trends analysis. The preselected journals as well as the design of the system are logically related to the kinds of trends sought. The Higher Education Media Scan Reference System, designed by Bissonnete and Dutton,[20] is an example of a bibliographic analysis system designed to detect certain kinds of trends in higher education. Key words are used to describe and retrieve articles appearing in *The Chronicle of Higher Education*, *Academe*, *Higher Education and National Affairs*, *Change*, the ERIC-ASHE series, and *New Directions for Institutional Research*. The determination of which journals to review was made on the basis of those having the widest circulation or the greatest respect among professionals in the field of higher education. The key words were selected on the basis of those areas of activity deemed most important to the future of higher education.

## Environmental Scanning

The technique of environmental scanning involves the systematic collection of information about the *external* circumstances and conditions associated with an organization or institution to detect the development of relevant social, technological, economic, and political trends likely to impact on the future of the organization or institution. Environmental scanning has been widely used by large corporations as well as by higher education as part of their planning processes. It is described by Brown and Weiner as "a kind of radar to scan the world systematically and signal the new, the unexpected, the major and the minor."[21] It is, in effect, a scanning of the environment for trends that may affect an institution's mission.

Over the past few decades, nationally based scanning networks have been established. Among the most widely used are those supported by the United Way of America and the American Council of Life Insurance Underwriters. These two networks support a number of public domain databases including legal–political trends, social demographic trends, and technological trends. It should be noted that bibliographic analysis is used in the building of databases by both networks. Raw data and analyses interpreting the meaning of the raw data are made available to the public.

Morrison and Held[22] of the School of Education at the University of North Carolina have described the process for establishing an environmental scanning system that is typically followed. To get started, key decision makers are often interviewed to determine those trends and events expected to be critical to the institution's environment in the future. The Delphi technique, discussed later, may also be used to achieve more objective results than are usually possible with direct interviews. Brainstorming sessions held among the leaders of the organization may be another approach followed in the initial identification of critical trends. It may be used alone or in combination with other interview techniques. Searches of bibliographic resources may also identify trends.

In this first step, according to Morrison and Held, the trends need to be stated in measurable terms so that the data will be amenable to objective analysis. Furthermore, the participants are expected to think broadly across the major sectors of human concern (i.e., social, technological, economic, and political) as well as on levels ranging from the local to the global as may suit the objectives of the trends analysis. In addition, the identified critical trends need to be expressed in as simple, clear, and straightforward a manner as possible so that their interpretation will be consistent among all the participants. An abbreviated set of examples follow:

**Critical Trends with Educational Relevance**
*Social*
Percent of annual increase/decrease in school-age children locally; countywide; statewide

Percent of children attending school living in poverty according to United States government guidelines locally; countywide; statewide

Ratio of minorities/mainstream youngsters locally; countywide; statewide

*Technological*
Percent of classrooms having microcomputers locally; countywide; statewide; nationally

Percent of increase in microcomputers expected annually for coming decade locally; countywide; statewide; nationally

*Economic*
Percent of increase in school tax levies expected in coming decade

Likely continuing/new sources for increased private support

New industries moving into local areas

*Political*
Ratio of conservatives/liberals on school board
Number of members in the local PTA

The result of this first step is the identification of critical trends whose changes could have a significant impact on the future of the institution and about which data are to be collected. In essence, the structure for environmental scanning has been established. Each critical trend will be monitored continually, and the raw data will be analyzed and interpreted using linear projections, cross-impact analysis, or other available procedures.

In the second stage, intended to increase the likelihood of catching a change in a trend's direction, participants develop a list of events that, if they were to occur, would significantly affect at least one of the trends or, more directly, the future of the institution. An event might include a nuclear plant disaster causing the largest local employer to permanently close down or the invention of a brain scanner capable of determining the intellectual potential of children without intervening cultural variables such as those posed when reading is necessary for measuring I.Q. Those charged with scanning would be especially alert to the identified events occurring.

The third stage involves the analysis and interpretation of the data collected during environmental scanning. A 1988 report on the future of work issued by the United Way of America[23] contains a representative example of this stage. Eight critical trends were established for scanning. These include: (1) personal and family concerns; (2) underused groups; (3) education, training, and retraining; (4) the corporate environment; (5) small business; (6) the global marketplace; (7) automation; and (8) employment prospects. Based on an analysis of the raw data, United Way presents a picture of these trends for the year 2000. For example, under personal and family concerns, it is suggested that personal and family issues will increasingly affect the workplace. Subtrends supporting this main effect include a continuing rise in the number of working mothers, a continuing increase in the number of dependent elderly, and a continuing rise in work-related illnesses. Each of the subtrends is based on an analysis of the raw data collected during environmental scanning.

*The Delphi Technique* represents a controlled means of combining the advantages of a survey instrument with panel discussions held among experts. Several rounds of questionnaires are presented to a selected group of experts. Each expert responds independently of the others to the first round, which usually represents an effort to determine the degree of consensus among the experts with regard to the identification of critical trends, the likelihood they will occur, the time frame for occurrence, and their expected impact.

The second round of questionnaires shares with each of the experts the overall results of the first round and invites the experts to reconsider their first responses and make whatever adjustments appear appropriate. A third round repeating the process may follow. In effect, the experts are interacting with each other while having ample time to consider their responses and being free from social influences arising from personality differences. One variation of this procedure would have the experts meet for face-to-face discussions after having engaged in several Delphi rounds.

*The Scenario Method* is not strictly a research method in the traditional, scientifically based conception of such methods. It is nevertheless an extremely useful planning tool and involves the study of sequences of possible events as a way of presenting viable alternatives during the decision-making process.[24] It takes the products derived from other research efforts and integrates them into holistic sets of occurrences. As the well-known futurist Herman Kahn noted, scenarios are really not forecasts even though they may make use of results from cross-impact analyses, the Delphi technique, and the like.[25] In the context of the definitions presented above, the scenario is a synthesized prediction based on prior research. It may also be conceived as a model of the future with multiple models being viable.

The purpose of a scenario will impact significantly on its final form. If a scenario is to be used to explore possible futures in an objective fashion, the models it presents will be quite different from those of a scenario intended to represent the ideal case or, possibly, the worst case. In a sense, the scenario is a tool that helps us to study not only the possibilities of the future but also our subjective involvement with those possibilities.

Numerous tools besides those mentioned above extend the power of human reason. Among these are:

The *computer*, the most important electronic tool presently available to futurists.

*Simulation models* based on mathematical models with equations to describe given situations in the future.

*Experience compression technique*, analogous to the conduct of a workshop in which participants from various fields discuss implications of probable events likely to take place in education, government, business, or industry in, for instance, a forthcoming 12-month period.

*PERT* (Program Evaluation and Review Techniques), a method for planning and developing new products rapidly.[26]

## Thinking about the Future

Human reason is certainly the most important tool for futurists. Like other researchers, the futurist may dispense with conventional procedures, engaging instead in "lateral reasoning" or probing unexpected "system breaks." Today we are surrounded by a "mega" set of perplexing crossroads; numerous decisions must be made concerning the kind of futures we hope to achieve.

Analyses of tomorrow's world may be undertaken from one of several spheres or perspectives: social futures, psychological futures (often included in social futures), economic futures, political futures, technological futures, and biological futures (often included in technological futures).[27] Of course, these perspectives are as inseparable as the parts of a human being. Whatever specific categories we settle on will help us to organize our study of the future and to view its possibilities from different vantage points. In essence, these future spheres of critical trends are at the base of a set of significant questions about what is possible, desirable, or even inevitable in our technological futures, in our social futures, and in our economic futures.

The future spheres lay out a kind of map describing what we shall think about, but they offer little guidance concerning how we shall approach the analysis of each sphere. In 1980, the Carnegie Council of Policy Studies in Higher Education issued a report entitled *Three Thousand Futures*.[28] In it are discussed those considerations that should inform one's thinking.[29] First, one must think about what is already largely determined because it already exists. Facilities, governance structures, and cultural heritage are among the major items that might be reviewed in this first approach to thinking about the future.

Then, one needs to think about those events or changes that are *likely* to occur although they are by no means certain. For example, a decline in new housing starts is likely to occur after the year 2000 because of an expected population decline among the age groups normally associated with new housing construction. Of course, this is a linear projection that may not hold up given the development of other related circumstances such as a growing trend among single heads of household to purchase their own home.

In this latter context, it is worth reminding the reader of the distinction noted before between *forecasting* and *predicting*. Forecasting involves projecting the future on the basis of the data on hand; prediction makes a metaphorical leap beyond the data to develop scenarios akin to prophecy.[30] It does not take much imagination to forecast a steady increase in the number of day care centers in the 1990s; predicting, however, that machines will be equipped with artificially developed bacteria and electronic computers in a new kind of synthesis that will endow real powers of intelligence upon the machines does involve going well beyond what is known now. The prediction may be highly unlikely, but many significant events of the future were not forecast because, on the basis of what was known, they were highly unlikely. The oil crisis of the 1970s initiated by OPEC was one such event. Few experts of the day had forecast a sudden drop in the supply of oil and the shocking rise in oil prices that resulted.

Another aspect of thinking about the future involves reflecting imaginatively about what might happen, whether desirable or not, that is either unknown or highly unlikely. In a sense, this is a form of prediction as one finds it in science fiction and as we have discussed it previously. An atomic war radically changes the face of social life and the futurist tries to predict what the changes will be; or a major new invention makes the production and distribution of solar energy very inexpensive and the possible impact of this innovation on our economic lives needs to be explored.

Finally, thinking about the future needs to involve an analysis of how current leadership and institutions are likely to react to a set of new events. Is the leadership or institution effective? Are new institutional policies needed? Indeed, are new institutions needed? Is the institution threatened and, if so, is it worth protecting?

### Structuring a Futures Study

There are numerous ways to approach a study of the future. However, we present a comprehensive system for studying the future that pulls together the various preceding discussions in one holistic procedure (Table 9.1).

**TABLE 9.1**  *Thinking about the Future*

| | Futures Spheres | | | | | |
|---|---|---|---|---|---|---|
| *Steps in Thinking about the Future* | *Bio-Futures* | *Socio-Futures* | *Econo-Futures* | *Poli-Futures* | *Techno-Futures* | *Psycho-Futures* |
| What exists now? | | | | | | |
| Forecast likely changes. | | | | | | |
| Predict imaginative reflection. | | | | | | |
| Reactions to change of leadership and institutions. | | | | | | |

Developing Forecast/Prediction Data

linear projections,
alternative futures projection,
cross-impact analyses,
trend impact analysis,
Delphi expert surveys,
simulation models,
scenarios,
etc.

Potential Outcomes
(Future forcasts/prediction)

We have not included education among our futures spheres because we consider all of the studies derived from the other spheres as contributors to the futures study for education. In other words, education serves to synthesize the other spheres into one holistic preparation for the future. Table 9.1 models the interactive activities that we would pursue in our effort to develop the synthesis.

### The Validity of "Futures" Forecasts

Because this chapter focuses on the need for educated foresight with a bearing on the curriculum as well as on more conventional educational prevision, it seems fitting to comment on the success with which scientists and other scholars anticipated both general and educational developments that had not yet transpired. Among general developments forecast in a poll of scholars conducted by John Elfreth Watkins[31] in 1889–1900 were:

> air conditioning
> color photography
> 150-mph trains
> disappearance of certain animal species
> universal free education
> fast food shops
> aircraft
> radio
> global TV
> free food and clothing for the underprivileged

All of these items were forecast at least four years before they actually occurred.[31]

Since the late 1960's, contemporary savants such as Daniel Bell and Konrad Lorenz have accurately foreseen future developments, a number of which now threaten humanity. Professor Bell, for example, identified urban decay, social conflict, economic imbalances, and diminution of the economic and military superiority of America.[32] Lorenz also presciently tallied the threats of overpopulation, damage to the environment, overuse and abuse of technology, internecine global commercial competition, and the breakdown of traditions that had provided much of the glue binding our cultures together. Any one of these predictions could become a hub of curriculum development.

Valid examples of educational forecasts from two decades ago can be found in the consensus among over fifty scholars obtained for a 1971 U.S. Office of Education study.[33] Images of the future that, for the most part, were correctly foreseen included: lifelong educational resources for those persons who became unemployed due to technological change; both greater community and corporate participation and penetration in education; upward extension of secondary schooling to encompass at least two years of college; teacher preparation stressing a knowledge of social and curricular change; increased interest in the school's rather than the child's accountability; research regarding the substantial increase in microelectronic equipment in the classroom; national data banks preserving student records; attacks on the dropout problems; education for mature and senior learners; and more carefully planned and directed work for paraprofessionals' preparation. Virtually all of the images scholars had in the 1970–1971 U.S.O.E. study have become realities.

### The Importance of Futures Studies for Curriculum Planning

We believe that alternative futures can be identified with considerable validity and that it is worthwhile to do so; that human reason, projections of various kinds, simulations, scenarios, and other tools used in futures studies can contribute to increased control over the future; and that awareness about *potential futures* can help us individually and as a society to achieve a better future.

We further believe that futures studies can contribute to making education more relevant and responsive to the needs of today's children. For instance, a cross-impact approach to curriculum planning could be based, say, in the field of the social studies of biology. The socioethical implications of advances in biology could be explored through scenarios of likely futures. Cross-impact analyses exploring critical trends in international relations could contribute to the development of a social studies curriculum from a totally different perspective. Instructional examples could be provided by current trends such as *glasnost* (openness) and *perestroika* (restructuring) in the former Soviet Union.

If content based on futures study were added to the curriculum, what content would be deleted to allow time for the study of critical trends? In biology, what should our approach be with respect to such controversial items as the current AIDS epidemic or ova transplants? The nature of the curricular response and whether there should be a curricular response would certainly be at issue. Even so, the very consideration of the question opens the mind toward future development.

The tools mentioned above need to be used by educators as they engage in the processes of curriculum study. Scenarios, the Delphi technique, cross-impact analysis, and the other identified procedures are of particular value when a conceptually new curriculum design is either being sought or considered for adoption. Active involvement in researching and thinking about the future contributes to the intellectual readiness necessary to free ourselves from our own cultural inertia, especially the inertia that appears to be an inherent part of our curriculum design. With a little tongue in cheek, we cannot help but think of our minds as being like parachutes—that is, functioning best when they are open.

The growing suspicion that we may have lost control of technological change and the futures instigated by innovation mandates that we educate ourselves with due regard for the shape of tomorrow. To borrow a term from Gulliver's travels, this is a Brobdingnagian task if we are to live successfully in a *utopian* rather than a *dystopian* age. Since Thomas More wrote *Utopia* in 1516, life on this imaginary little island has personified perfection—moral, social, and political. A dystopia is the exact reverse, and we do risk dystopia.

The futures approach, to retain its validity in the processes of curriculum planning, requires that certain of its principles be carefully maintained by teachers, supervisors, and administrators. These principles are essential as educated foresight is exercised in plans to improve teaching and learning.

First, there should be a multidirectional flow of information among educators and among experts of the various futures spheres as they work together in groups concerned with program improvements. Second, the problems, quandaries, and projected program developments considered should involve all parties concerned — parents, paraprofessionals, custodians, carefully selected representatives of community agencies, and competent consultants, in addition to the permanent school staff. Upon occasion student teachers and, perhaps, mature learners enrolled in the schools may need to be included. Third, the participants should be governed by carefully examined and clearly delineated values, and fourth, they should be governed by democratic group processes. Fifth, a distinct effort must be made by all the group participants to prepare themselves intellectually so that their contribution to futures planning is significant because it is based on a study of probable developments in the environments of the school districts involved.

### Concluding Comment: The Curriculum Should Anticipate the Tomorrows of a Changing World

Humankind has experienced seven major vectors of change or turning points since 5000 B.C. The first of these vectors occurred when people began to record and accumulate their knowledge — "knowing" began — when people realized they were thinking human beings and began to think and to work together.

Around 8000 B.C. agriculture was devised and many former hunters became farmers — the second vector of change. Other major intellectual watersheds include the development of religions (500 B.C.); the aesthetic era of the Renaissance (1300 to 1400 A.D.); the vast changes in production during the industrial revolution, which got under way around 1800; and the revolution of the twentieth century when scientific developments enabled us to begin methodically to "discover discoveries." From 1900 to date, as Alvin Toffler pointed out, we have been riding a high cresting information society wave — an increasingly microbioelectronic era, which is a seventh major turning point in human history.

### Educating for the Eighth Wave

We are already experiencing a modification of the information wave as we find our lives changing due to the impact of the microcomputer, related technologies, and the flood of information with which we and our children must cope. Hopefully, the deluge of electronic development will be used to support our going forward on an *eighth* wave — one on the crest of which we shall move from mere information or knowledge to wisdom based on knowledge and during which our heightening consciousness changes us from mere *human* beings to *humankind* beings.

The chapter that follows emphasizes the importance of education as we cross the threshold of a new millennium. It explores the various emerging elements on our planet which demand that teachers acquire the educated foresight and the broad command of knowledge that will enable them to help our young learners join us in creating a mature global wisdom and societies in which we do the right things for the right reasons!

## QUESTIONS FOR DISCUSSION AND REFLECTION

1. What major difference is there between preparing students for their future as adults in Napoleon's time and now?

2. What causes cultural inertia and how is it related to intragenerational disjuncture?

3. What are the effects of experience compression?

4. What are the premises underlying futures studies?

5. Define the following in terms of future research: *event*, *trend*, *fad*, and *issue*.

6. What is your understanding of trends analysis?

7. What is a critical trend? Can you identify a critical trend in education today? What important changes do you expect from this trend? Are you predicting or forecasting?

8. When would a particular issue be important to future studies?

9. What are the available methods of futures studies?

10. Describe the stages of classic or linear projection.

11. What advantages and disadvantages can you see in alternative futures projection?

12. What does cross-impact analysis add to the field of futures analyses?

13. What does environmental scanning involve? What reservations should we have about nationally based scanning networks?

14. Name eight critical trends that have been established for scanning on a national scale. Can you develop a list for educational scanning?

15. Describe the Delphi technique. Its advantages have been discussed in the chapter, but what are its possible disadvantages?

16. Can you identify interest groups in our society likely to support curriculum designs based on future studies? Explain your choices.

17. What groups do you think would *not* support curriculum designs based on futures studies, and why?

18. Choose one sphere and two ways of developing futures. Pick one trend to analyze.

## RECOMMENDED READINGS

Bell, Daniel. *The coming of post industrial society: A venture in social forecasting*. New York: Basic Books, 1972.

Boulding, Kenneth E. *The world as a total system*. Beverly Hills, CA: Sage, 1985.

Boyer, Ernest L. The future of American education: New realities, making connections. *Kappa Delta Pi Record* (Fall, 1988):6–12.

Brown, Lester R., et al. *The state of the world: 1989*. New York: W.W. Norton, 1989.

Cetron, Marvin J., et al. Class of 2000: The good news and the bad news." *The Futurist* (November-December, 1988):9–15.

Corn, Joseph J., ed. *Imaging tomorrow: History, technology, and the American future*. Cambridge, MA: MIT Press, 1986.

Godet, Michel. "Worldwide challenges and crises in education systems. *Futures* (June, 1988):241–251.

Grant, James P. *The state of the world's children 1989*. New York: Oxford University Press, 1989.

Harris, Louis. *Inside America*. New York: Random House, 1987.

Haub, Carl. Standing room only: The population period isn't over—it's worse. *The Washington Post* (Sunday, 24 July 1988):c-1.

Hodgkinson, Harold L. What's ahead for education. *Principal* (January 1986):6–11.

Larick, Keith T., Jr., and Fischer, Jock. Classrooms of the future: Introducing technology to schools. *The Futurist* 22 (May-June 1986):21–22.

Malik, Rex. Beyond the exponential cascade: On the reduction of complexity. *InterMedia* 14 (March 1986):14–31.

Shane, Harold G. *The educational significance of the future*. Bloomington, IN: Phi Delta Kappa Foundation, 1972.

Shannon, Thomas A. *100 Winning curriculum ideas*. National School Boards Association, 1987.

Solozano, Lucia, et al. Teaching in Trouble. *U.S. News and World Report*, 26 May 1986:52–57.

## NOTES

1. The reference is to a one-term study conducted at the University of Michigan–Flint and discussed briefly in: Engle, S. H. and Longstreet, W. S. (1978). Education for a changing society. In: Jelinek, J. J. (ed.). *Improving the human condition: A curricular response to critical realities*. Washington D.C.: Association for Supervision and Curriculum Development.

2. Tanner, D. and Tanner, L. (1975). *Curriculum development: Theory into practice*. New York: Macmillan Publishing, p. 185.

3. The following subjects were recommended: Latin, Greek, English, modern languages, mathematics, physical sciences, natural sciences, history and civics, and geography.

4. For a review of past proposals to maintain the dignity and efficiency of schooling, see: Harding, L. W. (1953). Influence of Commission, Committees, and Organizations. In: *The American elementary school*. New York: Harper and Brothers (*XIIIth Yearbook*, The John Dewey Society).

5. Centron, M. J. (1988). Class of 2000: The good news and the bad news. *The Futurist*, 22:6 p. 10.

6. For an extended discussion of encapsulation as the phenomenon relates to education, see: Zais, R. S. (1976). *Curriculum: Principles and foundations*. New York: Thomas Y. Crowell, pp. 218–229.

7. Platt, J. (1981). The acceleration of evolution. *The Futurist*, 15:1, p. 23.

8. Boulding, K. (1966). Nobel Conference Lecture, "The Prospects of Economic Abundance," made at Gustavus Adolphus College.

9. Hardison, O. B., Jr. (1989). *Disappearing through the skylight: Culture and technology in the twentieth century*. New York: Viking.

10. The phenomenon of experience compression was first identified in: Shane, H. G. (1973). *The educational significance of the future*. Bloomington, In: Phi Delta Kappa Foundation.

    The concept was more extensively developed in: Longstreet, W. S. and Shane, H. G. (1979). "Educating for the 80's: A transdisciplinary approach." Bloomington, IN: The School of Education, Indiana University. 10 pp. (mimeographed).

11. Toffler, A. (1970). *Future shock*. New York: Random House.

12. Shane, H. G. (1986). Educated foresight. *Computerworld* (Special 1000th issue of the publication). Vol. 20, No. 44, p. 52.

13. Selsky, J. W. and McCann, J. E. (1984). Social triage: An emergent response to hyperturbulence. *World Future Society Bulletin, 18*, May–June, 1–19.

14. Cited by de Jouvenel, B. (1967). *The art of conjecture*. New York: Basic Books, Inc., p. 15.

15. As cited in: Dale, E. (1967), What can literature do? *The News Letter*, November, p. 3.

16. Cited in the mimeographed U.S. Office of Education Report, *The Educational Significance of the Future*. Washington, D.C.: The USOE, 1972, p. 5.

17. Gordon, T. and Helmer, O. (1966). Report on a long-range forecasting study. In: O. Helmer with Bernice Brown and Theodore Gordon *Social Technology*. New York: Basic Books, 1966.

18. Meadows, D. H., Meadows, D. L., Jorgen and Behrens, William, W. III (1972). *The limits to growth*. New York: Universe.

19. Edited respectively by Edward Cornish and Guy F. Streatfeild.

20. As cited in: Morrison, J. L. (1986). "Environmental scanning activities in higher education." Unpublished paper presented at the 1986 joint annual meetings of AAHE, AIR, SCUP.

21. Brown, A. and Weiner, E. (1985). *Supermanaging: How to harness change for personal and organizational success*. New York: Mentor, p. ix.

22. Morrison, J. L. and Held, W. G. (1988). "Developing environmental scanning/forecasting systems to augment community college planning" (proceedings). Paper presented at the Annual Meeting of the Virginia Community Colleges Association, Williamsburg, VA.

23. United Way of America (1988). *The future world of work: Looking toward the year 2000*. Alexandria, VA: United Way Mission.

24. For a classic illustration of scenarios, see: Kahn, H. and Wiener, A. J. (1967). *The year 2000: A framework for speculation*. New York: MacMillan.

25. Kahn, H. and Weiner, A. (1967). *The year 2000*. New York: Macmillan, p. 264.

26. Booz, Allen, and Hamilton note that PERT contributed to making the Polaris missile ready for use two years ahead of schedule. Cf. their management firm book: *New Uses and Management Implications of PERT*. New York: Booz, Allen, and Hamilton, Inc., 1964, p. 1.

27. An extended discussion of these various perspectives on the future can be found in: Shane, H. G. (1973). *The educational significance of the future*. Bloomington, IN: *Phi Delta Kappa*.

28. Carnegie Council on Policy Studies in Higher Education (1980). *Three thousand years*. San Francisco: Josey-Bass.

29. *Ibid.*, pp. 83–85.

30. *Op. cit.*, Shane, H. G., *The educational significance of the future*, pp. 16–17.

31. For a more detailed list of dozens of accurate forecasts made in the 1899 study cited, see: Sojka, G. A. and Shane, H. G. (1982). John Elfreth Watkins, Jr.: Forgotten genius of forecasting. *The Futurist, 16* (October):8–13. For forecasts for the next 25 years see 1988–89 issues of *The Futurist* magazine published by the World Future Society.

32. Bell, D. (1972). *The coming of the post-industrial society: A venture in social forecasting*. New York: Basic Books.

33. "The educational significance of the future." A Report to the USOE, 1972. Contract OEC-0-73-0354. (Later republished, *op. cit.*, H. G. Shane)

# 10

# The Curricular Pursuit of
# Future Relevance

## Introduction

George Bernard Shaw, a dramatist and essayist who lived from 1856 to 1950 through an incredible series of cultural disjunctures, made a telling statement when he said that humankind is made wise not by its recollections of the past but by the responsibility it assumes for its futures. The previous chapter made the point that we can and indeed need to assume responsibility for our futures. Experience compression, the deepening of intragenerational disjunctures, hyperturbulance, and the exponential increase in both knowledge and the pace of change have thrust us into futures for which we are poorly prepared.

There is a widespread sense that the developments of technology have veered from our control and, almost against our will, have caught us up in their drift. From this perspective, gaining educated foresight means being able to envision a future essentially different from the present. It also means being willing and able to deal with perplexing, often insoluable problems, while not losing sight of the ideals and aspirations we hold for the future, including regaining control over technology.

## Preparing for the Future Wisely: An Array
## of Interpretations

Somehow, we must educate the young *wisely* for futures that are fundamentally different from the past, even their own personal past as children. In terms of education, this means developing curriculum dedicated to preparing the young to deal with circumstances that are, on one hand, reflective of current needs, however "needs" may be interpreted, and on the other hand, essentially disconnected from the present way of life insofar as the future is disjunctive.

However, even if the preceding statement were to garner unanimous agree-ment among policy makers and curriculum workers, in the real world of schooling there would probably be little agreement about how such a goal could best be achieved. Our words frequently hide a multiplicity of meanings. What, indeed, does it mean to prepare the young *wisely* for the future? Let us take, for example, the five philosophical categories that we discussed in chapter 6 and try to represent how each of these might translate "educating the young wisely for the future" in terms of the curriculum.

The perennialist's position would no doubt be that wisdom, whether for the future or any other purpose, must be rooted in the knowledge of everlasting prin-ciples of truth, goodness, and beauty. Children can best prepare for the future by studying what is universal and eternal. Regardless of the scenarios that might be envisioned for the future, regardless of the crises and disjunctures experienced or foreseen, the perennialist would pursue a curriculum based primarily on the great works and insights of the past. The meaning of "great" for the perennialist means what is universal and eternal. Wisdom can come only from such greatness.

The essentialists would be far more conscious of present and future circum-stances. However, they would want to avoid fads and concerns of only passing im-portance for society. Vocational education, for example, would not be appropriate since it would train students for current needs; it could not help them keep up with the accelerated pace of change that has characterized our progress toward the twenty-first century. For the essentialist, preparing wisely for the future would mean studying the most widely applicable, generalizable knowledge possible, such as one might find in the study of a discipline. The selection of subjects for the curriculum could be influenced by current circumstances and, possibly, by fore-casts of the future. However, esentialists would reject education designed to meet short-term exigencies. The study of genetics might be substituted for zoology be-cause of the tremendous increase in significant knowledge derived from that field. However, learning the technical skills needed in, say, restaurant management or sales would probably be relegated to on-the-job training.

The progressivists would see wisdom in a much broader range of possible studies than would either the perennialists or the essentialists. Vocational educa-tion, the disciplines, and the great works would all be acceptable content for chil-dren's curricula. No one content would be wise for all children; no one future would be clearly superior to all others. Empowering youngsters with the skills and processes necessary to engage in the decision-making activities of a democratic so-ciety would be, for the progressivists, the wisest preparation for the future. Pro-gressivists would begin instruction with the understanding and experiences that youngsters bring to their studies, even if these were relatively inconsequential. To prepare wisely for the future, youngsters would be helped to engage competently in reflective thinking and problem-solving activities. A broad range of issues or topics would be considered useful in developing these skills. The study of widely applicable, generalizable knowledge such as might be found in the disciplines would be pursued subsequently as students begin to understand the importance these may hold for them personally.

Reconstructionists have a vision of the future closely bound to their conception of democracy. Preparing youngsters wisely for the future would mean preparing them to live in a more perfect democracy as envisioned by policy makers and curriculum workers. Reflective thinking and problem-solving activities would be directed toward this end. Reconstructionists are political futurists who would use futures studies to develop a curriculum empowering the young to achieve and maintain an improved version of democracy in the future. While individual interests and differences would be important in their curriculum, the needs of a democratic society would supersede any personal consideration.

In responding to the question, "How can the young be prepared for the future wisely?" educational existentialists would probably be the only one of the five philosophical groupings to consider the question a foolish one with little relevance for the meaning of life. The perennialists might agree with them but would really sidestep the question by noting that true knowledge is timeless and that the curriculum they would pursue would necessarily be effective preparation for the future. In the view of the existentialists, studying and preparing for the future are irrelevant educational activities that ignore the self, which is the only true source of knowledge and understanding about life. All education must begin with an exploration of the self and its subjectivity.

In keeping with the eclectic nature of the American school curriculum, essentialists, progressivists, and reconstructionists form the philosophical base, albeit a murky one, on which the future-oriented curriculum is likely to develop.

## Reflections for a Future-Oriented Curriculum Design

Simply ascribing a futures orientation to the curriculum does not mean that basic disagreements about the purposes of schooling disappear or somehow become merged in one grandiose vision of the future. Additional goals rooted in the future may be incorporated into the design and activities may have a futures cast to them, but the problems and debates that have been a part of curriculum development since the inception of the field are essentially unchanged. Curriculum remains a cultural as well as a rational enterprise. Cultural inertia is unabated despite the acceleration of change; dealing with complex unknowns remains disquieting to the public at large and curricula that confront unanswerable conundrums are often rejected in favor of studies offering a clear set of answers.

This preference for what is simple, succinct, and delimitable runs contrary to our present circumstances. We are confronted repeatedly with decisions of a type that humankind has never known before. Uncertainty is a part of our social, political, and economic fabric. Somehow, someway the curriculum must acknowledge the immense complexity and indefiniteness characterizing our future.

Reconceptualizing the curriculum should be a rational enterprise. The kinds of studies to be pursued in schools ought to be determined by some reasoned analysis of our basic philosophy, the needs of children in the present, and the most likely circumstances of the future. Unfortunately, this is not a likely route in the United States because the curriculum design is deeply embedded in our cultural mindsets.

Furthermore, the bureaucratic system that is in place has interests to protect besides those of its students that are directly related to the status quo curriculum. Time available to the curriculum is limited, and there are increasing numbers of expectations laid at the door of public education. History teachers are usually quite eloquent in explaining the critical importance of history, and mathematics teachers are convinced that the very future of the nation depends on more time being dedicated to their subject. Of course, foreign language teachers make as good a case, and how can computer sciences be overlooked in this day and age! We are without the political or cultural will to set aside the traditions and our usual ways of operating. Despite vehement reform movements and a plethora of additions, the core of the school's curriculum is very much what it was at the end of World War II.

While understanding the problems and difficulties confronting society and its schools today cannot alone lead to reform, it is a necessary first step in undoing the cultural encapsulation that has blocked numerous efforts at reconceptualizing the curriculum, especially in the second half of the twentieth century. Planning wisely for the future means, at the very least, understanding current problems and their place in the curriculum. Let us therefore turn our attention to the many problems and opportunities with which we must work and the environments that encompass them.

## A Survey of Issues Confronting Schools as They Plan for a New Millennium

### Perspective from the Past

A number of educational writers have made prescient, sometimes accurate, often wishful predictions regarding probable developments in education. An excellent example is an essay prepared by Edgar Dale in the 1960s. A pioneer in various realms of the instructional technologies, Professor Dale made five predictions with respect to what he called "Things To Come." His predictions included the following:

1. The debates in the 1960s regarding acceptable values in a technological society would increase both in extent and bitterness.
2. The roles of teachers would shift. Rather than examiners of temporarily memorized materials, they would become exemplars of critical thinking and help students to confront important problems successfully.
3. Schools would become increasingly concerned with developing both a zest for learning and the power of continued self-education.
4. Teachers would begin to see students as persons.
5. Educators at all levels would increase their focus on individualized instruction.[1]

Generally speaking, Dale's images of tomorrow were more the expression of hope than forecasts representative of futures study. It is sadly true, however, that in the more than twenty years since the list was issued, massive social regressions in many areas of life in the United States have led to malaise and bitterness beyond anything conceived in item 1. The march out of poverty for America's poor seems to have been arrested, and our schools appear to be in a freefall of deterioration. Dale's predictions could be made today for there is not only a substantial distance to go before all five may be said to have come into being, they also remain desirable outcomes that most of us believe we can achieve. To see, however, our students as persons (item 4), we must also see and interact with their malaise. To give them a zest for learning (item 3), we must relate what they learn to their understanding of life; to confront important problems with them (item 2), we must also bring their understanding and experiences into the selection process.

## Contemporary Perspectives

Analyses made in the last several years by Richard D. Lamm[2] and Marvin J. Cetron[3] provide evidence of how technosocial changes have complicated both curriculum planning and classroom instruction and slowed progress toward attainment of Dale's ideal goals. Lamm, for instance, notes that our future prosperity depends on greater individual mastery of complex technologies, but this may be jeopardized, he tells us, since at present ". . . one in five Americans can barely read a menu."[4]

Cetron expresses great alarm regarding student performance. While recognizing the merit of goals such as Dale cited, he quotes many studies with findings such as one indicating that among high school seniors less than a third knew within fifty years when the Civil War occurred or that Columbus made his voyages before 1750. The implication of Cetron's discussion is that the lack of such knowledge reveals educational inadequacies that must be overcome for the sake of the future. This is a position that would be debated at some length among essentialists and progressivists who, for different reasons, would view the knowledge of dates as useful but not of central importance to education. Equally sad and possibly even more debatable is Cetron's finding, as presented in a Restaurant Association study, that by 1995 a half million jobs might go unfilled because job hunters lack the skills needed by waiters or cashiers.[5]

So many distressing observations could be made about the present circumstances of American education that we risk discouragement about the future of education. Children appear to be at risk today in a way not known previously: children from broken homes, children who are parents themselves, children who are drug addicts or whose parents are drug addicts, children who have greater loyalty to their gangs than to their families. Children bring problems to school in numbers unheard of a short while ago, and the emergence of this new kind of school population cannot be ignored while planning for the future.

We do need to remember that throughout the twentieth century we have been engaged in one of the greatest social experiments of all history, that of delivering universally available education to the entire population of a nation. As a society, we are still struggling with the translation of this concept into curricular offerings that will be both satisfying to the individual and useful for society as a whole. Its meaning for the future is one of the many conundrums to be faced.

### An Inventory of Trends and Representative Problems on the Horizon

Current problems having a direct bearing on curriculum and instruction may be sorted into five critical trend areas. These are:

1. dangers that have made our globe an imperiled planet;
2. social, political and economic phenomena of global importance;
3. social regression;
4. changes in family living; and
5. problems that at present are endemic to our schools.

Because all five categories are of coordinate importance, no priority is associated with the sequence in which each area is presented.

#### *Understanding Threats to Our Planet*

In all probability scholars in the field of history will, in retrospect, deem 1989 to be a turning point with respect to human beings and the earth that has supported them. A conspicuous sign of the times was the cover story in *Time* magazine for January 2, 1989. While *Time* traditionally had featured a "Man or Woman of the Year," the earth and its problems were the focus of attention.

There is growing concern about the world's ability to support life indefinitely. The world is at risk for an increasing variety of reasons.[6] Among them are world food problems, the greenhouse effect, threats to the ozone layer, exploding populations in many countries, land degradation, pollution and toxic waste, deforestation and desertification, the AIDS epidemic, deteriorating infrastructures especially in our largest cities, depletion of fuels, a growing water deficit, nuclear dangers, the need for global security and peace, and many others.

For example, American industry in 1988 pumped 2.4 billion pounds of chemicals and other toxic substances into the nation's air. The EPA concluded that over 100 million people in the fifty states breathed contaminated air as defined by federal standards. Among the toxics were such items as mercury, radon, asbestos, benzene, and arsenic. Since individuals inhale between ten and twenty thousands of liters of air each day, the potential for damage from toxins, especially in industrialized areas, is clearly evident.[7]

#### *Important Social, Economic, and Political Phenomena*

Our proliferating social, economic, and political problems have become so severe that they motivated W. Warren Wagar to comment that humans are akin to babies in wicker baskets, waiting on the doorstep of Doomsday![8] Interestingly enough, he made his remark nearly twenty years ago. Evidence has continued to accumulate to justify his pessimism. We are indeed in an "age of discontinuity,"[9] as Peter Drucker noted, and education may have become too important to be left entirely to educators. Nonetheless, there is much that needs to concern curriculum planners and teachers in the decades to come. Let us begin with a sample of social problems having such significance that ignoring them in the curriculum would most certainly undermine the relevance of the curriculum for the future.

### A Sample of Current Problems Likely to Hold Future Significance

#### An Aging Population
Those born at the beginning of twenty-first century will have an average life expectancy of 81 years.[10] Medicare costs, funds for social security payments, and education needed for senior (60 + ) learners suggest some of the fiscal problems that may become burdensome to the young.[11]

#### Increasing Debt and Foreign Property Purchases in the United States
As the 1980s drew to a close the aggregate debts of the government, corporations, and individual citizens had reached $7 trillion. The American taxpayer was obliged to work until May 5, 1989, to pay federal, state, and local taxes for that year. Furthermore, international investors (primarily from Japan and Britain) as of 1987–1988 purchased more than $170 billion in United States property such as hotels, office buildings, shopping malls, and corporations. Control and profits were preempted by the new owners.

#### The AIDS Epidemic
With an annual 1988 increase rate of over 72%, an obvious sociomedical challenge has arisen.

#### Violence
America has a deplorable record with regard to handgun killings. In a recent year 8,092 of these slayings occurred in our country. Canada reported 5, Britain 57, and Japan 121—and their *total* population was 203 million people versus 293 in the U.S.[12] Washington D.C., our "murder capital," had 75 homicides in the first 45 days of 1989, 13 in one day. The rise in violence and murder has continued in the 1990s.

#### Urban Jungles
A type of problem closely related to raw violence is the decline in urban safety. At least 200 youth gangs have been identified in Los Angeles, and in 1986, 287 gang-related homicides were attributed to their activities (a 24 percent increase in twelve months). Many people feel unsafe on the street and even in their homes. Areas such as Central Park in New York City can be dangerous to tourists, joggers, and others. Robbery during a recent ten-year period in one of our cities has grown from 1,072 to 12,236 break-ins.[13]

#### The Drug Problem
Another sample of the proliferating problems in the United States is the increased use of drugs by a large number of citizens, including many of our

youth.[14] This is a difficulty enhanced by gang warfare among drug pushers and between them and our law enforcement agents.

*Keeping the United States Habitable*

One last problem for our sample from among dozens more—for example involving the media, task disposal, the workplace, and uncontrollable immigration traffic—is keeping the country more habitable with respect to rapidly increasing automobile traffic. In 1988, Americans jammed the streets by driving an estimated 126,200,000 miles in a five-day workweek, often with one driver per car. Billions of dollars are needed to restore many roads and bridges that are both jammed and in unsafe conditions.

While the items selected above, and many others, are broadly based social, economic, and political problems, there is "spillover" from all of them into educational policy practices and the content of virtually all areas of the curriculum from driver and health education to the familiar language, social studies, math, and service areas.

### Social Regression: Lagging Social Progress

The nineteenth and twentieth centuries have been characterized by extraordinary progress in our industrial capabilities, in the influence and respect we have garnered world wide, in the availability of education for the entire population, and in our standard of living. As a people, we have come to think of ourselves as middle class. Even those families who fit the government's criteria for being below the poverty level consider themselves to be middle class.

In the 1980s and 1990s our social progress has slowed and this vast middle class has begun to feel the effects of regression to the mean. That is, the extraordinary social progress that we have grown accustomed to is becoming average and even less than average. When a 20-year-old left home in the 1950s and 1960s, he or she expected to do better than his or her parents had done and this was usually the case. Leaving home today often means experiencing a decline in one's standard of living and having far less hope than the preceding generation had that significant advancement in socioeconomic circumstances can be made.

This decline in our hopes for social progress, this regression to a mean that has not been part of our American history, brings new challenges to education. As in other instances, our schools seem unaware of the challenge or its potential significance in the curriculum.

### Multiplying Family Problems

Of the many changes we are confronting, none go so deeply to the core of our values and social encapsulation as those associated with the family. These are changes that have a direct bearing on the role of our schools in nurturing and guiding human growth and maturation. A brief sample follows.

1. Contributing to the disintegration of our traditional images of the family is the increasing number of working women. Indeed, over 68 percent of women were working by 1989. More than 52 percent of women in the work force have children

under three and often are unable to find adequate care.[16] Few can afford $300 a week nannies; day care and after-school centers have multiplied and "latch-key" kids by the thousands return from school to empty homes.

2. The point above introduces the next two serious problems, the child care crisis and child abuse. To ameliorate care problems, our schools and corporations are contemplating providing much more educational (not merely custodial) care at the early childhood level. An important aspect of the child care problem was reflected in a 1988 Census Bureau report showing that approximately 25 percent of American children lived with just one parent and over half, about 21 million, were in single-parent homes headed by a woman in nine cases out of ten.

3. Child abuse has become a conspicuous problem in the past decade. Social agencies, such as our schools, need to give much more attention to ways of protecting the well-being of the young who are harmed by abuse and neglect.

4. Children born out of wedlock are yet another sign of decline in conventional family status. About 45 percent of American children, as of 1988–89, were born to mothers who were not married, most of them teenagers. Also a number of employed women in their thirties and forties who want children now bear them out of wedlock. By the late 1980s over 100,000 babies were born in the United States to older mothers desiring a child outside the bounds of a conventional marriage.

5. The number of homeless children increased significantly throughout the 1980s. By the end of the decade, about 100,000 children of school age were members of families without a regular place of residence.

6. Media ecologist Neil Postman is among the number of scholars who have expressed concern over the inroads made in family life since TV and associated items such as VCRs have permeated virtually all of our homes. Young learners spend about 23 or 24 hours per week televiewing—a total of 16,000 hours as distinct from about 14,000 hours spent during 12 years in elementary and secondary school. Even more distressing is Postman's estimate that about 600,000 pupils stay up to watch video programs after midnight. Two national video dealers associations have announced that about 3,400,000 pornographic videocassettes are rented weekly in the United States. Undoubtedly, a number are viewed by youngsters either with or without parental approval. One other home TV-related problem may well be the time it subtracts from waning family activities, for example, reading stories to children; taking them to zoos, museums, and libraries; engaging in sports, and the like.

### Concomitant Problems in Our Schools

A roster of selected concomitant problems beleaguring American schools brings to a close the sample lists of some of the developments that have arisen and that are forcing a re-evaluation of virtually all policies related to curriculum development.

1. The growing amount of things to be learned in an information society is a source of heavy pressure on educators. Daniel Bell, of Harvard University, has esti-

mated that by the late 1990s the quantity of available information will double every twenty-four months. In effect, this means that learners in today's schools will be exposed to more information in a *year* than their grandparents were in a lifetime!

2. The proliferation of available information—and its accessibility—is made more complex by the number of families living below the poverty level, and many involving parents who are poorly educated and often homeless. Access to knowledge in more affluent homes undoubtedly is widening the "have" and "have-not" gap.

3. Ethnic and cultural changes are bringing new challenges to educators, too. Within the decade of the 1990s (assuming present trends continue) the *minorities* of the 1980s—Asians, Blacks, and Hispanics for example—will constitute the *majority* of pupils in fifty-three of America's 100 largest school systems.

4. Academic decline and poor performance have become increasingly intractable in recent decades. Failure to improve the United States educational systems with its enormous long-term costs has been noted by the congressional Joint Economic Committee.[17] The dropout rate and absences are further symptoms of our schools' problems. According to the 1989 congressional report mentioned above, the overall dropout rate in the United States had surpassed 25 percent—and approximately 13 percent of our 17-year-old Americans reportedly cannot effectively read, write, or count. A number of corporations have, as a result, felt obliged to instruct their employees in basic skills.[18] A U.S. Department of Education summary concluded, as of 1986, that there were between seventeen and twenty-one million illiterates in the United States and that the number is increasing by two million per year.[19]

5. Problems in the atmosphere of school and public libraries also have increased since a number of employed parents bring their youngsters to libraries where they hope their children will be exposed to a form of control and care. As one outcome, in some schools, the conventional library climate of quiet study and inquiry are disrupted.

6. Problems associated with sex, drug use, and teenage suicide have been so widely published by the media that further elaboration is unnecessary.

Many other problems and dilemmas spilling into or germinating in United States schools could be inventoried—for example, population shifts in various states ranging from increases in "sunbelt communities" to dropoffs of as much as 10 percent in a dozen of our "frostbelt states." The sampling provided above should suffice to stress both the extent and the seriousness of present situations and their significance for potentially alarming educational futures.

Certainly, the schools alone cannot begin to bear the weight of problems confronting us. The curriculum must become more responsive, but it can hardly become the total solution. It can be, however, a catalyst for coping with the upheavals of our time if we can somehow succeed in freeing it from the cultural mindsets that have so long kept it from changing.

## In Pursuit of Future-Relevant Curricular Designs

We need to invent new conceptions of education and respond to new questions. What would render a subject relevant for both today's circumstances and tomorrow's needs? Which subject matter areas would help youngsters deal with both the difficulties of their present and the ambiguities of their futures? What really makes up a basic core of studies when there are national networks of information and news shared by tens of millions of viewers on a daily basis? What can we do — and what ought we do — to govern the psychological relations between such technological resources as the computer and the human ability to use these resources wisely?

We propose pursuing the development of curricula based on enabling the young of today to deal with swiftly changing futures and the uncertainty and complexity of a society caught in an ongoing explosion of knowledge. We do not believe educational relevance can be achieved simply by including the study of current or even future problems in the curriculum. Learning the processes of engagement rather than the confrontation of any one set of problems is a key idea in the future relevant curriculum. However, a problem orientation to the curriculum involving student input does hold the potential for increased individualization, motivation and relevance and is one source of curricular renewal.

As change accelerates, current problems inevitably take on new forms and no single solution is likely to suffice. Nor is any one set of problems likely to satisfy the dynamic need of a relevant curriculum. The willingness to pursue multiple possibilities; the ability to search for, analyze, and utilize information; and the capacity to tolerate uncertainty and indecision even while having to confront problems requiring decisiveness are the kinds of characteristics that we consider of the utmost importance to the future of the young and must necessarily be among the goals of a future-relevant curriculum.

## Exploring Current Curricular Traditions for Future Relevance

In our pursuit of new curricular designs, we cannot ignore the traditions that are so powerfully a part of our cultural mindsets and that have stymied the many educational reforms undertaken since World War II. Lacking what we have called a major vector of change, new directions must necessarily depart from where we are, however confused that may be.

Our most long-standing curricular tradition bases school studies on knowledge for its own sake, particularly in the form of liberal studies derived from history, literature, foreign language, and mathematics. That tradition was augmented and greatly changed when the sciences were given a dominant position in the curriculum. A competing though less powerful curricular tradition places at the fore applied studies such as those embodied in vocational training, involvement in community affairs, and recreational pursuits. To a lesser degree, we have come to value as an outcome of schooling the existential development of each individual's innermost meaning.

Rather than trying to resolve the conflicts involved in supporting, say, both humanistic studies and vocational training, we would ask of each of our traditions, in somewhat modified form, Spencer's still crucial question: What knowledge is of most worth in preparing the young of today for a rapidly changing future full of disjunctures, complexities, and conundrums? This in turn would lead to a number of subquestions, the answers to which would serve as guides in designing and developing the curriculum. As illustrations: In what ways do the humanities speak to our futures? What kinds of vocational training can escape the inevitable obsolescence of the present? Can explorations of one's inner self be related to explorations of desirable futures? We would, furthermore, examine those problems and trends that have most left us with a sense of upheaval and disorientation. The insights derived from these explorations would form the bases for future-relevant curricular designs.

An example of a curriculum design that, in our view, holds the potential for future relevance was proposed years ago by Broudy, Smith, and Burnett.[20] They recommended the establishment of a "subject" that would help students to develop an interpretive map for organizing a vast array of information. As Broudy, Smith, and Burnett viewed this map, it would reorganize knowledge from a variety of fields to make it more useful "in solving problems of the social order."[21] As they noted, "problems confronting the citizen are rarely reducible to this or that combination of the basic sciences."[22] They called this new subject area "developmental studies" and included the following subcategories: *cosmos* (or the study of the universe and the rise of human life); *institutions*; and *culture*. A curriculum design that would place at its core developmental studies that explore from a futures perspective the problems and trends of the cosmos, institutions, and culture would be a significant departure from the discipline-based, subject design currently dominant in the curriculum. This design could establish certain fixed areas of study while still allowing for more open-ended and personalized involvement.

Indeed, if we were to pursue the question, "How can we utilize academic resources to produce more self-aware, community-minded, critical thinkers?"[23] posed by Professor Rachel M. Lauer, director of the Straus Thinking and Learning Center in New York, it is likely that the present emphasis on knowledge derived from the humanities and sciences would be significantly revised. Instead of pursuing at length the dates of the Civil War, the *Aeneid*, or the list of chemical elements, the curriculum would be about making connections, constructing arguments, and evaluating propaganda. The *Aeneid* or the Civil War might still be discussed but only as several among an array of useful topics supporting the processes of critical thinking. The development of community spirit would be likely to involve students in community-based activities outside the school and, of course, outside the full control of the schools. A part of the curriculum would necessarily come into being as it happens. Objectives involving self-awareness would also be beyond the direct aegis of the school and its fixed curriculum plan. As Lauer notes:

*If students are to become more knowledgeable about themselves, they're go-*
*ing to have to reflect upon their feelings, thoughts, motives, beliefs, and*
*behavior as they interact with one another in classrooms, clubs and lunch-*
*rooms. A discussion of early Mesopotamia, for example, will be ignored or*
*quickly forgotten unless it can illuminate something about the issues of per-*
*sonal, and contemporary, life.*[24]

A futures perspective could easily be added to this conceptualization of the curriculum. Reflections about one's feelings, motives, and the like would be directed
toward the conundrums of an essentially unknown adult life twenty years hence.
What is it that we want from the future personally? for the community? for our
world and even the universe? There are a lot of problems and a lot of problem
solving in answering such questions.

However, developing a curriculum along such lines would be a decisive departure from our curricular traditions. It is nearly thirty years since Broudy, Smith,
and Burnett issued their proposal for redesigning the curriculum; it is even longer
since the federal government embarked on its massive efforts to achieve a "new"
math or a "new" social studies. We have had a great deal of tinkering, a massive
increase in testing programs, and an essentially unchanged curricular design. Curricular inertia would appear to be the dominant theme.

### Taking the Route of Modest Change

One could be more modest and undertake the reform of a small segment of the
school's curriculum, leaving the overall design intact. Assuming that the current
curriculum design based on a set of subjects including English, mathematics, history, and science would remain unchanged into the foreseeable future, our modified, Spencerian question could still serve as a guide for curricular revision within
the context of each subject. We would examine, for example, mathematical knowledge to determine what in mathematics is most useful for the young to learn in
preparing for an enigmatic and swiftly changing future. This is really quite a different question from the one usually answered by today's mathematics curriculum,
which tends to reflect the fundamental structure and nature of mathematics regardless of its usefulness in dealing with the future. Thus, the vast majority of
students now study geometry in high school but have little experience with statistics, since geometry is seen as central to their understanding of the nature of mathematics and statistics is merely a useful offshoot. In our modest effort at curricular
revision, statistics would be made a required part of the mathematics curriculum,
while geometry would become an elective for those especially interested in pursuing the subject.

In similar fashion, the study of English could be viewed in terms of its usefulness to the future lives of children. The case for continuing to study the language itself would hardly be a difficult one to make. In addition, however, to such
traditional content as reading instruction, the development of literacy in televised
communications could be brought into the curriculum. Since a vast amount of the
information we acquire today is televised into our homes and since this is a trend

likely to continue in an accelerating fashion well into the future, "video" literacy would appear to be an important area of curriculum development in response to our question of what studies would be of the greatest usefulness in the future lives of the young.

Such "modest" changes, as we have referred to them, risk amounting to no more than mindless tinkering, an agglomeration of activities without direction or an underlying philosophical set of values. To avoid such a prospect requires, on the one hand, a foundational understanding of the curriculum and how children learn and, on the other, a careful analysis of the trends and issues most critical to the future of our children.

## QUESTIONS FOR DISCUSSION AND REFLECTION

1. How do the views of perennialists and reconstructionists differ with regard to educating children for the future? Can you see some areas of futures study in the school's curriculum on which both would agree?

2. How are the views of essentialists and progressivists similar with regard to educating children for the future? If they were to collaborate in the development of a future-oriented curriculum, what studies would they be likely to agree on?

3. How might existentialists deal with education for the future?

4. What kinds of problems might arise if a school district decided to implement a future-oriented curriculum?

5. We have traditionally expected a great deal from our schools and the curriculum. If we add educated foresight and preparation for the future to the claims made on public educatiom, what should we eliminate?

6. Would you revise the school's current approach to the teaching of factual knowledge? Defend your position; then defend the opposing view.

7. Toward the end of this chapter, a roster of problems was presented. Choose one of these for inclusion in the curriculum. How would you go about adding this new content to the curriculum? One possibility would be to develop a new course. Would this be viable? What else might you do?

8. Develop a set of problems that you would add to those included in our roster. Would you adjust the curriculum to reflect all these problems? Explain your position fully.

9. Should we develop different curricula for different populations? What are the positive and negative aspects of such an approach? Which of the educational philosophical schools would be most likely to agree with your position?

10. Ignoring political and economic difficulties, do you think a new curriculum design — one not based on the disciplines currently emphasized in our curriculum — needs to be developed? Why or why not? What underlying bases for

the design would you pursue? For example, would you establish a curriculum having a greater emphasis on the fine arts than is currently the case? To do so, in an already crowded curriculum, you would have to eliminate at least one traditional category of content. In sum, how would you redesign the curriculum? What would you do about futures studies?

## RECOMMENDED READINGS

Brandt, Ronald S. *Conversations with leading educators.* Alexandria, VA: The Association for Supervision and Curriculum Development, 1989, 145 pp.

Frymier, Jack (ed.). *One hundred good schools.* West Lafayette, IN: Kappa Delta Pi, 1984, 361 pp.

Jackson, Philip W., and Sophie Haroutunian-Gordon. *From Socrates to software: The teacher as text and the text as teacher.* Chicago, IL: The NSSE, 89th Yearbook, Part I, 1989, 235 pp.

Lapham, Lewis H. Notebook: Multiple Choice. *Harper's Magazine, 218*:166 (March), 1989, pp. 12–16.

Larick, Keith T., Jr., and Jock Fisher. Classrooms of the future: Introducing technology to the schools. *The Futurist, 10*:3 (May–June), 1986.

Naisbitt, John. *Megatrends.* New York: Warner Books, 1982.

Naisbitt, John, and Aburdene, Patricia. *Megatrends 2000.* New York: William Morrow, 1990.

Parke, Beverly N. Educating the gifted and talented: An agenda for the future. *Educational Leadership, 46*:6 (March), 1989, pp. 4–5.

Plummer, Joseph T. Changing Values. *The Futurist, 13*:1 (January–February), 1989, pp. 8–13.

Summers, Harry G., Jr. A bankrupt military strategy. *The Atlantic*, 263:6 (June), 1989, pp. 33–40.

West, Edwin G. Are American schools working? Disturbing cost and quality trends. *American Education*, January–February, 1984, p. 11ff.

## NOTES

1. Dale, E. (1969). Things to come. *The News Letter*, 34:4 (January), pp. 1–4.
2. Lamm, R. D. (1988). Post-crash institutions. *The Futurist, 22*, 4 (July–August), pp. 8–12.
3. Cetron, M. J. (1988). Class of 2000, the good news and the bad news. *The Futurist, 22*, 6 (November–December), pp. 9–15.
4. *Op. cit.*, Lamm, p. 10.
5. *Op. cit.*, Cetron, pp. 12–13.
6. For a superb and detailed resume of global problems cf. the report published annually by Brown, L. R., et al. (1984 to date). *State of the world.* New York: W.W. Norton.
7. An excellent guide to fathoming some of our problems is Brewster, J. A. et al. *World resources 1988–1989: An assessment of the resource base that supports the global economy.* New York: Basic Books, 372 pp.
8. W. Wager (1971). *Building the city of man*, New York: Grossman.

9. Drucker, P. (1969). *The age of discontinuity*. New York: Harper & Row.

10. The remarkable increase is underscored by the fact that life expectancy in the 1770s was 35 years and was 44 years in the 1890s. The 1986 life span for the newborn was 74.9 years.

11. By 1989 over $1 billion was spent each *week* for Medicare—one-third for terminally ill persons.

12. For more details see the *Time* cover story for February 6, 1989, 133:6, pp. 20–26.

13. Cited by *Insight* magazine, 10 April 1989.

14. The National Institute of Drug Abuse has reported that, as of 1988, 92 percent of United States graduating high school seniors had sampled alcoholic beverages and 54 percent had tried hashish and/or marijuana.

15. As reported in *The Atlantic*. 8:87, p. 44ff.

16. For more specific data see Working Parents. *Newsweek*, February 13, 1989, pp. 40–44.

17. The congressional report was cited by the Associated Press, Tuesday, April 18, 1989.

18. Conditions in Chicago, for instance, were sufficiently adverse by 1989 that state legislative action was taken to help remedy the fact that among 40,000 freshmen in the city's sixty-five high schools only 18,000 graduate. For specific details, see *Insight* magazine, 5:13, March 27, 1989, pp. 20–21.

19. As cited in: Losing the war of letters. *Time*, 127:18, May 5, 1986, p. 68.

20. Broudy, H. S., Smith, B. O., and Burnett, J. R. (1964). *Democracy and excellence in American secondary education*. Chicago: Rand McNally.

21. *Ibid.*, p. 202.

22. *Ibid.*

23. Lauer, R. M. (1990). Self-knowledge, critical thinking, and community should be the main objectives of general education. *The Chronicle of Higher Education*. XXXVI, *20*, pp. B1 and B3.

24. *Ibid.*, pp. B1 and B3.

# 11

# The Futures-Based Curriculum Design

### Introduction: Omitting the Future

Futures studies and trends analysis have greatly increased our ability to prepare for the future. Admittedly, some of the most significant events of the twentieth century were completely overlooked by forecasters. Most notable among these were the great oil crisis precipitated by the OPEC nations in the early 1970s, the invasion of Kuwait by Iraq in the early 1990s, and the near revolutionary upheaval of communist governments throughout Eastern Europe and the former Soviet Union in the last months of the 1980s and continuing in the 1990s. Nevertheless, engaging in analyses of possible futures is quite useful because it helps us to explore the range and nature of choices available to us. It can prepare us for sensible decision making. Our current images of the future are vague and often full of fearful spectres ranging from thermonuclear terrorism to tyrannical control of our genetic destinies by a handful of scientists. The most critical reality that we face today is long-range, profound uncertainty and the need to make decisions despite the uncertainty.

The curriculum has not ordinarily been designed to prepare us for any future that departs in significant ways from the present. Rather, the organization of the curriculum has tended to be based on one of several perspectives, which, with the exception of reconstructionism, hardly take into account potential futures.

In the wave of educational reform that occupied all the 1980s, objectively based knowledge that could be measured by nationally normed, standardized tests became the underlying bases for curricular decision making. Indeed, curricular decision making was largely taken over by lobbyists and lawmakers, whose awareness of many of the issues discussed in the first section of this work was minimal and whose primary concern appeared to be remedying the deficiencies measured by standardized tests. Educational accountability was equated to test performance.

For example, in 1988, the governing board of the National Assessment for

Educational Progress (NAEP), headed by Chester E. Finn, set out to establish a set of nationwide standards for performance *in the areas tested*, which include science, mathematics, and history. This is surely a formula for maintaining the status quo in curriculum. Instead of a national discussion concerning what the school's curriculum needs to become and then determining appropriate forms of evaluation, the curriculum would be driven by test makers deciding what should be studied to pass their tests. Regrettably, mindless and inexpert activity pursued in the name of educational excellence but responsive primarily to the political or cultural climate of the day, has defeated what efforts might have been made to achieve forward-looking renewal of the curriculum.

The future as essentially distinct from the present has rarely been given serious consideration and has never been, at least not consciously, a focal point for the design of the school's curriculum. Despite the many diverse concerns expressed by business and industry regarding what they perceive to be the declining capabilities of the American labor force, reforms have been limited to how to improve the test performance of youngsters in mathematics or reading or science as these are currently taught. We have not examined in terms of public education how we shall prepare the young to participate as citizens of a democracy in decisions that have never confronted humankind before. We have not sought to analyze learning as a function of an unknown future. Nor have we explored in terms of the curriculum and its offerings how education can contribute to regaining control over the course taken by technology. We have not even referred to futures studies and the results of trends analyses in selecting the content of the curriculum. Our collective future has been treated as though its scenarios were well known and could be taken for granted. We have, in sum, omitted from the curriculum any serious form of futures studies.

## The Cultural Inertia of Children

We often think of the young as being the hope of the future. In the sense that the forthcoming decades belong to them and their leadership, they are, of course, the bearers of the future. However, children are also the foremost bearers of cultural inertia. Their early enculturation is hardly mitigated by their intellectual powers of reasoning, which are still in various stages of cognitive development, and their experiences tend to be limited to their own immediate world and several hours of daily television.

One of the authors undertook an exploratory study with several elementary, junior high, and high school classes. The purpose was to gain some initial understanding of children's vision of the future. They were asked first to write brief compositions about what they thought the future held for them. On a subsequent day, they were asked to review their compositions and decide what they would need to study in school to be ready for their future. At all three school levels, students' visions of the future hardly went beyond what they knew in the present. This quote from a 14-year-old ninth grader is quite representative:

*Computers should still be advancing to help us economically and medically. I am hoping to see pollution and poverty well on their way to coming to an end.*

Another youngster in the same grade level wrote:

*When I enter the workforce, I believe the cities will be a lot more filled due to overpopulation. I also believe the quality of life will have deteriorated physically and morally.*

A thirteen-year-old wrote:

*I think that the future will be about the same. Cars may go faster and we may have more computers but life will be the same. However, we may have polluted our earth a lot more. Even though we're trying to fix our pollution, I think it will be worse in the future. We've done too much damage to fix it now.*

And one last representative sample in the same age group:

*I think we all kid ourselves and say that things won't change but I guess technology will leap ahead and pollution will be terrible. At my age, I feel there is nothing I can do to change that, but when I can, I will.*

In different ways, the youngsters involved in the study expressed the idea that there would not be much real change in the future. Cars might fly and there might be more computers, but pollution would probably continue to worsen. A number of them expressed the feeling that they really did not want much change, except to alleviate pollution, poverty, and other societal ills currently in the news. Not one of the fifty-eight youngsters who participated mentioned anything about genetic engineering or the growing global economy or the continuing revolution in communications. There seemed to be a profound naïveté about the future. The naïveté appeared to carry over into their views of schooling for the future. Recommendations from the 14- to 15-year-olds went something like this:

*I think schools are fine now, except I believe they should be cleaner and have more computers. Also, classes should be made more exciting.*

*Schools should be more cautious about who they let in. That is the major flaw in public education, they don't have a choice [sic].*

*In my opinion schools should project good morals and learning should come second.*

*Such studies as computer fabrications [sic], computer science, physics and robotics engineering should be greatly emphasized because the future depends on computer technology.*

*Science, English and math should be stressed. Ways to recycle, reuse and save should be taught. Schools should stress discipline and behavior. If we don't do these things, Japan will take over our country.*

*I feel that the real world should be studied. So much is going on and it's very interesting. We shouldn't have to study the past, it's gone. We should study now and the future.*

Most of the older students showed little insight into the needs they might have for the future, and they had obviously studied very little about the future. This chapter explores future-oriented curriculum designs and what the young might study so that the naïveté that was encountered in our small pilot study could be alleviated.

## Toward Future-Relevant Curriculum Design

### The Rational Ideal of Curriculum Design

What form might the curriculum design take if it were based on the idea of preparing the young for a future of accelerating change? In what way would school subjects be different? How would our expectations be changed? If developing curriculum were an enterprise wholly dominated by logical reasoning, the response to such questions could be quickly and straightforwardly presented. We would lay out our premises about the nature of important knowledge and how education can contribute to our conception of the "good" life; we would explain how and why dealing with an unknown future is a critical educational undertaking; and then we would link this rationale to a set of clearly expressed purposes. This would form the bases for selecting the subjects that would comprise the course of study.

School subjects do not have to be configured as they currently are, that is, based mostly on disciplines and arranged to facilitate instruction. Subjects may be based on current issues or on a cross-section of the sciences, as can be observed now in a general science course for the junior high or on a set of concepts that are only suggestive and open to the interests and decisions of teachers and/or students.

Determining the nature of the school subject is a key factor in designing a curriculum. During the curricular reforms of the 1960s, a good deal of discussion concerned the possible structure and design of subjects; the reform movement of the 1980s ignored the question altogether, emphasizing, instead, students' performance on standardized tests.

In a rational model of curriculum design and development, summative evaluation of student learning would be directly related to the objectives of classroom instruction, which, of course, would be representative of the goals and purposes of education. An evaluation that would not take into account what the curriculum set out to accomplish would be, in our nonexistent, wholly rational world, an unacceptable distraction.

## The Realities of Curriculum Design

At the broad level of educational purpose, as we have noted in previous chapters, there is likely to be widespread accord among both educators and lay people. As more specific goals and objectives are developed to guide practice, the accord dissipates quickly. There would, of course, be a question of different philosophical perspectives, for most certainly their influence on the kind of school subject(s) established would be significant. For instance, perennialists would seek a design based on the learning of "eternal" content, probably related to the great questions of all times, past and future, while progressivists would open the study of future problems to the interests and involvement of the young. Thus, perennialists would favor closed-ended forms of the school subject, whereas progressivists would most certainly favor more open-ended formats.

At this point, we need to reiterate that curriculum work is only partly a logical enterprise, although efforts at consistency are necessary to the ultimate validity of our educational activities. We do need a sense of why we are doing what we do. Nevertheless, curriculum work is laden with social, political, and economic concerns that repeatedly undermine acceptance of our more ideally designed curricular revisions. For instance, suppose we agree that the development of critical thinking skills ought to comprise a central strand of study. This does not preclude our disagreeing about whether those skills need to be a part of an independent study represented by the school subject "critical thinking," or wholly integrated into other subjects whose contents are considered especially important for society, or allowed to develop from choices made by students and teachers. Some of us may take the position that having a common core of content is politically desirable for the unity of the nation, while others may wish to relate critical thinking skills to the current needs of business and industry. Special interests of all kinds can and do influence the design and implementation of curriculum.

## Cultural Inertia and the Resistance to Curricular Reform

In addition, for most of us, schooling begins with kindergarten and even pre-kindergarten. The nature and design of the traditional curriculum is deeply embedded in us during our earliest stages of cultural development. The curriculum we carry in our mind's eye contributes to the cultural inertia that impedes so many of our efforts to achieve curriculum reform. Most of us are not only unwilling to change our curricular conceptions, we also lack the objectivity necessary to do so. While cultural inertia may contribute to the long-term stability of society and appears to be a characteristic found among all societal groupings, it has become, in our modern circumstances of disjunctures and uncertainties, an impediment to the achievement of a more relevant and effective curricular design.

Witness the curricular situation of the public schools at the beginning of the 1990s, after decades of vehement calls for educational reform. As Anne C. Lewis, former executive editor of *Education USA*, noted:

*Despite the efforts of more than 200 public commissions and task forces dedicated to improving academic performance in the schools, despite higher graduation requirements enacted in 45 states, despite consistent messages that amount to Uncle Sam pointing at young people and saying, "I want you to think smarter," it isn't happening.*[1]

The five basic school subjects, established early in the twentieth century, remain English (and, at the elementary school level, the language arts), social studies, science, mathematics, and modern languages. The Commission on the Reorganization of Secondary Education, in 1918, strongly supported the introduction of such nonacademic subjects as physical education and vocational preparation. These had enjoyed a period of extensive growth, only to be denounced as wasting precious resources and taking time from the five basic academic subjects by many of the reformers of the 1980s.

Even within the parameters of these five subjects, the reconceptualization of the curriculum has met with significant resistance and ultimate failure. The "New Math" of the late 1950s and early 1960s created an uproar among parents and teachers and has all but disappeared from our collective memory. The "new social studies" of the 1960s and early 1970s has had little impact on today's curriculum, and American history, Western civilization, civics, and a smattering of geography remain the fundamental content of the subject. Depending on school finances, we may still find a few courses in music and art and, though often derided, driver's education.

### The Practicality of Idealistic Curriculum Making

The resistance to curricular change is too significant a phenomenon to ignore. It may even be discouraging when viewed historically. But if we do allow ourselves to be discouraged, a static and inflexible curriculum will be the inevitable result. However "impractical" curricular ideas may appear to be from a social, political, or economic perspective, a well-defined, logically reasoned conception of what might be possible is the first step toward making our ideas practical. It is, at least partially, a way of reforming our expectations and the images that are the baggage of twelve and more years of schooling.

We will explore several reasonably innovative curriculum designs incorporating some form of future studies. In all likelihood, the effort is an intellectual one that will have little impact for the real world of the public schools. If, however, the reader's mind is opened to new curricular possibilities, it will have been a worthwhile undertaking.

### A Future Relevant Curriculum Design: Model I

Our first curriculum proposal starts from the progressive position. That is, we believe knowledge is continually in the process of reconstruction. There is no one set of knowings that supersede in importance all other knowing; child interest should be a primary motivator of learning; individuals are naturally social and desirous of being part of society; early involvement in the problem-solving processes of government contributes to the continued survival of a democratic form of governance; and the young need to be empowered to deal effectively with an essentially uncertain future.

Model I would reject the position of the reconstructionists that some ideal preconception of the future should undergird the curriculum. It would remain consistent with progressivism in considering the construction of the future as a function of each new generation. Control of the future, to the degree possible, needs to be in the rights, responsibilities, and capabilities of students; they are to assume the leadership roles while educators guide and consult.

Model I reflects the conviction that education must come to terms with a future of uncertainty. Given this perspective, the study of disciplines offers a poor basis for the development of school subjects. Knowledge and skills derived from the disciplines would be used in the course of study, and electives based on disciplines would be available. However, the major core of school subjects in this curriculum design are organized around processes and skills related to increasing individual understanding and capability for dealing with the future.

The discipline-based design that currently dominates the school's curriculum might support the study of future-oriented issues as well as efforts to involve students in decision-making activities, but not without considerable difficulty and confusion. The study of disciplines requires one to learn those structures and processes unique to each discipline. If chemistry, economics, or psychology is studied, the relevant set of concepts, facts, generalizations, and processes needs to be learned or else the discipline is not really being studied. Issues and processes that make use of the knowledge of a discipline to prepare for future challenges may be included but only as a secondary or minor addition to the discipline-based curriculum. If time grows short, these "extras" most certainly would be set aside to accomplish the real goals of the curriculum and, judging from present experience, that is often the case. Reflecting on the uncertainties surrounding an issue or involving students in a decision-making, future-oriented situation does *not* lead to an understanding of the nature and operations of the discipline, however important the activity may be. A discussion about humanity's pollution of the planet does not lead to the increased understanding of, say, chemistry as a discipline. Under typical circumstances, the disciplines close out an array of nondisciplinary concerns. This is true even in a humanistic undertaking such as the study of history. All too frequently, history teachers find themselves reluctantly ignoring significant, *current* events because the history curriculum has been designed to cover the chronology, say, of the rise of America from its founding to the present. This is rarely accomplished because 800 or so textbook pages stand between the beginning and the present.

Model I attempts to respond to the question: What knowledge is most useful in coming to terms with and controlling the future? Six areas of study are seen as responding in important ways to this question. They are (1) communication and information handling; (2) uncertainties; (3) values development; (4) democratic citizenship; (5) inquiries, and (6) Futures.[2]

The six subjects are treated initially as independent areas of study. Basic knowledge and skills relevant to each area would be studied in this initial phase. For example, under communication and information handling, knowledge of computer operations, filming and video techniques, reading, and writing would be developed. Under uncertainties, the concept of change and related phenomena would be pursued. Under inquiries, scientific methodology, historiography, and other forms of inquiry would be studied. Under futures, studies concerning such concepts as experience compression, intragenerational disjunctures, and hyperturbulence would be pursued, along with statistical analyses relevant to futures forecasting. Subsequently, the six subjects would be treated in a progressively more integrated fashion; collaboration and integration of studies across subject areas would characterize the more advanced portion of the curriculum.

Communication and information handling as a school subject would recognize the need for people to understand and exercise control over the production, uses, and dissemination of information, especially in relationship to the explosion of technology and change that continues to characterize our lives. Skills in working with and manipulating the range of modern communication devices from computers to television and radio would be an important aspect of this study. These devices permeate our lives and in many ways dominate the directions society has taken and is likely to take in the future. A significant proportion of youngsters today are not only reading illiterates but computer and video illiterates as well. They view television for hours on end without understanding how the information thus derived has been organized to manipulate not only their opinions but their wants as well. And while they may feel no hesitation in using various computer programs, they seem to have little insight into the limitations and unchecked premises found in most complex computer operations. Reading literacy is a crucial factor in the development of these other literacies.

The school study of uncertainties would be another major component of the design. Uncertainties are of many kinds and the school subject would be organized to cover a broad range. Intragenerational disjunctures, experience compression, cultural inertia, hyperturbulence, and significant vectors of change would be among the conceptual organizers of study. Specific topics might include Einstein's general theory of relativity and the upheaval that it has brought to our understanding of time and of the nature of the universe; the continuing failure to find adequate storage for nuclear waste and its possible repercussions for our way of life; and the hypothetical but not improbable decline in reading and the parallel rise in other means of communicating information. Studying the multiple possibilities in outcomes and repercussions and dealing with the kinds of decisions that might have to be made despite uncertainty would comprise the real content of this subject. Specific topics would be selected annually or biennially on the basis of their current significance and likely future relevance.

The subject of uncertainties is related to another subject of our Model I curriculum: values development. The content of this subject would have little to do with the traditional passing on of values from one generation to the next. Rather it would involve students in the active formation of their own values as individuals and as citizens of a democracy. The process of value formation as a school subject is perceived to be analytical, moving toward objectivity from a fundamentally subjective basis, and critically evaluative. The process would require an ongoing reappraisal of new conditions. A series of questions would organize the subject as well as to objectify the exploration of values. These would include: Why should we have values at all? Should individually based or societally based values take precedence? Are all values culturally relative, or are some values absolute and culture free? How should we go about establishing new values? absolute values? What comprises a good life?

Students' initial studies in this area would start with their own subjective responses to these questions. Later, their work would involve reasoned analyses and evaluation of their own responses. This would be followed by their pursuing creative works produced in a variety of media and including both fiction and nonfiction efforts that are relevant to one of the questions. These works would be dealt with in a critically evaluative fashion with students reaching their own *logically defensible* judgments. At the more advanced stages of values development studies, students would be actively engaged in establishing both their own personal system of values and a societally based system of values that would take into account the basic precepts of democracy.

Model I includes three other school subjects: democratic citizenship, inquiries, and futures. Democratic citizenship would involve basic studies concerning the development of American democracy as well as comparative studies with other democracies and other forms of governance. Emphasis, however, would be placed on the development of decision-making skills related to the exercise of democratic citizenship. The qualities describing such skills are somewhat nebulous for they are based on achieving the holistic, active involvement of citizens in their own governance. They involve taking decisions in the midst of conflicting values, being willing to confront complexity rather than settling for simplistic solutions, working toward long-term goals as well as short-term objectives, making tentative albeit firm judgments while remaining willing to revise judgments in the light of new input, and being knowledgeable about the realities of the political process. The subject, as conceived, would be closely linked to values development, but the content would stress political phenomena, governance structures, and the activities of citizens.

Specifically, the course of study would include active participation in local and possibly federal government along with studies of significant current issues of governance. As recommended by Engle and Ochoa in their 1988 book *Education for Democratic Citizenship*,[3] a one-year, one-day-a-week citizenship internship directed toward some socially useful enterprise would serve as the culmination of instructional activities based on active involvement. In addition, comparative studies in both international forms of governance and the historical rise of different forms of governance would be pursued. Common to all planned experiences would be the engagement of students in decision-making activities.

Inquiries as a school subject would involve the formal study of diverse research methodologies ranging from classical scientific inquiry to humanistic modes of inquiry to new, paradigm-breaking forms such as those developing in the science of chaos. This universal approach to seeking information and developing knowledge would support the comparative study of several disciplines and the kinds of knowledge their various structures lead to. It would provide the opportunity for students to sample various disciplines of study so that they might pursue one or more of them in greater depth as electives.

Futures would serve as the linking "hub" for the other five subjects since it would utilize the processes, attitudes, and skills learned to develop scenarios of likely futures. Research tools relevant to trends analysis and forecasting would be drawn from the subject of inquiries. Analyses pursued in values development and insights into the nature of democracy derived from studies in democratic citizenship would contribute to the quality of judgments made in laying out desirable futures. Uncertainties, of course, would contribute to students' abilities to envision multiple possibilities. Communication and information handling would provide the expressive skills needed in the development of scenarios. With regard to the latter point, scenarios could be presented using the video camera, the computer, written forms, or some combination of these.

The scenarios would be of several types ranging from linear projections based on quantitative data to more fanciful visions of an ideal life. In students' earlier years, scenarios would be built around small, concrete experiences subject to improvement or change. For example, a scenario could be developed around ways of improving the neighborhood or the components of an ideal school. Subsequently, more advanced futures studies would become involved in complex plans such as the achievement of a pollution-free urban environment or colonizing other planets in our galaxy.

Several important design questions remain to be resolved. Among these are the selection of specific content and its sequence; the nature of transition studies that would most effectively link basic skills and concepts to more complex, integrated studies; the degree of curricular openness desirable; and the kind of summative evaluation to be used. Examples of specific content have been suggested above and are, we hope, sufficient to give the reader an understanding of the kind of content each subject would pursue. The selection of what is most worthwhile is directly linked to its importance in the development of youngsters' abilities to deal with an unknown future.

Principles of sequencing have not been made explicit. For example, content selection would first be based on the experiences and capabilities of the students and then expanded to include more worldly and generalizable experiences. When viable, the relationship of contents from two different content areas would be underlined by having their study occur in close temporal proximity. Most important, sequences would move from clearly delineated components related to specific skills or conceptual understandings to complex issues involving all the skills and problem-solving capabilities.

A diagrammatic overview of Model I follows:

**Model I**

| | Communication/ Information Handling | Uncertainties | Values Development | Democratic Citizenship | Inquiries | Futures |
|---|---|---|---|---|---|---|
| Basic Studies | | | | | | |
| Transition Studies | | | | | | |
| Integrated Studies | | | | | | |

The emphasis on future uncertainties and active student involvement in the decision-making activities of government embedded in this curriculum design necessarily means that the specific outcomes of the curriculum cannot and should not be fully known in advance. The design needs to be open to outcomes that are of the students' making.

This openness to uncertain outcomes is a necessity and holds considerable significance for how the curriculum is to be evaluated. It is not reasonable to encourage students to deal with uncertainty while evaluating them on the basis of closed-ended, standardized tests characterized by the "correct" answers on a series of multiple-choice items. Possibly, portfolio assessments, such as those adopted by the state of Vermont in 1991, might be more suitable to this design. Portfolio assessments require each student to develop a collection of her or his best work for evaluation by a team of expert teachers selected from schools around the state. The evaluation would occur at the students' home school and would involve them in holistic performances capable of conveying the complexity of the studies undertaken.

Of course, as we have already noted, real change requires more than a new curricular design. If the uniform scheduling of classes continues along with the adoption of textbooks for a minimum of five years and teachers continue to lecture and emphasize a myriad of factual, often trivial detail, then, regardless of design, little significant change will occur.

## A Future Relevant Curriculum Design: Model II

If we were to take the existential perspective, a model such as the one described above would be inappropriate. Model I supports discrete subjects that may start with the backgrounds of children but posit certain broad objectives for learning linked to the study of an uncertain future not only for individuals but also for the larger social group. Societal needs are perceived to be at least as important as personal insight. The existential perspective views the development of personal understanding and inner meaning as essential to and more important than any other learning that may occur. To find meaning in one's life and be in touch with oneself are foremost because it is the individual spirit that creates order in the world; the universe is essentially indifferent to human existence. It is of the utmost importance that each human being, caught in an uncaring world, define his or her world, for otherwise personal existence verges on nothingness. The conscious being is burdened with anxiety-filled choices. Sharing and reciprocity is a necessary condition to protect each individual's freedom to explore and understand. Knowledge is essentially personal.

Within this context, is a curricular design directed toward the study of the future and intended for public school education as we have known it in the twentieth century viable? Only if the structure of the curriculum is perceived to be nonprescriptive in nature, offering guidance and openness to the needs of the developing individual and based on the personal experiences and observations of each individual. Mood, feeling, and rational concepts must all play a role in learning.

An existentialist's design for the curriculum would most likely start with the individual, the achievement of self-identity and of harmony between self and the world around. Important knowledge has to do with the understanding of the mystery of being. A need for understanding implies communication, and existentialists unanimously agree that awareness and "being with others" is an essential part of being human.[4] Kierkegaard[5] and Jaspers[6] both acknowledge that communication is deeply bound up in this state of being. They explored the phenomenon of communication, however, without fully probing its depths. Nevertheless, it may be said they "laid the first foundations for a sound phenomenology of human communication."[7]

It is with communication linked to the exploration of self and the world that we propose to establish a curricular framework that would support preparation for and exploration of the future. From Heidegger[8] we take the idea that the individual is his own "maker," by having projects into the future. There is an underlying unity between the past, present, and future.

The student is seen as an independent explorer of the world. Human existence is full of vectors, tendencies and new directions. Change is a basic phenomenon of life, and human existence involves a constant striving toward uncertain goals never, however, to be fully realized. The curriculum should empower students to achieve a sense of self and of a future of their own construction.

Symbolics, expression, and communication would form the existential triumvirate of study. The purpose of each of these subjects is to enable students to explore with the full range of their emotional and rational potential the meaning and value of their lives. Meaning is to be understood in terms of a future becoming as well as a present being.

The development of diversified processes of thought and self-expression is crucial for the achievement of meaning in a time when change and complexity have increased exponentially. Finding one's niche in the world and being able to nurture dialogue in an increasingly electronic context may be accomplished in school by supporting the acquisition of a broad range of expressive and communicative abilities. In addition, being capable of experiencing the world has come more and more to involve manipulating and interpreting symbolic systems from simple ones such as the international sign system to Mandelbrot fractals and dynamic geometry.

The three subjects would be offered to students in relatively small "packages," whose duration would vary but would almost always be shorter than the traditional semester. Instructional packages would be available on a continuing basis, and students could move in and out of specific studies at will. Sequencing might be implied in the arrangement of packages but would largely depend on the choices students make. Summative evaluation and "graduation" could also be related to the portfolio idea discussed above. However, in this case, instead of having external teams come and judge the quality of the portfolios, students and teachers would, through dialogue, reach a consensus of the criteria and standards to be used. In continued collaboration, they, themselves, would be the final arbiters of the success or failure of the project(s).

Examples of possible content to be pursued in each of the three subjects follows.

> *Symbolics*: mathematics, algebra, trigonometry, statistics, etc.; computer languages; musical composition; symbolic logic, set theory, information theory.
>
> *Expression*: painting, graphics, sculpture, etc.; playing musical instruments, choral singing, participating in musicals, etc.; filming, videotaping, and audio recording; writing essays, poetry, short stories, letters.
>
> *Communication*: writing/reading (as skills to be acquired in English), reading and interpretation of literature, uses of metaphor, semantic analysis, etc.; nonverbal systems of communication; television as a system of communication; foreign languages.

These three subjects would be presented early in students' careers and would offer active involvement as a primary means of learning. Creativity and self-expression would be encouraged.

Two additional subjects would become part of the teacher–student dialogue once students are able to sustain complex and abstract discussions. These are ethics and the history of future time.

For the existentialist, participating in a universal world-time in which the past is held stable while the future is projected leads human conscience to demand "authentic" action. "Authentic," however, remains to be specifically defined. Each culture, each individual must complete the ethical picture independently. The goal is to exist in the most positive and intensely human way into the future. The underlying ethics for such a goal can hardly be fixed, but rather must be continually related to shifting norms and circumstances. Ethics will provide students with the opportunity to explore choices and possible consequences not only as functions of rational analysis but also of human moods and feelings. Students will be encouraged to explore new ways of viewing and organizing morality in a future of uncertainty.

The history of future time would offer students numerous brief, future scenarios from which they may choose several to be pursued in-depth as a set of past, present, and future events. A list of possible, "brief" scenarios follows:

1. The European Common Market has come into being. This is placing United States business in jeopardy and many expect the dollar's value to collapse.
2. Nuclear waste will soon be stored in outer space.
3. Scientists will be able shortly to assist the body in regenerating its own organs.
4. Instead of getting hotter, as was predicted in the 1980s because of the greenhouse effect, the world has become much colder. Crops have suffered severely.
5. Half of the white-collar labor force is now working out of their homes. It is expected that the traditional office will soon disappear while customer service centers will multiply.
6. "Nonlinear dynamics" is contributing to the development of a science of chaos. Our understanding of the world we live in is undergoing radical change.

Students would select one of these future-oriented scenarios and develop a more complete description including past, present, and future events. Video taping, radio scripting, and collages are modes of expression that students could use to explore the full range and depth of their scenarios. Communicative skills would be used if the final scenarios are to be shared with others. If the student wished to pursue the effort in greater depth, an ethical study could be undertaken based on the question: Does this contribute to a better human existence?

A diagrammatic overview of Model II follows:

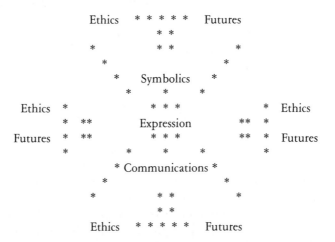

## A Future Relevant Curriculum Design: Model III

The essentialists believe that schooling is first and foremost about the intellectual development of children. They could probably be persuaded that education must prepare students intellectually for the upheavals and uncertainties of the future. However, it is highly unlikely that they would accept a curricular design without what they believe are the fundamental academic areas of study: English (including grammar, composition, reading, literary history), history, mathematics, and science. Subjects such as civics and physical education are seen as creating unwelcome diversions from the primary purpose of intellectual development. It is certainly improbable that a new subject such as futures, based on problems and issues rather than on a discipline, would receive their support.

Nevertheless, the essentialist curriculum would respond to new intellectual needs if they were felt to be of long-term benefit to students. The response would arise through a review of the disciplines included as subjects under each of the academic areas of study.

For example, under the general rubric of science, we typically study the disciplines of biology, chemistry, and physics. In assessing the relevance of these for likely future developments, other disciplines might be considered more appropriate. Genetics might substitute for the broader study of biology given the extraordinary developments in this field in the 1980s and that promise to continue into the twenty-first century. In mathematics, the study of statistics might replace trigonometry because statistics are used in many aspects of intellectual endeavor from the social sciences to quantum mechanics, while trigonometry maintains its importance within quite limited parameters.

However, until quite recently, dealing with uncertainty would have been out of the question in a discipline-bound, essentialist curriculum. The rising science of chaos[9] has changed this considerably. Non-Euclidean order and pattern have been discovered where once only randomness and the erratic would have been discerned. Chaos is becoming the science of disorder and the unpredictable. It is opening up a whole new way of viewing the world and might be added to science studies.

Unfortunately, the study of sociological change and future uncertainties in our socioeconomic and political circumstances has as yet no comparable disciplinary study and is unlikely to reach the essentialist curriculum except as an extension of currently included disciplines. In the study of history, periods of radical change and upheaval could be explored in depth and possibly compared to similar periods in our more recent history. In addition to the history of the Western world, global history is likely to become a part of the curriculum. In economics, the skills and processes related to forecasting and trends analysis could be brought prominently into the study of the discipline. In English, the development of future-based scenarios combined with critiques regarding the desirability of what has been predicted could be made a major component of composition.

Thus, Model III is one of additions and extensions. The learning of the disciplines and the increase of intellectual capabilities are central to the purposes of the curriculum. If the complexity and uncertainty of the future are to be dealt with at all, it must be within these parameters. The powers of reasoning and reflection must be brought to bear on the future through those disciplines that have yielded for humankind the greatest advancements. Control over an uncertain future is necessarily linked to the development of human intellect.

A diagrammatic overview of Model III follows.

| Area of Study | Current Disciplines | Revisions |
|---|---|---|
| Mathematics | Geometry<br>Algebra<br>Trigonometry<br>Calculus, etc. | *Add* Statistics (possible substitute for trigonometry) |
| Science | Biology<br>Chemistry<br>Physics, etc. | *Add* Genetics (possible substitute for biology)<br>*Add* Chaos |
| History | American History<br>Western History | *Integrate* historical views of crises and upheavals<br>*Add* Global |
| English | Grammar<br>Reading<br>Literature<br>Composition, etc. | *Add* development of future scenarios |
| Economics | Laws and history of economic development | *Integrate* skills in forecasting and trend analysis. |

## A Multiplicity of Curriculum Designs

The possible curricular designs are limited by our need, our imagination and our cultural willingness to consider new options. In this chapter, we ignored the limitations inherent in our current educational system and allowed ourselves to develop curricular solutions for a problematic future without considering the political or social circumstances that would surely enter into any equation for change. In the last section of this book we will look at the curriculum of today's schools and explore how it may be realistically revised to respond to the future more adequately.

## QUESTIONS FOR DISCUSSION AND REFLECTION

1. The authors have found youngsters to be rather naive in their views of the future. If you are currently teaching, why not explore the views of your students and decide for yourself whether your students are well prepared for the future. What should the goals of the curriculum be with regard to the future?

2. What primary forces drive curriculum design at the present time?

3. In what ways might a curriculum developer deal with cultural inertia within the context of the curriculum design?

4. What are the differences and similarities between Model I and Model II?

5. Is the method suggested in Model III for modifying the curriculum viable in your school? Explain your answer fully. What would make it viable or increase its viability?

6. What do you personally believe students need to become well prepared for a largely unpredictable future? Explain your answer fully and give specific examples.

7. Create a futures-oriented curriculum design. Be sure to establish the philosophical perspective underlying your model.

8. Should alternative schools be developed to give parents the possibility of choosing a school suited to their views and ideals? How would alternative schools support as well as interfere with the adoption of future-oriented curriculum?

## NOTES

1. Lewis, A. C. (1990). Getting unstuck: Curriculum as a tool of reform. *Phi Delta Kappan, 71,* 7, 534–538.
2. This model is an expanded version of one that appeared in an earlier chapter by one of the authors: Longstreet, W. S. (1979). Open education—A coming to terms with uncertainty. In Overly, N. V. (ed.). *Life-long learning: A human agenda.* Alexandria, VA: Association for Supervision and Curriculum Development.
3. Engle, S. H. and Ochoa, A. S. (1988). *Education for democratic citizenship: Decision-making in the social studies.* New York: Teachers College Press, p. 146.
4. Wild, J. (1959). *The challenge of existentialism.* Bloomington, IN: Indiana University Press, p. 206.
5. Kierkegaard, S. (1940). *Stages on life's way.* Princeton, NJ: Princeton University Press.
   Also: Kierkegaard, S. (1941). *Fear and trembling.* Princeton, NJ: Princeton University Press.
6. Jaspers, Karl (1951). *Way to wisdom* (Manheim, R., translator). New Haven: CT: Yale University Press.
7. *Op. cit.,* Wild, J. p. 214.
8. Heidegger, M. (1949). *Existence and being.* Chicago: Regnery.
9. Gleick, J. (1987). *Chaos: Making a new science.* New York: Penguin Books.

# 12

# The Mathematics Curriculum

## Introduction

The results of standardized testing are most disheartening in the area of mathematics. According to reports issued by the National Assessment of Educational Progress (NAEP), only about half of the 17-year-olds tested in 1986 could complete problems requiring the interpretation of graphs and the finding of averages.[1] NAEP found that a considerable number of 13-year-olds lacked the skills needed to do mathematics encountered on a daily basis, such as addition and subtraction. Furthermore, a high percentage of third and fouth graders lacked an understanding of the most rudimentary mathematical concepts and skills. The dropout rate from mathematical studies soars to fifty percent or more as soon as students have fulfilled minimum requirements.[2] According to Izaak Wirszup, professor emeritus of mathematics at the University of Chicago, only 12,557 bachelor's degrees in mathematics were awarded in the United States in 1983, which is a decline of over 50 percent compared to the 27,563 degrees in mathematics awarded in 1970.[3] The demand for qualified mathematicians in science, engineering, industry, and education will not be met if interest in advanced study continues at such low levels.

Negative statistics about mathematics education have become the norm over the last several decades, and calls for reform have come from every quarter. In part as a response, the U.S. Department of Energy announced in May 1990 that it would launch America into " 'a new Renaissance period' in science and mathematics."[4] Toward this end, a conference was held a few months earlier at the Lawrence Hall of Science in Berkeley, California, to plan for improving education in the sciences and mathematics. The agenda developed included establishing a K–12 core curriculum in mathematics; providing enhancement programs for teachers; increasing the number of minority, female, and disabled students completing advanced courses in mathematics; and expanding alliances between government, industries, and education.[5]

Interagency collaborations are a reality. For example, the Sandia and Los Alamos Laboratories have made arrangements to lend their expert workers to Native American schools as consultants for the math and science teachers. The University of Tennessee in collaboration with the Oak Ridge National Laboratory has developed a preservice math and science teacher education program for technically trained professionals wishing to change careers. Businesses across the nation have befriended local school systems.

The increasing number of collaborations does hold promise for innovation and renewal. However, most efforts appear to be directed toward improving the quality of instruction rather than toward a revision of the actual curriculum. Certainly, the most challenging item on the Department of Energy's agenda is establishing a K–12 core curriculum in mathematics. In the early 1980s, *A Nation at Risk*,[6] perhaps the most well-known of this era's calls for reform, proposed increasing the number of Carnegie units typically required in the average student's mathematics program. The report paid little attention to the actual content of the curriculum. Still serious questions concern the adequacy of the traditional mathematics curriculum.

John A. Dossey, past president of the National Council of Teachers of Mathematics (NCTM), has urged a complete overhaul of the mathematics curriculum and a revision of teacher training efforts.[7] In 1989, NCTM issued new standards for the mathematics curriculum that included several significant modifications. Talk of the *new* "New Math" has already entered the professional literature,[8] and discussions regarding how to meet the mathematical challenges of a new millennium abound.

Before exploring the NCTM recommendations followed by possible future developments, this chapter examines the problems and difficulties that have historically beleaguered the mathematics program and presents a brief history of mathematics and its school instruction. It further examines the mathematics curriculum that dominates in the schools. The University of Chicago School Mathematics Project, designed to change the present curriculum and turn the negative situation around, is also discussed.

## Historical Overview

### The Explosion of Knowledge — 16th Century into the Future

Until the mid sixteenth century, Western mathematics developed slowly and without remarkable discoveries. Early Italian mathematicians such as Leonardo Fibonacci (1170–1230) and Luca Pacioli (c. 1450–c. 1520) were largely indebted to Arabic sources for much of their work. In 1545, Gerolamo Cardana discovered an algebraic formula for solving both cubic and quadratic equations that led to Galois's theory of equations in the nineteenth century. In essence, the explosion in mathematical knowledge had begun and to this day has not ceased its extraordinary development.

In the seventeenth century, Napier discovered logarithms; Descartes discovered analytic geometry; Pascal and Fermat laid the basis for probability theory; and Newton, followed a few years later by Leibniz, discovered differential and integral calculus. Developments in the eighteenth century occurred even more quickly. Among the most important advances were Cantor's set theory and the discovery of Boolean algebra, which has been crucial in the development of computers. It could be estimated that "five times as much mathematics" had been produced in the nineteenth century than in all the previous centuries combined.[9] The French physicist Pierre Laplace could creditably put forth the idea that one day a mathematical equation would be discovered powerful enough to "explain everything."[10] We owe to the nineteenth century and to Charles Babbage's creative talents a computational machine that could be directed to carry out programs according to a series of instructions stored on punched cards—an idea inspired by Joseph Jacquard's invention of a loom using punched cards to guide the placement of threads. With the twentieth century and the arrival of the relay and the vacuum tube followed by the transistor, the programmable digital computer became a reality.

Mathematical knowledge increased many times over and continues to advance at an ever swifter pace. The computer has enabled the solution of problems once so time-consuming as to be thought unsolvable. The famous four-color problem is an example. The question was whether four colors would be sufficient to design a map, regardless of size, such that any two countries sharing borders would be of different colors. Proof of an affirmative response was achieved in 1976 on what was then considered a large-scale computer. Increasingly powerful computers have given impetus to the advancement of such diverse areas of investigation as differential equations, number theory, and topology.

We are on the threshold of a new science of chaos, which embodies the realization that in the midst of irregularity lies geometric regularity.[11] Patterns have been found in nature that are orderly in space but not in time or vice versa. Some are fractal, exhibiting recursive characteristics of self-similarity, while others remain in oscillating or steady states. At the heart of all this is the search for understanding how nature can be simultaneously both predictable and unpredictable— how snowflakes or trees can follow similar patterns while no two are alike. Already, applied uses are being sought for chaos in such areas as the epidemology of diseases, variations on the commodity exchange, and weather forecasting. The computer with its vast mathematical capabilities is providing new ways of working or, in Kuhnian terminology, new methodologies to suit a revolutionary paradigm.[12]

### Lagging Curriculum and Instruction

It would be reasonable to expect that an extraordinary increase in mathematical knowledge would lead to significant changes in the curriculum and its instruction. Curricular change, however, comes very slowly and with a reluctance born from deeply embedded cultural mindsets and from the political realities related to protecting one's "turf"; of possibly losing personal and institutional benefits if the current way(s) of functioning were to change. The lag between the recognition of new educational needs and the implementation of an adequately modified curriculum responsive to such needs has historically been great and remains so even in these times of perpetual innovation.

Until the 1600s, mathematics education remained essentially unchanged from the time of the Greek academy when mathematical concepts were considered an appropriate vehicle for the teaching of philosophy.[13] In fact, the role of mathematics in the curriculum before the seventeenth century was spotty and would certainly not have been included in the course offerings of the "better" schools such as Eton.[14] Budding commercial activity in Europe in the thirteenth century had led to a number of textbooks dealing with practical arithmetic problems including weighing, measuring, and money transactions, but these works were really not designed for the educated elite.

Significant curricular change ultimately depended on the coming together of several major historical events: (1) the development of efficient, oceangoing merchant ships in the fifteenth and sixteenth centuries leading to a rapid expansion of commerce, (2) the rise of a wealthy merchant class having significant political power, and (3) the growth of the sciences, whose progress was often related to advances in mathematics. A twofold development in the mathematics curriculum resulted. On the one hand, mathematics was increasingly presented to school children in the form of commercial arithmetic. On the other, to a lesser degree, there was a growing interest in the study of mathematical abstractions such as those embodied in the disciplines of algebra and geometry, which have become a fixed part of today's typical high school curriculum.

At the beginning of the nineteenth century, the English began to incorporate mathematics into their public school instruction, giving considerable emphasis to the benefits of mathematics as a mental discipline.[15] Both trends were ultimately reduced in the schools to the rote learning of systematic sets of rules primarily by drill and practice. In the twentieth century, the need for theoretical mathematicians has become progressively more acute. Even those more commercially oriented have expressed great dissatisfaction with the apparent lack of mathematical problem-solving skills among American students.

## Current Trends and Issues

### Knowledge and the Record of Knowledge

Reform movements and protests about ineffective instruction notwithstanding, the way we teach mathematics has changed very little over the years.[16] It is for the most part an approach based on "tell and show" with a single textbook as the main curriculum guide. Large-group instruction followed by seatwork is the dominant pattern. Students are told how to perform a certain computational procedure, are shown several examples, usually on the chalkboard, and then are assigned drill and practice.

Thomas Romberg, a mathematics educator at the University of Wisconsin, distressed by this persistent and increasingly unproductive pattern, has reiterated the distinction made by John Dewey between knowledge that is developed by the individual in the course of an activity and the record of the knowledge that has been communicated to students.[17] The latter may be turned into a "successful" effort at having students acquire information by rote and may even result in good scores on standardized tests, but until students actually experience the conceptual development of mathematics, they have not acquired knowledge.

The dominance of tell and show has been especially true at the very earliest elementary grades when students are expected to learn the multiplication tables by heart. As a result, young children's understanding of what is actually going on in a computational procedure such as multiplication may be quite limited. Most do not grasp conceptually, especially with multidigit numbers, that they are engaged in a form of addition.[18] Long division is even more likely to be learned as a memorized computational procedure (or algorithm). The understanding that they are actually engaged in a form of subtraction is only infrequently achieved by fourth and fifth graders. The teaching of fractions is repeated from the fourth grade to the eighth grade; junior high school teachers still complain that their students do not understand the meaning of fractions or how to use them correctly. Quite simply, a majority of students from their earliest school years are baffled by mathematics and become, at best, technicians capable of employing the procedures necessary for passing the test.

The need for theoretical mathematics has greatly increased with the continued development of the computer. Virtually all scientists—indeed, all professionals—encounter mathematical models in the course of their work.[19] The public schools, on the whole, have not come to grips with the fact that computers have changed the way we deal with mathematics and the extent to which mathematics permeates our lives.[20]

## The Philosophical Spectrum

Across the philosophical spectrum is widespread agreement that the achievement of conceptual understanding and problem-solving capabilities ought to be central to mathematics instruction. This agreement, however, hides important differences. Perennialists would prefer to follow the ancient Greek academies in their use of mathematics as a vehicle for the study of philosophy. Of course, they support a conceptual development of mathematical knowledge. Essentialists would pursue abstract, conceptually based, generalizable studies considered to be supportive of the mathematical needs of society. Vocational mathematics expected to satisfy immediate needs would be unacceptable. Progressivists and reconstructionists would begin with applied mathematics, engaging students in problem solving linked to their experiences. Broader, more conceptual understandings would be developed as students' interests move beyond their immediate realm. Existentialists, true to their view that the curriculum must be derived from each individual child's personality and needs, would support students in their mathematical investigations and help them to extend their knowledge but without establishing any programmatic sequence of study.

"Official" goals typically set forth for mathematical studies have long given a great deal more importance to gaining knowledge of concepts than to the rote mastery of computational skills.[21] The development of problem-solving abilities, the understanding of logical relationships, the capacity to use mathematics in real world settings, and the encouragement of mathematical creativity are nearly always presented by curriculum guides as among their intended outcomes.[22]

We have nevertheless become increasingly involved in pursuing records of knowledge rather than in the conceptual development of knowledge. With mindless eclecticism at the fore, there has been widespread support for standardized tests that have, in fact, a conservative, traditional effect on current curricula. It appears we lack not only the clarity but the cultural will to make the changes in the mathematics curriculum that most would agree are necessary.

### The Content of the Current Curriculum

Few empirical studies have been undertaken to describe the "implemented curriculum," that is, the curriculum that actually is presented in the classroom.[23] In a summary review of two such studies, Porter concludes:

> There was not a single example of consensus among teachers to emphasize a topic having to do with conceptual understanding or applications.
>
> These findings of heavy emphasis on skill development and slight attention to concepts and applications may help to explain the United States' relatively poor standing among other nations on mathematics problem-solving ability of students. Can we expect our students to learn what they are not taught?[24]

There is, of course, the planned or "intended" curriculum. The topics currently included in the K–12 mathematics curriculum have been essentially unchanged for decades and most of us are quite familiar with them. The earliest grades deal with learning the numeration system, addition and subtraction of whole numbers, performing very simple measurements and in-depth reviews with repeated drills of these topics through the third grade.

Problem solving is presumedly introduced in kindergarten and is expected to receive progressively more attention with each passing grade. That the skills of problem solving are not successfully acquired by a substantial portion of students has already been noted. Teacher avoidance of problem solving is likely to be one source of the problem. Another source of difficulty may relate to the instructional methodologies pursued. Word problems are first encountered by youngsters in the third grade and are often the only real effort to engage students in the solving of problems through the twelfth grade.

In the earlier grades, word problems have proved to be especially unsuccessful because most children are still in the preoperational and concrete stages of thought development as described by Piaget.[25] That is, they need to deal with concrete problems that are close at hand, rather than in abstractions which can be more readily handled during the formal operations stage of development when propositional thinking is within their capabilities. In fact, there is research to suggest that some two thirds of high school seniors may not have reached the formal operations stage.[26] In any case, problem solving in the early grades needs to be based on specific, concrete factors that youngsters can perceive for themselves and manipulate.

Instruction in multiplication of whole numbers may also begin in the third grade but is especially stressed in the fourth grade together with long division. The addition and subtraction of fractions is usually taught in the fifth grade and then repeated for the next three school years. Decimals are introduced in the fifth grade as well and then reviewed in the sixth and seventh grades.

Learning fractions appears to be the first real hurdle in most students' mathematical experience. Many students have difficulty understanding them especially when multiplication and division of fractions are introduced in the sixth grade. It may be that the level of abstraction required is beyond the cognitive developmental stage of a good percentage of the students. In any case, it has become part of the tradition to review fractions extensively in the seventh and eighth grades.

The ninth grade typically introduces the study of algebra and marks the beginning of high school mathematics and the first real departure from an arithmetic base. Given that fractions mystify many eighth graders, the shock of encountering algebra must indeed be overwhelming. Geometry and trigonometry at introductory levels of study comprise the remainder of the typical secondary curriculum, although calculus is increasingly found among high school offerings. As noted above, mathematical studies become progressively unpopular among students as they advance to the upper grades. Efforts at reform of the curriculum, however, have not met with success.

## Computers and Calculators

Although diminishing, there has been significant resistance among math educators to incorporate calculators and computers into instruction, especially in the earlier grades. In 1974, the NCTM urged the integration of calculators into the curriculum. Eight years later, Suydam[27] reported that less than twenty percent of elementary teachers allowed the calculator to be used during mathematics instruction. At the secondary level, only 36 percent of teachers used calculators.[28] No doubt, the image that nearly every supermarket shopper has of the young cashier unable to figure change when the register has not indicated the correct amount contributes greatly to this reticence. Math teachers are especially concerned that students not be hindered in their acquisition of basic arithmetic skills. The fear is that students will learn how to press the buttons without really knowing what they are doing. Studies conducted by Wheatley et al.[29] and Roberts[30] among others appear to support the contrary conclusion that the use of calculators actually improves the average student's basic skills with paper and pencil both in working exercises and in problem solving.

Avoiding the use of electronic supplements, which has persisted into the 1990s although to a lesser degree than in the eighties, has done little to reduce the number of students lacking conceptual grasp of the mathematical algorithms they have memorized. It is likely that relieving students of the onerously long computations often found in the midst of problem-solving activities will contribute to increased conceptual understanding by diminishing the number and burden of rote activities. Such activities consume inordinate amounts of time and may actually become distractors interfering with the concentration needed for conceptual understanding.

The extraordinary advances in mathematics supported by computers has made the reconsideration of the role of calculators and computers in the school's curriculum a professional necessity.[31] The reprioritization of skills vis-à-vis the electronic revolution is clearly under way. In addition to basic arithmetic and problem-solving skills, students need competence in the use of estimation techniques, statistical modeling, probability, forecasting and prediction, geometry and measurement. All these activities have greatly increased in frequency of use and importance with the advent of the microcomputer era. Should we modify the school's curriculum to reflect our new mathematical realities, instruction would move radically away from rote drill and practice to involving students both actively and conceptually in the collection, organization and analyses of data. Making well-founded forecasts, evaluating statistical models, and running statistical experiments are among the kinds of activities now possible even for the less affluent schools because of the declining costs and widespread availability of computers.

Whether we have reached a point culturally to support significant curricular change even within the limits of a long-established subject is an unknown. The experience of the "New Math" about a quarter of a century ago is worth exploring in this regard. There was federal funding, intellectual leadership, and a cadre of enthusiastic supporters, but there also was little lasting change.

## The New Math

From the late 1950s to the early 1970s, a major curricular reform effort in mathematics was undertaken to shift from drill, practice, and rote memorization to an emphasis on meaning and concept. The effort at revision, which was dubbed the "New Math," was largely a response to the vastly increased use of mathematics in industry as well as in the physical, biological, and social sciences. At a conference sponsored by the School Mathematics Study Group (SMSG) in 1959, the importance of elementary mathematics to secondary school success was recognized and an agreement was reached to revise the elementary program so that it would be supportive of the expected outcomes of the secondary program. Historically, this was the first time that reform was to flow from the elementary grades to the secondary grades rather than vice versa. With SMSG leading the way, New Math programs and materials were developed.

The intent was to teach the underlying theories of mathematics as a discipline, thereby giving students insight into what they were doing and why. Instead of practice in the basic skills, the New Math presented set theory including the union, complements, and intersection of sets. Different number bases and how they functioned was another important topic. While youngsters were being introduced to subtraction, they were also presented with the beginnings of algebra. In the earliest grades, these ideas were introduced without formal definitions and took the place of such traditional activities as memorizing the multiplication tables.

The long-standing tension between mathematics as a commercial, practical study and mathematics as a theoretical discipline reached a fever pitch for the public and teachers alike. The new curriculum was exceedingly abstract, a major departure from the traditional one, and difficult to understand especially for the parents of elementary school children who would come home expecting some help. Most of all, it neglected the practical. The rote memorization of the multiplication tables and repeated drill and practice with the other basic mathematical operations were dispensed with while children became familiar with sophisticated, conceptual theories that were often not well explained by teachers whose backgrounds had not prepared them for a content of this kind. Students did not do as well in making change or in other simple transactions with money as they had done under the old system; nor did they reach the conceptual level of understanding hoped for. Standardized tests had generally not adjusted to the new curriculum and test scores continued to decline. Criticism of the New Math was widespread. Typical was Morris Kline's position that sound mathematics was not the same as sound pedagogy in mathematics.[32] By 1974, the "Back to Basics" movement, meaning a return to the mathematics curriculum of the first part of the century, was in full swing. The New Math, which represented for the experts the kind of theoretical mathematics necessary to maintain America's technological leadership, was out!

### The University of Chicago School Mathematics Project

Despite this apparent failure at curricular reform, the objectives of the New Math have remained in public discussions as desirable ends. Curriculum projects continue to be mounted in an effort to incorporate advances in the sciences and technology and to increase students' knowledge and skills especially with regard to problem solving. Among these, the University of Chicago School Mathematics Project (UCSMP), sponsored by the Amoco Foundation for six years beginning in 1983 and extended with funding from the Carnegie Corporation, the General Electric Foundation, and the National Science Foundation, has received a great deal of attention from the media. Its purpose is to meet "the growing need for a mathematically literate public in a technological age."[33] Izaak Wirszup, UCSMP's principal investigator, is intent on revising school mathematics for the 1990s so that the curriculum will emphasize mathematics of contemporary importance, incorporate advances in technology, and increase students' proficiency in problem solving.[34]

The project is organized into five components designed for a coordinated

K–12 curricular reform.[35] The Elementary Component is responsible for the development of the K–6 pilot curriculum and related teacher preparation. The Secondary Component deals with the 7–12 curriculum and related teacher preparation. The Resource Development Component is responsible for maintaining international contacts, conducting surveys of foreign mathematics resources, and translating selected materials for use in the project. The Evaluation Component undertakes experiments and research designs to provide empirical evidence of effectiveness; it also observes classroom and teacher activities, giving feedback to the project staff. The Administrative Component is responsible for the integration of the activities of the other components.

It is this emphasis on integration, along with plans to develop both teacher skills and adequate instructional materials, that holds promise for avoiding the mistakes of the New Math era. The idea of adapting the best materials from Western Europe, Japan, and the former Soviet Union may contribute in a significant way to the opening of new vistas for American mathematics education. Wirszup is especially frustrated by the current poor quality of instructional materials, which he says are a waste of time.[36] He also believes that involving students in problem solving will spark the kind of interest necessary for improved performance.[37]

The features of the UCSMP curriculum are in several respects similar to those of the New Math. Algebra is introduced in the elementary grades with the same informality that was part of the New Math effort. Geometry and statistics are also informally integrated into the elementary curriculum.

Reflecting the electronic progress of the 1980s, UCSMP utilizes simple, handheld calculators throughout the K–6 curriculum. Scientific calculators are introduced in the seventh grade. The seventh grade is reserved to a course in transition mathematics designed as a bridge between arithmetic and the formal study of algebra and geometry. This is a new curricular idea and may serve to alleviate the difficulties that many youngsters experience in moving from elementary to secondary mathematics. Statistics and probability, algebra, and geometry are major components of the secondary curriculum in addition to a twelfth grade course in discrete mathematics. It is in this course on discrete mathematics that the UCSMP curriculum clearly distances itself from the curricular recommendations of the New Math.

As the use of digital computers expands, the need for discrete mathematics has surpassed the need for classical, continuous mathematics and calculus.[38] Currently, at the college level, calculus dominates the first two years, which has, in turn, impacted on the high school curriculum. Many high schools offer calculus as the culminating course in the precollegiate, mathematics curriculum. Very few, if any, offer discrete mathematics comprised of such topics as graph theory, the design and analysis of algorithms, set theory, number theory, abstract and linear algebra, combinatorices, and mathematical logic.[39]

Eric W. Hart of the Maharishi International University suggests that the content of the New Math was based on "formal axiomatic and existential proofs," whereas discrete mathematics is based on "algorithmic-constructive proofs."[40] In other words, the approach of new math was "axiomatic and holistic" while discrete mathematics is "algorithmic and recursive."[41]

No doubt, the reader with limited mathematical background is having some difficulty following this discussion. It emphasizes the theoretical character of both the New Math and the curriculum of the UCSMP project. A major mistake of the new math reform movement was its disregard for the commercial, practical uses of mathematics. Furthermore, reaction to excessive drill and repetition of topics often ends in overcorrection, that is, in the elimination of the kind of reiterative practice with basic math operations that make them second nature to most of us, allowing us to conduct our daily business transactions without having to resort to paper and pencil figuring.

It remains to be seen whether the errors of the past are being repeated by a new generation of scholars. In 1989, an estimated 35,000 students were using the materials developed under UCSMP and another 15,000 were studying with teachers trained using the project's materials.[42] Summary evaluation beyond enthusiastic testimonials remains to be published. In the meantime, a national consensus about what needs to be done appears to be coalescing and strengthening.

### The NCTM Standards

The National Council of Teachers of Mathematics issued, in March 1989, a report from its Commission on Standards for School Mathematics.[43] The report includes three sets of curriculum standards for grades K–4, 5–8, and 9–12, respectively, and a related set of fourteen evaluation standards to be used in program evaluation and the assessment of student performance.

Five general curriculum goals are established for all students at all grade levels, as follows:

1. To become mathematical problem solvers
2. To learn to communicate mathematically
3. To learn to reason mathematically
4. To learn to value mathematics
5. To become confident in one's own ability to do mathematics[44]

In the course of explaining the curriculum standards, problem solving is defined as being able to use a variety of strategies in solving a wide range of problems from a number of diverse sources. It includes being able to discuss alternative solutions, to generalize solutions and strategies to new situations, to formulate problems from the mathematical as well as the real world, and to apply mathematical modeling techniques to real situations and problems.

Communicating mathematically is presented as being able to use a language, including symbols, to represent and expand mathematical ideas. It also means being able to model situations in a variety of ways including pictorial, graphical, and algebraic modes and to work with different means of representation to solve problems and validate hypotheses. In the secondary grades, 9–12, being able to express mathematical ideas in writing is added.

Mathematical reasoning is described in the curriculum standards as involving the capacity to find relationships and extend patterns, to explain and justify solutions, to make and validate conjectures, and to recognize both deductive and inductive arguments. In the upper grades, students are expected to go beyond recognizing logical arguments to being able to formulate valid arguments as well as to judge the validity of arguments.

The fourth goal of valuing mathematics is expressed more vaguely in the NCTM curriculum standards than are the preceding three. Valuing mathematics is expected to permeate all of the standards. Students are to come to appreciate the importance of mathematics for contemporary society and for our cultural development.

Becoming confident in one's own ability to do mathematics is also not included in any one curriculum standard but is expected, as in the preceding instance, to permeate all the standards. The curriculum is seen as using many experiences related to the development of mathematics to help students understand that mathematics is a product of the human mind that they are capable of controlling.

The lack of more extensive elaboration in the curriculum standards with regard to learning to value mathematics and to become confident in one's own ability to do mathematics is a cause for concern. In fairness, it should be noted that there is an evaluation standard that refers to "mathematical disposition." It includes among its important characteristics the willingness to persevere at mathematical tasks, interest, curiosity, and the like. However, given our cultural mindsets about the importance of learning mathematical operations and of passing the standardized test, there is reason to doubt that much importance will be given to the evaluation of mathematical disposition and the teacher's ability to ameliorate in children such dispositional traits as perseverance and a positive attitude toward the study of mathematics. Nevertheless, the consideration of disposition is certainly a step away from the traditional, memoriter approach to mathematics.

As noted previously, the curriculum standards are presented in three separate sections representing grades K–4, 5–8, and 9–12, respectively. The underlying assumptions of the twelve standards set forth for the K–4 group include that the curriculum is conceptually oriented, that it is developmentally appropriate, that it actively involves youngsters in the doing of mathematics, that it emphasizes the interrelationships of mathematical knowledge, and that it makes full use of calculators.

Grades 5–8 are seen as a time of emotional and intellectual instability for youngsters and self-esteem must be especially nurtured. The incorporation of problem situations into the curriculum is seen as a way of motivating students and creating for them the need to comprehend new mathematical ideas. Intellectual excitement rather than a mere review of grades K–4 is seen as the primary factor driving the 5–8 standards.

Underlying assumptions for the fourteen curriculum standards set forth for grades 9–12 include the expectation that students entering the ninth grade will already have an enriched background as outlined in the standards for the earlier grades. In addition, students will have achieved computational proficiency, although they are not to be denied access to mathematical studies if they lack the expected proficiency. It is also assumed that scientific calculators will be available to students at all times and that there will be a computer in every classroom for demonstration purposes. It is further assumed that at least three years of mathematical studies will be the minimum requirement for high school graduation and four years will be required in precollegiate study. Of course, any increase in the study of mathematics means a decrease of time for other subjects in the curriculum such as modern foreign language.

For many of our schools and their students, the assumptions appear to be at least doubtful if not unrealistic. For example, it is unlikely that most inner-city schools will be able to supply scientific calculators for all their students or that there will be a computer in every math classroom for demonstrations. Assuming computational proficiency while not excluding students who have not achieved such proficiency poses considerable instructional difficulties apparently overlooked by the commission.

As Alan Bishop noted in a review of the new NCTM standards,[45] there appears to be very little recognition of the social milieu and its constraints on the instructional environment. The standards appear to assume that the improvement of the instructional act is primarily a question of how students and teachers relate to each other. The very real and complex problems of the typical inner-city school are hardly considered: poverty, drugs, racial and social inequality, among others are ignored as is the encapsulation of scholastic tradition that imbues students and teachers alike. Bishop puts it quite aptly: "Education is about goals and ideals, but schools and educational institutions are places of work and are about rules, which have their own existence and morality."[46] Students come to school with a great deal of baggage and to ignore this, as the standards do, creates an irrelevance about them that is unfortunate for they are proposing reforms of the utmost urgency.

Notwithstanding such reservations as expressed here, the report of the Commission on Standards for School Mathematics represents a determined effort to move away from the memorized mastery of basic computational skills that has continued to typify mathematics education in the United States despite beliefs and efforts to the contrary. Even at the secondary level where such traditional subjects as algebra, geometry, trigonometry, and functions are assigned a central role in the curriculum, the commission calls for increased emphasis on conceptual understanding, modeling, multiple representations and connections, and problem solving.

If the standards were adopted, instructional strategies would change radically from current practice. Setting and investigating problems, group work, peer instruction, and oral and written defense of conjectures would become the norm. Students would be engaged actively in a variety of problem situations, using, when necessary, both calculators and computers. Paper and pencil calculations would occur infrequently while mental arithmetic, estimation, and approximation would be frequent occurrences. Students would be transformed from passive spectators to creative problem solvers.

# Scenarios for the Twenty-First Century

## The Future of Content

Whether we have the cultural will to make the kinds of curricular changes recommended by the NCTM Commission is still, in the early nineties, questionable. That we are facing a continuing technological revolution having enormous impact on our uses of mathematics and on the discipline itself can hardly be doubted. Whether we look to the practical, commercially oriented traditions of math education or to the traditions of abstract, theoretical mathematics, we see fundamental change. On the one hand, as Steen notes, "technology has mathematicized the workplace and statistics have permeated public policy debates."[47] On the other hand, chaos and the theory of complexity are revolutionizing not only how we look at reality but also how we conceive order, set the parameters of our problems, and go about solving them.[48] We stand on the threshold of a paradigmatic upheaval in mathematics of major proportions.

If the public school's curriculum continues to ignore the *new*, new math — that is, statistics, mathematical modeling, and estimation remain minor topics in the curriculum, chaos and complexity theory are ignored altogether, and basic skills are repeatedly reviewed with drill and practice as the typical means of learning — the study of mathematics in the public school will surely be reserved for the non-college-bound student whose aspirations do not surpass requirements for the simplest of service-level jobs. The public schools may become the conservator of paper and pencil mathematics, while other agencies such as private foundations take over leadership in math education.

Possibly, though this is admittedly a grim scenario, the inadequacy of the mathematics curriculum will become a symbol for the disengaged of our society — for those not participating in the full benefits and privileges of being in America. Those who are able will pass examinations or pay the requisite amount and will thus be admitted to the "foundation" able to offer an updated curriculum. Advanced mathematical studies will serve a gatekeeping function to all the major technological studies and offer both status and power to those who succeed.

This grim scenario is not a necessary one. A substantial retooling of teachers' mathematical background could be supported by state or federal funding; business and industry could become more active partners with education; and the study of mathematics itself could move out of the classroom, at least some of the time, and into locations with advanced computer facilities staffed by experts knowledgeable in the newer mathematical content. Collaborations of all kinds could typify the conduct of the mathematics curriculum. The teacher would be the manager of a community effort to maintain currency in the curriculum. It is largely a question of how strongly we feel, as a society, that significant mathematical knowledge must be made available to all.

## The Future of Pedagogy

There is broad consensus with respect to the need to incorporate computers into the curriculum. By the year 2000, computers will be ubiquitous and the hours of drill dedicated to learning basic arithmetical operations will be a phenomenon of the past. Computers will be used for visualizing geometric proofs, for the multiple representations of information, for the statistical analysis of large quantities of data, and for exploring fractals and other mathematical images of irregularity contributing to the developing theory of complexity or of chaos.

As the future unfolds, the classroom will become a laboratory for mathematical explorations and students will use technology to investigate, conjecture, and verify findings.[49] Multiple options will be available to students. That is, they will be able to choose what they study from a list of possibilities prepared by their teacher or team of teachers. Teachers will continue to explain basic mathematical procedures and algorithms, but their primary focus will be to facilitate the work of students in their investigations. Collaboration with other students and with external experts will also be an important component of the new pedagogy.

Finally, the classroom laboratory will collaborate intermittently with the community at large on a needs basis. For example, students could collect data for an environmental assessment of some sort and undertake an extensive analysis and interpretation of the data to be used in a written report submitted to the local governing body. Another community project could involve an assessment of employment patterns and future trends. As mathematical vistas open, so must its pedagogy.

## QUESTIONS FOR DISCUSSION AND REFLECTION

1. What did you most like/dislike about mathematics in elementary school? junior high school? high school? Are you finding it difficult to answer this question because you think you have forgotten most of the mathematics you studied? Is it *really* true that you have forgotten it "all," or can you think of instances in your life when what you learned in mathematics was or is useful? What is your attitude toward mathematics now? Could more have been done to improve your attitude?

2. How would you change the way mathematics was taught to you? Do you think the new NCTM standards are moving in the right direction? Explain your answer.

3. What group or groups do you think would be the most resistant to a major change in mathematics curriculum, and why?

4. Suppose a majority of students in a junior high school mathematics class had not yet reached Piaget's cognitive stage of formal operations while the curriculum clearly involved teaching mathematics requiring formal operations. What *ought* to be the function of a teacher in this situation? Realistically, what *can* the teacher do?

5. What were the problems involved in adopting the New Math curriculum? Can we avoid those same problems today?

6. Where do you stand on the use of computers and calculators in the teaching of elementary mathematics? Explain your position fully.

7. Assuming that a future-oriented mathematics curriculum has been developed that takes into account the impact of technological advances on mathematics, how would you convince and prepare the following groups to accept the changes: teachers? business people? parents? the general public?

8. You have been selected as the chairperson of a committee to develop a new mathematics curriculum for K–12 for your school district.
   a. You have the freedom to choose other committee members from among both your colleagues and the community at large. Who would you choose and why?
   b. What issues would you want your committee to consider and why?
   c. Outline an overall design for this new curriculum.

9. It is now the year 2025. What changes do you think will have to be made in your proposed mathematics curriculum developed for the turn of the century?

## NOTES

1. Rothman, R. (1988). Student proficiency in math is 'dismal,' NAEP indicates. *Education Week, VII*, 38, pp. 1, 23.
2. Steen, L. A. (1989). Teaching mathematics for tomorrow's world. *Educational Leadership, 47*: 1, 18–22.
3. Wirszup, I. in testimony before The Task Force on Women, Minorities, and the Handicapped in Science and Technology, Chicago, IL, October 29, 1987.
4. Rothman, Robert (1990). Energy secretary unveils science-education projects. *Education Week, IX*: 36, p. 17.
5. *Ibid.*
6. Commission on Excellence in Education (1983). *A nation at risk: The imperatives of educational reform*. Washington D.C.: U.S. Government Printing Office.
7. *Op cit.*, Rothman, R. (1988).
8. See, for example: McKenna, B. (1989). The new new math. *On Campus* (April), p. 8, 12.
9. Sherman, Helene (1987). A historical perspective in teaching mathematics: Numeration. *WCCI Forum, 1*, 2, 38.
10. Briggs, J. and Peat, D. F. (1989). *Turbulent mirror*. New York: Harper and Row, p. 21.
11. Gleick, J. (1987). *Chaos: Making a new science*. New York: Penguin Books, pp. 304–305.
12. Kuhn, T. S. (1970). *The structure of scientific revolutions* (2nd ed., enlarged). Chicago: University of Chicago Press.
13. Shepherd, G. D. and Ragan, W. B. (1982). *Modern elementary curriculum* (6th ed.). New York: Holt, Rinehart and Winston, p. 302.
14. *Ibid.*, p. 303.
15. Mehitens, H. and Bos, H. (1981). *Social history of nineteenth century mathematics*. Boston: Schneider, p. 10.
16. Weiss, I. R. (1978). *National survey of science, mathematics, and social studies education*. Washington D.C.: U.S. Government Printing Office.

17. Romberg, T. A. (1983). A common curriculum for mathematics. *Individual differences and the common curriculum*, 82 Yearbook. National Society for the Study of Education. Chicago: University of Chicago Press, pp. 124–126.

18. Lampert, M. (1986). Knowing, doing and teaching mathematics. *Cognition and Instruction*, *3/4*, 305–342.

19. Steen, L. A. (1988). A 'new agenda' for mathematics education. *Education Week*, *VII*, 3 (May 11): 28, 21.

20. *Ibid.*, p. 28.

21. *Op. cit.*, Shepherd and Ragan, p. 300.

22. *Ibid.*
    More recently: National Council of Teachers of Mathematics (1989). *Curriculum and evaluation standards for school mathematics*. Reston, VA: Author.
    Also: National Research Counil (1989). *Everybody counts: A report to the nation on the future of mathematics education*. Washington, D.C.: National Academy Press.

23. Porter, A. (1989). A curriculum out of balance: The case of elementary school mathematics. *Educational Researcher 18*, 5:9–15.

24. *Ibid.*

25. Inhelder, B. and Piaget, J. (1958). *The growth of logical thinking from childhood to adolescence*. New York: Basic Books.

26. Renner, J. W., Stafford, D. G., and Ragan, W. B. (1979). *Teaching science in the elementary school*. New York: Harper and Row, p. 342.

27. Suydam, M. N. (1981). *The use of calculators in pre-college education: Fifth annual state-of-the-art review*. Columbus, OH: Calculator Information Center.

28. In addition to Suydam (*Ibid.*): Travers, K. J. and McKnight, C. C. (1985). Mathematics achievement in U.S. schools: Preliminary findings from the second IEA mathematics study. *Phi Delta Kappan, 66*, 407–413.

29. Wheatley, G. H., Shumway, R. J., Coburn, T. G., Reys, R. E., Schoen, H. L., Wheatley, C. L., and White, A. L. (1979). Calculators in elementary schools. *Arithmetic Teacher, 27*, 18–21.

30. Roberts, D. M. (1980). The impact of electronic calculators on educational performance. *Review of Educational Research, 50*, 71–98.

31. Corbitt, M. K. (1985). The impact of computing technology on school mathematics: Report of an MCTM conference. *Mathematics Teacher, 77*, 380–381.

32. Kline, M. (1973). *Why Johnny can't add*. New York: St. Martin's Press.

33. *Op. cit.*, Wirszup, I. p. 11.

34. *Ibid.*, p. 12.

35. *Ibid.*

36. McKenna, B. (1989). The new 'new math.' *On Campus* (April), pp. 8–12.

37. *Ibid.*, p. 12.

38. Hart, E. W. (1985). Is discrete mathematics the new mathematics of the eighties? *Mathematics Teacher*, (May) pp. 334–337.

39. *Ibid.*, pp. 335–336.

40. *Ibid.*, p. 336.

41. *Ibid.*

42. *Op. cit.*, McKenna, B., p. 12.

43. Working Group of the Commission on Standards for School Mathematics (1989). *Curriculum and evaluation standards for school mathematics*. Reston, VA: National Council of Teachers of Mathematics.

44. *Ibid.*, pp. 12–14.

45. Bishop, A. J. (1990). Mathematical Power to the People. *Harvard Educational Review, 60,* 3:357–369.

46. *Ibid.*, p. 366.

47. Steen, L. A. (1989). Teaching mathematics for tomorrow's world. *Educational Leadership, 47,* 1:18.

48. Doll, W. E., Jr. (1989). Complexity in the classroom. *Educational Leadership, 47,* 1:65–70.

49. Fey, J. T. (1989). Technology and mathematics education: A survey of recent developments and important problems. *Educational Studies in Mathematics,* (August) pp. 233–272.

**13**

# The Science Curriculum

## Introduction

In none of the subjects of the traditional curriculum is the long-standing dichotomy between the traditions of the elementary school and those of the secondary school so starkly drawn as in science. The resistance of the Committee of Fifteen to young children studying the scientific method and its insistence that history, geography, grammar, literature, and arithmetic comprise the main core of the elementary curriculum contributed to a long period of neglect for the sciences at the elementary level. In fact, most states did not begin to develop separate curriculum guides for elementary science until the 1940s.

At the same time, the Committee of Ten supported greatly increased prominence for the study of the sciences at the secondary level. This involved introducing physics, chemistry, astronomy, and biology into the curriculum — disciplines still held to be crucial to the education of college-bound students.

In 1987, almost a century after the Committee of Ten completed its work, then Secretary of Education William J. Bennett presented what he considered an "ideal" program of studies for the high schools.[1] He recommended three years of study from astronomy, geology, biology, chemistry, physics, and principles of technology. The only significant addition to the secondary science curriculum in Bennett's proposal is the course in principles of technology, which would be based on such applied engineering topics as the design of buildings, bridges, machines, and electrical circuits. Content would include studies of force, vibration, resonance, energy, digital circuits, momentum, power, heat transfer, and so forth.[2] This course is a departure from the discipline-based science courses that have characterized the curriculum of the twentieth century. Its suggested content, however, appears to be a reorganization of many of the topics typically found in the traditional science curriculum.

Bennett's proposal is a part of the reform movement of the 1980s and 1990s that was initiated with the April 1983 publication of *A Nation at Risk* developed by the National Commission of Excellence in Education.[3] The commission's great-

237

est concern was the deterioration of academic studies in American schools. Their remedy was the strengthening of academic requirements for those courses traditionally considered part of the college-bound program. Little real curricular change was pursued.

Recommended increases in science requirements[4] have not led to the increases in funding necessary to implement the additional requirements. According to Eichinger, there is insufficient state and federal support to do an effective job.[5] Inadequate supplies, inadequate facilities, and lack of time to prepare new methods and materials are reasons cited by teachers for not becoming more deeply involved in the latest reform movement.[6]

A very different kind of reform movement took place in the late 1950s and 1960s. Although the movement was under way before the Russians succeeded in placing a satellite in space ahead of the United States, that event sparked the federal government to spend millions of dollars to support the development of more adequate science courses for all grade levels. Not only did public education have to contend with the accelerating explosion of scientific knowledge, it was now also being asked to "win" the race for worldwide technological dominance. Efforts were concentrated on developing prototypes of new science courses that could fit into the overall curriculum design. For the most part, scope, sequence, and purpose of the overall curriculum were not involved.

The courses developed in this earlier reform movement shared the goal of improving the science performance of academically able students. They shared, in addition, a desire to expand the use of instructional media beyond textbooks to include laboratory and field experiences, films and film loops, transparencies, artifacts, and computers. Many of the methodologies pursued in this period involving multimedia continue to influence our presentation of the science curriculum today, although the general program of study has changed very little. The courses developed in this period were neither coordinated with each other nor with the traditional curriculum. They often differed significantly in their assumptions concerning both what was important to learn and how children learn.

The attention that was paid to the elementary study of science, especially in such federally funded projects as the "Elementary Science Study," "Science Curriculum Improvement Study," and "Science — A Process Approach" was literally a first for the twentieth century curriculum. Improvement in the science performance of students was seen to be directly linked to the quality of students' early science studies. In fact, recent research supports this view. A study investigating when students become committed to science and mathematics indicates that interest appears in elementary school and reaches its maximum level shortly before ninth grade.[7] By high school, the level of interest among students declines.

This emphasis on the early acquisition of scientific processes and concepts was greatly reinforced when the Woodshole Conference was held. This involved a group of well-known scientists, mathematicians, and psychologists who had been recruited to improve the nation's science curricula. The Conference issued its report, *The Process of Education*,[8] written by Jerome S. Bruner in 1960. In particular, it proposed that any subject could be taught to young school children in some intellectually honest, albeit simple fashion.

There also were numerous secondary projects that tended to reflect the curricular triumvirate that has dominated the entire century—biology, chemistry, and physics. There were, for example, the "Chemical Education Material Study," sponsored by the National Science Foundation for the purpose of developing an effective high school chemistry course, as well as the "Biological Sciences Curriculum Study" and the "Physical Science Study Committee." The goal of helping students understand the theoretical underpinnings of the discipline was clearly reflected in each of these efforts. As McNeil notes, students who were not interested in becoming scientists found the materials developed in these efforts rather uninteresting.[9] In the early 1970s, with a rising interest in the social responsibility of scientists as well as in the earth's ecology, interdisciplinary approaches to the study of science were introduced. They proved to be short-lived as the nation moved toward increased standardized testing, a greater concentration on the acquisition of factual knowledge, and a renewed emphasis on the study of the disciplines as traditionally embodied in chemistry, physics, and biology.

Notwithstanding the major efforts of the 1950s and 1960s to improve student performance in science, the indicators representing the state of scientific knowledge among American youth continued to decline. Scores on standardized tests steadily declined for 17-year-olds through 1982 when, as already noted, a very different kind of reform movement took hold. In the following four years, according to a National Assessment of Educational Progress (NAEP) report cited by Bennett, test scores of 17-year-olds moved upward to nearly reach 1977 levels.[10] Some educators who do not support the increased emphasis on standardized tests suggest that the improvement in scores reflects an improvement in test-taking skills rather than in the level of students' scientific knowledge.

In fact, despite the reform movement of the 1980s and the doubling of positions in engineering and the sciences,[11] a steady decline in the actual number of recipients of bachelor's degrees in the physical and life sciences has persisted since the 1960s.[12] This was in sharp contrast to the early decades of the twentieth century when enrollment of students in the sciences increased steadily in the high schools and universities.[13] Further, the percentage of minority students entering the sciences remains negligible, as has long been the case.

In addition, many comparisons of Americans' scientific knowledge with that of other nationals yield a dismal picture of our science literacy. For example, while 72 percent of 13-year-old students in British Columbia and 56 percent in French Quebec performed adequately when asked to analyze experiments, only 42 percent of American 13-year-olds were able to do so.[14] According to Carl Sagan, considerable evidence indicates that 94 percent of Americans are scientifically illiterate.[15] A pamphlet presenting *Project 2061*, initiated by the American Association for the Advancement of Science in the 1980s to totally revise the science curriculum, expresses the sense of crisis that many feel about the state of science (and mathematics) education:

*When fewer than half of all Americans know that the earth goes around the sun once a year and when one-third believe that boiling radioactive milk will make it safe, it is time to take a fresh look at why our citizens are learning so little about their world.* [16]

In this context of a nation deeply concerned about the scientific competence of its young and about its ability to compete in an increasingly technological world, this chapter explores the science curriculum as it is pursued in American schools today. It scrutinizes more closely the changes recommended in the science curriculum at both the elementary and secondary levels—changes that have been widely discussed in the professional literature since the 1950s. The curricular work of several of the science projects of the 1960s is examined in depth. Several futuristic scenarios will also be explored. First, however, an historical overview of science and its school instruction will be undertaken.

## Historical Overview

### The Explosion of Knowledge–Sixteenth Century into the Future

In the thirteenth century, several scientific works from ancient Greece were discovered. They led to considerable controversy among the scholars of European universities concerning the most appropriate approach to scientific methodology. On the one hand were those who supported the idealist views of Plato, and on the other were those who preferred the Aristotelean emphasis on studying the empiricals of the actual world. However, the enormous upheavals caused by the Black Plague and the Hundred Years' War that followed effectively cut off the renewed interest in science for several centuries.

In the 1540s, the Polish astronomer Nicholas Copernicus issued his revolutionary paper on the movement of the heavenly bodies, and the Belgium anatomist Andrea Vesalius, published his work on the structure of the human body, laying the basis for the discovery of the circulation of the blood. In the late 1500s, the mathematician Johannes Kepler discovered, without the benefit of the telescope (yet to be invented), that Mars moved about the sun in an eliptical orbit obeying predictable rules of nature, rather than in the circular path associated with ideal perfection that had been assumed by Pythagoras, Plato, Ptolemy, and all subsequent Christian astronomers. Kepler proposed that physical laws applying to the earth also applied to heavenly bodies. This was a fundamental change in the scholarly study of the universe. Along with the great mathematical advances in algebra made by Cardano, the work of Copernicus, Vesalius, and Kepler initiated the era of modern scientific development.

The origins of the scientific method as we know it today can be traced back to Francis Bacon's work on induction, John Locke's empiricism, and Gallileo's carefully devised methods for developing evidence to support his theories. It was Gallileo and his work with the telescope who added to the ancient Greek traditions of induction and deduction the concept of systematic verification. The thermometer, telescope, microscope, barometer, and exhaust pump were developed in the seventeenth century largely in conjunction with scientific experimentation.

The publication of Isaac Newton's *Philosophiae Naturalis Principia Mathematica*, which set forth what is known as the universal law of gravitation, represents not only the culmination of Kepler's vision, but a kind of watershed, a turning of Western civilization from both religious and philosophical idealism to a scientific materialism that was the precursor of the Age of Enlightenment. Confidence in human capabilities for logical analysis and an increasing propensity to undertake empirical experimentation characterized the Age of Enlightenment. Characteristic of the period was the work of Lavoisier, *Treatise on Chemical Elements*, published in 1789, which initiated what may be considered the field of quantitative chemistry.

By the nineteenth century there was a veritable explosion of scientific knowledge. John Dalton revitalized the ancient Greek atomic theory of matter, using it to develop the law of partial pressures. Michael Faraday developed the first dynamo and lay the bases for the electromagnetic theories elaborated by James Clerk Maxwell. James Joule established the mechanical theory of heat, and Charles Darwin developed a comprehensive theory of evolution in his *On the Origin of Species by Means of Natural Selection*.

Science and mathematics were virtually indistinguishable in this period. Newton's theories were mathematically represented, predictions were based on the formula set forth, and observations either confirmed or disproved the predictions. The tremendous progress in mathematics noted in the preceding chapter was also the tremendous progress of science. It was only in the nineteenth century that pure mathematics was acknowledged to be a field based on the logical analysis of relations essentially independent from the laws of nature and was recognized to be a field distinct from the sciences.

## Science as Differentiated Fields of Endeavor

The Pythagorean scholars of ancient Greece accepted four subjects as fields of science: music, geometry, arithmetic, and astronomy. By the time of Aristotle, science included studies in physics, zoology, mechanics, optics, and meteorology. The long period between the fall of the Roman Empire and the reawakening of scientific interest in the thirteenth century returned science to a largely undifferentiated study of nature.

Specializations grew slowly at first. Chemistry became an important, mainstream specialization only in the seventeenth century with the work of Robert Boyle. Geology was not even considered a science until the eighteenth century. By the nineteenth century, chemistry and physics were the major specializations of the physical sciences while botany, zoology, anatomy, and genetics were dominant disciplines in the life sciences.

The classification and subsequent specialization of science led to more powerful results than might otherwise have been possible had science remained undifferentiated. With specialization, the parameters of an investigation could be strictly limited to a very small segment of reality while all else in the surrounding physical world was assumed to remain unchanged. Results from studies could be accumulated according to the organization of each specialization, often leading to an in-depth understanding of the area under investigation. Knowledge thus obtained has proven to be especially fertile in expanding our understanding of the physical universe. It has not proven to be as fruitful for the social sciences.

### Defining "Science"

When one considers the span of disciplines from music and optics to anatomy and zoology that have been included under the rubric of science, the difficulty in defining the term "science" is understandable. There is no lack of definitions, simply a good deal of difference among them. For some, science refers to all those studies that seek to understand the order of nature.[17] For Carl Sagan, it is "a way of thinking,"[18] rather than a body of knowledge. In his words:

> Science invites us to let the facts in, even when they don't conform to our preconceptions. . . . It urges on us a fine balance between no-holds-barred openness to new ideas, however heretical, and the most rigorous skeptical scrutiny of everything — new ideas and established wisdom.[19]

In a different and broader sense, the term has been used to refer to systematized knowledge in any field. Thus, it has not been unusual to find scholars referring to, say, the science of morality or the science of culture even though the scientific method as we have come to know it is hardly applicable.[20] Perhaps the most useful definition in an educational context was put forth by Paul Dehart Hurd in 1969. His three-part definition proposes that science is "a process of thinking," as well as "a means of acquiring new knowledge" and "a means of understanding the natural world."[21] This definition supports science both as a generalized enterprise and as a set of specialized disciplines organized to collect new knowledge. It supports a curriculum design for science that would turn the memorization of science facts into a relativity minor objective.

## Current Trends and Issues

### The Content of the Secondary School Curriculum and Its Resistance to Reform

So much knowledge has been developed under each of the sciences that it is virtually impossible for an individual to know any one of them completely. Out in the field, need has tended to dictate the specializations pursued; in the schools, tradition and what we have called "cultural mindset" have been more influential in determining the nature of what is studied. Once the content of the science curriculum was established in the early 1900s with the work of the Committee of Ten, the high schools hardly changed their science offerings for decades. General science, biology, chemistry, and physics comprise the science program in the vast majority of American secondary schools.

College-bound students almost always take the latter three and may take general science in the seventh or eighth grade as well. Biology is most often the first of the science disciplines encountered by students, usually in junior high or middle school program. About 75 percent of all high school students take a class in biology. Of this group, approximately 30 percent will continue to pursue science with the study of chemistry. The number of students who then choose to go on by studying physics declines sharply to about 50 percent of those who have taken chemistry.[22]

The average student's high school science experience has remained essentially unchanged for decades. This condition has been deadly to the sustained study of science. As Bill Aldridge notes, high school students are presented with complex abstractions from day one and there is no letup for the next 179 days.[23] The traditional curriculum design is developed around broad content strands such as the human body, the solar system, heat and its actions, and so forth and is replete with factual information. Whether chemistry, physics, or biology, students are confronted with an onslaught of descriptive materials full of mathematical symbols, difficult scientific jargon, abstractions, and generalizations for which they have had little prior experience.

Satisfaction with the teaching of biology is at a particularly low ebb. In September 1990, a panel of biologists and educators organized by the National Research Council issued a report stating that middle and high school teachers were "poorly trained and the textbooks they used were inaccurate and outdated."[24] It also was the panel's view that all areas of science education were in need of reform. Their recommendations included improved teacher training, textbooks that emphasize ideas rather than the learning of terminology, and decreased emphasis on standardized tests.[25]

The panel also recommended that biological studies in the middle school should be related to topics of particular interest to adolescents, such as the functioning of the human body and health, rather than, as they are now, being an anemic version of high school biology.[26] They further suggested that the high school curriculum, whether in biology, chemistry, or physics, concentrate less on technical language and deal in depth with a relatively few, key concepts.[27] According to the panel, science studies in high school are a series of exercises in memorization rather than an intellectual exploration.

The recommendations tend to remind those old enough to remember of the science reform movement undertaken in the 1960s when, despite the efforts of scientists, educators, and the federal government, little sustained change was achieved. There were pressures back then to abandon the emphasis on memorizing facts in favor of involving students in conceptual learning and the processes of discovery. For example, the Physical Science Study Committee (PSSC) undertook to update and improve the high school teaching of physics in 1956. One of the major objectives of the committee was to develop a unity of curricular structure for what had long been a patchwork collection of topics overloaded with factual details that students had to memorize. The committee tried to diminish the emphasis on technology so that students would study the true science of physics. It was their intention to provide "a sound foundation" to students planning to study engineering or science at the college level.[28] Two major themes were selected to unify the instructional materials developed. These were wave propagation and the laws of momentum and energy. Thirty-five concepts including the atomic structure of matter, distance, time motion, magnetism, and measurement were explored in support of the themes.

Another example of the 1960s reform movement, the Biological Sciences Curriculum Study (BSCS), was sponsored by the American Institute of Biological Sciences with funding from the federal government. The study developed materials based on nine themes as follows:

1. Evolution and change in living things across time
2. Unity and diversity in the patterns of living things
3. The genetic continuity of life
4. The complementary relationship of the environment and living organisms
5. The biological origins of behavior
6. The complementary relationship of function and structure
7. Genetic continuity: the preserving of life in the face of change
8. Science as inquiry
9. The history of the development of biological ideas[29]

To support the study of these themes, BSCS developed a hierarchical scheme of basic biological systems that progressed from the simplest and least inclusive unit of matter to more complex and inclusive entities of existence. The molecular system formed the initial basis for the development of instructional materials and the community and world systems topped the hierarchy.[30] The three major types of living organisms—protists, plants, and animals—were to be studied at each level of the hierarchy and in light of each of the themes noted above. This rather elaborate, three-prong curricular design integrating several kinds of biological concepts proved to be both flexible and capable of supporting different implementations. In fact, BSCS developed three distinct sets of materials based on the design. One version emphasized physiological and biological ideas, another stressed genetic and cellular processes, and the third focused on ecology and its community and world effects. All the materials have been widely recognized as being innovative, representative of current scientific knowledge, and requiring a higher-than-average level of student performance.

In the mid 1970s, courses in earth sciences began to displace the hodgepodge of units that had typically comprised the general science secondary school curriculum. Several science disciplines, including astronomy, geology, meteorology, oceanography, and physical geography were integrated around a few basic scientific principles with the purpose of studying our human environment. The "counterreform" or back-to-basics movement that followed in the late 1970s curtailed the increase in earth sciences courses. Interest in the earth's ecology has supported a smattering of courses in environmental sciences around the country, but their impact on the high school curriculum has been negligible.

As the proverbial explosion of scientific knowledge accelerates into the next millennium, the pursuit of interdisciplinary work out in the field has intensified. The essential arbitrariness of the divisions among the sciences, especially those dominating high school study — that is, chemistry, physics, and biology — has become even more obvious. The need to understand broader, often interlocking relationships as they exist in the natural environment has led to the ongoing revision of specialized fields, especially in business and industry. The study of science from a holistic, conceptual perspective is widely recognized as important to scientific creativity and the future development of new, increasingly productive specializations. In sum, good reasons for a fundamental revision of the science curriculum are accumulating and intensifying.

It is worth emphasizing here that even though there was a major effort to redesign the science curriculum in the 1960s, the dominant position of biology, chemistry, and physics in the secondary curriculum was not challenged even then. While there had been widespread awareness since the 1950s that the content of the science curriculum was not keeping pace with the developments in science and probably could *not* keep pace as organized, it appears not to have occurred to the scientists and educators involved in updating the school study of science that the curriculum design based on biology, chemistry, and physics might need overhauling. The revisions undertaken were wholly contained within the disciplines typically present in the schools.

Groundbreaking materials developed during that period have not been widely incorporated into the traditional curriculum and there is little evidence in today's schools of the work accomplished in the sixties. As Sidney Besvinick notes in his 1988 discussion of science materials:

> *The texts that scientists, professors, and teachers worked so long and so hard to produce are no longer even adopted for use. In their place, I have found practices and structures that were popular forty years ago. The emphasis is on fact acquisition through lecture and "cookbook" lab activities.*[31]

The materials of the 1960s were directed toward involving youngsters in the processes of scientific investigation and toward the achievement of conceptual understanding, objectives ill-suited to the standardized tests that currently dominate evaluation. While much of the more recent rhetoric refers to helping students understand the societal problems that have arisen because of the successes of science and technology, students are still being evaluated primarily on the facts they know.

Confronting questions concerning what is most important to teach *about* science and *in* the sciences remains crucial but largely ignored, at least if we are to judge from the unchanged and inflexible curricular offerings of most high schools.

As we have already noted, the reform movement of the 1980s and early 1990s has contributed little to the revision of the secondary science curriculum, although it has strongly endorsed a minimum of three years of science study.

## The Content of the Elementary Curriculum and the Effort toward Curricular Change

Traditionally, the goals set forth for the elementary science curriculum are not directed toward the understanding of particular science disciplines or the accumulation of a significant factual base. Rather, they involve broader intellectual, emotional, and social outcomes. Children will experience the joy of discovery through hands-on activities; they will attain the attitudes and values appropriate to science; they will gain sufficient conceptual understanding and adequate skills to perform experiments; they will learn to observe, describe, and classify, and so forth.

This tendency to set relatively broad guidelines for science instruction has often led to very uneven elementary science experiences among students. Science has often been neglected in favor of the other instructional areas, in particular, reading, writing, and arithmetic. Freelance writer, Deborah Fort described her daughter's experience as being like that of most elementary students, that is, as consisting, "of reading textbooks and listening to lectures for about one hour a week."[32]

While the quality of science teaching in the elementary schools has left much to be desired, teachers in the lower grades are generally without the pressures to prepare students for college typically imposed on the secondary curriculum. As a result, they have responded positively to the learning-by-doing approach to instruction and the emphasis on concept learning fostered by the reforms of the 1960s. Having children do as scientists would do out in the field held a certain attraction for teachers and a substantial number of schools embraced the new curricula.

The Elementary Science Study (ESS), sponsored by Educational Services, Inc. in conjunction with McGraw-Hill Publishing Company, was especially compatible with the more open qualities of science study found in the elementary school. This curriculum project of the 1960s sought to involve students in the processes of science from the very beginning. There was no specific set of concepts or facts that youngsters had to learn. The materials supplied for instruction and experimentation were intentionally similar to objects ordinarily found in the child's environment rather than typical scientific equipment. Unlike most of the other science education curricula developed then, ESS hoped, above all, to help children to explore the world around them and thereby encourage them to develop a more personal but greater interest in science.

The Science Curriculum Improvement Study (SCIS) project, funded by the National Science Foundation, was organized quite differently. It was concerned with the development of a well-defined scientific literacy for young children. A broadly based conceptual understanding of the natural world was a key purpose of the curriculum. Units were organized around systems such as life cycles, populations, environments, energy sources, and models. Clusters of concepts supported each of the units, and a wide range of activites were available to teachers.[33]

Still another, quite different approach to the development of science curriculum was pursued by the American Association for the Advancement of Science in its project, Science — A Process Approach (SAPA). Basic to the materials developed was the view that the processes used in doing science, rather than concepts, embodied what was most unique in all of the sciences. The design was organized around such scientific processes as classification, observation, measurement, and inference.[34]

The work of ESS, SCIS, and SAPA, among others, was readily accepted by elementary school teachers, although their efforts soon waned when, in 1976, federal funds for improving science education were terminated. Standardized testing, especially in reading and language arts grew significantly in the period following, and science education in the elementary schools returned to its more typical state of a potpourri of studies. It also returned to being a somewhat neglected subject area because a major portion of the elementary school teacher's time and attention goes into the teaching of reading, writing, and arithmetic.

In effect, with the cut-off of federal funding, science curriculum reform, which had a real chance of succeeding in the elementary school, was cut off in midstream. The return to the haphazard traditions of the elementary schools came like a rubberband snapping back that had been stretched but not broken.

The 1990 report on the state of biology education issued by the National Council on Research was initially limited to secondary school biology. However, the panel of experts soon became concerned with the low quality of elementary science studies. On the premise that learning about science is cumulative and thus any real improvement must begin in the early grades, the panel included elementary school science in its report. According to the panel, "The elementary-school years present an opportunity for teaching about the natural world that the Nation's schools have failed to grasp."[35] They strongly recommend the introduction of science studies in the very earliest elementary grades and an increased focus on the teaching of natural history. They would develop "intuitive understanding" through "hands-on" projects involving, for example, raising animals or plants.[36]

### The Success / Failure of the 1960s Reforms

The impression left by the end of the 1970s was that, K–12, the 1960s science curriculum reforms had failed. Declining test scores at the secondary level seemed to support the idea that general science knowledge had been sacrificed to the emphasis on concepts and process. However, comparisons between the achievement of students who had studied under the new science curricula with those that had pursued a more traditional program indicate that students of the innovative programs did considerably better on standardized tests.[37] Furthermore, a research study conducted in 1984 by Kyle and Bonnstetter comparing attitudes toward science between SCIS and non-SCIS students found significant attitudinal differences with 51 percent of SCIS students choosing science among their favorite subjects as opposed to only 21 percent in the other group.[38]

Penick and Yaeger reviewed a number of sucessful elementary science programs. They found these programs all shared a set of characteristics: a greater than average amount of time dedicated to science study (145 minutes per week versus the average of 100 minutes per week), a significant level of local and parental involvement in curriculum development, and an unusual level of student involvement through hands-on activities, inquiry, and decision making.[39]

### The Teacher as Key to a Successful Curriculum

On the whole, teachers' backgrounds in science have been found to correlate positively to students' achievement in science.[40] Evidence also links teacher enthusiasm to increased student learning.[41] At the elementary level, these factors may easily translate into a greater or lesser amount of the school day being dedicated to science studies as well as to greater or lesser competence in the actual content of instruction. At the secondary level, a clearly allocated amount of time is assigned to science study. However, it is more difficult for the secondary teacher to remain current with the developments of the scientific fields, and the curriculum may suffer from the teacher's inadequate background even though all prerequisites in science studies have been met. At both the elementary and secondary levels, a strong, teacher-based interest in the sciences contributes to an improved science program.

The National Science Teachers Association (NSTA) recommends that all preservice elementary teachers take at least twelve semester hours in the sciences including studies in the biological, physical, and earth sciences. However, only 34 percent of all elementary teachers actually meet this standard.[42] Elementary teachers tend to concentrate their science studies in biology, neglecting earth sciences to a considerable degree. The participation of females in science studies is notoriously low notwithstanding significant improvement in recent years. Because a vast majority of elementary teachers are women, the weakness of science instruction at the elementary level is certainly comprehensible although not less disquieting.

### The Philosophical Spectrum: A Crisis of Expectations

What are the purposes of science studies in the schools? We have just discussed the curriculum projects of the 1960s, which have, themselves, become the object of growing interest in the early 1990s. Some of these projects tended to treat students as novice scientists working in the field. Involving students in the dynamic processes of such disciplines as chemistry and physics certainly had an air of relevance and excitement well beyond anything generated by the traditional treatment of these disciplines. We needed to ask then and we still need to ask whether developing young specialists capable of becoming future scientists really is what we hope our children will gain from their science studies.

Philosophical essentialists would be the least likely to disagree with the proposition that all youngsters should receive a scientific education reflective of the structure of the major disciplines. Theory and the learning of basic facts and principles should always precede in their view, applications and the firsthand experiences of the learner.

Essentialists do not agree, however, on the curricular configuration that would best prepare youngsters to deal with an ever-changing, unpredictable scientific future. For some, the study of basic concepts and processes as configured in the 1960s is most appropriate, whereas for others the development of a fundamental base of scientific knowledge including a solid understanding of established principles is the essential first step. Some support the widespread use of standardized tests as a way of determining how well essentials have been learned, while others find students' abilities to think about what they have learned at a low ebb and tend to blame the short-answer items of standardized tests for the shallowness of students' thought processes.

Those of a progressive persuasion would certainly note how difficult to read and understand the materials developed in the sixties were for a significant percentage, if not a majority, of students. They would also note that students' differences and interests were ignored, in all likelihood contributing to a negative attitude toward the study of science and possibly causing the steep decline in the number of students majoring in the sciences at the college level. They, like many of the essentialists, want to see more thoughtful, active involvement in the doing of science and in the solving of problems. Unlike the essentialists, they do not perceive the study of the disciplines as the most effective curricular vehicle for achieving scientifically literate, reflective citizens able to question and think clearly about the results of science and technology. Importantly, scientific literacy for the progressivists is based on being able to participate intelligently in the decisions of society relevant to science and its impact on the quality of our lives. Making "little scientists" is, at best, a secondary goal that some students may move toward because of their own talents and interests.

In both curriculum design and instructional methodology, the progressivists would place student involvement in the doing of science foremost. From their perspective, the study of science must first be a reconstruction of youngsters' own experiences. Stimulating children's natural interests is of crucial importance, as is involving students in social problem solving related to the impact of science and technology on society.

As we noted in the foundations section of this work, there is often not a clear demarcation betweeen the thinking of essentialists and progressives. Essentialists tend to accept that some insight into the social implications of scientific progress is desirable as is the realization that science is both full of inconsistencies and empirical orderliness. Progressives hope that a good percentage of students will move into disciplinary studies as they mature and become more keenly interested in the sciences.

The work of Jerome S. Bruner during the reforms of the 1960s integrated the essentialists' emphasis on disciplinary structure with the progressives' view that learning by doing is the most effective way to reach youngsters and develop their problem-solving abilities. Because funding was cut short in the 1970s and interest in educational reform turned toward a more traditional approach, it has been virtually impossible to assess the real effectiveness of the eclecticism that came to typify many of the projects.

It seems, however, that as interest in the curricular work of the 1960s continues to grow, perennialists have become even more strident in their appeals for chemistry to be taught as chemistry, physics as physics, and biology as biology. They want increased requirements and the removal of frills in the program of study in general as well as in the sciences. They offer examples of hardworking Japanese students who attend school many more hours than the typical American student. Meeting children's personal learning needs leads, for them, to trivial studies that ought not be a part of the curriculum.

The reconstructionists see the study of science as contributing to citizens' control over important elements in their future. Reshaping society for its ultimate betterment needs to be for them the underlying purpose of all science studies. Critical evaluation of the problems and issues arising from the continued progress of science is likely to be foremost among their curricular objectives. Students need to become involved in the social, political, and economic planning of the uses of science so that a more humane and democratic society may be achieved. New, issue-oriented courses in ecology and environmental preservation would certainly be favored by the reconstructionists.

Of course, existentialists reject prescribing studies of any kind to students and would, at best, encourage students to pursue science studies of their own choosing. In essence, this means that students would do their own personal curriculum planning, a feat that would require some prior research. Possibly, they could establish a set of issues to explore or investigate what the progress of science will mean in their individual lives.

Typical of American eclecticism, the public seems to waffle without too much awareness of its waffling between the different philosophies. Sometimes it embraces the view that teaching students how to think is far more important than acquiring basic factual knowledge of a discipline. It accepts that children come from different backgrounds and have different needs and these must be met for real learning to occur. At other times, the public demands increased requirements for the "tough" subjects without regard for the differences among children. It demands accountability through objective measures such as may be obtained from standardized tests. At the same time, it may also be in favor of students having hands-on, practical experiences so that they will internalize what they learn. Above all, the schools need to help business and industry maintain the technological lead that has been America's for most of the twentieth century. The future of America is linked closely to the willingness and capability of the young to both control and contribute to the progress of science.

All of the views expressed above, given an appropriate context, would be accepted almost without question by a significant portion of the public and are indeed often espoused by the same politician on different days. Mindless eclecticism dominates our information media and public thinking. There is an ongoing crisis in our understanding of what we expect students to gain from their science studies, and its resolution does not appear to be forthcoming. We continue nevertheless to seek ways to improve the science curriculum and its instruction.

### Project 2061

In 1985, the American Association for the Advancement of Science (AAAS) established the National Council on Science and Technology Education, assigning it the responsibility of initiating Project 2061, intended to become a major revision of the K–12 science curriculum. The council planned its work in three phases, as follows:

> *Phase I:* defining what people should know;
> *Phase II:* redesigning the educational system; and
> *Phase III:* making it happen.

Phase I was completed in 1989 with the publication of a summary report entitled *Science for All Americans* [43] and five panel reports dealing with such topics as mathematics, biology and the health sciences, and technology. The council established a set of basic premises for its initial effort that clearly distinguished its efforts from other reforms of the 1980s.[44] These were: (1) reform must be comprehensive, that is, involving all grades (K-12), all subjects and all aspects of schooling from curriculum to community support; (2) it must be zero-based, that is, beginning with a clean slate rather than with the existing subject arrangement; (3) it must emphasize the understanding of key principles rather than the memorization of unrelated facts; (4) it must involve, at every phase of development, the views of teachers; (5) it must be based as well on a broad collaboration of educators and citizens; and finally (6) it must view change as a long-term undertaking.

The summary of Project 2061, based on four years of deliberations involving scientists, mathematicians, engineers, historians, and educators, focused on the nature and substance of scientific literacy. The key questions that the council confronted dealt with what high school graduates need to understand about science, mathematics, and technology. What is most important for them to know about how the world works and about the changing nature of scientific knowledge? What kinds of skills and ways of thinking do they need to acquire to be scientifically competent? The purpose of Phase I was to establish the basis for choosing the knowledge, skills, and attitudes to be included as part of the curriculum's objectives.

The recommendations put forth by the council form the broad outline of the work to be undertaken in Phase II, which was initiated in 1990. The scientifically literate high school graduate should:

> be familiar with the natural world including its diversity and unity;
>
> understand the basic concepts and principles of science;

be cognizant of the more important ways in which science, technology and mathematics are interdependent;

be aware that science, mathematics, and technology are human endeavors exhibiting the limitations and strengths typically associated with the human condition;

be capable of thinking in scientific ways; and

use scientific knowledge and ways of thinking for both personal and social purposes.[45]

As the council itself notes, many of its recommendations are already represented in the school's curriculum by such topics as the structure of matter, the transformation of energy, and the prevention of disease.[46] It does, however, believe that there are two major differences, one in the intention to "soften" boundaries among traditional subject-matter categories and the other in the greatly decreased quantity of detail that students are expected to memorize in favor of their developing ideas and thinking skills. The council's recommendations also imply topics not ordinarily included in science studies such as exploring the interdependence of science, mathematics, and technology and studying their relationship to the social system in general.[47]

In discussing the future, the council emphasizes that the current K–12 science curricula were not designed to deal effectively with the kinds of goals set forth in its recommendations. According to the council, new curricular models must be developed that will support a reduction in the quantity of materials covered; that will allow the blurring of rigid disciplinary lines and the exploration of the interdependence of science, mathematics and technology; that will emphasize the social aspects of the scientific enterprise; and that will foster scientific ways of thinking.[48] Developing several curriculum designs to meet these requirements is part of Project 2061's work in Phase II.

### The Science and Technology for Children Project

In 1987, the National Academy of Science and the Smithsonian Institute established the National Science Resources Center (NSRC) to support a major project for the improvement of science teaching. This project, called Science and Technology for Children (STC), is developing twenty-four modular units for grades 1–6. Topics in life science, earth science, physical science, and technology are to be studied by involving youngsters in hands-on investigative experiences. The materials are to develop children's problem-solving and critical thinking skills as well as their basic science knowledge.

One of the important functions of the NSRC after the materials have been developed and tested in a network of schools is continued dissemination and improved delivery. The center will help school systems to implement the materials as effectively as possible, offering in-service workshops for teachers and sharing successful uses of the materials with schools around the country.

There is a certain *déjà vu* quality in this discussion of the STC project for very similar undertakings were pursued in the 1960s, although the emphasis on dissemination and delivery was not as great. The development of exemplary materials, the emphasis on hands-on involvement, and the setting of objectives based on problem-solving and critical thinking skills are characteristics shared by a period driven toward a radical modification of the school's curriculum that just was never achieved.

### The Success / Failure of the Reforms of the 1960s–Again

The directions taken by both Project 2061 and the STC project are similar to and yet quite different from those pursued in the 1960s. The mandate in Project 2061 for interdisciplinary curriculum is clearly distinct from the efforts of the 1960s, which undertook to represent the unique nature of each of the science disciplines and to have youngsters act as scientists would out in their respective fields. The council's emphasis on a comprehensive approach to curriculum revision and on students' understanding principles rather than on factual recall appears to be a continuation of the reform efforts of the 1960s. On the other hand, the intention to design the curriculum "from scratch," to deeply involve both the community and teachers in every phase of curriculum development and implementation, and the recognition that real change requires a significant time commitment appears to be a concerted effort to avoid what many have thought of as the mistakes of the 1960s.

Linkages to the projects of the 1960s are even more apparent in the STC project. Objectives involving children gaining control of scientific processes and problem-solving skills recall the rhetoric as well as the materials developed in that earlier reform movement. The production of modular materials involving children in hands-on experience undertaken by STC also recalls the kinds of materials developed then. At the beginning of the 1990s, there has certainly been an awakening of interest in the work of the 1960s and much professional ruminating about why it failed.

In the course of this work, we have presented several reasons why curriculum reform may fail. We have said that deeply embedded cultural mindsets impede the acceptance of quite reasonable reforms. We have repeatedly noted the tendency among the public to subscribe to contradictory philosophical positions leading to compromises that are often no more than mindless eclecticism. All too frequently, innovations function more poorly than the traditional curriculum because the existing instructional milieu is likely to be ill-suited to the smooth functioning of a program involving significant change. Certainly, the political pressures within both the school system and the community increase during a period of change and add to the hurdles that new programs must overcome. The apparent failure of a curricular innovation also seems to lead to greater public support for the very tradition that the innovation was trying to change. To add to the difficulties, evaluations based on standardized tests do not adequately measure objectives directed toward the acquisition of process skills and conceptual knowledge. The measures work better under more traditional programs because they developed within the framework of these programs. A study of the science reforms of the 1960s quickly reveals all of these problems.

## Scientific Scenarios for the Twenty-First Century

### The Future of Content

What we believe is important to know about science has been a conundrum since at least the 1960s. As scientific knowledge has continued to grow exponentially, it has become increasingly obvious that ground-covering, introductory level courses overwhelm students with detail while alienating their interest. Furthermore, preparing students to be knowledgeable in even one specialization has become progressively impossible. There is so much to know in any one field that only a set of core principles and skills seem to be truly viable as a content of instruction. Even so, we continue to evaluate students' knowledge of science with standardized tests that emphasize knowledge of terminology and rote applications of laws and formulas.[49]

The challenges that science and technology pose to our way of life—the decisions with which we will be confronted because of the continued progress of science and technology—will necessarily direct the science curriculum toward a values-oriented, experiential base supportive of citizen's decision-making activities. Daniel Boorstein expresses this challenge to citizenship posed by the progress of science with great eloquence when he states:

> *We are baffled and dazzled today by new concepts and "entities"—from double helixes to black holes—that defy common sense, yet we are still expected to have an opinion on what to do about them. Should we legislate against genetic experiments? Dare we venture a defense program in outer space?*[50]

The decisions are momentous, the knowledge mind boggling, the uncertainty great!

From time to time, we have moved toward a discovery- or process-based curriculum, or we have tried to have students deal with the underlying concepts of all sciences. Rarely have such efforts been related to the kinds of decisions students will need to make in their lives as citizens. Many reform efforts have proven uninteresting to a large number of students because content presented to children that is devoid of some relevance to real world activities tends to become a meaningless set of abstractions.

The grimmest scenario from our perspective is that the science curriculum will persist in its assiduous pursuit of the disciplines as first set forth by the Committee of Ten. The content will remain suitable for evaluation through multiple-choice tests. There is much discussion of developing "standardized" tests based on a variety of tasks and activities,[51] but the technology for developing objective, standardized techniques capable of assessing conceptual and true problem-solving skills and qualitative responses remains far beyond our current measurement capabilities.

In an ideal future there will be increasing public recognition that understanding the social impact of scientific progress is a key characteristic of scientific literacy in a democracy.[52] Good scientists are not necessarily good citizens. Participating actively and effectively in a democratic form of governance implies sufficient knowledge and understanding to participate wisely in the decisions of society. It also implies a clear understanding of the valuing that always accompanies human behavior. Project 2061 certainly has recognized the importance of understanding the social impact of scientific progress and appropriate curricula are being planned. In general, however, the curricula of today's schools hardly take note of social implications or even of current advances that may become the subject of legislative action, social debate, or economic change. The emphasis tends to be on preparing students for advanced study at a university.

In the ideal curriculum of the future, students will behave not only as scientists but also as citizen–scientists studying topics of relevance both for the learning of science and the judgment of citizens. The earth's ecology, food production, world population, exploration of the universe, genetic manipulation, and birth control represent the kinds of topics that will be included in this citizen–scientist curriculum.

The interdependence of the scientific disciplines will be emphasized; the objective, value-free methodolgies of science will be studied, and the doing of science will occur frequently. Unlike what happens in today's schools, students will be confronted with value-laden social, political, and economic questions directly linked to their studies of fundamental scientific processes and concepts. Rather than memorizing facts, they will learn to gather, store, retrieve, and evaluate facts. They will come to understand the difference between scientific evaluation and critical evaluation, and they will engage in an ongoing assessment among our ideals, what science is capable of accomplishing, and where technology is directed. This can and should occur in the early elementary grades as well as in the upper grades.

In conjunction with content based on significant social questions related to science or technology will be a minimum but basic set of scientific principles and processes taught as core science learning. Topics may change, possibly from year to year, but the core will be stable since it will be related to the foundations of doing science. Core content such as the scientific use of classification, making predictions, and the taking of measurements will intersect with each of the selected topics. Sources for the topics to be pursued will vary and students will regularly participate in the selection process.

The design of such a curriculum is clearly more open to changing events than the discipline-based, subject design currently dominating the school study of science. Depending on circumstances, topics may be selected from a variety of scientific areas rather than being, as is now the case, restricted to one of three specializations (i.e., biology, chemistry, and physics).

An example of an initial source of content is *The Chronicle of Higher Education*'s regular listing of major science projects under current consideration for support by the United States Congress. For instance, the listing for the week of September 12, 1990, included seven projects: (1) the moon and Mars initiative, which would return an astronaut to the moon and then to Mars; (2) the establishment of a permanently manned space station; (3) the strategic defense initiative; (4) the human genome project, which would map the entire human genetic code within fifteen years; (5) the earth observing system; (6) the superconducting supercollider, which is planned as the world's most powerful particle accelerator; and (7) the National Aerospace Plane Program, which would develop a plane capable of flying at 4000 miles per hour and hence capable of putting itself into orbit.[53]

Students might well explore the scientific principles and concepts underlying, say, the genome process. They might gather data about the project and ultimately make their own decisions concerning whether the project should or should not be supported, presenting a fully reasoned argument based on both scientific and social considerations for the position taken.

### The Future of Pedagogy

In the future, increased flexibility of the instructional milieu is likely to open the citizen–scientist curriculum to an increased variety of study experiences. For example, the transformation of the daily class schedule in the junior and senior high schools from one based on equal time allocations for all subjects to one arranged according to instructional needs would radically change the nature of study possible in the science curriculum. To some extent, lower-grade elementary teachers do have greater flexibility in their time allocations, although they tend not to take advantage of the possibilities.

When necessary, an entire school day could be turned to the study of a single, especially significant topic involving all the students of a class, of a school, or even of a school system. For instance, in celebration of Earth Day, toxic waste could be the topic of study. In preparation for this special day, groups of students, assisted by their teachers, could prepare reports on the topic from the perspective of the various disciplines. These reports would be presented to the student body early in the day. Experts could be interviewed later in the day regarding, say, the restoration of a site—whether it is possible, what would be required to succeed, how to avoid a repetition of site pollution, what methods could be used to take care of future disposal of waste, and so forth.

Also as preparation for the Earth Day presentations and in collaboration with their teachers, *who would act as consultants rather than as lecturers,* students could be asked to analyze soil samples from several neighboring sites either known or suspected of being contaminated, take appropriate measurements, and carefully record their observations. They could set up several original experiments strictly following the requirements of the scientific method while taking care to note the limitations of their study. The directions they choose for their experiments would be related to the decisions that need to be made by citizens. The

Earth Day forum would review the evidence, determine, if possible, the most urgent issues, and discuss what might be done and how it might be accomplished. The student groups would each draw up a set of recommendations to be submitted to and voted on by the entire student body, and, depending upon the vote, forwarded to the appropriate local and federal agencies.

The pedagogy of science teachers will need to be transformed from all-knowing lecturing to questioning and collaboration with students helping them to accomplish projects without dominating the decision making. Teachers will need to know how to both lead and follow. They will need to accept performances and objectives that may be without right answers, helping their students to become used to the uncertainty typical not only of the scientist's world but the citizen's world as well.

The citizen's decision making is almost always done in the midst of inadequate evidence and inconclusive insights. The scientist can continue to collect data and suspend judgments until the evidence is sufficient; all too frequently, the citizen cannot do so and judgments must be made whatever the state of knowledge may be. The citizen–scientist must be capable of doing and respecting the importance of both.

## QUESTIONS FOR DISCUSSION AND REFLECTION

1. Explain in your own words the differences in the curriculum materials developed by ESS, SCIS, and SAPA.

2. The science reforms of the sixties were both a success and a failure. Explain this seemingly contradictory statement.

3. What problems do you think would be typically associated with the development of a new science curriculum? Don't overlook such "touchy" issues as the study of creationism.

4. What should the goals of the science curriculum be in your opinion? Are your goals future-oriented? What are the distinctions between goals based on current concerns and goals directed toward problems of an unknown future? Give specific examples.

5. Summarize the activities and goals of Project 2061. What aspects of Project 2061 do you think:
   a. might contribute to its success?
   b. might contribute to its failure?

6. If the design of the science curriculum were based on a values orientation:
   a. what problems might interfere with its implementation?
   b. what kind of a design would be suitable? (For example, would the science disciplines continue to dominate the curriculum?)

7. Children often find the study of science "boring" in school. What are some of the reasons for this state of affairs? What are some of the remedies that you would pursue?

**8.** What is your future scenario for the study of science? Be sure that your scenario is consistent with your philosophical position.

## NOTES

1. Bennett, W. J. (1987). *James Madison high school*. Washington, D.C.: United States Department of Education.
2. *Ibid.*, p. 31.
3. National Commission on Excellence in Education (1983). *A nation at risk*. Washington, D.C.: U.S. Government Printing Office.
4. *Op. cit.*, Bennett, W.
5. Eichinger, J. (1990). Science education in the United States Are things as bad as the recent IEA report suggests? *School Science and Mathematics, 90,* 1:33–39.
6. *Ibid.*
7. Berryman, S. E. (1983). *Who will do science?* New York: Rockefeller Foundation.
8. Bruner, J. S. (1960). *The process of education*. New York: Vintage Books.
9. McNeil, J. D. (1990). *Curriculum: A comprehensive introduction*. Glenview, IL: Scott, Foresman/Little, Brown Higher Education, p. 333.
10. Bennett, W. J. (1988). American education: Making it work. Reprinted in *The Chronicle of Higher Education* (May 4, 1988), A29–A41.
11. Darling-Hammond, L. and Hudson, L. (1990). Precollege science and mathematics teachers: Supply, demand, and quality. *Review of research in education, 16* (Courtney B. Cazden, ed.). Washington, D.C.: American Educational Research Association, p. 225.
12. Rotberg, R. C. (1990). Resources and reality: The participation of minorities in science and engineering education. *Phi Delta Kappan, 71,* 9:672–679.
13. United States Office of Education (1962). *What high school pupils study*. Washington, D.C.: U.S. Government Printing Office, pp. 117–118.
14. International Assessment of Educational Progress (1989). *A world of differences: An international assessment of mathematics and science*. Cited in: Baker, C. O. and Ogle, L. T. (1989). *The condition of education*, vol I. Washington, D.C.: National Center for Education Statistics.
15. Sagan, C. (1989). Why we need to understand science. *Parade Magazine* (September 10), 6–12.
16. American Association for the Advancement of Science (no date, first issued 1990). *Project 2061: Educating for a changing future*. Washington, D.C.: American Association for the Advancement of Science.
17. Henry, N. B. (1960). Introduction. *Rethinking science education* (59th Yearbook, National Society for the Study of Education). Chicago: National Society for the Study of Education.
18. *Op. cit.*, Sagan, C., p. 6.
19. *Ibid.*
20. In fact, John Dewey wrote extensively about the science of morality and Leslie A. White, the noted anthropologist, published one of his major works under the title, *The Science of Culture*.
21. Hurd, P. D. (1969). *New directions in teaching secondary school science*. Chicago: Rand McNally, p. 20.
22. The New York Times (1990). Biology teaching under fire by panel. *The Times Picayune* (September 7, 1990), p. A–9.

23. Aldridge, B. G. (1988). *Essential changes in secondary science: Scope, sequence and coordination*. Washington, D.C.: National Science Teachers Association.
24. *Ibid.*
25. *Ibid.*
26. *Ibid.*
27. *Ibid.*
28. Haber-Schaim, U. (1967, March). The physics course. *Physics Today*, pp. 26–31.
29. *Op. cit.*, Hurd, P. D., p. 153.
30. Grobman, A. B. (1969). *The changing classroom: The role of the Biological Sciences Curriculum Study*. Garden City, NY: Doubleday.
31. Besvinick, S. L. (1988). Twenty years later: Reviving the reforms of the '60s. *Educational Leadership, 52* (September).
32. Fort, D. C. (1990). From gifts to talents in science. *Phi Delta Kappan 71*, 9:664–671.
33. Karplus, R. (1962). The science curriculum—One approach. *Elementary School Journal, 62*, 5:243–252.
34. Gagne, R. M. (1966). Elementary science: A new scheme of instruction. *Science 151*, 3706:49–53.
35. West, P. (1990, September 12). Academic calls for a panel to oversee efforts to reform science education. *Education Week X*, 2:5.
36. *Ibid.*
37. Shymansky, J. A., Kyle, W. C. & Alport, J. M. (1982). Research synthesis on the science curriculum projects of the sixties. *Educational Leadership, 40* 1:63–66.
38. Cited in: Kyle, W. C. (1984). What became of the curriculum development projects of the 1960s? How effective were they? What did we learn from them that will help teachers in today's classroom? *Research within reach: Science education* (Holdkom, D. and Lutz, P. B., eds.). Washington, D.C.: National Institute of Education, p. 13.
39. Penick, J. E. and Yaeger, R. W. (1983). The search for excellence in science education. *Phi Delta Kappan 64*:621–23.
40. Druva, C. A. and Anderson, R. D. (1983). Science teacher characteristics by teacher behavior and student outcome: A metaanalysis of research. *Journal of Research in Science Teaching, 20*, 5:467–479.
41. Murnane, R. J. (1985, June). Do effective teachers have common characteristics: Interpreting the quantitative research effort. Paper presented at the National Research Council Conference on Teacher Quality in Science and Mathematics, Washington, D.C.
42. Weiss, I. R. (1987). *Report of the 1985–86 National Survey of Science and Mathematics Education*. Research Triangle Park, NC: Research Triangle Institute.
43. American Association for the Advancement of Science (1989). *Science for all Americans: Summary*. Washington, D.C.: American Association for the Advancement of Science.
44. *Op. cit.*, American Association for the Advancement of Science, *Project 2061: Education for a changing future*.
45. *Op. cit.*, American Association for the Advancement of Science, *Science for all Americans: Summary*, p. 4.
46. *Ibid.*, p. 5.
47. *Ibid.*
48. *Ibid.*, p. 10.
49. Shavelson, R. J., Carey, N. B., and Webb, N. M. (1990). Indicators of science achievement: Options for a powerful policy instrument. *Phi Delta Kappan, 71*, 9:692–697.

50. Boorstein, D. G. (1988). The shadow of democracy. *U.S. News & World Report* (November 14), p. 61.

51. *Ibid.*

52. Forte, D. C. (1990). From gifts to talents in science. *Phi Delta Kappan 71*, 9:665.

53. Cordes, C. (1990). Big science and technology projects near important milestones in face of federal budget crunch and mounting criticism. *The Chronicle of Higher Education XXXVII*, 2:23, 28.

# 14

# The Social Studies Curriculum

## Introduction

While all of the school's subjects are currently objects of reform and may be thought of as being in a transitional state, there is a traditional and more or less clear public image of English, science, and mathematics. The same cannot be said of the social studies, which has meant virtually everything to everyone, from rote memory of state capitals to discussions of current events and analysis of the hypothesis construction techniques of historians. Edgar Wesley, a well-known authority of social studies education, described the uneasy state of the field with these words:

> *The field of the social studies has long suffered from conflicting definitions, an overlapping of functions, and a confusion of philosophies.*[1]

Wesley, of course, was not referring to a dictionary definition but rather to the very nature and structure of the field. What purposes are served by having a special field designated as the social studies? How does the field differ from the social sciences, if it does differ? What is the nature of the content to be included in the school's curriculum?

Currently, much of what is studied is claimed to lead toward the development of citizenship. Over the past several decades, all kinds of studies have been included in the curriculum with the purpose of achieving better citizenship. Jack Fraenkel's description of the knowledge from which social studies draws its content would literally make all of life the appropriate object of study:

> *For the most part, the content of the social studies is drawn from the disciplines of history and the social sciences — traditionally geography, political*

*science, and economics; more recently anthropology, sociology, and social psychology. But that is not all — certainly art, literature, music, ethics, occasionally the natural sciences — indeed all of life itself — might be considered as a data bank for the social studies.*[2]

If Fraenkel's view were accepted, whatever anyone said was social studies would be social studies!

To people unfamiliar with the social studies, it may be surprising to learn that the question of definition has plagued the field continually since its inception in 1916. There appears to have always been general agreement that a major purpose of the social studies is the preparation of the "good" citizen. It has usually been recognized that the term "good" is a difficult one to define particularly in a pluralistic democracy where a wide range of citizen behavior is expected and accepted. What has been less well understood is the ambiguity of the concept of *citizenship*. The ambiguity relates to the term in general as well as to its usage in a democratic society. For example, do the significant differences among different forms of governance (e.g., republicanism, oligarchy, democracy) affect the objective definition of citizenship?

We often talk of the inevitability of global citizenship as technology slowly turns our world into a global village, but we rarely deal with what that means to us as citizens. Everywhere, global interaction affects the ways we behave as citizens: contacts with remote peoples are steadily increasing, requiring us to deal publicly with fundamentally different value systems; our environmental frailty and interdependence are becoming more obvious; the European Common Market is already a reality; and the United Nations has shown its worldwide organizational potential during the Kuwait–Iraq crisis. What obligations do citizens of the United States have to their world citizenship? Is local citizenship comparable to global citizenship, and is it likely that there will be significant conflicts between the activities of local citizenship and those of a global nature?

One searches in vain through all the reports of the major national committees charged with revising curricula, starting with the Committee of Ten, for a definition of the term "citizenship." The definitions that we find hardly respond to the kinds of questions posed above. For instance, in developing a scope and sequence for the social studies on behalf of the National Council for the Social Studies (NCSS), a task force headed by John Jarolimek defined citizenship as meaning that the "individual is fully franchised as a member of a political community."[3] Despite the apparent precision of the definition, none of our questions can be clarified because of it, and the goal of developing citizenship continues to contribute to the intellectual "wandering about" that has been so characteristic of social studies curriculum development. In sum, the scope of the curriculum — that is, what the curriculum ought to cover — is in grave doubt and this, in turn, affects the sequencing of the content.

Curriculum workers always bring to their efforts their own conceptions of citizenship although these usually remain unexpressed. Lacking some explicit consensus about the most salient characteristics of democratic citizenship, the curriculum has become a catch-all for social remedies and reforms. A variety of courses have been added from time to time to the social studies curriculum depending on the definitional interpretation given to the field and its central purpose of citizenship development. Aside from courses in the social sciences, students are often encouraged to study consumer education, law education, family living, career education, travel in the United States, technology in society, and even sex education.

Despite the many significant challenges confronting today's young from intragenerational disjunctures to experience compression, stimulus overload, and a genetic/values revolution, the results of social studies instruction continues to be measured by standardized tests based on multiple-choice questions requiring clear and discrete answers. Citizens must deal with perplexing, often unresolvable problems, while American students are expected to respond with direct and definite answers.

Before stepping down from his position as Secretary of Education in 1988, William Bennett presented a report to the nation on the state of its schools based on the standardized testing conducted under the auspices of the Scholastic Aptitude Testing (SAT) program, the American College Testing (ACT) program, and the National Assessment of Educational Progress (NAEP). According to Bennett, only 51 percent of 17-year-olds enrolled in history classes could respond correctly to twenty-six questions "of basic historical chronology."[4] Over a third of students tested could not correctly identify the Mississippi River on a map of North America.[5] The gravest deficits appeared to be in civics where 60 percent of the students tested did not know why the *Federalist Papers* were written and 40 percent were unable to recognize a definition of checks and balances, considered such a unique characteristic of American governance.[6]

In Bennett's report, these academic failings are seen as a serious deterioration in the rigor of American education. The fact that students' knowledge of American history and of the documents forming the bases of our government is greatly wanting does disturb most Americans; we share the belief that such knowledge forms the core of our common heritage and ought to be a part of our background. Yet, there is little evidence linking the effective practice of democratic citizenship with such knowledge. Knowing about the history or geography of America does not appear to lead to active civic involvement, nor does it help students develop the reflective skills and willingness to make decisions in the face of complex and probably unresolvable conflicts necessary to the survival of a democratic governance. The question of what content would best contribute to the development of good citizenship for a democracy lies at the heart of the definitional debate that has for so long plagued the social studies.

A multitude of recommendations for reform have been derived from very distinct conceptions of the social studies and of citizenship. Before exploring several of these, this chapter presents an overview of the history of the field of social studies. In the process, it seeks to clarify the origins of what is currently taught in the schools as part of our educational effort to develop good citizenship. The chapter also compares the existing curriculum with several proposals put forth with great fanfare at the end of the eighties, and ends with an exploration of possible social studies futures.

# Historical Overview

## Origins

The establishment of the United States in the late 1700s was a vector of change such as we have discussed in the first section of this work. Developing loyalty to the new nation became an important purpose of education, easily rivalling the religious purposes that dominated the colonial period. Few materials were suited to this new direction and it is likely many of the quaint stories lauding the greatness of our founding fathers had their origins in the lectures of teachers who lacked appropriate printed materials. The study of American history appeared early in the curriculum as a way of developing patriotism in the young.

This was also a period of vast land settlements. There was a growing consciousness of the American continent and the great opportunities that were afforded from the seemingly unlimited availability of land. Geography became an exceedingly popular subject especially with the publication of Jediah Morse's textbook, *American Universal Geography*, in 1784.[7]

The years leading up to the Civil War saw a continued diminution of religious purpose, a rise in the instruction of morality often associated with patriotism to the nation, and a greatly strengthened industrial economy requiring ever increasing numbers of factory workers. The demise of slavery and the end of the Civil War allowed a divided nation to come together again. The need to spark a sense of patriotic unity and civic responsibility among the whole populace was even greater than in the period following the Revolutionary War.

This need was exacerbated when millions of non–English-speaking European immigrants arrived in the United States between the 1880s and 1921. Their labor was urgently needed if America's factory economy was to continue to grow. Their customs and ways, however, were sufficiently different to cause the resident population great concern and a sense of urgency in "Americanizing" the new arrivals.

It should be noted that the immigrants themselves were willing to be "Americanized" for most of them had known the most abject poverty in their homelands and neither expected nor desired to return. For them, in that period of increasing industrialization, the idea of being part of a great melting pot was the equivalent of a promise that at least their descendents would know not only the political but also the economic benefits of being American. This conception of a "melting pot" represents a unique moment in history when the inculturators (i.e., the natives) and those to be inculturated (i.e., the immigrants) agreed. Both looked to the schools to carry out the task. To a considerable extent, today's social studies is a product of that unspoken agreement.

The immigrants did not spread out evenly across the country but rather gathered together in large groupings close to their places of employment. The cities of the Northeast and the Midwest were most affected, and their schools especially showed increasing concern for instruction in citizenship. Civics or the study of American government was added to the curriculum. History textbooks, sometimes beginning with Biblical creationism before moving on to the American Revolution, multiplied in this period. Patriotism, morality, and the socialization of the young were closely bound together with the history of the United States, its Constitution, and the ideals of society. A quote from two historians at the turn of the century characterizes well the attitude that existed prior to the twentieth century:

> *The principal reasons for the study of history are that it trains the memory, is a steady practice in the use of materials, exercises the judgment and sets before the students' minds a high standard of character.*[8]

The concept of "social studies" was in the educational air at the beginning of the twentieth century, but its roots were deeply embedded in history, somewhat less so in geography and more recently in civics. In the 1880s, the American Historical Association (AHA) was among the first groups to make recommendations concerning the improvement of the schools' curricula. Quite naturally, as George Maxim points out, the historians reserved a substantial portion of the curriculum for history.[9]

Historians were by far the largest group to participate in the report issued by the National Education Association's Committee on the Social Studies in 1916. Thomas Jesse Jones, a sociologist, chaired the committee, coining the term "social studies" in a 1913 preliminary report.[10]

From the beginning, good citizenship was to be the purpose of the new subject. The committee defined the social studies as "those [studies] whose subject matter relates directly to the organization and development of human society, and to man as a member of social groups."[11] This is a definition as broad as life itself and clearly laid the basis for the kind of definition put forth by Fraenkel that we have cited in the introduction.

The committee added in its discussion of aims that the 7–12 social studies curriculum should develop in the young a sense of responsibility toward their social group and a willingness "to participate effectively in the promotion of the group's social well being."[12] They went on to say that the "cultivation of good citizenship" should be the constant purpose of high school social studies.[13] In essence, it was their position that whatever did not contribute to the betterment of the citizen was not to be a part of the subject's content and, vice versa, that content far afield from traditional history, geography, and civics could become a part of the curriculum only if it contributed to improved citizenship. The committee hoped to achieve greater educational efficiency by changing the emphasis of study from one based on the study of disciplines to one based on studying content that would relate to the student's future role as citizen. However, notwithstanding goals such as these, the committee proposed a curriculum for the secondary schools based largely on the disciplines of history and geography.[14]

Jones, as director of research for the Hampton Institute, had designed a program of study for American Indians and Blacks to help them acquire the skills of the middle class. When the committee issued its final report, it endorsed the

Hampton program as an excellent illustration of its proposals.[15] The committee proposed a two-cycle pattern for the social studies so that the majority of youngsters who would drop out before the eighth grade could receive some citizenship preparation. The secondary sequence of courses was as follows: grade 7—geography and European history; grade 8—American history; grade 9—civics; grade 10—European history; grade 11—American history; and grade 12—problems of democracy.

### Debating the Sources of Content: History's Holding Power

The design of the social studies curriculum is closely linked to what one believes are the essential characteristics of democratic citizenship. Does knowing about history or how to do social science help the citizen to function more effectively in a democracy? What does help? And how does all this rational discourse relate to the real world of curriculum making? Cultural mindsets and political realities can never be ignored.

The remarkable holding power that history has had over the social studies is reflected in the Committee on the Social Studies' proposed secondary sequence of courses and is a case in point. Despite the openness (and ambiguity) that was introduced by the committee itself as it discussed the meaning of developing good citizenship for the content of the curriculum, history was assigned a dominant role in the social studies program, reinforcing a tradition that was established in the late nineteenth century and that affects us to this day. Indeed, the inclusion of geography and civics in the seventh and ninth grades, respectively, was a further imbedding of traditions that had already set their roots by the time the committee's report was issued in 1916.

It is clear that, from the beginning, there was tension between those who held objectives related to citizenship education foremost and those who believed history and geography were of the utmost importance. Knowing the facts about the Civil War or some other major event may be seen as unifying the nation and its many disparate cultural groups or it may be interpreted as ignoring the significant conditions of being a citizen in a world fraught with problems. Although tradition has dominated the curriculum throughout the twentieth century, repeated efforts have been made to go in other directions.

There has also been tension between those who would favor the social scientific disciplines over the traditional history curriculum. Like the historians, the social scientists saw the content of their disciplines as directly useful to the development of citizenship in a democracy. In discussing Alan Griffin, a major follower of Deweyian thought and a member of Ohio University's faculty until his death in 1964, Shirley Engle[16] describes the tensions between the various sources of content quite well:

> . . . he [Griffin] accepted social problems as a proper concern of study. He thought it imperative that so called "touchy" areas in our society be opened up for full scrutiny, arguing that this would never be done with even hand-

*edness if not done in the schools. But while he embraced a problem ap-proach, he warned against over [sic] dependence on it. He also saw usefulness in the study of disciplines, providing the study was done in the reflective rather than in the expository mood.*[17]

Engle further indicates that Griffin reacted to a plea for more history in the school's curriculum as a way of ensuring the continued growth of democracy by noting there was little evidence to support the idea that a relationship exists between the study of history and the growth of democracy. According to Griffin, democratic institutions develop prior to and independently of the study of history.[18]

The eclectic flavor of this discussion is quite typical of the American educational scene. In Griffin's case, it was no doubt a reflective eclecticism; in the case of many public schools, mindless eclecticism has led to a hodgepodge of social studies curricula. Content has been drawn from whatever source would appease the particular political furor of the day.

## The Social Sciences

Deciding which activities do or do not contribute in a direct fashion to the betterment of citizens has remained a perplexing undertaking. It has been the target of many scholarly efforts across the years. Defining the social studies is really about what citizenship is in a democracy and how it can be best supported in the public schools.

Many would undo the central role of history and make it, instead, only one of a number of socially oriented disciplines useful to the goals of the social studies. In the 1930s, the American Historical Society (AHA) issued a series of reports on the social studies that tended to treat the social sciences as though they were the social studies.[19] Sociology, psychology, economics, political science, and anthropology were thus added to history and geography as appropriate sources of content. Faith in science and the scientific method was still at an acme, and the AHA reports represented a sincere belief that the application of the sciences to social problems would contribute to their resolution as well as to the improvement of citizenship in America. Charles Beard, the famous historian, issued his book *The Nature of the Social Sciences*[20] in 1934. He explored each of the social science disciplines to determine what content could be used in the social studies to further citizenship.

In a sense, using the social sciences as sources of content for the social studies is a contradictory undertaking because *all* sciences have as part of their intellectual ethic the goal of being value-free. Social studies, with its aim of developing good citizenship, is clearly a value-oriented undertaking. Linking value-free social sciences to value-oriented social studies in a noncontradictory fashion is, at the very least, a major challenge.

Typically, the term "social sciences," when applied to the school's curriculum, includes sociology, psychology, anthropology, political science, and economics. These disciplines have two major characteristics in common: they study human behavior and they utilize scientific methodology in their studies. Each views human behavior from a unique perspective that in broad terms may be represented by a set of concepts.[21]

Anthropology, for example, studies *patterns of culture*, their underlying universal similarities, and their differences. Sociology concentrates on *societal institutions* as a holistic, interactive system, exploring how, why, and when they change. Psychology involves the scientific study of *individual behavior* as it is observed in personality, attitudes, motivation, perception, innate skills, and learning. Economics is the study of *scarcity* and how this relates to the numerous, unlimited wants of humankind. Like sociology, political science observes, measures, and generalizes the patterns of human interaction in society, but it does so primarily from the perspective of *power* and how it is originated, allocated, and used.

Quite often, both geography and history are included as social sciences, but each has characteristics that make it difficult to assign this label without acknowledging the caveats. Geography is both a physical and a human science. On the one hand, it studies the many features of the earth's surface, the association of features that distinguish one area from another, and the nature of interaction among different physical areas. On the other hand, it explores the interactions between cultural, political, economic, and social processes with the physical features of the earth. While clearly in the realm of science, the kinds of studies pursued are significantly physical in nature rather than social (as this adjective is used in the term "social sciences").

History is without a doubt social in content. The question is whether the very nature of its content, the story of past events, often reported by participants heavily involved in the most controversial activities of their period, can ever achieve the detachment and objectivity required by science. Of course, pure objectivity is never fully achieved, but the narrative and interpretive qualities of history have often led professionals to classify it as a humanity. The broad generalizations about democracy or the wars we have fought in the name of democracy — useful generalizations but often lacking what would be thought of as scientific evidence — and the values of society transmitted to students as givens embedded in narratives about the past correspond more closely to the humanities than to the sciences.

In 1937, Edgar Wesley issued a definition of the social studies that, if accepted by the field, would have diminished the importance of the traditional curriculum based on history, geography, and civics. Wesley posited that the social studies *were* the social sciences simplified for pedagogical purposes.[22] Regardless of Wesley's belief in his later years that his definition was being misinterpreted, implicit in this very simple, clearly expressed definition was the idea that the individual who was knowledgeable about the social scientific disciplines had the tools necessary for being a good citizen. Active participation in citizenship activities was made secondary to engaging in scientific methodology. In complementary fashion, the knowledge of history, even "patriotic" historic, was being given a diminished role in the education of citizens. Of course, such a position would not stand long without major challenge. It was especially attacked by those supportive of a content based on social problems.[23]

The structure of the social science disciplines became an especially important source of study during the reform movement of the 1960s. The emphasis on the structure of the disciplines that had been pursued in the federally funded curricular revisions of physics, chemistry, and biology served as models when finally the National Science Foundation began funding curricular revision in the social studies. It was soon followed by a number of other foundations and professional associations.

The results of the Woodshole Conference, as reflected in Jerome S. Bruner's *The Process of Education*,[24] served as the conceptual bases for what was called the "New Social Studies." Scientific inquiry skills were to be pursued by youngsters at various stages of intellectual development and the structure of the social science disciplines was to be the chief source of content. Students were to study human behavior with objectivity and with the inquiry skills of social scientists working in their respective fields.

Among the best known programs of this period were: the Harvard Social Studies Project,[25] which alone among the projects clearly focused on citizenship; *Our Working World*,[26] which tried to demonstrate how the disciplinary structure of economics could be used to understand economics even at the earliest grade levels; the Sociological Resources for the Social Studies,[27] which produced high school materials from 1964 to 1971 intended to teach scientific inquiry skills as reflected by the discipline of sociology; *The Family of Man*[28] K–6 program, which focused on developing worldwide cultural understanding; and *Man: A Course of Study*[29] (MACOS), which incurred widespread criticism for its efforts to have fifth and sixth grade children study basic questions about human social life from the objective perspective of scientists.

### Social Problems

For many, the study of disciplines, whether history or the social sciences, is irrelevant for the development of citizenship. In a democracy, citizens are continually involved in decision-making activities often concerning complex social problems that defy any straightforward resolution. Inquiry based in the disciplines can proceed according to accepted scientific methodology; inquiry, however, used to help solve problems confronting citizens must often function without the necessary definitional precision and in the midst of value conflicts that make objectivity an impossibility. John Dewey and his followers understood this well.

In 1896, some twenty years before social studies was conceived as a school subject, John Dewey established an experimental school at the University of Chicago. A student governance was organized, and students were directly involved in making decisions about the running of the school and their curriculum. For Dewey, learning was best achieved by starting with the needs and interests of children. It followed that learning to be a citizen needed to be based on children's active involvement in social problems concerning them directly. In later years, as children's interests matured, they would pursue more objective, discipline-based studies such as those represented by the disciplines. Dewey certainly would have replaced history, geography, and civics with a social studies curriculum based on social problems.

Dewey's influence was felt by the 1916 Committee on the Social Studies. It recommended that schools focus on problems of interest to students. Somewhat in contradiction to this position, however, was its strong recommendation for the continued study of history as preparation for citizenship. Even while the social sciences were being supported as appropriate content for the social studies in the 1930s, Lucy Sprague Mitchell was offering a social studies program called "Here and Now."[30] It had as its first step helping youngsters experience things for themselves. This was in direct opposition to the still popular method of having students memorize, or at least know well, the facts about historical events, people, and places without any firsthand experience. In the 1960s reform movement, as noted above, only one of the new social studies programs, the Harvard Project,[31] was clearly directed toward the development of citizenship through the consideration of social issues. By presenting public issues in a historical context, students were guided into discussions about the problems and values faced by people needing to make judgments. Issues dealt with such topics as freedom of the press and the propriety of violent demonstation.

The scarcity of social problems programs, especially in the second half of the twentieth century, is probably related to the general confusion that developed in the late 1940s among school people concerning what the content or scope of the social studies ought to be. When research in the early 1950s began to show that students had a poor grasp of basic historical information, the problems orientation supported by the progressives received much of the blame. This situation was similar to the 1980s when test scores revealed shocking inadequacies in students' historical knowledge. In both instances, there was a call to return to the basics and to increase the amount of history studied in the schools. In reality, while there was a good deal of public discussion about adopting a social problems approach, the traditional curriculum emphasizing history remained dominant.

## Concepts and Processes

Among the reforms of the 1960s were several efforts to develop social studies curricula based on concepts and processes useful in their own right to the citizen independently of possible associations with the disciplines. Under a grant from the U.S. Office of Education, the Social Studies Curriculum Center at Syracuse University undertook to identify social science concepts appropriate for social studies instruction.[32] The work focused on concepts not restricted to a single discipline and that could shed light on our understanding of human social interactions. Reflecting the structure of the disciplines was not a part of the objectives. The final list was comprised of thirty-four concepts organized under the following categories: Substantive Concepts; Value Concepts; and Aspects of Method, which was subdivided into Methodological Concept and Technique of Method. Among the eighteen substantive concepts were: culture, conflict, scarcity, input and output, sovereignty of the nation–state, morality and choice, power, and social control. Included in the eight techniques of method was observation, classification and measurement, skepticism, and evidence.

Just a few years earlier, Shirley H. Engle, well known in the social studies field for his support of the social problems orientation, suggested that there were several recurring concepts useful to the study of problems throughout human history.[33] These included: (1) culture, (2) man in culture interacting with nature, (3) social group, (4) economic organization, (5) political organization, (6) freedom, (7) interdependence, (8) science, and (9) the suprarational (which includes philosophy, aesthetics, and religion).

Both the social science and the social problems camps agree on the usefulness of basic concepts in a curriculum for citizenship development. It is likely that a curriculum based on concepts and processes could be devised that would satisfy both for it is clear that neither would emphasize learning specific facts but, rather, how to obtain and use facts. Basic concepts encountered at relatively simple levels during early studies of the social sciences and history could be pursued later in greater depth as part of an effort to solve current social problems. This is certainly what Engle intended when he proposed his list of recurring concepts. His recent work with Anna Ochoa, *Education for Democratic Citizenship*,[34] appears to confirm this view. It proposes a problem-centered treatment of the social studies integrated with sets of questions likely to lead to broad generalizations.

This organization of content based on returning to concepts already studied with the purpose of enlarging and deepening their meaning is known as the spiral curriculum. Hilda Taba developed such a curriculum in the late 1960s. She organized basic concepts according to their level of complexity and abstraction and drew concepts from all the social sciences, encouraging students to analyze and generalize about social issues.[35] As an example, the concept of work can first be studied by young children through a series of observations in their own community. At first, they can simply collect their descriptions. Later, they can begin to group and classify the different kinds of work to be found in American society. This can lead to the development of a small database about work in America. In spiral fashion, the complexity can be increased by examining questions related to work such as why some work is valued more highly than other work. Relationships of various kind can thus be pursued and explanatory statements or generalizations developed.

## The Three Traditions

As we have noted, debates concerning the nature of the social studies have characterized the field since its inception. After more than half a century of debate, a book that tries to sort out the various traditions that had come to characterize social studies instruction in the schools was issued in 1977 by three university professors, Robert Barr, James Barth, and Sam Shermis. Because this work, *The Nature of the Social Studies*,[36] responded to a deeply felt need for greater clarity in the field, it quickly became standard reading for preservice and in-service teachers.

An initial analysis of the conflicting conceptions of what needs to be taught in the social studies was undertaken by Professors Barth and Shermis in an article published in 1970, accompanied by commentaries from their student, Robert

Barr. Barr, the year before, had conducted research for his dissertation concerning teachers' perceptions of the social studies.[37] These efforts led directly to what has become one of the most widely cited works in the field. The authors suggest that three traditions have dominated social studies instruction in the schools. These are:

1. *Citizenship transmission* based on the belief that patriotism and cultural heritage should be "transmitted" by the schools. This tradition is most closely linked to the content of history, geography, and civics as currently taught in the schools.

2. *Social science* based on the belief that mastery of the concepts, processes, and problems associated with the disciplines will promote improved citizenship. Although dominant in the new social studies reform movement of the 1960s, its only influence on today's curriculum is found in high school programs offering introductory social science courses in psychology, economics, and sociology. These are usually electives.

3. *Reflective inquiry* based on the belief that the learning of inquiry processes related to citizens' decision making will best prepare students to deal with democratic citizenship problems. The many efforts, especially in the lower grades, to develop thinking skills are related to this tradition. The problems of democracy course recommended by the 1916 Committee on the Social Studies for the twelfth grade persists in many high schools. The work of the Syracuse Social Studies Curriculum Center and the recommendations made by Shirley Engle, both in the 1960s, also relate well to this tradition.

### The Philosophical Spectrum

The conception of the social studies, in which the development of citizenship plays a central role, is to a certain degree a philosophical statement. Giving so much primary importance to the participation of people in their society and governance ignores the existential self. Social studies assumes that people are members of society, that they must learn how to exercise not only their rights but also their responsibilities, and that their identity is largely acquired through successful social interaction.

Within these parameters, there remains for the social studies a philosophical continuum, which has at the more conservative end perennialism and at the more liberal end progressivism along with its variant reconstructionism. The three traditions, as proposed by Barr, Barth and Shermis, can be arranged along this continuum. Citizenship transmission, along with the passing on of cultural heritage, satisfies in varying degrees both the perennialists and the essentialists. The perennialists, once they have discovered all great knowledge, or, from a religious perspective, have received insight into the will of God, would wish to transmit this to students in as unchanged a manner as possible. The essentialists do expect knowledge as well as governments to transform themselves *slowly*. They, too, believe in cultural transmission, but because they also believe that new knowledge can be developed by science, they would support as well a conception of the social studies based on the social sciences although probably not to the exclusion of the study of history. The progressives, who see knowledge and all of human life in an ongoing state of change and who conceive of people as being social by nature, would certainly embrace the reflective inquiry tradition and social problems as the main source of content. The reconstructionists would agree with the progressives, but they would insist on a curriculum design directed toward a set of well-planned outcomes closely related to a more perfect, democratic future.

The selection of content based on concepts and processes not directly associated with the disciplines would most likely not be acceptable to the perennialists. They would see this as the study of empty vessels without any "cargo" or meaning. Great works cannot be reduced to a set of concepts or processes; they must be experienced holistically. However, since the perennialists give great value to logical reasoning, some grudging support could probably be found among them for the study of processes.

In all likelihood, a substantial portion of essentialists would also be uncomfortable with a study of processes or concepts not directly related to a specific content. However, as the quantity of knowledge has continued its exponential increase and deciding what specific content ought to be learned has become more difficult, the essentialists have exhibited greater willingness to accept studies of processes such as thoses related to scientific methodology independently of any one discipline.

The progressives would certainly embrace a curriculum design based on concepts and processes because the specific content could then be varied according to the individual student's background and interests. Although closely related to the progressives in their view of the nature of knowledge, the reconstructionists would be more reluctant to accept a "directionless" study of concepts and processess that could embrace ideals other than democracy.

Figure 14.1 represents the correlations between the philosophical continuum, the three traditions, and the sources of content. It is intended as a summary as well as an approximate representation of the different continua.

**FIGURE 14.1**   *Correlated Continua for the Social Studies Curriculum*

PERENNIALISTS    ESSENTIALISTS    PROGRESSIVISTS    RECONSTRUCTIONISTS

*The Three Traditions*

←Cultural Transmission ——————→

        ←——— Social Science Tradition ——→

                        ←——————————— Reflective Inquiry ——————→

*Sources of Content*

←Traditional Content ——————————→

←——— The Social Sciences ——————→

                        ←——————— Social Problems ——————————→

        ←——————————— Concepts and Processes ——————————→

## Current Trends and Issues

### Reforms of the 1980s–1990s

In our most recent period of school reform, which reached a peak in the mid 1980s but is continuing in the early 1990s, many have taken the view that "watered down" studies accompanied by social promotion and insufficient time on task has rendered American education mediocre. The results of innumerable standardized tests has seemed to confirm this position.

Among the recommended remedies are extending the academic calendar to 220 days and requiring all students to pass a series of objectively normed examinations before graduating from high school or advancing from one to another academic level. In the latter recommendation, we have an instance of the continued deepening of what is fast becoming the standardized testing tradition. For the curriculum, this has meant a renewed emphasis on the academic subjects that became "standard" with the recommendations of the Committee of Ten almost a century ago and that are typically "examined" by nationally normed tests.

In the sciences and mathematics, this renewed emphasis on the traditional disciplines has necessarily included the most recent conceptual advances in each field. In the social studies, however, it has tended to mean increasing the study of history for the sake of achieving a more unified and patriotic citizenry. Since there has been almost no advancement in our understanding of the nature of citizenship, how to be a more effective citizen in a democracy, or what it means to be a citizen of both a nation and the globe, the social studies curriculum has added little to its conceptual base.

It should be noted that the increased dependence on standardized tests for evaluating the success of a social studies program is a form of de facto support for the traditional citizenship transmission curriculum based on history, geography, and civics. These are the subjects receiving the lion's share of attention via multiple-choice questions requiring a single correct answer. Whenever the results of these tests are discussed, whether by former Education Secretary William Bennett or some other dignitary, student ignorance about a major historical or geographical fact is pointed to (usually with despair) as an example of the failure of schooling. It is rare indeed for students to be queried about public affairs in their own community or about the current activities of PAC committees and lobbyists. Complex questions that might have more than one answer are generally excluded from the standardized test as are decision-making and reflective thinking activities related to a social problem of current significance. In sum, the widespread acceptance of standardized evaluations in history and geography as measures of success for social studies programs not only reflects a cultural mindset about the nature of studies relevant to citizenship but also contributes to the deepening of that mindset.

### Standard Curriculum — the Elementary Grades

The traditional social studies curriculum has exhibited a stability not unlike the school's curriculum as a whole. History, geography, and civics are the long-standing, traditional mainstays of citizenship preparation. There are few prospects that will change in the near future.

Typically, one finds in the early elementary grades some form of the "expanding environments curriculum,"[38] which sequences study beginning with the child's home and school, moving on to the neighborhood, and then expanding to increasingly greater and more remote entities — the community, the state, the region, the nation, and the world. This sequencing reflects both the cognitive developmental characteristics of young children and the progressive's view that instruction must start with the needs and experiences of each child.

In our most recent reform movement, the content of this curriculum, usually based on human activities typical of each of these environments, has received much criticism. The contention has been that too much precious time is spent on content of too little consequence such as the child's immediate environs. Certainly, these early studies do little to improve children's performances on standardized social studies tests.

In 1987, the California State Board of Education adopted what is popularly known as the "California Framework."[39] This is the set of guidelines that the board has established for the development of social studies curriculum. The "expanding environments curriculum" is recognizable in the recommendations but has been significantly modified to included an early, greatly increased emphasis on history and geography.

For example, the scope of the first grade is entitled "A Child's Place in Time and Space." This heading is to be responsive to such goals as expanding children's economic worlds and developing awareness of cultural diversity, now and long ago.

The second grade scope would be based on "People Who Make a Difference." The topics recommended under this rubric range from the people who supply our needs, which could certainly be interpreted as the immediate needs of each child's typically egocentric world, to people from many cultures, now and long ago.

Not only is there a clearly historical underpinning in the recommendations of the early grades, there is also much greater emphasis on broader and conceptually more inclusive studies than has hitherto been characteristic of content in the expanding environments format. For example, not only are young children to study the cultural diversity of their local region, they are to look at cultural diversity in the past as well as in many different geographic locations of the present. By the third grade, both local and national history is to be covered through the reading of biographies, stories, folktales, and the like.

The framework continues what has been a long-standing tradition of the social studies curriculum by recommending the study of American history and geography in the fifth grade. Geography, map reading skills, and civics (usually interpreted in the early grades as the learning of appropriate social behaviors) round off the content.

It is difficult to tell from a set of guidelines how cognitive developmental stages of youngsters would be treated. It may be that a first grade youngster would come to understand her own immediate economic world, that is, what she can purchase with the money she has, the relationship of work to money, and so forth.

Helping the youngster to organize these models is an instructional approach that would move from the known to the unknown and from the concrete to the conceptual. It is a significantly different instructional undertaking to help her organize the economic models functioning in the United States today or in times gone by. Instruction would be at the level of conceptual complexity at one fell swoop and well removed from her own realm of experience.

The Brunerian claim that any subject can be taught in some conceptually accurate fashion in the very earliest grades[40] leads to an instructional approach that would start with greatly simplified concepts in all likelihood derived from the child's sphere of understanding. Subsequently, the concepts are presented in more comprehensive and complex forms, building on the initial learning in the spiral curriculum approach. While it is possible that children will learn more historical and geographical facts if they begin to deal with advanced concepts (such as cultural diversity in the distant past) earlier, we must ask whether this is the most effective way to approach the social studies. If early instruction and testing push children to a frustration level of not understanding and of repeatedly failing tests, are they not likely to resist the continued study of that subject in later years? In our view, good evidence is scarce, and there is not a clear answer to the question. Still, many of the current reformers seem to have concluded that they have found the solution to our educational problems and are deeply engaged in efforts to reinforce the academic traditions of our social studies past.

### Standard Curriculum — The Secondary Grades

In the secondary grades, one year of American history is typically studied at both the junior and senior high levels. Geography of the United States and the Western world is well ensconced in the junior high curriculum and is rarely pursued as an independent subject in the higher grades. World history, which in most instances is the history of the Western world, and civics usually complete the required program of study in the high school. In addition, there has been a persistent presence of the social science disciplines especially in the high school curriculum. Even in the 1940s, one could find psychology, economics, and sociology among the offerings of the high school curricula in large cities. There may also be an elective offered in problems of democracy.

Somewhat erratically and not really in keeping with the emphasis on disciplinary studies, but rather as an occasional response to public pressure, urgent social problems have been turned into social studies units or even courses. Thus, teenage pregnancy, consumer education, career education, and drug education, to name a few, may be found among social studies offerings as well.

The most recent wave of reformers appear to be reacting to this occasional potpourri of courses as well as to the poor performance of students on standardized tests. In part, they blame the social problems orientation for the ignorance demonstrated on tests even though the traditional subjects have never ceased to overwhelmingly dominate the curriculum. Strengthening the history and geography components seems to be their primary objective.

A case in point is the recent report of the Bradley Commission on History in Schools. It proposes boosting history instruction as a way of improving scores on standardized tests.[41] The report takes the position that the schools ought to place their primary emphasis in the social studies on the history of the United States and Western civilization.

Another report, entitled *Charting a Course: Social Studies for the 21st Century*,[42] was issued in November 1989 by the National Commission of the Social Studies in the Schools. This group was formed by the American Historical Association, The Carnegie Foundation for the Advancement of Teaching, the National Council for the Social Studies, and the Organization of American Historians. Not surprisingly, the commission recommends three years of world history for the high school curriculum. Whether one prefers world history to the history of Western civilization is certainly an important point to be considered in its own right; in the context of this presentation, however, it is more important to recognize that whatever discussion may develop between those of the Bradley Commission's persuasion and the members of the National Commission, the discussion is about history. It appears that history has not only maintained but increased its hold over the social studies curriculum especially at the secondary level.

### Curriculum Recommendations

In discussing the elementary grades of study, the National Commission on Social Studies states:

> By the end of grade six, pupils should know much factual information from the disciplines of history, geography, government and economics and have an elementary sense of how that information relates to national and global understanding. . . . Students should know what "long ago" means locally as well as in relation to their work in grades 4–6. They should know how mound builders of Ohio or Neolithic sites in New Mexico fit into the big picture and where such events as the founding of Williamsburg or the Civil War or the Dust Bowl fit into the time line of national history.[43]

While the commission certainly sees the understanding of such key social science concepts as chronology and climate as important, their vision of what young students should know is so comprehensive that one must wonder whether the school's curriculum, as typically implemented today, can really accommodate their vision.

The commission sees grades 7 and 8 as being the critical period in the curriculum when students need to "develop the knowledge, skills and ethical attitudes necessary for effective, active citizenship."[44] They therefore recommend two courses, one a study of the local community and the other a study of the nation. According to the commission, state history and geography, when mandated, can be studied as a part of the local community course. This same course would also study how changes in the past altered the community culturally as well as physically. In addition, students would pursue in their readings, research, and classroom activities local public issues such as housing, environmental pollution, and transportation. As a result of the course, according to the commission, they would come to understand that practicing good citizenship requires "a clear knowledge of the issues," as well as an awareness of how diverse opinions and interests are reconciled.[45] Local history is seen as a means of linking the schools with the larger world. Habits of community service are expected to evolve naturally as a result of students vigorously studying their own community.

The second junior high course pursues the economic and political development of the United States as well as its changing relationships with the rest of the world. An in-depth understanding of the impact of the United States Constitution on the social and economic shape of the country would comprise an important strand of this course. Also included would be beginning legal studies as well as comparative studies in capitalism, socialism, and communism. The influence of foreign events on the way the nation has developed along with local, national, and international public policy questions would be studied as well.

According to the commission, these studies will further "develop students' knowledge of their responsibility for active civic participation."[46] This two-year sequence of study based first on the community and then on the nation is described as leading youngsters to a better understanding of their overlapping roles and loyalties as citizens. The commission appears to have unlimited confidence in the power of historical and social scientific studies to develop desirable citizenship qualities. They expect their curriculum to develop thoughtful, involved citizens but present little evidence or logic to support their claims. It is unclear how the quantity of reading and library-based investigating necessarily tied to their plan will lead to *active* student involvement.

Students in grades 9 to 12 are seen by the commission as being more mature and analytical and better able to study an in-depth history of the United States and the world. Indeed, the commission would prefer an integrated historical study of national and world change, but, in acknowledgment of various state requirements, accepts the separate teaching of United States history. The proposed scope and sequence for high school studies is as follows:

1. World and American history and geography to 1750. The major civilizations from early times on would be studied along with their unique cultures.
2. World and American history and geography, 1750–1900. This course would highlight three major transformations in modern times: the democratic revolution, the industrial and technological revolution, and modern population growth and mobility.
3. World and American history and geography since 1900. This course revolves around the three dominant movements of the nineteenth century — marxism, fascism, and democracy — and their development in the twentieth century.

In all three courses, case studies of particular times and places are to be studied although the specific content may vary. The commission considers especially important that overarching themes and the interplay among local and more general patterns be kept in view and understood.

In the twelfth grade, an increased range of options is to be made available to students, who are expected to take two semester-long courses. The options are: government/economics, either singly or as a combined course; social science courses in anthropology, sociology, and psychology; multidisciplinary study of contemporary or recurring issues; and a supervised experience in community service.

The option for a one-semester community service experience is the only active student involvement in the exercise of citizenship skills included in the curriculum. The contemporary issues course is the only one that would deal with current problems. Unfortunately, the proposed sequence would make it likely that students would have to choose between them. The academic, albeit enlightened study of history and geography are clearly dominant in this curriculum proposal and "reform," despite the greatly increased emphasis on world history, amounts to strengthening what already exists.

Numerous references to democratic values and ethics[47] are made in the commission's report, but what these mean in terms of the proposed curriculum is perplexing. Does studying marxism, fascism, and democracy in objective and comparative fashion lead to the development of ethical values in the young? Will knowledge of world history and awareness of the interaction of our history with world history lead to the development of citizens deeply committed to democracy? What can we reasonably expect from the kinds of studies recommended?

Certainly, the commission's proposed curriculum lacks conceptual consistency. While history and geography are emphasized throughout, community service, citizen involvement, and ethical behavior are repeatedly referred to as "desirable outcomes." What is striking, as James Shaver, a former president of the National Council for the Social Studies, points out is "the failure to deal with citizenship in an adequately comprehensive way."[48] Curricular goals directly associated with history, geography, and the other social science disciplines have persistently fared better in the schools in terms of status and time allocated for study than has the goal to develop citizenship, even though everyone seems to agree that the latter goal is the most important one for the social studies. Indeed, the National Commission on Social Studies places civic responsibility and active civic participation at the top of its list of goals.

## Global Studies

The task of defining global education, usually included among the social studies, poses considerable difficulty. In part, as Steven Lamy notes, the tendency to think of global education in terms of contemporary issues and advocacy positions has impeded the serious theoretical work that needs to be done if the scope and objectives of the field are to have form and direction.[49] As in the case of citizenship, there is much rhetoric about the need to develop global understanding in the young but little that actually happens in terms of curriculum. Furthermore, we hardly know what we ourselves believe about globalism. There are all sorts of usually unspoken questions. What do we have in common culturally with the people of the Amazon jungle or the sheiks of Saudi Arabia? What do we gain once we know about our similarities and differences? Will we lose some of our patriotism in the process of developing a world view? Is global studies worth the limited time of youngsters, many of whom are woefully ill-prepared in basic academics? Despite some reluctance, the sense that global studies must gain a place in the curriculum is growing in urgency.

The report by the National Commission of the Social Studies takes into account the increasing need to view our existence from a world perspective. However, its recommendations remain almost entirely within the context of the study of history, whereas global studies are widely accepted to be interdisciplinary in nature.

Global studies also need to be, as Lamy points out, capable of varying with the world view of the students and their community.[50] That is, they need to reflect the values, priorities, and assumptions used by the individual and the community in the interpretation of conditions and events. Such a shifting perspective hardly contributes to a well-defined field. In fact, Lamy presents several clear, albeit contradictory definitions depending on the particular constituency.[51] The multinational corporate world sees the mastery of skills necessary for the conduct of business in a worldwide community as the crucial ingredients for global studies. The scope of the content would include geographic awareness, foreign languages, cultural studies, history, economics, and decision-making skills as well as the basic skills of reading, writing, and arithmetic. Then, there are organizations that pursue global studies from a particular vision for a better quality of life on earth. World peace and a protected environment are two such perspectives. Each group offers an explanation of how the world functions and then proceeds to propose how it should function based on the priorities and values they hold. Based on this foundational discussion, a global curriculum proposal is put forth. In all these instances, very little effort is made to critically evaluate the particular world view that underlies what is being proposed. If social studies is worth anything to a democracy it is in its ability to support critical evaluation of *all* positions taken.

Looking at world-centered curriculum from a more objective perspective, the Andersons suggest that five major goals of schooling should underlie the selection of content. These are, as cited by James Becker in *Schooling for a Global Age*:

1. To develop students' understanding of themselves as individuals.
2. To develop students' understanding of themselves as members of the human species.
3. To develop students' understanding of themselves as inhabitants of the planet earth.
4. To develop students' understanding of themselves as participants in global society.
5. To develop students' competencies for living responsibly and intelligently as individuals, human beings, earthlings, and members of global society.[52]

As Becker indicates in his discussion of these goals, "identities, loyalties, and competencies as well as rights, duties, obligations and privileges are associated with each of these goals."[53] For example, documents such as The Universal Declaration of Human Rights could be analyzed from the individual, human being, earthling, and global perspectives. In the upper elementary grades, the United Nations document "The Rights of the Child" could be studied in some simplified form so that the relevance for each student's life could be emphasized.

The conflicts arising among the various interpretations of the documents could provide a social problems basis for the global studies curriculum. For instance, the rights of fishermen worldwide could be contrasted with the rights of those who wish to preserve the environment for the sake of future generations. The uncertainty of not being able to think of one party as clearly right, the lack of straightforward solutions to problems, and the need to make decisions despite the confusion of contending rights are circumstances arising from the intersection of rights with the various levels of human participation in society that can be used to advantage when preparing youngsters to participate actively in the affairs of their own governance.

The potential for global studies appears to be all in the future. While there is considerable awareness that we are living in a shrinking world, relatively little evidence exists in today's curriculum of that growing awareness.

## Social Studies Scenarios for the Twenty-First Century

### Ignoring the Future

Of all the school subjects typically found in today's curriculum, none lend themselves so readily to explorations of the future as the social studies. Much of what will happen to us in the future depends on the decisions citizens make today. When does life begin? Who shall decide when life should end? What shall we do about pollution? the ozone layer? the greenhouse effect? What role shall we allow the increasingly powerful media to play in the education of our children? Should we go on exploring space, a costly undertaking, while social problems from homelessness to hungry school children persist?

Neither the Bradley report nor the curriculum proposed by the National Commission on Social Studies provides for the study of future-oriented issues. Despite the title of the Commission's report, *Charting a Course: Social Studies for the 21st Century*, the twenty-first century is hardly a consideration in its proposal.

Cultural universals that lend themselves to the historical study of the past dominate the commission's thinking and are undeniably useful in reflecting on future possibilities. However, as we have previously discussed, the future is full of disjunctures that have not previously been known. Very little in our current school experience prepares us to deal wisely with a future of unpredictable and difficult problems in a context of constant uncertainty. Surely, a major purpose of education is to help children achieve insights into the kinds of difficulties they will face as adults.

The resistance to using the future as content for the curriculum may in part be due to a popular tendency to view the future from the perspective of a science fiction writer. That is, the future is described in terms of novel inventions—cars that fly, robots that talk as though they were the next-door neighbor, machines that travel through time. Problems, if there are any, tend to be trivial—how to repair the flying car or the quirky robot. While this may all be very amusing to youngsters, it is not the kind of content that leads to more reflective thought about the nature of our future and the enormity of the decisions we will need to make. It is not simply that we need to prepare ourselves to function effectively with new discoveries and marvelous inventions, but rather that we need to reflect on the effects these may hold for the quality of our lives—effects that we might reject and wish to stop if we were less naive about technological progress.

For instance, once people sat outside on the porches of the country or the stoops of the city to escape the summer heat. In the process they came to know their neighbors well and feel a sense of real community. Then air-conditioning became widespread and available to even modest homes. The porches and the stoops were abandoned as people stayed inside to enjoy the cool. Getting to know your neighbor became a lot more difficult. In other words, air-conditioning contributed to the undoing of "community" as we once knew it. If we had been less naive and more aware of the potential impact, we might still have embraced air-conditioning, but we could have thought more cogently about ways of sustaining the community of our neighborhoods.

Where in the social studies curriculum is there a place for such reflection and analysis? From the perspective of current trends, the future of futures studies appears grim indeed.

The study of the future as social, political, and economic phenomena must be issue oriented and exploratory. For example, a study of the social impact of computer technology would involve exploring the problems as well as the benefits arising from such usage and weighing pros and cons so that students could arrive at cogent decision-making positions. The social problems curriculum has been much discussed, especially by university professors, but rarely implemented.[54] It is especially out of favor in the early 1990s.

A wishful but more positive scenario for futures studies would posit an increased popularity for the study of social problems and a realization that one of the most important purposes for the social studies is to prepare the young to be decision makers with regard to their own futures.In addition to a course in problems of democracy, long a favorite of those who support the problem-centered curriculum, there could be a course in problems of the future. The content could include exploring the desirability of the "global village"[55] based on a network of electronic media, the potential impact of genetic manipulations on humans and other life forms, the effects of television on democratic practices, the benefits and demerits of the computerized workplace, the future of the environment, global multiculturalism, and so forth.

In an ideal, problem-centered curriculum of the future, numerous, integrated meetings would occur between the science and social studies classes. The members of the social studies classes could establish, with the help of their teachers and as a result of careful analysis and evaluation, the questions related to a given scientific advancement that they as citizens of a democracy would need to answer to make cogent decisions. The members of the science classes would pursue the data required with the assistance of their teachers. Later, all the classes could meet to develop a series of reports to be distributed to the entire student population.

As we have suggested in discussing an ideal science curriculum, an entire school day could be turned over to the study and discussion of these reports. The activities might end with a list of options drawn up by an elected student leadership and voted on by the student body. When viable, the school or local newspaper could publish an account of the proceedings. This activity could contribute to a sense of importance beyond the letter grades assigned by teachers.

### Decentralizing the Curriculum

Advanced computer technology and the communication power of television have made distance education a viable alternative even for those who live in cities or for members of classes able to have routine, large-group meetings. In the latter case, instead of always meeting at the same time and place (i.e., the school), work could be carried out by students in various community facilities, say, the main public library, a NASA facility, and the science museum. After dinner, the class could meet via televised hookup and interactive, computer-based communication to present the work accomplished at the separate community sites.

In this form of decentralized social studies education, involvement of parents and members of the community as a whole becomes quite practical. While the number of adequately equipped science laboratories is necessarily limited by cost factors, there is no better laboratory for democratic citizenship education than working with the community at large. For students to be involved in problem presentations and critical analysis of real situations, even by long distance, and to observe the reaction of adults to their work and conclusions about problems of general concern represents a level and quality of experience well beyond anything now available in social studies courses.

Other possible benefits from a system of distance education could include individualized tutoring based on the academic needs of students and on a selection of carefully developed CAI modules. In addition, class schedules could be varied both in the nature of instruction and in the amount of time assigned per meeting. That is, some classes could be wholly based on interactive CAI materials transmitted electronically to class members at their homes, while others could involve televised, teacher-based discussion/lecture. A computer-based student bulletin board could be used to encourage small-group discussions and research-based sharing of knowledge.

The vision of tomorrow's education that we have put forth here is technologically possible today. Perhaps expense alone impedes our ability to reconceptualize how we deliver instruction. Perhaps, as we have suggested for the curriculum, we cannot overcome the cultural mindsets of our past, and perhaps we really don't want to give up the factory-like organization of our schools that ensures youngsters will come together in a variety of social situations.

## Opening the Curriculum to the Hypothetical

If one is of the view that the curriculum is the scope and sequence planned by the central administration, a futuristic content for the social studies is virtually impossible. Clearly, if we are confronted by an array of possibilities of which only a few can actually occur and a number of those are based on unpredictable events, what we study must be opened to the hypothetical as well as to uncertain outcomes.

Specific performance objectives would be a foolish enterprise in a future-oriented social studies curriculum. This does not mean that general areas for study and critical evaluation would not be selected beforehand, but rather that the specific nature of the outcomes could be known only after studies are completed. For example, the role of robotics in America's workplace could be a preselected topic to be explored along with implications and possible undesirable directions. The kind of content teachers and students would specifically pursue would depend on what *they* conclude is most important to understand in their roles as citizens. Basic knowledge that is important to their decisions would be studied but, again, what they study could not be specifically determined months, possibly years, before it is studied, as is now the case. If we are to study the hypothetical, the curriculum must be open to the uncertainty it implies. John Dewey understood this well long ago.

## The Future of Pedagogy

A pedagogy of the social studies that would involve the local community as well as the students and that would deal honestly with possible futures and inevitable uncertainty must necessarily be premised on the hypothetical mode rather than the expository one. Of course, teachers can render student learning more efficient by making well-organized presentations of known data and processes in typical expository fashion. However, the dominant mode of instruction must be one of questioning what is likely to happen and of exploring problems that have no answers or, possibly, too many answers. "What-if" conundrums need to be at the heart of social studies content directed toward an exploration of the future and its many problems. Teachers working in the hypothetical mode would help students explore social problems while ensuring a climate open to questions and full of uncertainty. Students would engage in a series of decision-making activities and often take on a leadership role in determining exactly what problems would be pursued.

## QUESTIONS FOR DISCUSSION AND REFLECTION

1. The goal of the social studies that receives the most support from professionals in the field is the development of good citizenship. However, several problems are associated with the meaning of citizenship that need to be worked out if we are to understand fully the goal. What are the problems? Is there any way to resolve them?

2. Do present social studies curricula meet the goal of developing good citizens? Explain your position.

3. What specific processes, skills, and topics should be included in a social studies curriculum whose goal is the development of good citizenship? What should the role of history be in this curriculum?

4. What is/ought to be the relationship between the social sciences and the social studies curriculum?

5. A curriculum based on current social problems has been implemented in San Francisco and in Council Bluffs, Nebraska. Should the students in both places study all of the same problems, some of the same problems, or none of the same problems? Justify your answer.

6. List and explain the three traditions put forth by Barr, Barth, and Shermis. Based on your own experience, do you think these three traditions cover the full range of possible approaches to social studies instruction? What could be added or changed?

7. Do you agree or disagree with this statement: social studies is a progressive's conception of citizenship education, while an essentialist would prefer to emphasize history in the preparation of citizens. Please explain your position fully.

8. What do you think are the two strongest factors working against the creation and implementation of a future-oriented social studies curriculum, and why?

9. If a future-oriented social studies curriculum with a global perspective were to be adopted by a school district, what problems would be likely to occur? How might these problems be dealt with?

## NOTES

1. Wesley, E. B. (1978). Forward to *The nature of the social studies* (Barr, R., Barth, J. L., and Shermis, S. S., authors). Palm Springs, CA: ETC Publications.
2. Fraenkel, J. R. (1973). *Helping students think and value: Strategies for teaching the social studies*. Englewood Cliffs, NJ: Prentice-Hall, p. 92.
3. Jarolimek, J. (1984). In search of a scope and sequence for social studies: Report of the National Council for the Social Studies. *Social Education 48*, 4:250–261.
4. Bennett, W. J. (1988). American education: Making it work. *The Chronicle of Higher Education*, (May 4), pp. 29–41.

5. *Ibid.*

6. *Ibid.*

7. Maxim, G. W. (1987). *Social studies and the elementary school child*, 3rd ed. Columbus, OH: Merrill Publishing, p. 7.

8. Channing, E. & Hart, A. B. (1903). *Guide to the study of American history*. Boston: Ginn and Company, p. 1.

9. *Op. cit.*, Maxim, G. W., p. 12.

10. *Preliminary statements by chairmen of committees of the Commission of the National Education Association on the Reorganization of Secondary Education* (1916). Bulletin 28. Washington, D.C.: Bureau of Education, p. 16.

11. Dunn, A. W., compiler, (1916). *The Social Studies in Secondary Education*. Washington, D.C.: U.S. Government Printing Office, p. 9.

12. *Ibid.*

13. *Ibid.*

14. *Ibid.*, p. 12.

15. Kliebard, H. M. (1987). *The struggles of the American curriculum: 1893–1958*. New York: Routledge and Kegan Paul, pp. 126–127.

16. Engle, S. H. (1982). Alan Griffin 1907–1964. *Journal of Thought* 17 3:45–54.

17. *Ibid.*, pp. 45–46.

18. *Ibid.*, p. 48.

19. See, for example: Beard, C. A. (1932). *A charter for the social sciences in the schools*. Report of the Commission on the Social Studies, Part I. New York: Charles Scribner's Sons.

      Tryon, R. M. (1935). *The social sciences as school subjects*. Report of the Commission on the Social Studies, Part XI. New York: Charles Scribner's Sons.

20. Beard, C. A. (1934). *The nature of the social sciences*. New York: Charles Scribner's Sons.

21. For an in-depth, comparative discussion of the various social sciences, see: American Council of Learned Societies and the National Council for the Social Studies (1962). *The social studies and the social sciences*. New York: Harcourt, Brace & World.

22. Wesley, E. B. & Wronski, S. P. (1958). *Teaching the social studies: Theory and practice*. Boston: D. C. Heath, p. 4.

23. Shirley H. Engle, former president of the National Council of the Social Studies, was especially vocal in his opposition. See, for instance: Engle, S. H. (1965). Objectives of the social studies. In: Massialas, B. G. and Smith, F. R. (eds.). *New challenges in the social studies*. Belmont, CA: Wadsworth.

24. Bruner, J. S. (1960). *The process of education*. New York: Vintage Books.

25. Shaver, J. P. and Knight, R. S. (1986). Civics and government in citizenship education. In: Wronski, S. P. and Bragaw, D. H. (eds.). *Social studies and social science: A fifty-year perspective*. Washington, D.C.: National Council for the Social Studies, Bulletin 78, pp. 71–84.

26. Senesch, L. (1965). *Our working world*. Chicago: Science Research Associates.

27. For an in-depth discussion of the activities of the Sociological Resources for the Social Studies project, see: Haas, J. (1977). *The era of the new social studies*. Boulder, CO: ERIC Clearinghouse for Social Studies/Social Science Education.

28. Mitsakos, C. L. (ed.) (1971). *The family of man: A social studies program*. Newton, MA: Selective Educational Equipment.

29. Bruner, J. S. (1974). "Man: A course of study." Social Studies Curriculum Project. Cambridge, MA: Educational Services.

30. Mitchell, L. S. (1934). *Young geographers*. New York: John Day.
31. The materials from the Harvard Social Studies Project were reissued in 1988 by the Social Science Education Consortium under the earlier title, *Public issues series*. Revisions have been made by Giese, J. R. and Glade, M. E. under the direction of the original authors, Oliver, D. W. and Newmann, F. M.
32. Price, R. A., Hickman, W. and Smith, G. (1965). *Major concepts for the social studies*. Syracuse, NY: Syracuse University Press.
33. Engle, S. H. (1963). Thoughts in regard to revision. *Social Education 27* (April), 182–184, 196.
34. Engle, S. H. and Ochoa, A. S. (1988). *Education for democratic citizenship: Decision making in the social studies*. New York: Teachers College Press.
35. Taba, Hilda (1967). Implementing thinking as an objective in the social studies. In: Fair, J. and Shaftel, F. (eds.) *Effective thinking in the social studies*, 37th Yearbook. Washington, D.C.: National Council for the Social Studies, pp.25–50.
36. Barr, R., Barth, J. L., and Shermis, S. S. (1977). *The nature of the social studies*. Palm Springs, CA: ETC Publications.
37. Barth, J. L. and Shermis, S. S. (1970). Defining the social studies: An exploration of three traditions. *Social Education 34* 2:743–751.
38. Hanna, P. R. (1957). Generalizations and universal values: Their implications for the social studies program. *Social studies in the elementary school*, 56th Yearbook of the National Society for the Study of Education (Part II). Chicago: University of Chicago Press, pp. 27–47.
39. California Department of Education (1987). *History-social science framework*. Sacramento, CA: State Department of Education.
40. *Op. cit.*, Bruner, J. S. (1960).
41. Rothman, Robert (1989). Social-studies panel shuns call for radical changes. *Education Week* (Sept. 6), p. 9.
42. National Commission on Social Studies in the Schools (1989). *Charting a course: Social studies for the 21st century*. Washington D.C.: National Council for the Social Studies.
43. *Ibid.*, p. 11.
44. *Ibid.*
45. *Ibid.*, p. 12.
46. *Ibid.*, p. 13.
47. *Ibid.*, p. 10, 11, 16, 17.
48. Shaver, J. P. (1990). Defining (conceptualizing) social studies. *Louisiana Social Studies Journal* XV 1:20–24.
49. Lamy, S. L. (1987). "The definition of a discipline: The objects and methods of analysis in global education." Occasional paper. New York: Global Perspectives in Education, p. 1.
50. *Ibid.*
51. *Ibid.*, pp. 1–2.
52. Becker, J. M. (1979). The world and the school: A case for world-centered education. In: J. M. Becker (ed.). *School for a global age*. New York: McGraw-Hill, p. 41.
53. *Ibid.*
54. Evans, R. W. (1990). Reconceptualizing social studies for a new millennium. *Louisiana Social Studies Journal* XV 1:30–33.
55. A term coined by Marshall McLuhan in the 1960s.

# 15

# The Changing Language Arts and Foreign Language Curricula: Emerging Needs for Improved Communication Skills

## Introduction

The language arts in the elementary school and its secondary school counterpart, English, are considered an essential "core" study of today's curriculum. Skills in both expressive and receptive communication undergird teaching and learning in *all* fields of educational activity. The mastery of language skills is a prerequisite to overall academic success at every stage of development from childhood to adult years.

Despite widespread acknowledgment of the importance of studying English and the language arts, there are questions concerning what the true identity of the subject should be.[1] There is the tendency to juxtapose content and process; the greater emphasis is on process while content is neglected as though its selection were hardly an important concern. Speaking, listening, reading, and writing are the major communication processes. Some professionals, such as Moffett and Wagner, take the position that children can learn these processes well regardless of the particular content chosen.[2] This emphasis on process supports a selection of content based on the interests of students rather than on a prescribed set of literary and grammatical studies and is often considered an anti-intellectual concept of the language arts.

However, many in the field consider the content and its selection of the utmost importance. They think of the language arts as a vehicle for transmitting

America's literary, creative, and moral heritage to youngsters. Whether content would be pursued in depth or in the superficial mode of cultural literacy promoted in the 1980s by E. D. Hirsch,[3] it is perceived to have values of greater significance than the mere acquisition of communicative processes. The cultural and intellectual content of the curriculum becomes a crucial point of debate as does the relationship between the communication processes and the content.

An emphasis on content poses a new set of questions for curriculum decision making. For instance, in what way does the study of English, American, or world literature contribute to a better, possibly happier life? Are there some contents for the study of English more appropriate to the concerns of business and industry? Can we identify content that would support the instruction of communicative processes more effectively than others? What possible importance can knowledge of the history and development of the English language have for a community of diverse cultural backgrounds? What role should creative expression have in the content plan? Or should creative expression be considered a frill perhaps to be relegated to co-curricular activities?

The secondary curriculum is more preoccupied with the reading of major literary works and knowledge of their historical importance than is the elementary curriculum. Composition develops in two distinct directions, one involving literary analyses and library research reports and the other involving personal exploration and the meeting of practical needs such as the writing of business letters.

In considering the nature of the English language arts curriculum, the categories organizing language arts studies at both the elementary and secondary levels have hardly changed over the years. From the beginning of our national government to 1929, reading, writing, spelling, grammar, composition, and the study of literature comprised the major areas of study. Art, drama, and listening skills were added in the fifty odd years preceding the great depression.[4] Linguistics and semiotics are quite recent albeit sporadic additions.

There appears to be a widely accepted expectation that the language arts process skills are acquired in the elementary grades and may be taken for granted at the secondary level. Support for advancing students' reading skills diminishes greatly in the high schools. If it occurs at all, it is either included as a minor part of teaching literature or as a remedial course for those with serious deficiencies. Listening comprehension skills are ignored altogether, even when public speaking is offered as an elective study. Since there is widespread recognition that a good portion of American secondary students have not achieved acceptable levels of reading literacy, it is difficult to understand why such neglect has persisted into the 1990s.

Composition has been the exception to this tendency to ignore process at the secondary level. It takes on increased importance probably as a response to university and job-related requirements. Teaching of composition may evolve in three distinct directions. One, based on utilitarian considerations, emphasizes competence in writing to meet business and personal needs; another emphasizes expository writing involving such activities as literary criticism, library research reports, and essays of opinion; the third emphasizes creative writing and the development of the individual imagination.[5] In addition to improving expressive skills, objectives usually include developing logical thinking skills.

Handwriting, spelling, punctuation, and capitalization are treated with varying degrees of emphasis often depending on the teacher's own philosophy. Grammar receives considerable attention at the secondary level as a means of teaching correct usage. It is usually taught independently of composition but the carryover to writing is expected. In recent decades, grammatical studies have sometimes been taught from a linguistic/scientific perspective, that is, as a study of how language forms meaning and undergoes change. However, traditional sentence parsing still remains the mainstay of grammatical studies.

In addition to curriculum decisions regarding content and process, challenges confront curriculum developers related to such attributes as the learners' age, socioeconomic status, native language, ethnicity, and the nature and quality of home or family relationships. Specific problems may include such concerns as life in a single-parent home, neighborhood violence, relationships with siblings and parents, substance abuse in households, the homeless child, and past experiences of individual youngsters with literature and electronic gear and in other schools they have attended. In none of the other subjects of the school's curriculum are a child's background and experiences so directly related to the skills needing development. Topics for compositions are frequently connected to personal experience, while listening skills are, of course, linked to how people listen in the child's home environment. The appropriate curricular responses to this inevitable "personalism" are still evolving.

This chapter explores the past, present, and future nature of the K–12 English language arts curriculum. A historical overview is followed by descriptions of the kind of curricula typically found in the school. In addition, several curricula that have affected the thinking of the field, such as the Carnegie-Mellon program that was instrumental in the development of the "New English" movement, the experience curriculum, and the life adjustment curriculum are described and placed in their historical contexts. The debates concerning what ought to be the nature of the English language arts curriculum are viewed from the various philosophical perspectives as well as in relationship to diverse cognitive learning theories. New trends in the English language arts curriculum are also discussed, and their likely impact on future directions explored. As Marshall McLuhan[6] noted over a quarter of a century ago, the way we communicate and handle information has undergone profound changes—changes that are only slowly being reflected in today's curriculum. Scenarios exploring possible responses to these new realities are proposed in an effort to start us all thinking together about directions we hope the schools will take in the new millennium.

## Historical Overview

### The Public Elementary School and the Early Establishment of the Traditional Curriculum

In the early nineteenth century, there was growing concern about the general disarray of American schooling, especially at the elementary or common-school level.

Whether education was even available to youngsters largely depended on the resources and disparate interests of the various localities. Educational reformers, such as Horace Mann and Henry Barnard, advocated systematic, universal elementary education supported by the states as a way of transforming the nation into a more completely democratic and stable society. In 1852, Massachusetts passed a law making free, compulsory elementary education a reality. By 1918, every state in the union had compulsory attendance laws.

This was a period of significant educational upheaval as well as of limited public financing for education. Reading, spelling, and writing nevertheless remained fundamental to whatever efforts to educate the young were implemented, regardless of the funding sources. Ideas about what and how native language studies should be pursued were deeply embedded in the cultural mindset well before universal elementary education supported by public funds had become a reality. The amazing advances in science and mathematics and the greatly expanded addition of these subjects in the school's curriculum resulted in more significant curricular change in the early 1900s than was the case for language arts and English.

To be sure, there had been, in the period following the establishment of the Union, a great awareness of the differences between American and "English" English and an almost passionate desire to distinguish what was uniquely American from its European roots. Noah Webster's work, *The American Dictionary of the English Language*, completed in 1828, is especially representative of the effort to achieve a national identity by cataloging the unique characteristics of American English. In the 1780s, Webster published a series of textbooks for language instruction including *The Blue-Backed Speller*, the first of three parts comprising *A Grammatical Institute of the English Language*. The remaining two parts consisted of a reader and a grammar. It has been estimated that over 60 million copies were sold of the speller alone in the century following its publication.[7] The purpose of these works was to foster in elementary school children both the American language and culture. These widely circulated textbooks helped to set native language instruction in American schools.

At the secondary level, academies grew in importance during Webster's lifetime and began displacing the Latin grammar school. The curricula of the academies were quite disparate for their major purpose was to prepare youngsters for the requirements of their own lives—requirements that often had little to do with attending college or the study of the classics and that were prone to widely differing interpretations.[8] Although Latin and Greek remained among the more popular subjects for advanced studies, English grammar, composition, rhetoric, and declamation were also among the subjects typically offered by academies. The study of English literature was less frequently included but was still among the twenty subjects most often found at the academies.[9] The kinds of reading adopted varied widely since most of the youngsters were not expected to go to college. Among the sciences, physiology and physical geography were by far the most popular with zoology, botany, chemistry, and astronomy included at the tail end of the top twenty.[10]

By the twentieth century, the English language arts curriculum was firmly

fixed in our scholastic traditions. Reading, writing, spelling, grammar, and literature formed the underlying structure for the selection of content. The school subject, K–12, hardly participated in the major revisions of the curriculum that
occurred in the first decades of the century, although there was and continues to be
a good deal of debate about how reading should be taught and what literature is
most suitable for children. There were also several far-reaching proposals for basic
change in the underlying curriculum structure, but none had lasting impact.

First of all, there was the resistance of the Committee of Fifteen to the col-
lege-orientation and scientific emphasis of the reforms proposed by the Committee of Ten. Also, a group of English teachers working through the National
Education Association (NEA) resisted what they believed were the efforts of college
presidents to control what was read in the public schools through the issuance of
booklists.[11] This group founded the National Council of Teachers of English
(NCTE). By 1917, with the NEA report, *Reorganization of English in the Secondary Schools*, long lists of both modern and classic works were published. Teachers
could presumedly choose from among these without following any particular set of
norms. In actuality, rather than choosing, most secondary teachers have clung to
textbook anthologies dominated by the British literary heritage. This was true even
after the great wave of immigration had significantly changed the ethnic composition of America's population.

At the elementary level, the legendary McGuffey *Eclectic Readers*, a textbook of readings for young children, sold some 120 million copies between 1836
and 1920, leaving an indelible mark on American primary education for generations. The *Readers* were revised periodically but the fundamental nature of their
content was never changed. It was based on simple moral lessons, excerpts from
American and English literature, fables and poetry. Obviously, it, too, ignored the
significant changes that had taken place in the ethnic heritage of Americans.

From the 1920s to the early 1970s, the teaching of reading was dominated by
the "look-and-say" method, which emphasized the recognition and verbalized
identification of whole words. A smattering of phonics was used in the process. In
the next decade, there was a decided increase in the use of phonics for reading
instruction. However, it is unclear how much real methodological change actually
occurred. There is no research concerning this point and judgment must be made
on the basis of the greatly increased quantity of phonics instruction included in
basal readers.

Unlike Latin and Greek, English language arts were widely perceived as necessary whether one went to college or directly into the work force. As the sciences
grew in curricular importance, Latin and Greek diminished, nearly disappearing
altogether in the secondary schools by the 1980s. Language arts (elementary) and
English (secondary), in slightly varying forms, remained a significant component
of the curriculum throughout. If one wonders why a subject area with so much
inherent flexibility has changed so little in the twentieth century, a partial explanation may be found in the cultural encapsulation of native language arts studies
that existed long before the major curricular revisions at the beginning of the
twentieth century. Reading had to be taught, literature had to be read for both

practice and cultural enlightenment, and writing, supported by the study of grammar, needed constant effort. These are expectations that have remained unchanged from the founding of the common school to our own times.

## The Experience Curriculum

There have been efforts to change the basic curriculum design of the English curriculum, but these efforts have not succeeded in modifying the curriculum of the schools even when the professional literature was quite taken with a particular curricular model. For example, a curriculum based on life experiences was proposed in a highly influential work written by Hatfield and issued by the National Council of Teachers of English in 1935.[12] The design of the curriculum was to be based on an analysis of people's everyday communication needs. The selection of literature was to reflect the emotional and intellectual range of students. A list of several hundred works, including many written by American authors, was developed to help teachers select more relevant reading materials. Business activities such as letter writing and conducting interviews; listening activities, especially those related to classroom instruction; and radio broadcasts and even activities related to enjoying films were also to be used to establish the nature and scope of the content. Classroom instruction was to reflect the reality of life "without deception or pretense."[13]

Occasionally, one finds activities in the schools today that reflect the experience curriculum, especially at the elementary and junior high level or in general studies for non–college-bound and often academically weak high school students. The increased proportion of American literature among the reading selections is probably the most permanent contribution of the life experience movement. Typically, curricular variations are found more frequently in the earlier grades and disappear almost altogether at the secondary level.[14]

## The Life Adjustment Curriculum

The life adjustment curriculum, successor to the experience-based model, emphasized meeting the physical, emotional, and mental needs of students. The developmental stages of children, as understood in the 1940s and 1950s, were to determine the kinds of activities to be pursued. This movement, too, has had little real effect on what actually occurs in the schools, especially in the high schools. As Margaret Early of Syracuse University notes, the "recommendations of scholars and national committees influence classroom practice only indirectly and with considerable dilution. . . ."[15] In the case of the English language arts, the traditional academic curriculum has remained dominant. Early continues:

> *Publishers only "dictate the curriculum" when they give textbook committees what they want. . . . If Dick and Jane reappear decade after decade*

*in only slightly new guises, the publishers are responding to teachers'*
*invitations.* [16]

Louise Rosenblatt recommended as far back as 1938 that students' responses
to reading literature were more important considerations for English instruction
than the content of the literature selected. [17] This transactional position must
surely have been influenced by the life adjustment movement. However, long after
that movement had been forgotten, Rosenblatt's classic work, *Literature as Explo-*
*ration*, [18] first published in 1938, advocated a student-centered, process-oriented
program based on the exchange of ideas rather than the coverage of a selection of
literary works. Her pioneering work in the field of subjective criticism was especially important to the development of both pedagogy and criticism in the 1970s
and 1980s.

### The Advent of the Paperback–A Renaissance in the Reading of Literature

In the 1950s, the paperback came into its own and it became possible to purchase
literature of all kinds at a minimum cost. For the first time, schools could afford to
purchase currently popular works such as *Catcher in the Rye* and *A Coney Island of*
*the Mind* and school libraries became increasingly varied in their holdings. Twentieth century American literature became a part of the curriculum. Howard Fast,
Richard Wright, Pearl Buck, John Dos Passos, Theodore Dreiser, and F. Scott
Fitzgerald were among the many American authors to be added. With them came
a rise in censorship from the political left, the political right, and commercial publishers fearing to offend one or another interest group and thereby lose sales. [19]

The amount of reading Americans engage in appears to have increased
steadily. Between 1967 and 1984, the number of books produced in the United
States rose by 160 percent. Books continue to be a growth industry despite the rise
of television and the often-noted decline in verbal ability as measured by the average score of the Scholastic Aptitude Test (SAT). [20] The 1990–91 SAT verbal scores
continued a five-year decline, which may indicate the reverse of the trend toward
more reading. It may also indicate that scores are being lowered by proportionally
more people reading than used to be the case but at a lower level of competence so
that scores of the reading population as a whole are being skewed toward the lower
performance level.

### Sputnik and Beyond

The success of Russia's space program with the flight of Sputnik is often credited
with a return in the late 1950s to an academic emphasis for all school subjects.
However, many publications had been issued —from Bestor's *Educational Waste-*
*lands* [21] to Flesch's *Why Johnny Can't Read* [22] —demanding a more solidly academic

curriculum years earlier. Neither the experience curriculum nor the life adjustment curriculum had ever really taken hold in the nation's schools. Complaints about falling academic standards in the 1950s probably should have been directed at the increasing proportion of the population attending high school and college and at the fundamental confusion about the nature of the goals set for the schools.

The real significance of America's reaction to Sputnik lay in the greatly increased federal government involvement in the nation's curriculum. This involvement has persisted with the publication of *A Nation at Risk* in 1983, with the establishment of the National Education Goals Panel by the Bush administration in 1990, and with the pursuit of a nationally based evaluation program by the NAEP in the early 1990s.

Initially, the government-funded programs of the 1960s were directed toward updating and improving academic content in the sciences and mathematics. By 1964, however, federal funds were directed to the social sciences and English language arts as well. The shock of Sputnik was already receding in the national consciousness, and the approach to language arts supported by university experts was increasingly holistic. That is, the separation of the curriculum into literature, composition, grammar, and speech was beginning to be seen as counterproductive since such divisions were not part of people's real life experiences. The "New English" movement of the mid and late 1960s, supported largely by federal funding, was very much in this vein.

The Project English Curriculum Study Center at Carnegie-Mellon University developed one of the best known secondary programs of the movement. Among its more notable features was the inclusion of literature from other countries in the first year, followed by American literature in the second year, and British literature in the last year.[23] In the first year, love, the search for wisdom, and other universal concerns were explored. In the second year, the cultural impact of America and the American character on universal concerns was studied, followed in the third year by a focus on such literary art forms as satire, tragedy, and drama of social criticism.

Under the influence of the "discovery" movement in the teaching of the sciences, the Carnegie-Mellon program also stressed an inductive approach to reading literature. Students were first to read a literary work and then were encouraged, under the guidance of the teacher, to make discoveries about the work in question. Editorial explanations typically found in high school anthologies were omitted whenever possible to avoid distracting the student from the literary experience itself. Student compositions were to be directly related to the literature read. The literal grasp of the literature was to be reflected in the students' ability to relate and reorganize ideas into generalizations of their own.

While the 1950s and early 1960s saw considerable emphasis on structural lingistics, a more humanistic approach to English language arts, as represented by the Carnegie-Mellon program as well as Rosenblatt's response-centered work, dominated curricular thinking until the back-to-basics movement took hold in the mid 1970s. Little had really changed in what was done in most English language arts classrooms regardless of what the experts were proposing. The 1970s represented a kind of backward-looking shift from the newer thinking about possible curricular directions to what has essentially become several decades of political talk about "returning" to academic tradition (which, of course, we had never left).

## Current Trends and Issues

### New Knowledge for the School Subject

The curriculum design for English and language studies has been rather fixed in a traditional academic vein, but this should not be taken to mean that the English language or knowledge about English has not developed significantly. It is important to understand that the existing curriculum can accommodate new knowledge and perspectives about language arts without undergoing any significant design modification. Reading, composition, and the study of grammar and literature may change in specific content selections while they remain the unchanging categories of study and form the basic design of the curriculum.

We could, for example, make video literacy a part of the curricular structure and at least as important as reading literacy. This would fundamentally change the nature of what we study in the language arts curriculum. At present, if we study video literacy at all, we make it a minor addition to literary studies, composition or, possibly, public speaking. As a major component of the curriculum, we might, say, pursue the development of a set of skills that would help us to become expert in ciphering the full range of meaning conveyed by a video experience. We might dedicate a number of hours to viewing different video genre and identifying some great video works of the past.

In sum, a traditional and unchanging curricular design may lead to serious omissions in what we study. However, this does not have to mean that new knowledge or new perspectives will necessarily be ignored.

### Vocabulary: An Ever Changing Affair

It has been estimated that the English vocabulary has doubled in size since the 1933 edition of the *Oxford English Dictionary*[24] was published. Scientific and technical terms comprise a significant portion of this increase along with borrowings from many foreign languages and slang. Presently, the English vocabulary continues to grow through such processes as onomatopoeia, addition of prefixes and suffixes (e.g., "pro-," "-ness"), combination of words or word parts, and so forth. Spelling lists and reading materials have accommodated easily to these changes without any fundamental structural change in the curriculum.

However, changes to content, even within the existing curricular framework, have not been as extensive as could be expected. There are several reasons for this. In the early grades, children bring to school a core of vocabulary functional in the context of their daily lives. The schools have traditionally based vocabulary development on this core. It is only in the fourth or fifth grade that students begin to study the structure, origins, and changes of words. The generation of new words, the analysis of connotations, and the effects of context on word meaning begin to be studied in the latter years of the elementary experience. Once students start changing classroom teachers, usually in the seventh grade, moving from subject to subject several times during the day, vocabulary instruction tends to diminish and take a back seat to the content areas. Even in English classes, vocabulary is studied in terms of the literature assigned for reading, most of which dates back at least fifty years before the students were born. Thus, the study of vocabulary as a set of semantic and morphological concepts is hardly pursued in the typical public school secondary curriculum, and almost no attention is given to the rise of new vocabulary.

## Spelling and Vocabulary Development

One of the explanations for some of the novel characteristics of spelling and the vocabulary used in American English can be traced to the many linguistic sources from which our language has evolved. Among the more common "loan word" sources are Greek, Latin, Spanish, French, and German. Obviously, the various sources of our language complicate vocabulary development and spelling. Consequently, they have an important bearing on the curriculum planning and instructional methods that are most suitable in a given classroom through the secondary level.[25]

Certain problems in developing spelling are illustrated by such examples as "infernal," "colonel," and "journal" which are rhyming words but with spellings that vary greatly. The same may be said of the following terms, which also have both different meanings and divergent spellings: *rough* and *bluff*; *blue*, *blew*, and *through*; *snow*, *foe*, and *although*; *sight*, *cite*, and *site*; or *niece*, *lease*, and *peace*. The list of fifty "demons" that follows is representative of widely used words that also are very likely to be spelled incorrectly — even by persons at the graduate level! We list them partly to intrigue readers with examples of reasonably familiar terms that are often misspelled and partly to make the point that such well-known terms as *gauge*, *judgment*, *moccasin*, and *occurred* often are among those incorrectly written, sometimes even by teachers.

### Fifty Words Often Misspelled in Our Language[26]

| | | |
|---|---|---|
| Accommodate | Discernible | Inoculation |
| Asinine | Diphtheria | Judgment |
| Asylum | Dyeing | Likable |
| Battalion | Embarrass | Liquefy |
| Braggadocio | Euphoria | Lose |
| Changeable | Gauge | Mayonnaise |
| Clientele | Harass | Millennium |
| Colossal | Hemorrhage | Mischievous |
| Consensus | Imposter | Moccasin |
| Desiccate | Impresario | Naphtha |
| Dietitian | Indispensable | Oases |

| | | |
|---|---|---|
| Occurred | Rarefy | Tenement |
| Paid | Resuscitate | Titillate |
| Paraphernalia | Rococo | Uncontrollable |
| Pavilion | Saccharine | Vermilion |
| Perennial | Sacrilegious | Weird |
| Permissible | Supersede | |

Typically, children study short lists of words and their spelling so that they may pass the "test." However, what many educators refer to as a "functional approach" has gained favor over the past couple of decades in both spelling and vocabulary instruction. New words and their spelling are presented *for a reason*, such as preparing a research paper or reading about a current event or a new invention. Rather than rote practice, students are required to use the words several times in various contexts.

## Understanding Abbreviations

Well before they complete elementary school, students begin to encounter abbreviations. This occurs most when references are encountered in books or articles read in connection with the preparation of library-based reports. A number of the items below such as "Chapter II," "Fig. 7," or "Sec. 4" typically appear in secondary school textbooks.

### Glossary of Abbreviations

| | |
|---|---|
| abr. | abridged |
| annot. | annotations, annotated |
| anon. | anonymous |
| art. iii | arts. (articles) |
| b. | born |
| c. | copyright |
| Cf. | confer, "compare" |
| Cf. ante | "compare above" |
| Cf. post | "compare below" |
| chap. II | chaps. (chapters) |
| ca./circa | at, in, or approximately |
| col. 6 | cols. (columns) |
| comp. | complied, compiler |
| div. III | divs. (divisions) |
| ed., edit. | edited, edition, editor |
| e.g. | exempli gratia, "for example" |
| et al. | et alii, "and others" |
| et passim | "and here and there" |
| Fig. 7 | Figs. (figures) |
| Ibid. | for ibidem, "in the same place" |
| i.e. | id est, "that is" |

| | |
|---|---|
| Infra | below |
| illus. | illustration, illustrator |
| introd. | introduction |
| loc. cit. | loc citato, "in the place cited" |
| Ms., ms. | manuscript |
| n.d. | no date |
| n.n. | no name |
| no., nos. | number(s) |
| n.p. | no place |
| op. cit. | opere citato, "in the work cited" |
| o.p. | out of print |
| orig. | original |
| p., pp. | page(s) |
| pp. 5–7 | pages 5 to 7 inclusive |
| pp. 4f., or | |
|    pp. 4 et seq. | page 4 and the following page |
| pp. 5ff., or | |
|    pp. 5 et seq. | page 5 and the following pages |
| pref. | preface |
| pseud. | pseudonym |
| Pt. | Pts., parts |
| rev. | revised |
| Sec. 4 | section(s) |
| ser. | series |
| Supra | above |
| t.p. | title page |
| [sic] | thus (also "error in quotation") |
| Vol. I | Vols., volume(s) |
| [viz.] | namely |

## Interpreting Acronyms

Recently, there has been a substantial increase in the use of acronyms, words formed from the first letters, or from several letters, of a series of words. *Radar*, for example, stems from *ra*dio, *d*-etecting, and *ra*nging[27] and WAC is derived from *W*omen's *A*rmy *C*orps.

While many acronyms such as I.Q., A.M., and P.M. are usually learned at an early age, their nature and derivation need to be explained to youngsters. Some of those most widely used might well be objects of instruction. NATO, IBM, YMCA, and P.O. [box] are frequently encountered and can be confusing as in the case of NEA, which represents both the National Education Association and the National Endowment for the Arts. A large number, such as WFUNA (World Federation of United Nations Associations) may be conundrums to adults as well as youngsters.

### Oral Comprehension and Critical Listening

The increasing diversity of the population in the United States underscores the need to emphasize comprehension of oral language since at least 15 percent of our young speak a language other than English as their first language. Moreover, younger children often find some aspects of English to be quite confusing, with resultant misinterpretation of meaning as the following anecdote illustrates:

> *The teacher of a group of six-year-olds was reading aloud a number of Mother Goose nursery rhymes such as "Hickety-Pickety, My Black Hen," "Little Miss Muffett," and "Diddle-Diddle-Dumpling, My Son John." At the end of the activity, she passed out sheets of drawing paper and asked the group to draw pictures illustrating with crayons the images that the verses brought to mind. One little boy drew a recognizable picture of "My Son John" who went to bed with his stockings on. The quilt spread over the bed in the drawing even had a rather intricate embroidery of tiny creatures.*
>
> *"Well," the teacher exclaimed "that's a nice pattern you've drawn on the bed covers!"*
>
> *The boy looked surprised. "That's not a pattern," he said. "Those are the mice!"*
>
> *"Mice?" the teacher repeated in surprise.*
>
> *"Sure. Those are mice on the bed like in 'Diddle-Diddle-Dumplin', Mice on John,' " he responded.*

Obviously, learners both young and old do not always hear or comprehend the messages or verbal images that are communicated. An understanding of synonyms and the importance of garnering information from the context are necessary components of language arts instruction. Knowledge of the use of similar sounding words such as "wood" and "would" also is essential.

Closely related to *comprehension* in our schools is the skill of *listening with understanding*, an art sometimes referred to as "auding."[28] Critical listening, as distinct from merely hearing, involves translating the verbal symbols expressed by others so that they convey the meanings a speaker intends them to convey. The following example illustrates the need to give heed to how children endow with meaning what they hear.

A middle grade teacher was reviewing the familiar American "Pledge of Allegiance," which was to be recited in unison by the pupils before a forthcoming high school basketball game. He decided to review the meaning of some of the terms and phrases involved and was surprised at the following lack of skill in understanding the familiar terminology of the pledge.

When asked about "I pledge allegiance to the flag . . ." one youngster said that "allegiance" referred to "an organization that gets together." Another boy when asked about "and to the Republic for which it stands" said that "republic" meant that the flag belonged to the public. Finally, a girl in the group thought that "one nation under God indivisible. . ." referred to the fact that God was not visible.

Formal instruction in oral English usage includes such items as the subtleties of stress and pitch as well as the pauses and gestures used in communicating ideas. Often these elements can markedly alter meaning and sometimes even reverse it. Story-telling and oral reports by teachers or pupils and the use of "show-and-tell" time where objects are displayed or explained, or when youngsters tell of interesting out-of-school experiences, are important (albeit informal) elements during the elementary classroom day. They are far less frequently encountered in the secondary school but that may very well be to the detriment of students' acquisition of advanced expressive skills.

### Grammar and Its Continuing Development

The school study of grammar has generally been pursued to prescribe proper English usage. The parts of speech are defined and norms about how to put the parts together are set forth. Prescriptive studies of grammar are considered "practical" because they are thought to help youngsters speak and write correctly. Research indicates that this widely held belief is incorrect and that prescriptive grammatical studies may even be harmful to the improvement of writing.[29]

However, the public remains convinced of the productivity and practicality of prescriptive grammar in the curriculum. The widespread expectation persists that its study will lead to the use of correct form and style. Errors in language usage are widespread and often attract the disapproving attention of leading public figures. James Kilpatrick, a professional writer, found in 1990, for instance, that the verbs *lay* and *lie* were incorrectly used in such newspapers as the *Portland Oregonian*, *The Miami Herald*, *Morning News* (Savannah, GA), and *The New York Times*. A typical error from the *Times*: "Many tough tasks lay ahead."

Grammatical studies undertaken to produce knowledge about language rather than to prescribe its proper usage are not typically pursued in the school's curriculum. Historical studies concerning how a language has changed over the years, comparative studies that explore the relationships among languages, and sociolinguistic studies that examine the functions of language in social contexts are almost completely ignored—quite possibly because they are not perceived to be useful for youngsters who are learning to speak and write correctly.

Only one form of nonprescriptive grammatical studies has had any impact on the school instruction of grammar. The descriptive/transformational grammarians approach the study of language from a theoretical perspective. The early descriptive linguists developed objective and rigorous methods for describing the structures of speech as these occur among a community of speakers. The transformational-generative grammarians, led by Noam Chomsky,[30] sought a theory of language that would describe how language generates meaning and how human beings become competent in communicating meaning regardless of the language spoken and stay competent despite continuing growth and change. In the early 1960s, an effort was undertaken to bring this approach to grammar into the school's curriculum. Roberts 1–12 grammar textbooks turned structural linguistics into a new way of teaching grammar.[31] For a short while, the program was widely adopted, but its departure from traditional grammatical analyses and declining skills in writing and composition combined to create a good many protest among teachers and the public at large, blocking its continued usage. These textbooks all but disappeared from the classroom in the 1970s.

### Linguistics

Technically speaking, linguistics is a discipline that is not a part of the language arts per se but one that both permeates and transcends our activities in writing, listening, speaking, and reading. The Roberts grammar textbooks tried to introduce into the schools some of the thinking of linguistics. It was poorly understood then and continues to be misunderstood in terms of its potential for increasing youngsters' grasp of language. As the objective study of language progresses, it is more than likely that linguistics will have a significant impact on the language arts curriculum. The well-informed curriculum planner and classroom instructor needs to be knowledgeable about the field.[32]

First, linguistics is a social science that links language and culture. Second, it is a behavioral science that is concerned with behavioral changes in humans that are wrought through the use of language. Finally, linguistics is a discipline with a scholarly focus on various grammar systems, dialects, and how various ethnic groups use their native tongue.

Due to its varied dimensions, it is difficult to define linguistics precisely. In broad terms it can be described as the scientific study of human speech including its evolutionary changes, structure, and general nature. The broad study of language is known as *macrolinguistics*, a field with three major components: *prelinguistics* (biophysical dimensions of speaking and hearing), *microlinguistics* (concerned with speech sounds, grammar, and semantics), and *metalinguistics* (which probes and explores the relationships between language and the subsequent behavior of humans).

While the role of linguistics in the English language arts curriculum may be deemed superfluous by some curriculum planners and an intrusion on time needed for conventional and more basic language arts instruction, its pursuit gives us new insights into the nature of language and the development of meaning. As we move into an age of multiplying systems of communication, learning how to approach the objective study of language becomes increasingly important. Certainly, the linguistic analysis of how we go about reading, writing, and speaking promises new insights and new approaches to instruction still largely unexplored. It appears likely that the results of linguistic studies will make a significant difference in our understanding of the more traditional components of the language arts curriculum.

### Reading: A Crucial Problem Area

The teacher's skill in helping children to read well and to *like* to read has grown steadily in importance over the years. An increasingly unqualified work force has made improving reading skills a crucial problem area. According to former Education Secretary Lauro Cavazos, students are "dreadfully inadequate in two basic tools of learning — reading and writing."[33] He released two reports with findings including these:

- Since 1980, the percentage of 9-year-olds with basic reading skills — the ability to understand specific or sequentially related information — has declined from 68 to 63 percent. Seven percent lack rudimentary skills.

- Forty-two percent of all 13-year-olds lack the skills needed to read at the next highest level, which calls for the ability to interrelate ideas and make generalizations.

- Nearly 6 out of 10 — 58 percent — of 17-year-olds cannot read at the adept level, which is defined as the ability to find, understand, summarize, and explain relatively complicated information.

- Less than 5 percent of the nation's 17-year-olds are reading at the advanced level.

Developments in the American work force that have been widely recognized have particular significance for curriculum planners in all academic areas, but especially in the language arts. Consider the following:

> *As much as a quarter of the American labor force — anywhere from 20 million to 27 million adults — lacks the basic reading, writing and math skills necessary to perform in today's increasingly complex job market. One out of every 4 teenagers drops out of high school, and of those who graduate, 1 out of every 4 has the equivalent of an eighth grade education. Already the skills deficit has cost businesses and taxpayers $20 billion in lost wages, profits and productivity. For the first time in American history employers face a proficiency gap in the work force so great that it threatens the well-being of hundreds of U.S. companies.*[34]

The extent of the problem is further emphasized by the fact that since the late 1980s more and more American corporations have been obliged to provide remedial instruction for employees. The problem is not only that too many Americans are inadequately educated, but also that jobs in our technologically inundated society are placing more complex burdens on the work force. Various research studies document the need for improved literacy levels in the United States. Among them is the Hudson Institute's 1987 document, *Workforce 2000*, which concluded that the United States "will become, sometime after the turn of the century, a Third World country" because of the shift from low- to high-skill jobs.[35] The alarming perspect of America becoming an intellectual ghetto can presumably be avoided by restructuring education.

### "New" Perspective — The Whole Language Approach

In the traditional reading curriculum, children have first been taught to read by moving them carefully through succeeding stages of readiness from learning the names of letters of the alphabet to instruction in phonics and exercises for accomplishing hand–eye coordination tasks. The acquisition of prereading skills has then led to brief encounters with readings of little consequence. Teaching youngsters to write has usually been delayed until reading is well under way.[36]

There is considerable evidence indicating that children who study phonics — that is, the relationship of spoken sounds to printed letters — have an initial advantage in learning to read.[37] A 1988 report from the Commission on Reading recommends teaching phonics through the end of the second grade.[38] This same report, however, also recommends providing children numerous opportunities for reading that would reinforce not only their knowledge of phonics but their enjoyment of reading as well.

There is growing criticism among experts of the position that youngsters' early reading experiences should be supplemental to the teaching of phonics and other readiness skills, rather than being enjoyable literary experiences. Basal readers and their emphasis on phonics have been widely blamed for presenting children with piecemeal, uninteresting materials of low literary quality. The "whole language" approach to reading instruction would immerse youngsters in the reading of literary works from the earliest grades and would diminish the role of phonics.

Since the 1970s, Tierney suggests, reading comprehension has undergone a major redefinition.[39] Instead of reading speed and the ability to rephrase the content of a passage being used as measures of comprehension, a much broader view of reading has taken hold. The subjectivity of meaning-making and the shared schemata of the community of readers have been recognized as essential to the process of comprehension. To achieve understanding, readers need to use their own background in interpreting the meaning of text. Typically, they engage with the meaning of the text by visualizing people in their experience, by asking themselves questions about how they would feel, or by assessing the plausibility of events. In Tierney's words, "a mechanical view of reading has given way to a view of reading as a holistic and creative enterprise."[40] In a sense, it is a return to the kind of holistic studies recommended in the "New English" program proposed under the aegis of Carnegie-Mellon University.

The whole language approach has been gaining favor since the mid 1980s. It emphasizes the simultaneous teaching of reading and writing in a total literacy context based on activities meaningful to the young child. Although specific skills and concepts are taught, these are not arranged in a set order or presented separately. Rather, children are immersed in a print environment, and different learning experiences are orchestrated by the teacher to help them understand the overall patterns of their language.[41]

Carol J. Fisher has contributed an important idea to achieving an integrated reading–writing program—the readers' theater.[42] She suggests that scripts, written by students and based on well-liked literature, can provide educational experiences and involve critical examination of literature. As the story or poem is converted into a script, students have both practice and fun in purposeful oral reading. In readers' theater, a small group of readers, scripts in hand, portray the characters and re-create the events in the story they are sharing. Most of the real learning comes as students work together to choose the best story, select the parts to use or convert into dialogue, and write the necessary narration.

The IBM Corporation has produced computer software entitled "Writing to Read" that integrates speaking, writing, listening, and reading skills.[43] During the initial creative process, little attention is paid to spelling thereby freeing children to compose creatively. Correct spelling and grammatical usage are approached during the revision process, which is based on oral editing and written modifications.

A quite unusual, K–2 program produced by Scott Foresman & Company to integrate reading and writing skills while relating students' real life experiences to their language arts activities is known as "Success in Reading and Writing."[44] Teachers are given a skeletal outline to follow, but no workbooks, ditto masters, or basal readers. Children are to use magazines, newspapers, and a well-stocked library. The program was originated at Duke University based on the principle that "children should be taught to read and write using the materials they will rely on later in life."[45] The curriculum design does not include a predetermined sequence for the learning of skills; rather, children learn new skills, concepts of language usage, and vocabulary as these may arise while engaged in reading.

### Creative Writing

The assignment of work in creative writing tends to be difficult for students of all ages. At least part of the difficulty may be created by asking learners to express themselves before they have the psychological maturity or a range of experiences that nurture the creative *thinking*, which is a prerequisite for *writing* creatively. The fact that children mature at different rates, plus the wide-ranging differences in their home and family backgrounds, requires curricular flexibility often not present in the curriculum.

The school's curriculum probably should not stress creative written expression too early at the elementary level. Rather, there should first be time allocated for developing readiness and a child's sense of purpose. Creative *oral* experiences serve the subsequent development of skill in *writing*. Reading suitable stories to children also is a means of developing youngsters' ideas that may manifest themselves in creative written form in both the language arts and other academic fields in which term papers and reports are assigned at upper grade levels.

All things considered, creative writing is probably the most fragile and delicate component in teaching communication skills at all levels. It should be broadly construed to include compositions, anecdotes, the dramatization of creative play-lets conceived by the students, poems, stories, and presentations made for parents' meetings or analogous adult gatherings in the classroom or school auditorium.

### Literature and the "New" Reading Lists

If a strict process approach to language arts instruction is taken, what is read or written about represents no more than a tool for learning skills. Within this context, however, there can be a significant divergence in the nature of the content pursued. For example, reading may be perceived as a series of exercises for skills development, as already has been noted. A study of basal reader textbooks, conducted by Woodward in 1986,[46] found that in the 1950s the teacher's guides contained extensive supplemental reading materials. By the early 1970s, few references to student interests or independent reading were made and topics were presented in magazine-like formats. In Woodward's words: "Reading had become a matter of the mastery of hundreds of skills and sub-skills and the completion of worksheets, workbooks, [and] remedial exercises."[47]

Alternatively, teaching reading as a set of processes, the content for which is open to whatever interests the students or teachers, may be perceived as a significant opportunity to help students explore their own personal and social meaning. In this context, the selection of literature for reading might be made by teachers or the students themselves. This approach overcomes the criticism of many that the emphasis on process skills distances reading from real world experience.

It is important to keep in mind, however, that if literature is viewed as a major vehicle for passing on the cultural heritage or a set of ethical standards, then the criteria for its selection become a critical area of discussion and far more likely to be a "central office" decision. The view held of children and their roles in society will profoundly affect the selection of readings.[48] The excessively didactic materials selected for children at the turn of the twentieth century reflected a perception of the appropriate relationship between adults and children that was formal and rule-based. Current lists, such as the one issued recently by the Children's Literature Association, lead one to believe that a return to great literary works of the past is in the offing. The intragenerational disjunctures that most of our children will confront in the new millennium suggests, however, that not only does the reading of new works need to be included in the curriculum but the development of skills for their critical evaluation as well. The reflection involved may serve children very well in the future.

Questions about what ought to comprise literary studies have been especially important since the post World War II period. Should "literature" include the reading of pulp magazines, comic books, and the like? Should British literature continue to dominate what high school students read? Should translations of great classics from all nations of the world be included? Should readings be organized around the development of specific reading skills?

For most of American education's history, the selection of high school literature has meant primarily British literature—typically a standard set of selections such as *Julius Caesar*, *Great Expectations*, and *Silas Marner*. However, in the 1960s, as a more humanistic approach to language arts instruction came to dominate professional discourse, bringing popular literature into the curriculum gained in acceptance. Relevance to the times and to the needs and interests of individual students was given far greater importance than had hitherto been the case. Critics of the movement felt the curriculum had been rendered trivial and incapable of cultivating a lasting interest in literature and the reflection it leads to. However, as Charles Suhor points out, even though the classics dominated the curriculum for generations preceding the "relevancy" craze of the 1960s, Americans had not "typically become avid adult readers of the classics or anything else."[49]

Certainly, for generations what was read in the schools could be considered an unchanging "canon" of literary works. In recent times, however, there is growing evidence that the notion of a set of standard readings comprising the literary component of the curriculum is no longer the case.[50] According to Sandra Stosky, a research associate at the Harvard Graduate School of Education, it is probable that a majority of American students do not read even a small body of literature in common.[51]

The addition of American writers to the standard list of readings starting in the middle of the twentieth century and the increased emphasis on the relevancy of readings to students' daily lives in the 1960s may have led to what many perceive to be a serious, possibly dangerous decline in the knowledge of our literary heritage. Furthermore, television and videocassettes have begun to transmit so much material based on both literary classics for young people and newly written works that educators are beginning to question whether the microelectronic age is enriching or diluting — or possibly even devastating — the field of conventional "between the covers" story books.[52] Reading as a way of sharing and reflecting on one's heritage appears to be losing ground in favor of high stimuli, quickly communicated messages of the electronic media.

It should be noted, however, that a 1989 study by Arthur Applebee of the Center for the Learning and Teaching of Literature found that Shakespeare continues to dominate the nation's reading lists.[53] Films based on Shakespeare's plays have given far greater visibility to these works than had been possible in earlier times. Certainly, the movement toward whole language instruction that gained momentum in the 1980s is related in part to the view that a shared core of literary studies is essential for all Americans.

One of the important but sometimes overlooked benefits of introducing children and youth to classic tales with which many of their parents and most of their grandparents were familiar is that of bridging the "literary generation gap." The minds of adults are full of literary materials to which they make allusions in their speech and that appear in the press. These include references to such widely known tales and fables as:

"The Boy Who Called 'Wolf' "
"The Lion and the Mouse"
"The Ugly Duckling"
"Aladdin and the Magic Lamp"

"Robin Hood"
"William Tell, The Archer"
"Tom Sawyer" tales

—and many many others, including adult-level literature encountered by second-ary pupils.[54] Literature in the curriculum, if properly selected, can become a door-way to what E. D. Hirsch has called "cultural literacy."[55]

### Making Choices about What to Read

If the teacher is involved in determining the selection of reading materials, the following suggestions could be helpful in making choices:

1. Teachers need to work closely with the school librarian. She or he is usually delighted to be helpful, knows what is available and popular, and is a mainstay in reminding teachers of classics that bridge the literary generation gap. Restricting the selection of literature to *vintage* preapproved lists of books needs to be avoided because so many of these works are distant from the realities experienced by children. Student choice as well as *informal* suggestions from teachers are increasingly important at the secondary level.

2. The differences in the socioeconomic and ethnic backgrounds of students need to be taken into account. As a general rule, during the primary years animal stories, fairy tales, and stories in which children are the main characters are favored. Beginning with 9- and 10-year-olds adventure stories and amusing yarns become popular. The preferences of *individual* elementary and secondary pupils do not conform to a fixed pattern. Interest in poetry is especially varied as students move into higher grade levels.

3. Oral reading and story-telling need to occur often, and a good portion of the reading materials selected should be suited to these activities. Well-told tales are an art form enjoyed by everyone, helping to sustain interest. Story-telling and brief oral book reports by students of all ages should be encouraged. These develop students' language power, increase their imagination, and facilitate their interpersonal relationships from primary through high school levels.

### The Philosophical Spectrum

As the discussion in this chapter has proceeded from one to another approach in the teaching of the English language arts, it must surely have occurred to the reader that beneath it all is an underlying philosophical debate not only about the nature of important knowledge but also about how learning best occurs. Those who would preserve a "canon" of literature—a set of great works that all students would read and share—are likely to be educational perennialists. Lectures inter-spersed with analytical discussion probing even more deeply into the meaning of the works under study would characterize instruction.

The classification, however, may be too glibly assigned. Many who are not perennialists would consider having all citizens share a set of literary experiences, images, and values "essential" for the continued strength of our pluralistic nation. There is, in their view, a core of knowledge and understanding that all Americans should have in common. The language arts is—must be—at the center of that core.

A good number of essentialists might also conceive of the language arts as primarily a set of processes that are best learned in relationship to the needs of business, industry, and technology. Reading technologically complex explanations, being capable of interpreting studies in several disciplines, and even conducting routine business affairs may be viewed by this group as being "essential" to the continued strength of our economy and nation.

Progressivists could probably accept this view of the English language art curriculum because of its potential linkages to real life experiences and to the interest that many youngsters might hold in business, industry, and technology. However, the progressivist's position that learning must start with the interests and needs of the child would most certainly support a broader spectrum of content for the process-oriented approach to the language arts. In all likelihood, teachers and students together would decide what is to be read or the topics to be written about. The study of usage, vocabulary, and spelling would probably occur as the need were encountered.

Reconstructionists would certainly go along with the process orientation of the progressives but would no doubt want to add a critical-evaluative strand that would have students assess and interpret the social, moral, and economic values contained in a literary work. They would probably look for readings that would lead students to question the organization of society and the values of their own times. Literature and writing and thinking about literature would become a means of helping youngsters achieve the ideal of a perfect society.

The existentialists would support a process-oriented curriculum as well, but hardly one that would engage in long analyses of the social order. The language arts are, above all, the tools to help each of us explore more deeply our own inner meaning. What can be more personal than a composition about how one "feels," whatever the topic may be? Content takes on meaning only as the individual gives it meaning.

With so many points of agreement among the different philosophical perspectives, the public curriculum is bound to be an eclectic one. Personal expression happens as a part of learning to communicate, and the reading of literary works is generally recognized as being a source of great pleasure. Experts of every philosophical bent tend to share these views. Reading and writing are practical for our daily affairs, they are crucial for societal communication, they are tools in the processes of logical analyses, and they are inevitably child-centered. The reading of Shakespeare's plays could even be accommodated by the existentialists who might see the soul-searching characters of his plays as a way of helping youngsters explore their own inner thoughts.

It may be that so much "agreement" has contributed to the inertia that has afflicted the English language arts curriculum. It appears that we are unable to conceive of significantly different curricular designs for the study of the language arts. Notwithstanding the creativity, thoughtfulness, and flexibility associated with the language arts by their very nature, the subject is deeply encapsulated in the existing school culture.

### Creating a Positive Language Arts Climate

When it comes to the question of how to increase the success of language arts studies, first and foremost we need to recognize the enormous differences between learners at all age levels. Among the variables that need to be considered are:

1. ethnic background
2. physical or psychological handicaps
3. socioeconomic status
4. the language used in the home (about 15 percent of the children in America in 1990 come from homes where English is not the first language used)
5. the educational experiences provided by parents (such as reading to children or taking them to a zoo or museum)
6. I.Q. test scores, and other analogous factors that support or impede the development of communication skills
7. the nature, quantity, and quality of electronic involvement in each student's home

The climate for learning language arts skills can be enhanced in many ways. First, instruction should include a number of terms that the children already understand. This allows them to start from a familiar context and then move to the unknown. New vocabulary needs to be integrated among the known terms and fully explained whenever possible.

Second, because of the many individual differences noted above, the instructional procedures used need to be varied accordingly. With classes of thirty students on the average, it is often difficult to pinpoint the exact methods that will be most effective, and planning a set of varying methods is likely to be the most efficient approach.

Third, it should be recognized that any teaching *in* English is also the teaching *of* English. Learning and discovery in all subject fields—in the sciences, in mathematics, or in the social studies—extend vocabularies, reading comprehension, and writing skills. Integrating language arts with the other subject areas is productive from the point of view of process as well as content.

For all practical purposes, strategies for creating a positive classroom climate are infinite, but one more needs to be stressed. This is the tactic of treating pupils with dignity and respect. Without realizing it—possibly because of ethnic differences—teachers may appear to be ridiculing written or verbal errors when they intend only to correct. None of the school subjects are so prone to misunderstanding as the English language arts for we ask children to express themselves and then we set about correcting the products of their expression.

### The Spread of Minority Groups' Languages

Population has been steadily increasing among America's major minority groups, bringing new and urgent challenges to the English language arts curriculum. Early in the twenty-first century, projections indicate that the minority population will outnumber the traditional white majority by approximately six percent.

In 1989, Census Bureau data indicated that in the United States over ten percent of the residents spoke a language other than English when at home. Furthermore, in Los Angeles more than half of the population is made up of persons who speak Spanish, and there are 1,500,000 Hispanics in New York City.[56] There are also 300 television stations and 200 newspapers in America that are for Spanish speaking people.[57]

As minority groups become a majority, the impact of their languages on American English underscores the need for continuing to assimilate new terms into our vocabularies. There is, of course, a precedent for doing so. We have already adopted from Mexican Spanish some 500 words such as fiesta, coyote, canyon, buffalo, burro, and mustang.

We need also to view language instruction from a broad, linguistic perspective, possibly tracing the development of Indo-European languages, their impact on each other, and the ways in which they have diverged. The phenomenon of English as an international language would be a promising avenue to pursue as would be the importance of foreign literature for the development of American literature. It is clear that the English language arts cannot continue to ignore the influence of foreign languages and literature on American development. The multicultural language arts curriculum is a fast-approaching challenge.

### The Concomitant Video Curriculum

As we work to meet the new and growing needs of a multicultural society, we must bear in mind a trend that may ultimately be even more important than the increasing number of people whose native tongue is not English. Since the 1950s, we have been surrounded by a barrage of high-level stimuli full of all kinds of information. The major sources are radio programs, microcomputer networks, television, comic books, paperbacks, increasingly sophisticated telephone systems. Of these, the video screen has certainly been the most powerful. It is redolent with visual and audio messages that penetrate our lifestyles.

A flood of concepts — visual and verbal — have engulfed the minds of the young and may well be an increasing threat to their intellectual development. Curriculum planners have become more and more harassed as they seek an answer to the query, "What shall we do in the language arts to use and cope with this milieu of sounds and images that has invaded all of our minds?"

The concomitant video curriculum includes on-the-spot news often rife with terrorism, political confusion, or conflict in our government, or the threats of war. Also available at the touch of a button are films ranging from depictions of life in space capsules to dramatizations of life in ancient Rome or medieval Britain, athletic contests, pictures of prehistoric animals, or simulated Indian attacks on a covered wagon train. The magnitude of one aspect of the problem is underscored by the fact that two national video dealers' associations agreed in 1988 interviews that approximately three and a half million pornographic video-cassettes were rented to American customers each week! Many were probably viewed covertly by youngsters.[58]

Let us now confront the question of what we can do to cope with the challenges posed by the concomitant video curriculum. What can—ought the schools do? The nature of the problem with respect to TV was made clear by a distinguished media ecologist, Neil Postman. His research indicates that American students in the elementary and secondary school spend twenty-three to twenty-seven hours per week televiewing.[59] On an annual basis, Postman calculates that young learners spent 12,000 hours in grades 1–12 but 18,000 hours in front of the TV set! Can the school's curriculum possibly compete?

Control over the concomitant curriculum is really the problem. Should the schools try to reach out and bring video and possibly other electronic experiences into their curriculum? This would no doubt be at the expense of our more traditional studies, which have been none too successful in recent years if we are to judge from SAT and other standardized scores. Should parents and the community at large exercise greater responsibility in controlling what their children view? What kind of collaboration among the schools, parents, and the community would be most productive? Who should edit vulgarity, terrorizing scenes, bigotry, and sexual promiscuity that appear so frequently in our video experiences? How do we achieve and retain for our youngsters the sense of a wholesome and honorable life that once was so powerfully conveyed in the thoughtful reading of literature and now appears to be so quickly undermined by a daily succession of flimsily developed video sitcoms often utterly without literary, moral, or cultural value?

Some simple and probably not very effective activities could be pursued under the current curricular structures. For example, teachers could review the daily listing of video shows with their students and encourage discussions of what they plan to view and the criteria they would pursue in making their selections. They could also watch several popular video programs in the classroom and discuss their merits and demerits, modeling the behavior they would hope students would engage in at home. In addition, they could discuss the question of selectivity with parents during parent–teacher conferences. As the curriculum is currently implemented, there is little time for any of these activities.

To effectively confront the problems posed not only by television but by the other electronic media as well, a major revision in the design of the English language arts curriculum is necessary. It may well be that the time is right for such a revision. The numerous crises that we have referred to in this chapter and elsewhere in this book may have already brought us to a cultural vector of change sufficient to overcome the encapsulation that has so dominated our efforts to change the curriculum in the second half of the twentieth century.

# Foreign Language Instruction

### Brief Historical Overview

Historically, Latin was the preeminent foreign language taught. For most of this history, it was taught by the learn-grammar-and-translate method, a method reasonably appropriate for a language that had not been spoken actively for centuries. It was the language of the Church and the power structure and was studied by a very small percentage of the population. Whether Latin or Greek, the second most widely studied language, were of any practical use was hardly relevant especially since it was believed that their study improved students' reasoning and analytical skills.

Although the post-Revolutionary period saw a decline in the study of Latin and Greek and an increase in the study of such subjects as surveying and book-keeping, even the Committee of Ten retained their study as part of the recommended high school curriculum. The committee did, however, include the study of modern foreign languages as well, recognizing the growing regard for their study that came from the scholarly as well as the commercial world. Throughout the twentieth century, improving systems of transportation and commerce gave added importance to learning modern foreign languages.

After World War II, with millions of American soldiers returning from abroad, interest in studying foreign languages reached a peak. Instructional methodologies emphasized oral skills. The Audio Lingual Method (ALM), based on the oral practice of typical sentence patterns, became especially popular. Its parrot-like repetition, however, alienated many students, and the grammar-and-translate method, which most of us who have studied languages in precollegiate programs know well, continued to dominate the curriculum. After years of such studies, few are able to form a simple sentence to order a meal in a foreign country. A period of significant decline in foreign language enrollment followed.

### Increasing Importance of Foreign Language Study

Only in the late 1970s did we begin to find a renewed interest in the study of foreign languages. According to the American Council on the Teaching of Foreign Languages (ACTFL), enrollment grew by more than a million students between 1982 and 1985.[60] The U.S. Department of Education reports that the number of students earning foreign language credit in high school rose from 50 percent in 1982 to 66 percent in 1987.[61] To some extent, this renewed interest may be attributed to the 1979 report of the President's Commission on Foreign Language and International Studies, entitled *Strength through Wisdom*. The commission expressed alarm over Americans' growing lack of knowledge about any language other than English and the impact that could have on our economic future and our relationships with other nations. They recommended a greatly increased level of study extending to the elementary school.

Other reasons have been offered to both support and explain increased foreign language study. In particular, it is believed that a better knowledge of English grammar and usage is acquired as one learns another language. The merits of this point are particularly important at the secondary level, when it is hoped students will achieve a more sophisticated grasp of their mother tongue. Students often do not begin to fully understand the cultural roots of their native English until they are exposed to other languages. In addition, foreign language study is a challenge to the gifted as well as occupationally important to an increasingly polyglot American work force.

## Global Literacy in the New Millennium

It is no longer possible for any nation to exist in isolation. While English has become an international language, the vast majority of people still speak only their native tongue. Knowledge of a second language is not only useful in communicating with people of other nations but also for deepening one's cultural understanding of other people through the reading of their literature and history and the experience of firsthand communication.

There is a pressing need for a new kind of global literacy in a world of cultures drawn closer together by an array of technologies and media. Of course, there remains the need for increased reading literacy worldwide. In fact, the United Nations passed a unanimous resolution proclaiming 1990 as International Literacy Year (ILY). According to UNESCO statistics, as recently as 1980 there were 889 million illiterates fifteen years of age or older (27.7 percent of the world's population). As the Paris Office of UNESCO noted, the deplorable extent of illiteracy has impeded industrial production and severely impaired the ability of tens of millions of people to support and to participate significantly and with informed wisdom in attacks on problems of political and social significance.[62]

These comments and related statistics refer primarily to the ability to read one's native tongue, undeniably a first step toward global literacy. Global literacy, however, refers to the ability to communicate intelligently and effectively with other peoples of the world. Key to global literacy is knowledge of a foreign language and, when viable, multiple foreign languages.

For foreign language studies in the United States, global literacy implies that the number of different languages offered by our schools needs to be greatly increased. In addition to traditional courses in French, Spanish, and German, such languages as Japanese, Russian, and Arabic need to be studied. The ability of school systems as currently supported and organized to offer such a wide array of languages is nearly nonexistent. Significantly increased offerings are not expected before the new millennium. Notwithstanding what could surely be considered an undue delay, achieving global literacy is a likely part of our educational futures and one for which the current rebirth of interest in foreign language study may be a precursor.

### Trends in Elementary Foreign Language Instruction

Interest in foreign language study has grown rapidly not only for secondary but elementary students as well. Instruction in a second language is a relatively new area in the curriculum for grades six and below, although some schools in the United States and many European elementary schools have featured foreign language instruction or FLES (*Foreign Language in the Elementary School*) for many years. In 1941, no more than 5,000 children were exposed to second language instruction in the elementary grades. By the mid 1950s, well over 300,000 younger children were receiving instruction, predominately in French and Spanish. The number of pupils involved in such programs exceeded 500,000 by the 1959–60 academic year but declined drastically in the late 1960s and 1970s. Consistent with the overall trend, interest in FLES is again on the rise.

Most youngsters who come to the United States to live acquire a working knowledge in a few months and a modest command of English in less than a year. The potential for learning a foreign language among young children is considerable. Introducing the study of a foreign tongue as early as age five or six represents an effort to take advantage of this potential. However, how to go about teaching a second language to children who are neither in full command of their abstract intellectual abilities (necessary for a full understanding of grammatical principles) nor in their first years of life (when willingness to learn spoken language by repetition is at its height) remains a significant conundrum. FLES efforts in the 1960s did not meet with the kind of success that was expected, and the public's disappointment was probably a significant factor in the steep decline that followed.

The purposes associated with the establishment of an elementary foreign language program need to be clear at the very outset. What will be the expectations that govern the program? Several fundamental questions should be asked and their responses clarified before a program is undertaken. Among these are:

- Is it to provide—at the elementary level—a foundation for secondary instruction?

- Is it to acquaint the children of a community with the language and culture of a minority group present in the community?

- Is it primarily to become familiar with the literature and culture of a foreign nation?

- Is it to prepare students for the everyday, practical use of a second language?

- Is it to prepare students for commercial activities and a better economic future?

The way we determine the success of a program will depend largely on how we respond to these questions. If we concentrate on translating and understanding the literature of a nation and then expect our children to speak the language well enough to deal with the daily activities of life, we will no doubt be disappointed with the results of language instruction. The lack of clarity about our purposes has in the past undermined support for foreign language study.

Other less important but still crucial questions need to be confronted for the success of an elementary foreign language program. For example, what is the best second language to be introduced in a given school district? At the elementary level, is instruction in more than one foreign tongue to be offered? To whom and at what age should second language instruction be offered? Should the curriculum be designed for all learners? for the fast achievers? for those who elect to study or whose parents want them introduced to a second language?

In general, foreign language programs for the elementary grades are viewed under three groupings: FLES; FLEX (Foreign Language Experience); and immersion.[63] Each of these represents a different approach to foreign language instruction for young children and a different set of purposes for curricular outcomes.

FLES classes meet several times a week for twenty to forty minutes. Much of the time is spent in activities using both the foreign language and English. The intention is to teach some oral and written skills in a foreign language as well as to develop sensitivity toward a culturally different group. FLES programs may start as early as kindergarten or as late as the fourth grade.

FLEX programs are usually taught in English. Youngsters are introduced to foreign languages with an effort to increase their cultural awareness of other nations and peoples. On the whole, they will acquire rather limited skills in speaking a foreign language.

In contrast, immersion programs are taught, to the extent possible, in the foreign language itself. Youngsters are to gain fluency in speaking the language. Often, reading and writing skills are addressed as well. Currently, there are more than 16,000 students enrolled in immersion programs in twenty states.[64] Given the greater success they appear to have in helping youngsters to achieve oral fluency, these numbers appear likely to increase. The expectation, however, is that FLES and FLEX programs will continue to dominate elementary foreign language instruction,[65] especially since they are less demanding on the skills of teachers and talents of students.

### Trends in Secondary Foreign Language Instruction

The current revival in secondary foreign language study has been accompanied by a new curricular emphasis on "communicative proficiency," that is, the ability to communicate effectively in an authentic context. Communication rather than grammar is the organizing curricular principle. The emphasis on grammatical accuracy is downplayed while students learn to use the skills of speaking, listening, reading and writing in terms of real world situations.[66]

The content of the foreign language curriculum is determined by first generating a list of communicative purposes. These are then related to the settings in which communication is expected to occur. Being able to satisfy basic needs in a foreign land may be established as a purpose, and shopping at a store, living at a hotel, and eating at a restaurant may be the settings selected to accomplishment this purpose. Materials derived from audio and video tapes, newspapers, magazines, and original literature would support the authenticity of the contexts developed.

Those favoring the communicative proficiency approach believe that, as students move into more sophisticated contexts, their grammatical skills will improve. There is, however, little evidence to support this position other than the knowledge that before the age of puberty children can learn second languages as though they were mother tongues. Students with limited time to devote to foreign language study have not achieved in the past the kind of progress made by youngsters who have immigrated to a foreign land and are surrounded by a second language. There is little reason to believe that secondary foreign language study will exceed the two to five hours weekly typically assigned to it during the academic year.

There is also a good deal of support for teaching grammar in ways relevant to authentic contexts. For example, in discussing the communicative proficiency movement, Met takes the position that grammar should be learned in the way that it is actually used by beginning speakers.[67] He suggests that instead of teaching only the present tense and practicing this tense for an extended period of time before introducing the past tense, both tenses should be introduced and practiced together because they are so frequently encountered together in typical communication activities.

The communicative proficiency movement in foreign language instruction has had a powerful effect on secondary textbooks. According to Edward Scebold, ACTFL executive director, textbooks have been improving in quality and in their approach to a proficiency orientation.[68] There are nevertheless problems to be faced. The vast majority of teachers are instructionally knowledgeable in ALM and grammar-and-translate methodologies and would need training in new methods. Furthermore, the fluency required for the proficiency orientation may be beyond the skills of many teachers. A partial solution may be to use as "paraprofessionals" students who are skilled speakers of the second language. Whatever procedures may be adopted, the role of grammar is to become meaning-oriented rather than rule-oriented.

## Language Arts Scenarios for a New Century

### The Challenge of a New Millennium

We are just beginning to understand the meaning of living in a global environment. Our interdependence is becoming slowly and painfully apparent. War in the Persian Gulf affects the small economies of Third World countries; disasters in nuclear power plants spread noxious fallout around the globe; deforestation undertaken by a developing nation threatens air quality for everyone. We are, in sum, creating and using powers without understanding how to use them wisely, and our lack of wisdom is of global consequence.

Because of the undeniable fact that humankind is making the planet less and less capable of supporting the growing crowd of billions which inhabit it, a distinct and increasingly important role is emerging for the language arts. This is the challenging multifold task of helping us (1) to become well informed, (2) to develop sound values by properly interpreting the vast audiovisual input to which most of us are exposed, (3) to communicate clearly and intelligently with the world's inhabitants, and (4) to use our verbal skills to find ways of communicating with those who share our global environment so that together we may cope with the dilemmas facing us all.

## Revising the Traditional Curriculum: the Expanding Communications Horizons

Receptive and expressive abilities form the cultural essence of what keeps us together as a society. These have traditionally been represented in terms of four interrelated systems: (1) listening and interpreting what is heard, (2) reading, (3) writing, and (4) speaking. If our social, economic, and intellectual lives were to remain essentially unchanged into the twenty-first century, these four systems would certainly need to continue their domination of the language arts curriculum. Taken as a group, they were once viewed as analogous to the four legs of a chair, supporting the weight of a vast network of shared communication and created meanings.

However, other symbolic systems have come to the fore and have become the object of formal study. The traditional abilities are increasingly viewed as an incomplete representation of modern communication. Despite what is an already crowded curriculum, the widely recognized, broader array of communicative systems appears destined for a role in the language arts. Especially important among these are the newly understood systems called kinesics and proxemics, both of which represent forms of nonverbal communication, and semiotics, which undertakes the scientific study of signs and signals. In addition, we cannot ignore the new forms of communication developing with the continued growth of computer systems and the increasing interaction of people with video screens. Clearly, our understanding of what is involved in communications has broadened greatly in the latter part of the twentieth century.

### Kinesics and Proxemics

Kinesics[69] is the study of body movements and their meanings. This nascent field has developed a good deal of evidence indicating that gestures are not idiosyncratic movements used by individual speakers as a way of expressing personality. They are, rather, established as a result of early social contacts with other members of one's cultural group and are a basic form of communication. Kinesics has been widely recognized as especially useful in analyzing and comparing the nonverbal communications of people from different cultural backgrounds.

Proxemics[70] is the study of systematic spatial arrangements and their meanings. Like kinesics, it promises major contributions to the development of global literacy and improved international communications, as well as an increased internal understanding of pluralistic relationships, so crucial to our sense of nationhood and the harmony of our multicultural populations.

Several concrete examples follow to explain more fully how these systems function and can be studied. We smile, for instance, at someone while we are giving him bad news. Are we being kind or are we showing a lack of concern? That would depend upon the kinesic background of the individual receiving the bad news. Do we understand about each other's culturally diverse, nonverbal systems well enough to understand the diversity of interpretations? Certainly, the language arts study of kinesics would go a long way toward ensuring that we do understand each other well enough.

Take another example. A young man and woman are standing quite close together while conversing — say, fourteen inches apart. Are they lovers or merely good acquaintances engaged in a conversation? Again, the interpretation would depend on the proxemic understanding of the interpreter. Both kinesics and proxemics promise increased objective knowledge of culturally different, nonverbal systems of communication. If the language arts curriculum continues in the cultural encapsulation of recent decades, these new conceptions of communication will continue to be ignored. If that is the case in the future, it will be at the risk of continued misunderstandings both globally and nationally.

### Semiotics

Another field likely to impact on the future language arts curriculum is semiotics, or the study of signs and signals. It deals with the symbolism and meaning derived from the use of signs and signaling, both verbal and unspoken. The range and nature of signs and signals include not only those of human origin but also those used by animals. Furthermore, semiotics has become increasingly involved with communication in a microtechnological sense. This development took place as our sign and symbol relationships became more interactive with satellites, computers, robots, and analogous electronic gear.

### The Video Message

The video screen presents a powerful set of messages about values and appropriate behaviors that we have hardly begun to understand. Television is basically a new communicative medium with its own rules and grammar of meaning. Its sounds and visual images compose messages at least as effective as the printed text. A tremendous amount of information is contained in each video frame. How this information is manipulated and interpreted remains largely unstudied. Nevertheless, there is widespread agreement that television is having a significant impact on the ways we think and how we assimilate information.

Video literacy is, in today's world, fast becoming as important as reading literacy and is certainly on a track toward increasing importance in the future. While children spend years learning to read and critically analyze literature, they are given little assistance in interpreting the images and sounds of television. Students need techniques and insights for the proactive deciphering of video messages. They need to be in control of video message rather than controlled by them.

While the study of video messages is in its infancy, it is apparent that the language arts curriculum of the future will need to find room for a major new strand of study — that of video or media literacy. As we expand the curriculum to include additional communication systems, we realize that our traditional conception of the language arts, based solidly in the study of English and its literature, is fast going by the wayside. Communication has been generalized to include an array of nonverbal systems. In this context, English literature studies seem almost out of place, as though we were forecasting, reluctantly, a study of communication systems not directly related to the reading of literature.

### *Literature for Increased Global Literacy*

In truth, we have largely ignored the question of literature and what its position in the curriculum needs to be. Typically, English and American literature have comprised a major portion of the language arts experience, especially at the secondary level. Given the greatly increased range of communication skills that may need to be included in the curriculum, it may be necessary to do what has hitherto been unimaginable — eliminate the study of ethnocentric literature from the language arts.

Admittedly and most importantly, the study of literature helps us to explore the images of good living that we hold in our mind's eye. It gives us insight into different ways of thinking about the human condition. There are phenomena such as intragenerational disjunctures and experience compression that have profound effects on how we live and create meaning together. Fundamental conceptions of community, family, and work are under radical revision even as we look to them to order our ways of living together. Were the days of a past most of us have only heard about better? Should we try to return, can we return, to that past? Surely the school's curriculum ought not continue to ignore the economic, social, political, and moral upheavals that have only increased as the twentieth century has progressed. The study of literature offers us both affective and cognitive insights into what is happening to our world.

However, it is hardly necessary to read only English and American works to gain such benefits. Nor is it necessary to use great literary works for the purpose of improving our communicative skills. Indeed, in the past this has often undermined appreciation for the works themselves. In the future, literary studies may be profitably undertaken independently of communication studies as a part of our effort to develop global literacy and intercultural understanding about questions that touch on our fundamental humanness worldwide.

In sum, assuming that the school's overall curriculum design continues to be based on subjects with an emphasis on the disciplines, especially the sciences, we envision a transformation of the English language arts into two distinct subjects. The subject of communication systems would include such studies as video literacy, kinesics, and semiotics, as well as reading, writing, speaking, and listening in English and, possibly, a foreign language. Literary studies would comprise a separate subject involving the analysis and interpretation of great literature *not* as a way of learning English but as a way of building one's beliefs and values about the nature of a good life. We envision the future role of literary studies as that of serving as an agent for better tomorrows.

## QUESTIONS FOR DISCUSSION AND REFLECTION

1.  What did you most like or dislike about the English language arts in elementary school? junior high school? high school?
    As you think back on your own experience, have you found your high school studies relevant to the needs of your adult life? Would you change anything in the curriculum? Why or why not?

2.  In the long-standing, traditional language arts curriculum, there is an ongoing dispute between those who would emphasize process and those who would emphasize content. What differences would one or the other emphasis make on the kinds of learning experiences that would be planned for students? What is your own position with regard to this dispute?

3.  Discuss the historical and educational importance of Noah Webster's *The American Dictionary of the English Language*.

4.  Describe the experience curriculum design. Have you ever encountered this kind of curriculum in your school experiences? Would you support its adoption in today's world? Explain your position fully.

5.  The advent of the paperback is often seen as a major turning point for the language arts curriculum. What has been the role of the paperback for language arts instruction? What connections have been made between the increase in censorship and the paperback?

6.  What are some of the most notable features of the "New English" movement?

7.  What are some of the benefits attributed to the study of grammar? In your opinion, should grammar continue to be a major component of language arts studies? Explain your position fully.

8.  Describe the whole language approach to reading and writing. Specify how it is different from the phonics approach. Which approach is preferable, and why?

9.  In selecting reading materials for students, what considerations should be taken into account by teachers?

10. Explain the difference between FLES, FLEX and immersion programs for elementary foreign language programs.

11. How does the proficiency-oriented approach to secondary foreign language instruction differ from ALM and grammar-and-translate?

12. Explain each of the following terms representing important new considerations for the English language arts curriculum: (1) transformational-generative grammar, (2) global literacy, (3) semiotics, (4) video literacy, (5) kinesics, and (6) proxemics.

## RECOMMENDED READINGS

### I. Selected Classic Language Arts Publications from the Past*

Applegate, Mauree. *Helping children write*. Evanston, IL: Row, Peterson, 1954.

Arbuthnot, May Hill. *Children and books* (rev. ed.). Chicago: Scott, Foresman, 1957.

Dawson, Mildred A. and Marion Zollinger. *Guiding language learning*. Tarrgtown-on-Hudson, NY: World Book, 1957.

Herrick, Virgil E., Leland B. Jacobs, et al. *Children and the language arts*. Englewood Cliffs, NJ: Prentice-Hall, 1955.

Hildreth, Gertrude. *Teaching spelling*. New York: Henry Holt, 1955.

Stone, Laurence J. and Joseph Church. *Childhood and adolescence*. New York: Random House, 1957.

Strickland, Ruth. *Language arts in the elementary school*, (rev. ed.). Boston: D.C. Heath, 1957.

Witty, Paul A. *Reading in modern education*. Boston: D.C. Heath, 1949.

### II. Selected List of Current Writings Related to the Language Arts

Adler, Mortimer J. *How to speak, how to listen*. NY: MacMillan, 1983.

Barton, Bob and David Booth. *Stories in the classroom*. Portsmouth, NH, 1990, p. 128.

*Benet's Reader's Encyclopedia* (3rd ed.). New York: Harper and Brothers, 1987.

Bering-Jensen, H., Tongue tied by foreign languages. *Insight* 6:5 (January 29), 1990, p. 46f.

Bettman, Otto L. *The delights of reading*. Boston: David R. Godine, 1987.

Bowman, Barbara T. Educating language—minority children: challenges and opportunities. *Phi Delta Kappan*, 71:2 (October 1989), pp. 118–120.

Brandt, Ronald S. Preparing today's students for tomorrow's world. *Educational Leadership*, Arlington, VA: The ASCD, September 1989, 47:1. (See entire "theme issue.")

Bromley, Karen D'Angelo. *Language arts: Exploring connections*. Boston: Allyn and Bacon, 1988, 490 pp.

Bryson, Bill. *The mother tongue English and how it got that way*. New York: William Morrow, 1990, 270 pp.

Carrier, Carol A. Note taking research: Implications for the classroom. *Journal of Instructional Development* 6:3, 1983, pp. 19–25.

Cheek, Earl H. *Reading for success in elementary schools*. New York: Holt, Rinehart, and Winston, 1989.

Connolly, Paul (ed.). *Writing to learn mathematics and science*. New York: Teachers College Press, 1989.

DiSilvestro, Frank R. Effective listening in the classroom. *Teaching and Learning at Indiana University*. Bloomington, IN: Indiana University Press, 1989, pp. 1–4.

Feigenbaum, E.A. Toward the library of the future. *Long Range Planning*, February 1989, pp. 118–123.

Gorman, Christine et al. The Literary Gap. *Time*, 132:25, December 19, 1988, pp. 56–57.

Haas, John D. *Future studies in the K–12 curriculum* (2nd ed.). Denver, CO: Social Science Educational Consortium, 1988, 100 pp.

Lado, Robert. *Teaching English across culture*. New York: McGraw-Hill, 1989.

*Note: A deliberate effort has been made to include a few "classic publications" from years past when the content has remained valid. Today's teachers need this background information.

Levy, Mark R. (ed.). The VCR age: *Home video and mass communication*. Newbury Park, CA: Sage Publications, May 1989, 274 pp.

Newark, Thomas. *More than stories: The range of children's writing*. Portsmith, NH: Heinemann, 1989, 240 pp.

O'Neil, John. Foreign languages: A new focus on 'proficiency'. *Curriculum Update*. Alexandria, VA: The Association for Supervision and Curriculum Development, January, 1990, pp. 1–8.

Parker, Jeanette Plauche, *Instructional Strategies for Teaching the Gifted*. Allyn and Bacon, 1989, 341 pp.

Petty, Walter T., et al. *Experiences in Language* (5th ed.). Boston: Allyn and Bacon, 1989, 505 pp.

Potter, Rosemary L. *Using reading in the middle school*. Phi Delta Kappan Fastback, 1990.

Robinson, Sandra R. *Bringing words to life*. New York: Teachers and Writers Collaborative, 1990, 168 pp.

West, Woody. English secures the melting pot. *Insight* 6:21, May 21, 1990, 64 pp.

Whaley, Charles E. and Helen F. Whaley. *Future images: Futures studies for grades 4 to 12*. Trillium Press, 1986, 92 pp.

## NOTES

1. Suhor, C. (1988). Content and process in the English curriculum. In: Brandt, R. S. (ed.). *Content of the curriculum*. Washington, D.C.: Association of Supervision and Curriculum Development.

2. Moffett, J. and Wagner, B. J. (1983). *Student-centered language arts and reading, K–13*. Boston: Houghton Mifflin.

3. Hirsch, E. D., Jr. (1987). *Cultural literacy: What every American needs to know*. Boston: Houghton Mifflin.

4. Sheperd, G. D. and Ragan, W. B. (1982). *Modern elementary curriculum* (5th ed.). New York: Holt, Rinehart and Winston, pp. 446–447.

5. Cornett, J. D. and Beckner, W. (1972). *The secondary school curriculum: Content and structure*. Scranton, PA: Intext Educational Publishers, p. 74.

6. McLuhan, M. (1964). *Understanding media*. New York: Bantam.

7. Cited in the *Funk & Wagnalls new encyclopedia*, vol. 27, p. 222.

8. Cubberley, E. P. (1920). *The history of education*. Boston: Houghton Mifflin, p. 697.

9. See: Cubberley, E. P. (1947). *Public education in the United States* (rev. ed.). Boston: Houghton Mifflin; and Monroe, P. (1940). *Founding of the American public school system*. New York: Macmillan.

10. For a more complete discussion of subject popularity in the academies, see: Ornstein, A. C. and Hunkins, F. P. (1988). *Curriculum: Foundations, principles and issues*. Englewood Cliffs, NJ: Prentice Hall, pp. 64–71.

11. Early, M. J. (1983). A common curriculum for language and literature. In: Fenster, G. D. and Goodlad, J. L. (eds.). *Individual differences and the common curriculum*. 82nd Yearbook, Part I, National Society for the Study of Education. Chicago: University of Chicago, p. 187.

12. Hatfield, W. W. (1935). *An experience curriculum in English*. Urbana, IL: National Council of Teachers of English.

13. *Ibid.*, p. 134.
14. Purves, A. C. (1981). *Reading and literature: American achievement in international perspective*. Urbana, IL: National Council of Teachers of English.
15. *Op. cit.*, M. Early, p. 192.
16. *Ibid.*, p. 193.
17. Suleiman, S. and Crosman, B. (eds.) (1980). *The reader and the text: Essays on audience and interpretation*. Princeton, NJ: Princeton University Press.
18. Rosenblatt, L. (1976). *Literature as exploration* (3rd ed.). New York: Noble & Noble, Publishers (first published in 1938).
19. See: Burress, L. (1989). *Battle of the books: Literary censorship in the public schools, 1950–1985*. Metuchen, NJ: The Scarecrow Press.
20. Dodge, S. (1990). Average score on verbal section of 89–90 SAT drops to lowest level since 1980. *The Chronicle of Higher Education* (September 5), pp. A33–34.
21. Bestor, A. (1953). *Educational wastelands*. Urbana, IL: University of Illinois Press.
22. Flesch, R.(1956). *Why Johnny can't read*. New York: Harper and Brothers.
23. *Op. cit.*, Cornett, J. D. and Beckner, W., pp. 332-3.
24. *Funk & Wagnalls New Encyclopedia*, Vol. 9. (1986). Chicago: Rand McNally, p. 276.
25. For a readable, scholarly, and comprehensive overview of English, including spelling, vocabulary, etc., cf. Bryson, *Mother Tongue, op. cit.*
26. Compiled from over 100 term papers prepared for the authors' doctoral level university classes.
27. Cited in *Webster's new world dictionary*.
28. For a classic review of early studies of listening skills, see: Caffery, J. G. (1955). Auding. *The Review of Educational Research* 25:121 (April).
29. Braddock, R., et al. (1963). *Research in written composition*. Champaign, IL: National Council of Teachers of English.
30. See, in particular: Chomsky, N. (1965). *Aspects of the theory of syntax*. Cambridge, MA: M.I.T. Press; and Chomsky, N. (1969). *The acquisition of syntax in children from 5 to 10*. Cambridge, MA: M.I.T. Press.
31. Roberts, P. (1964–66). *The Roberts English series for grades 1 to 12*. New York: Harcourt Brace Jovanovich.
32. For a detailed and still historically relevant study of the field based on more than 700 publications, cf. Harold G. Shane, *Linguistics and the classroom teacher*. Washington, D.C.: The Association for Supervision and Curriculum Development, NEA, 1967, 120 pp.
33. Cited by the Associated Press, January 10, 1990. (Reproduced in the Bloomington, Indiana, *Herald Times*, January 10, 1990, p. A-3).
34. The Literacy Gap. (1988). *Time*, 132, 25:56–57.
35. Cited in the *Hudson Institute Report*, Fall, 1989, p. 4. See chapter XVII for proposals to remove the growing obsolescence of our schools created by the technological revolution engulfing the United States.
36. Strickland, D. S. (1990). Emergent literacy: How young children learn to read and write. *Educational Leadership, 47*, 6:18–23.
37. Commission on Reading (1988). *Becoming a nation of readers: The report of the Commission on Reading*. Champaign, IL: ERIC.
38. *Ibid.*
39. Tierney, R. J. (1990). Redefining reading comprehension. *Educational Leadership* 47, 6:37–42.

40. *Ibid.*, p. 37.
41. *Ibid.*, p. 21.
42. Fisher, C. J. and Terry, C. A. (1974). *Children's language and the language arts.* New York: McGraw-Hill, Chapter 9.
43. Spillman, C. and Lutz J. (1986). A writing to read philosophy. *Childhood Education* 62, 265–267.
44. George, C. (1986). "Success"ful reading and instruction. *Educational Leadership* 44, 3:62–63.
45. *Ibid.*, p. 78.
46. Woodward, A. (1986). Taking the teacher out of teaching reading. *The Education Digest* 52, 4:50–53.
47. *Ibid.*, p. 52.
48. Vandergrift, K. E. (1990). *Children's literature.* Englewood, CO: Libraries Unlimited, pp. 78–79.
49. *Op. cit.*, Suhor, C., p. 39.
50. Viadero, D. (1990). Notions of "literary canon" in schools not valid, report says. *Education Week.* X, 14:5.
51. *Ibid.*
52. For an outstanding and detailed elaboration of the field with regard to younger children, see: Huck, C. S., Hopoler, S., and Hickman, J. (1987). *Children's literature in the elementary school* (4th ed.). New York: Holt, Rinehart, and Winston.
53. *Ibid.*
54. For added information see: Hirsch, E. D. (1987). *Cultural literacy: What every American needs to know.* Boston: Houghton Mifflin.
55. *Ibid.*
56. Bryson, B. (1990). *Mother tongue: English and how it got that way.* New York: William Morrow and Company, p. 239.
57. *Ibid.*
58. For a provocative series of four consecutive statements entitled "How TV Is Shaking Up the American Family," cf. Joanmacie Kalter's articles in the *TV Guide*, 36:30ff. July 23–August 13, 1988. Especially see her July 23 essay, "How TV Helps Shape Our Values."
59. For an early report on how TV research is pursued, see: Postman, N. (1981). The day our children disappear: Predictions of a media ecologist. *Phi Delta Kappan* (January), pp. 382–386.
60. Chastain, K. (1989). The ACTFL proficiency guidelines: A selected sample of opinions. *ADFL Bulletin* 20, 2:47–51.
61. Kolstad, A. (1989). *Changes in course-taking patterns from 1982–1987.* Washington, D.C.: U.S. Department of Education.
62. Also see Neil Postman's vintage but still prescient article: Postman, N. (1970). The Politics of Reading. *Harvard Educational Review*, (May) pp. 244–252.
63. *Op. cit.*, O'Neil, J.
64. *Ibid.*, p. 6.
65. *Ibid.*
66. *Ibid.*, p. 3.
67. Met, M. (1988). Tomorrow's emphasis in foreign language: Proificiency. In: *Content of the curriculum* (1988 ASCD Yearbook). Alexandria, VA: Association for Supervision and Curriculum Development.

68. *Ibid.*, p. 6.
69. For an extensive discussion, see: Birdwhistell, R. L. (1970). *Kinesics and context*. Philadelphia: University of Pennsylvania Press.
70. For an extended discussion, see: Hall, E. T. (1959). *The silent language*. New York: Doubleday; and Hall, E. T. (1966). *The hidden dimension*. New York: Doubleday.

# 16

# Electives and Co-Curricular Studies

## Introduction

We have discussed the typical school program and the five subjects that have dominated its curriculum — mathematics, science, social studies, the English language arts, and foreign languages. Other subjects are found among school offerings, but none have received the kind of attention and regard of these five over an extended period of time. Their central importance in meeting college admission requirements has contributed significantly to this state of affairs.

It would be difficult to find anyone who would take the position that the study of music, art, health, or physical education is unimportant or irrelevant. Nevertheless, we must look at what we do and not at what we say. In 1979, only two states mandated a course in the fine arts for high school graduation.[1] It is expected that this number will increase to 29 states in 1992; this is certainly a sign of growing support for the fine arts but still academically insignificant.

For the most part, the fine arts, along with health and physical education, have been assigned a peripheral role in the formal education of children. If these subjects are pursued in any depth, it is almost always as electives or as co-curricular activities. When a graduation requirement exists for the study of music or art in high school, it almost never goes beyond a single semester of study. English, on the other hand, must be studied every semester; mathematics, social studies, and the sciences are required for six semesters or so; and foreign language is pursued for a minimum of four semesters. Performance in mathematics, science, history, English, and geography is repeatedly evaluated on national assessments. Poor performances in any one of them is likely to receive a banner headline. One, however, is unlikely to see a similar headline lamenting, let's say, that only 40 percent of school-aged youngsters are able to use the vocabulary and notation of music or play an instrument.

Typically, if a child excels in music or art, he is thought to have an innate talent that cannot be achieved by simply increasing study and effort. If he does not perform well in music, his parents may express regrets but that is usually the end of the discussion. If, instead of music or art, the subject were science or mathematics, a great deal more concern would surely be expressed by parents. The child will probably feel "pressured" to improve his or her performance no matter what the level of talent may be. By such behavior, we assign status to school subjects, making some academically important and others peripheral. We do this often without any rational discussion—it is simply a part of our cultural mindset. On the whole, electives in the school's curriculum, like co-curricular activities, are comprised of subjects having peripheral academic status.

Notwithstanding these realities, there is among educators and the public at large a positive attitude toward electives and co-curricular activities related to the belief that these offer ways of letting youngsters express their individuality and develop talents and interests otherwise ignored by mainstream academics. In fact, Goodlad concluded on the basis of hundreds of classroom observations conducted on a national scale that "activities associated with students' own goal setting, problem solving, collaborative learning, autonomous thinking, creativity, and the like," are conspicuously absent in the school's curriculum.[2] Activities free of formal curricular requirements are widely seen as a way of redressing this imbalance.

Playing music, creating art, publishing a newspaper, participating in a sport—activities capable of yielding gratification from the sheer pleasure of performance—have long been emphasized in co-curricular activities. This is somewhat true among electives as well, although some of these subjects are often considered academically innovative, such as environmental studies, Black history, and even psychology and sociology.

Electives and co-curricular activities are perceived as having other functions as well. They are viewed as a means for expanding and revising the curriculum without undertaking a major structural reorganization. An after-school computer club or a special interest group in holographic arts expands the curriculum not only according to youngsters' interests but also in new academic directions.

Concomitant learnings that are associated with the conventional content discussed previously have become more important as the complexity of our information society has increased. Electives and co-curricular activities often act as liberating and creative avenues of study complementing the traditional classroom curriculum. As Lewis Perelman of the Hudson Institute points out, unless full-scale reconstruction of our schools takes place, our technological revolution ". . . will have made conventional classrooms as obsolete as livery stables and blacksmith shops."[3]

This chapter first reviews co-curricular activities as they now function in the schools and then explores the needs they fulfill and possible future directions that they could pursue profitably for American education. The fine arts, health, and sports, academically peripheral subjects found both in the school's regular curriculum and as co-curricular activities, are also explored, especially in terms of their double role and possible future contributions to the school's curriculum.

# Co-Curricular Activities Today and Tomorrow

### Five Perspectives on Co-Curricular Activities

Five somewhat different ways of approaching school studies are associated with the term "co-curricular." The general term "co-curricular" pertains to the experiences that learners have under the sponsorship or direction of the school in addition to content often prescribed in some form of curriculum guide or handbook.

While music, art, health, and physical education are usually included as an integral part of the curriculum, many schools also sponsor co-curricular groups in these fields. Such groups meet before or after scheduled work in the classroom. Likewise, some, but not all, students may participate in a choral group or sports. A junior or senior class play would fall into this category, too, as would a teacher- or parent-sponsored hobby group such as stamp collecting or painting.

Activities frequently labeled as *extracurricular* are analogous to the co-curricular cluster, but these activities tend to be more limited in scope. Organizing a fund drive for a fellow student who is ill, for example, qualifies as an extracurricular activity because of its "onetime," short-term characteristics. Also, generally at the secondary level, extracurricular activities are likely to be more closely directed or supervised by the staff than are the wide-ranging co-curricular ones.

Many schools offer a variety of *electives*, that is, choices not specifically required by the curriculum guide. For purposes of discussion, electives may be deemed to be loosely related to the co-curricular or extracurricular genre. Specifically, a student may elect to take a particular language from among three or four that are offered. The total number of years of study beyond the minimum of two also generally is elective. The option of choice underlies our view of electives as one form of co-curricular choice.

The term *special activities* is included here because it is used in some school districts as a synonym for the three varieties of activities discussed above. Rather than extending our notions of co-curricular studies, this is simply a more inclusive label.

The term *paracurriculum* pertains to an important, recently recognized type of activity likely to receive increased support because of the present problems that vex schooling. A relatively new term, paracurriculum pertains to valuable activities of co-curricular merit but ones that are not operated or directed by a given school system. The term was coined as a result of eighty-two interviews with futurist scholars participating in a USOE survey.[4] More explicitly, the term paracurriculum is a label for a variety of parallel *out-of-school activities* that increase knowledge and competence, build useful skills, and generate mature sophistication. Examples of such activities include membership in a Scout troop, YMCA or YWCA participation, part-time or weekend employment, certain types of church-related involvement, and various forms of community service. Obviously this type of real life experience promotes learning in a way that often has the impact of co-curricular work. Also, under some circumstances, it may pave the way toward subsequent employment, a better grasp of social problems, and possible access to some types of information that generally are not included in conventional academic content surveyed in the classroom.

The fifth and last item in this brief overview of diverse conceptions of co-curricular activities is concerned with *professional innovation of novel forms of co-curricular study and work experience* often initiated by teachers. This form of creative educational leadership is a bright star in the constellation of strategies for extending knowledge in unique ways.

### Contemporary Problems Demanding Co-Curricular Innovations in Education

Most schools are caught in a quagmire of proliferating problems with which the conventional curriculum is unable to cope. The range and scope of these problems have been discussed at some length in the first sections of this work. From a different perspective, contemporary newspapers and magazines have done a thorough job of commenting on school problems ranging from faulty scholarship, unwed mothers, and working parents to drugs and an array of difficulties such as those referred to by Susan Tifft in a *Time* magazine article:

> *Race and ethnicity, two of the touchiest issues in American life, have become an increasing source of friction and inspiration for the country's frayed public educational system.*[5]

Possibly, the schools will move toward completely ignoring the many problems burdening our youth and society in general. The reports that have appeared since the National Commission on Excellence in Education produced *A Nation At Risk* in 1983[6] have emphasized increased academic studies, either ignoring or underestimating the problems of broken homes, of parents who pay little attention to their youngsters, and of children who watch television late into the night and return from a day at school to an empty home when both parents work full time.

Furthermore, curricular flexibility in terms of elective studies and co-curricular activities have been given almost no attention in these many reports. Even the fine arts, physical education, and health have been largely ignored. Indeed, in recent times, scant attention has been paid to the instructional potential of informal studies.

While the curriculum has thus become more academic in its offerings and requirements and in many ways less responsive to the problems confronting students, educators have continued to view electives and co-curricular activities as adding flexibility to school studies. In the meantime, their conceptions of electives and especially of co-curricular activities lack current relevancy.

Co-curricular activities have long been conceived as opportunities to socialize the young, to develop their citizenship and leadership skills, and to direct their energies toward worthwhile projects.[7] However, like the formal curriculum, traditional co-curricular activities have diminished in effectiveness over the years. The kinds of activities pursued—student governance, athletics, clubs, school newspapers, and bands—have remained essentially unchanged for decades and really do not respond well to the kinds of problems that have burdened both students and teachers. They also have not responded well to the swift advancement of science and technology. While one may find computer clubs in many schools, clubs exploring, say, chaos or fractal geometry or computer visualization as art or even futures forecasting are almost nonexistent. Of course, finding teachers who are able to serve as advisors poses an obstacle to any effort to update club activities.

Moreover, parental attitudes and a wide-ranging array of community opinion—from liberal to conservative and from conventional to unconventional—have a direct bearing on whether such school facilities as the cafeteria, bookstore, and so on, may be used in novel ways to develop new kinds of skills for students. For instance, the local high school's cafeteria might be open after school hours to elementary school youngsters whose parents both work. The high school students would make all arrangements from developing a financial plan and determining costs to maintaining discipline and devising productive activities for the children. Of course, without the willingness to use facilities in novel ways, such a co-curricular activity could not even be considered.

### Guiding the Syntax of Learning in Co-Curricular Activities

Just as there is order in spoken languages such as English, so there is a form of sequence in the curriculum development involved in educational planning which may be thought of as *syntax*. To illustrate, note how word order changes meaning as in "the batter struck the ball" versus "the ball struck the batter." The way words are arranged to show various relationships and meanings among and within sentences and their phrases and clauses is a form of order or *syntax*, which these two sentences aptly illustrate.

Albeit order of a different quality, there is a form of order or syntax for us to recognize and acknowledge if we are to grasp and achieve coherence in the development of co-curricular activities that supplement work in the basic skills. A highly stuctured syntax having precise objectives would contradict the nature and overall purpose of co-curricular activities. Flexibility and openness to a variety of activities are necessary characteristics in the co-curricular syntax. Activities introducing students to electronic devices can be encouraged, but the specific activities need to be selected by the students themselves possibly with some help from the faculty advisor. The sequence of studies needs to be able to move in multiple directions. For example, in a formal curriculum situation, the level of conceptual difficulty would be a major factor in determining the sequence of topics for study. It certainly would not be ignored. In the co-curriculum, if students wish to proceed according to interest and ignore complexity, their interest would determine the sequence. At this point, the advisor would need to take on a supplementary role to help students with difficult content and be prepared to discuss students' experiences after the fact. Co-curricular syntax organizes as the curriculum unfolds. While there have been several proposals for such an open-ended curriculum design in the public schools, implementation has been both rare and brief.

Instructors can use a variety of methods to govern the order in which each student encounters the flow of co-curricular experiences as they supplement the curriculum. Sensitive teachers develop an awareness of the variations in their pupils' maturity, home background, and motivation as these relate to the co-curricular experience. Some very young children, for instance, may achieve at an early age a rather distinct interest and a considerable degree of skill in, say, music or art if their parents have instilled or encouraged such skills as drawing, painting, or playing the piano. Of course, the reverse could also be true with, for instance, a young learner being told by a parent to keep away from the piano, expensive phonograph records, or delicate microelectronic gear. It also should be kept in mind that many children come from "have not" families, families too poor to provide an environment that facilitates these skills and aptitudes. Often, too, these youngsters come from low-income homes and belong to the 70 percent of American families in which both parents are employed. In such a context, carefully selected co-curricular experiences acquire increased value and importance, particularly as they permit teachers to explore and to identify the humanness and the potential of young learners from poverty-stricken or disintegrating families.

In guiding the syntax of students' individual learnings, the teacher who is working with children in special realms (such as music or physical education) also needs an understanding of how students are performing in the various basic subjects such as mathematics or English. This is especially important when a given co-curricular activity has a bearing on the standard curriculum content being pursued. To give a simple illustration, if a physical education instructor is using a skilled young pianist's abilities at the keyboard to play for dance exercises or rhythmic movements in regular gym classes or during after-school hours, the music teacher should be aware of both the students' co-curricular gymnasium work and the added exercise of musical skills. It is through knowledge of students' overall school performance that the teacher associated with one or more special areas acquires insight into the total scope and sequence involved when assessing pupil performance in a special area. Since co-curricular work is not graded or evaluated in any conventional fashion, it is essential for the "regular" teacher to seek out the assessments made of individual student performance in co-curricular activities if a broad and insightful understanding of the student's performance is desired.

### The Co-Curricular Role of Special Fields and Materials

Educational co-curricular materials used in United States schools virtually always *supplement* rather than *replace* the explicit assignments and responsibilities of teachers. As Albert Shanker, President of the American Federation of Teachers, has indicated, our current reform movements, often mediated by teaching aids such as computers, will not ensure many of the education reforms, per se, that the years ahead mandate. In his words, to build schools for the next century "we must do more than put a new coat of paint on an old structure."[8]

Important as co-curricular studies promise to remain, our educational challenge is not merely to "build intelligence" in each special field with supplemental functions but to nourish knowledge in the spectrum of the *total* curriculum of which concomitant educational activities must become a part. We must not merely add "a new coat of paint."

The study and appraisal of human development—of the quality of individual learning prowess—spreads across all aspects of the curriculum and must be recognized as significant for the success of co-curricular programs. Also, as an integral part of their experience, young learners, too, need to be evaluated on a personal basis. Howard Gardner, a Harvard psychologist, has made some important and relevant points in this regard with his discussions of multiple intelligences.[9] He has identified seven forms of intelligence that have a direct bearing on the breadth of human activities within special fields in the curriculum. In addition to conventional and generally accepted mathematical-scientific and linguistic skills, Gardner lists five areas of intelligence that are related to our special curriculum fields. They include: (1) spatial, (2) musical, (3) bodily-kinesthetic, (4) interpersonal, and (5) intrapersonal (self understanding).[10] Patently, these multiple intelligences are cultivated not merely in conventional curriculum content but also in the array of representative "special aspects" of the curriculum—the co-curricular components.

In all of the concomitant curricular realms involving the assessment or appraisal of learners' progress in music, art, and so on, the following points should be borne in mind:

1. A *positive approach* should be taken with regard to pupil performance in all co-curricular activities.
2. Guidance based on assessment and evaluation of work students are doing in special fields should be informal and casual, not critical. It also should in general be *confidential* and not the object of faculty "coffee break" conversations.
3. Individuals *constantly are changing* and appraisal of their work in special fields is forever in an emerging state of flux and is likely to vary from day to day.
4. *Diverse and broad aspects* of human development should be kept in mind in lieu of what pupils are or are not accomplishing in various special, or academic, areas.
5. The fact that learners "differ from themselves" from day to day is a crucial insight when evaluations are made or when testing is under way.
6. The assessment of pupils' co-curricular learnings by individual teachers has limitations. Even teachers working with the same elementary or middle school learners in all of their daily classes and activities must remember that they can never know "all about" a given pupil at any time.

## Redirecting Co-Curricular Activities

Among the increasingly important contributions for guiding pupils' skills and intelligence through forms of co-curricular experiences not always inherent in standard curricula is the art of helping learners develop the ability to cope with the closing years of the twentieth century and beyond. With the passing of time, ". . . the imbalances and conflicts we generally called 'issues' have grown into 'big messes'."[11]

Some of the items that complicate the prospect of living in years to come are:

- being a member of a population with an average age approaching 50 years

- anticipating how to cope soon after 2000 A.D. with the rapidly rising costs of healthcare, housing, and other services when approximately one-third of our work force will have retired and have a median life expectancy of eighty or more years

- preparing women for workplace equality and for greater roles in government

- determining how to deal with what appears to be more single person–single parent households and the sustained disintegration in traditional family life reflected in such things as out-of-wedlock habitation

- learning to adjust (say by 2025 or 2030) to an American population in which the Asians have doubled in number and the persons speaking Spanish as a mother tongue outnumber the African-American population

- introducing pupils to the need for and availability of continuing *lifelong* education.

To guide students and provide intellectual input, our co-curricular programs must become more effective. The basic questions that need to be confronted are: How can we redirect co-curricular activities and concomitant learnings so that their contribution will be more effective in dealing with our many problems and new challenges? What comprises balanced mental, physical, and emotional well-being in our world of uncertainty? Can we ignore the challenges of technology and have balance in our program? What needs to be done with regard to a swiftly changing technology that appears at times to have escaped our control? Some educators believe that balance can be achieved through intellectual development alone. Others are convinced that active involvement in real world activities is an essential component of sustained intellectual growth. There is no simple way to redirect co-curricular activities that will ensure greater success. However, exploring potential directions is an important first step toward improvement.

## An Array of Promising Co-Curricular Activities

New ways of dealing with traditional activities is one route for renewal. That is, the astute supplementation of conventional curriculum content with co-curricular experiences can both update and increase the relevancy of the traditional curriculum. Among the range of potentially useful activities are: (1) field trips, (2) collaborative programs involving parents and students, (3) use of community resources, (4) educationally significant auditorium programs including films or dramatizations, (5) active involvement in school and local governance, and (6) production of films, tapes, newspapers, and the like.

### Field Trips

Although they take time to arrange and require teacher cooperation and often parental help at all levels, off-campus trips have many virtues, especially when made an integral segment of the curriculum. For instance, in a middle grade classroom, visited by one of the authors during an arduous Cincinnati winter, the students had spent about four weeks operating a classroom weather bureau. They learned to use a number of the tools employed by meteorologists, such as the barometer and wet- and dry-bulb thermometer; tracked weather systems; and posted daily forecasts on a corridor bulletin board. After a few weeks, with parents providing transportation, the class made a half-day visit to the local weather bureau. Trips to airports, museums, the zoo, and many other places add to and increase the relevancy of the curriculum for youngsters.

### Collaborative Programs and Activities

When a unit of study is nearly completed, it can be stimulating to invite parents to the classroom or auditorium to learn in greater detail what their children have been studying. Student presentations might include a puppet show based on what has been studied, a debate revolving around a current issue and the research undertaken by the students, or a pageant of different kinds of creative works including poems, paintings, inventions, gymnastics, and so forth.

The direct involvement of parents in co-curricular activities can also add an element of novelty and excitement. At the beginning of each academic year, the school could solicit recommendations concerning community problems for which parents and students would like to join together to seek solutions. A list of parental suggestions could then be circulated, and parents and their children could join with others in studying a problem that they wish to pursue in depth. A short-term, special interest group could be established to share information and invite local experts to discuss the problem. The group could decide on an appropriate action to be taken and, to the extent possible, would follow up on its own recommendations. At this point, the group would consider either its own dissolution or establishing a standing club.

In this approach to co-curricular activities, adults would work in collaboration with youngsters and a faculty member would serve as advisor. This might offer a route for bridging the age gap that seems to be opening between a very large older population and a relatively small younger generation. It would also help to maintain real world linkages between the school's curriculum and the concerns of daily life.

### Using Community Resources

Museums, aquariums, public libraries, and the like are often objects of field trips. They are, more importantly, valuable community resources whose uses for research and extended studies can lead to the opening of vast new vistas. Involving young-sters regularly in their use, making them both competent and aware of the possi-bilities while allowing them to explore directions of interest to them personally is perhaps one of the most productive directions co-curricular activities could take. An after-school club designed to explore the academic potential of community resources is one possible format in this context.

### Technology and the Media

In addition to continual updating of the *content* of instruction, co-curricular offer-ings can add creative enhancement to traditional studies. Of particular importance in co-curricular activities is their use to compete with television as a source of learn-ing. They offer youngsters active engagement in achieving goals as opposed to the passivity of televiewing. In 1990 the A.C. Nielsen Company, which measures time spent televiewing, announced that 6- to 11-year-olds spend twenty-three or twenty-four hours weekly watching television. Preschoolers spend even more time.

Furthermore, after-school clubs involved in developing videotapes of various genres from news coverage to dramas can contribute significantly to the video liter-acy of youngsters. Students who learn the nuances of shooting different kinds of scenes also become more knowledgeable in understanding how both information and the audience can be manipulated by the video camera. Another approach to the co-curricular development of video literacy could involve clubs based on the analysis and evaluation of new television offerings. Possibly a "Critics' Circle" newsletter could be distributed to the student body and responses to the various reviews invited.

Other areas of technology are equally promising for co-curricular activities. Following the NASA space program closely is one possible direction. Club activi-ties could involve studying inventions necessitated by space flight that have im-pacted on our daily lives, an analysis of manned versus unmanned flight, and an overview of the historical-political contexts that have impacted on the develop-ment of the space program.

Environmental watchdog clubs are another route that might be pursued as co-curricular activities. While becoming increasingly mainstream, many environ-mental questions are still very controversial and are either avoided in the formal curriculum or discussed at such a level of generality that the real problems involved are ignored. The voluntary participation of students and the support of their par-ents would be likely to ensure a greater depth of study.

### The School as Co-Curricular Resource

Educators can find many ways to use various aspects of school life as resources for enhancing the basic curriculum. At the outset, when we think of the school itself as a co-curricular teaching aid, it is essential to bear in mind two major points. One is that each school—even those in adjacent districts—may well have student clients who differ, for instance, the 15 percent of our youth for whom English is a second language. There also is the 14 percent who were born out of wedlock, the 30 percent who are latchkey children, and so on. Second, financial resources are varied and often meager, limiting versatile use of school plants. (In 1990, UNESCO reported that the United States financial support was among the four lowest in the educational programs of sixteen major industrial nations!) There are, nonetheless, many dimensions of special or co-curricular fields in which the total school program can serve as a teaching aid if these fields are adequately funded.

*A Sampling of Ways in which the School Has Been a Resource for Co-Curricular Activities.*    Some middle grade and secondary schools blessed with creative, competent leadership have developed a variety of novel approaches that portray the innovative use of the school setting as an aid to acquiring experience and knowledge. Here is a sampling of a few such ventures that, with faculty sponsors, have been encountered by the authors:

- The students who helped the management clean up the cafeteria and do dishes were unionized by the educational director of a national union and worked out a financial contract each spring for the coming academic term. The idea was developed by the cafeteria director.

- Concomitant to the point above, several pupils opened a low-cost on-campus insurance company to enable students to obtain reimbursement for dish breaking for which their school charged them a fee. A social studies supervisor initiated this venture.

- Student employees in a school system's bookstores became bonafide participants and members of a national cooperative movement at the suggestion of a staff member who managed the school district's four bookstores.

- With the advice of a local banker, a group of pupils and their mathematics teacher sponsor established a school loan office to subsidize youngsters who needed to borrow money for a day or two for lunch or other items, such as books for which there was a school charge. A modest loan fee was charged and the small profits were divided among those pupils who put some of their spending money in the "loan office" coffers in order to make a bit of profit.

- A group decided to invest, with teacher cooperation, in setting up beehives and having periodic honey sales to learn about business and investing and, of course, to make pocket money.

Beyond a doubt, ventures like these suggest how the school plant itself, if sufficiently flexible and managed by a dedicated, imaginative group of qualified faculty members, can help to "create" excitement and stimulate real life experiences for various segments of the pupil population. These experiences, it should be noted, are significant departures from conventional classroom content. Winston Churchill once commented that we shape our buildings and then *they* shape us. By the same token, we shape our schools and then they shape experiences from which children learn. Redirecting some of the uses to which school facilities are put can contribute importantly to the reshaping of education.

# The Peripheral Subjects

### Electives

As we pointed out earlier, the traditional school curriculum assigns very little time to electives, notwithstanding widespread acknowledgment of the benefits to be derived. Since the mid 1970s, as the emphasis on traditional academic subjects has increased, support for electives has decreased. Financial stress in many school districts has added to the neglect. The national concern with improving scores on standardized tests measuring academic achievement in such subjects as science and mathematics has only worsened the scholastic situation of electives.

A small percentage of elective credit is typically used toward high school graduation. Sometimes, elective credit is given for employment off campus or conducting a project for the community, blurring the definitional lines between electives and co-curricular activities. Electives are often perceived as giving students the kinds of experiences not readily available in the more "important" academic subjects. This attitude is unfortunate in terms of the status assigned to electives, but fortunate in terms of the increased flexibility acquired by the formal curriculum.

Electives are usually offered to students in their junior and senior years of high school. For the most part, they are one-semester courses on such topics as urban geography, international relations, and social psychology. For the college-bound, advanced placement courses in science, mathematics, and so forth are also considered electives.

### The Fine Arts

Music and art are often required studies for high school graduation. Still, like electives, they are viewed as having only peripheral importance because they are neither necessary for college entrance nor subjects typically measured on standardized assessments.

To some limited extent, the undervaluation of music and art in the formal curriculum may be compensated for by the fact that both are often supported in co-curricular activities. However, while we have talked positively about the syntactical flexibility of the co-curriculum, its voluntary nature tends to undermine studies involving theory and historical background. Today's co-curriculum emphasizes the doing of music and art—rehearsing for a forthcoming performance, painting a mural for a school wall, and so forth. Co-curricular activities can be meaningful experiences for youngsters and supplement their regular school studies in ways not viable in the traditional classroom. The key word here, however, is "supplement." With so little "official" school time assigned to the fine arts, there is almost nothing to supplement and co-curricular activities literally become the program. This state of affairs may be changing somewhat with more school districts requiring at least one half Carnegie unit in the fine arts for high school graduation, but hardly to a degree that would modify what we think of as the neglect of the fine arts by American schools.

## Music

When music *is* a part of the regular curriculum, developing sensitivity to and appreciation of its basic qualities usually comprises the core of study. This involves gaining a conceptual understanding of melody, rhythm, tone, harmony, tempo, dynamics, style, notation, and so forth. Often, performance skills on an instrument or singing in a group are included. Listening to various kinds of music and being able to identify compositions are found at appropriate levels of difficulty throughout the curriculum. A historical knowledge of America's musical heritage, when included, is usually found at the secondary level. On the other hand, moving rhythmically to music is more typically found at the elementary level. There is a good deal to learn about music, but objectives couched in terms of appreciation and sensitivity are poorly accepted in today's academic world where specific performance objectives are given more credence.

Another challenge confronts the traditional music experiences of students that involves ethnic diversity among the young. Some of our cities already have a majority of former minority groups, and fifty-three of America's 100 largest cities are expected to enroll a *majority* of today's *minorities* early in the twenty-first century. What are the implications for music experiences when, for example, Hispanics and Asians may became majority groups in many of our classrooms?

We are in a difficult situation with respect to the future of instruction in music as we try to ensure that learners will not be cheated out of the inheritance that is a part of their socioethnic backgrounds. We are neglecting traditional American music and its various antecedents, which is certainly a source of concern. Even more serious for an Anglo-dominated society that aspires to achieve a well-balanced pluralism is the neglect of the music of the many varied cultural groups that inhabit its territories.

Music education in the curriculum is generally uneven in this country and depends largely on the preparation and background of teachers. Often no specialist is available for music instruction, especially at the elementary level. Furthermore, the integration of music with the regular academic subjects, although widely recommended,[12] is not really pursued. It is not often, for example, that a history teacher has her students study the beliefs and customs associated with an important event of the past through the songs of the period. Nor are youngsters usually encouraged to explore the scientific aspects of music making. The reality is that the American school has turned its back on music as a significant source of cultural development.

## Art

Art education in the earlier grades places great emphasis on performance activities such as drawing, painting, clay modeling, origami,[13] and the like. As in music education, youngsters are encouraged to express themselves and to become knowledgeable about the basic elements of graphics—line, form, shape, texture, shading, and color. In upper elementary and junior high, children are introduced to perspective, composition, and three dimensional relationships. They are encouraged to analyze their own works and improve their performance with self-evaluation.

At the high school level, there is a distinct shift away from performance. Objectives, in contrast to music, emphasize developing a sensitivity to visual relationships and an appreciation of art's emotional impact and symbolic value. Western art history is often a part of the secondary curriculum, certainly to a far greater degree than is true for music. Comparisons of culturally different art traditions are, however, less frequently pursued.

While music performance grows in popularity throughout the secondary grades, the active involvement in art production diminishes greatly. Children come to school loving to draw and exhibiting a good deal of creativity. By the middle grades, they become more literal and less willing to paint or draw. High school students, unless they are especially talented, tend not to engage in art at all.

As in music education, there is little integration of art studies with other subjects of the curriculum. Life sciences and art, for instance, could be productively integrated but this rarely occurs. Precise drawings of plants and animals could be analyzed for both their scientific value and their aesthetic value. The study of perspective, light, and color could also be viewed both scientifically and artistically. With regard to perspective, mathematics could certainly be integrated with art. Many more examples of integration are possible, and some teachers probably make an effort to utilize integrated studies in their instructional presentations. However, planned integration at the level of curriculum design appears quite unlikely, at least in the near future.

Art education has never gained a solid position in the school's curriculum. Possibly, the inability or unwillingness of artists and art critics to define the nature of their enterprise has interfered with the acceptance of art as a subject in the traditional curriculum.[14] One of the most important questions that a definition would need to confront in terms of the curriculum is whether one studies art for the purpose of communication or for the sake of inner expression.[15] Are art studies undertaken purely for personal expression? Are they a way of understanding one's own cultural heritage? Do they extend one's ability to communicate with others? Without some clear understanding of what we expect youngsters to gain from the study of art, there is little likelihood that its position in the curriculum will improve.

## Health and Physical Education

Health and physical education are also peripheral subjects in the regular curriculum. Unlike the fine arts, they are consistently present in the K–12 curriculum. Neglect for them is really of another kind; it is one of status and having both youngsters and their parents really pay attention to their content. Of course, both health and physical education are seen as important components of a complete fitness program. However, neither are perceived to be contributions to the academic program. They do not generally fulfill college entrance requirements, nor are they included among the subjects tested for achievement.

Since most secondary schools have athletic teams and since gym classes are usually an integral part of the regular curriculum, the degree of neglect tends to be underestimated. It is essential, however, to point out that in the elementary school and in the middle grades, sports and physical activities are often poorly managed. Teachers with little background in sports instruction are frequently responsible for supervising games and other gym or playground activities such as exercise sessions. It is not often that school size and available funds permit the hiring of specialists in health and physical education in the lower grades. Yet, this is the period when the bases for life-long health habits and physical *recreation* skills are laid. Harried teachers under increasing academic pressures and with little professional background must include this duty in an increasing array of responsibilities.

Recess periods in the morning and afternoon are an integral part of most elementary school programs. If properly handled by teachers, such periods can do a great deal to improve children's attitudes toward health and fitness. "Proper handling," of course, pertains to planned, developmentally oriented group activities. Such activities are superior to free play or the random use of such items as swings and slides.

Although physical fitness is often associated with productive human activity, because physical education is tied to the stages of growth and physical development, it is given almost no instructional importance. This, in turn, often means that insufficient resources are assigned to the program and students do not take the program with sufficient seriousness. Well-developed after-school sports programs, however, do compensate for these difficulties, especially for those students who are athletically inclined.

### Physical and Psychological Health

Of key importance is recognition of the point that physical welfare and psychological health are closely associated. Generally speaking, gym classes and various sports are quite adequately scheduled in the curricula of most districts and at the various age levels. However, in all too many of our schools too little in-depth attention is given to the sometimes serious mental and emotional health problems children may have. Closer cooperation and better communication are needed among parents, classroom teachers, and special personnel employed in health and physical education. In the last analysis, the overall physical well-being and configurations of mental emotional health are intimately related.

Everyone involved, from professionals to family members, needs to work together to ensure that pupils are not pushed around either literally or figuratively and that physical health definitely includes careful attention to the role of emotion and mental hygiene in all settings: classrooms, playgrounds, or gymnasiums. The increasingly varied cultural and socioethnic backgrounds of our student body in the United States also make an awareness of the need for continued examination of mental-emotional health significant.

### Health Education

Health studies are often associated with the school's health services or with a particularly urgent community health problem such as AIDS. The school subject is rarely taught as an applied science based on the research of such disciplines as the physical and life sciences. Its content varies widely from instruction about the need for cleanliness, grooming, sleep, and a healthy diet at the elementary level to consumer and environmental health issues at the secondary level. Sexual behavior, drug use and misuse, nutrition, and the like are variously included or not included in the school's curriculum depending on the community's sense of urgency with regard to one or another topic. No one denies the importance of such studies. The subject is simply, and, in our opinion, unfortunately, not viewed as an academic component of the curriculum.

As Donna Lloyld-Kolkin has noted, the health education curriculum in the United States does not even follow a consistent pattern of delivery.[16] Sometimes it is part of the physical education program or a course in family life; sometimes, it is an independent, one-semester high school course. At the elementary level, its instruction is largely dependent on the attitudes and interests of the teacher. It is very frequently no more than an afterthought in the teacher's busy day.

As in the fine arts, there is the possibility of integrating health studies into the core subjects. However, most teachers have insufficient background to achieve such integration on their own. Furthermore, many believe the program should be skill-based as well as content-based.[17] That is, students need to be involved in the active pursuit of health, not merely in discussions about health. Integration into the core subjects would hardly support this kind of active involvement.

The debate between skills and content is really one about the purpose of health studies in the schools. Are we trying to give students a background sufficient so that in future years they will be able to make wise decisions about health, both in the public arena and personally, or are we trying to change their immediate behaviors—for example, teaching them how to avoid AIDS? While the latter goal provides more impetus and support for health studies, it also undermines the academic role the subject might have and its status in the curriculum.

## Considering Possible Futures for Co-Curricular Studies

Because they can become widespread in a school and because they often have an influence on the work of various faculty members, co-curricular offerings confront us with a wide array of questions and issues. Any conclusions that educators seek to reach will be profoundly influenced by the impact of rapid change in an increasingly high-tech school milieu and by social change.

Among the many items shaping *both* curricular and co-curricular futures are the following: Our need for a better prepared work force, our need for a million or more teachers in the coming decade, a national debt of over $3 trillion as of 1991,[18] a growing public school enrollment that will approach 44 million early in the new millennium, and closer business and education relationships.

In view of such considerations, educators must consider questions such as the following:

1. How can the quest for excellence in student performance be supported by co-curricular activities?
2. How shall we strike a proper balance between the current emphasis on control by a school bureaucracy and the role of the teacher as a creative agent in devising curriculum change?
3. How shall we avoid using computer skills as an end in themselves rather than as a means to learning in education?
4. How can we achieve more significant goals in our microtechnological life by coordinating man–machine relationships in co-curricular guidance sessions? Or should computer skills become a part of regular class sessions?
5. How shall we improve the varied quality of students' enrollment in co-curricular work and at the same time avoid a nationwide lockstep in these activities?
6. How can we approach co-curricular activities so as to lessen the problems young people face?
7. How can we increase the contributions of wide-ranging concomitant activities yet retain the integrity of basic classroom learnings?
8. What are ways in which co-curricular work can increase pupils' understandings of an "international world" importance, which many learners have yet to fully sense?
9. How can we reflectively develop a body of desirable human values through our choice of co-curricular work?
10. Do we need to be more authoritative and directive in encouraging students to engage in co-curricular activities?
11. In view of the developments in research pertaining to the deterioration of our global environment, what should be done in the co-curricular realms to ensure a return to a healthy planetary milieu?
12. What information and guidance policies should govern us in helping learners understand and appreciate economic and ethnic groups other than their own?
13. How shall we select co-curricular experiences of the greatest value for a particular student?
14. What shall be the model of the man and woman that we hold up in helping students to participate in co-curricular groups?[19]
15. Assuming that it is possible to design and modify the future, what educational tomorrows should we endeavor to anticipate in the classroom and in concomitant activities?
16. How can ideas and support for co-curricular work best be obtained from parents?

## Concluding Comment

It is not easy to make a succinct concluding comment in regard to creating or cultivating intelligence through interesting and challenging work in the co-curricular field. Part of the difficulty is that extracurricular or co-curricular activities tend to be so varied. Fields of activity vary appreciably from each other as well as from one grade or age level to another and from one child, adolescent, or adult to another. Furthermore, no minimum body of skills or accomplishments must be mastered by *all* learners in special fields of activity at the same time. Their varied maturities, health and physical skills, personal interests, and involvement are all important factors. In addition, ethnicity and family backgrounds bring uniquely personal qualities to any learning situation. We must recognize that many individuals march to the beat of different drummers. Therefore the place and co-curricular role of each individual needs to be considered in an atmosphere free of instructors' preferences and of educational jargon.

A further observation is in order. This is related to the fact that educators must keep the significance of probable futures in mind as co-curricular and elective experiences are explored or modified. Some awareness of the implications of the future is often reflected in such changes as introducing work with computers, videocassettes, and the like. However, a substantial number of changes can and should be made in terms of co-curricular offerings. This is particularly desirable when there is no specific place in the standard curriculum for certain forms of future-related content such as increased technical literacy.[20] Often, emerging future educational needs can be probed or even included by providing concomitant experiences such as introducing the study of global cultures or work designed to meet some of the after-school needs of latch-key children.

We are hopeful that co-curricular and elective learning possibilities will become increasingly varied and may well provide the basis for a state of *transition* in the 1990s as the world becomes increasingly involved in its own remaking. In short, young people will need to learn in schools that have the capacity to reeducate them three or four or even more times as they grow toward their later years and confront a continuing need for new talents and insights for life in a changing world.

At this juncture the words of English philosopher Bertrand Russell may well be kept in mind. His uncanny image of what the twentieth century held for humanity led him to write, "One of the troubles of our age is that habits of thought cannot change as quickly as techniques, with the result that as skill increases, wisdom fades." The challenges of the twenty-first century lend added meaning to Russell's statement as we contemplate curricular and co-curricular changes that anticipate the ways humans will be living in tomorrow's world.

## QUESTIONS FOR DISCUSSION AND REFLECTION

1. In your own words, characterize peripheral studies. Compare peripheral studies and co-curricular activities; explain both the differences and similarities.

2. Why should students study art, music, health, and physical education? There appears to be considerable ambiguity about the purposes of school

study for each of these subjects. What are the sources of ambiguity, and how can the situation be clarified?

3. Some educators would prefer integrating music, art, and health studies into the core subjects of the curriculum rather than having special courses for each. Do you agree? Explain your position completely.

4. Suggest several practical ways of integrating music into the language arts, science, mathematics, and social studies. Do the same for art and health education.

5. Suppose a school district were encountering financial difficulty and had to cut back on its offerings. Would you, as a member of the school board, eliminate the electives, music, art, physical education, or health? Why?

6. Explain and distinguish each of the following terms:
   a. co-curricular activities
   b. extracurricular activities
   c. special activities
   d. paracurriculum

7. What are the advantages of the co-curriculum for the school's formal curriculum? Do you see any disadvantages?

8. Music and art studies are often found in both the regular curriculum and the co-curriculum. Is this advantageous? Would you change how these subjects are currently included among school studies? Specifically, what would you do?

9. In what ways can co-curricular activities contribute to the updating and modification of the curriculum?

## RECOMMENDED READINGS

Arms, Caroline (ed.). *Campus strategies for libraries and electronic information*. Bedford, MA: Digital Press, 1990.

Biklen, Douglas et al. *Schooling and disability*. Chicago, IL: University of Chicago Press, 1989 (88th *Yearbook* of the NSSE), 287 pp.

Boulding, Kenneth E. *Human betterment*. Beverly Hills: Sage Publishing, 1985.

Cappo, Joe. Future scope: Success strategies for the 1990's and beyond. *Futurist*, November 1989, p. 14ff.

Connecticut ASCD. *Supervision and curriculum for the new millennium: Trends shaping our schools*, Arlington, VA: The Association for Supervision and Curriculum Development, 1988.

Didsburg, Howard F. Jr. Beyond mere survival: A report in a poll of Nobel laureates. *Futures Research Quarterly* 6:2, Summer 1990, pp. 7–25.

Hamburg, David A. "Early adolescence: A critical time for interventions in education and health. New York: The Carnegie Corporation, 1989, 16 pp.

Johnson, Julie, et al. Shameful bequests to the next generation. *Time Magazine* 136:15, October 8, 1990, pp. 42–46.

Kubey, Robert, and Mihaly Csikszentmihalyi. *Television and the quality of life: How viewing shapes everyday experience*. Hillsdale, NJ: L. Erlbaum Associates, 1990.

Loraine, John. *Global signposts to the 21st century*. Seattle: University of Washington Press, 1980.

Moreland, Jennifer. *Renaissance: 1300–1600 A.D.: Man, the measure of all things*. Tucson, AZ: Zepher Press, 1987.

Ornstein, Allan C. *Strategies for effective teaching*. New York: Harper and Row, 1990.

Shane, Harold G. Educated foresight for the 1990's *Educational Leadership* 47:7, 1989.

Tifft, Susan. Reading, writing and rhetoric. *Time* 125:7, February 12, 1990, p. 54ff.

Tyler, Ralph W. *Education: Curriculum development and evaluation*. Berkeley, CA: University of California, 1990, 466 pp.

Yaffe, Stephen H. Drama as a teaching tool. *Educational Leadership* 46:6, March 1989, pp. 29–32.

# NOTES

1. O'Neil, J. (1990). Music education: Experts take new look at performance, general music. *Curriculum Update* (June), p. 2.

2. Goodlad, J. L. (1983). Individuality, commonality, and curricular practice. In: Fenstermacher, G. D. and Goodlad, J. L., (eds.) *Individual differences and the common curriculum*. Eighty-second Yearbook of the National Society for the Study of Education. Chicago: University of Chicago Press, p. 305.

3. Perelman, Lewis. (1989). The Learning Revolution. *Chalkboard*. Bloomington, IN: Indiana University Alumni Association, Fall/Winter, p. 12.

4. The term *paracurriculum* appeared in a mimeographed report, *The educational significance of the future*, prepared for the United States Commissioner of Education, Sidney P. Marland, Jr., in 1972. Washington, DC: USOE Contract No. OEC-072-0354. 70 pp. (Later expanded to 116 pp and published by the Phi Delta Kappa Foundation: Bloomington, IN, 1973.)

5. Tifft, Susan. (September 24, 1990). Of, by and for—Whom? (Education Essay). *Time* 136:13, p. 95.

6. For a substantial summary of reform reports, see: Beatrice Gross, B. and Gross, R. (eds.) (1985). *The great school debate: Which way for American education?* New York: Simon and Schuster.

7. Oliva, P. F. (1972). *The secondary school today* (2nd ed.). Scranton, PA: Intext Educational Publishers, pp. 174–175.

8. Dr. Shanker's comments were made in a *U.S. News and World Report* interview, May 26, 1986, p. 57.

9. Howard Gardner, *Frames of mind: The theory of multiple intelligences*. New York: Basic Books, 1983.

10. For a succinct, helpful overview of Gardner's ideas, see: (1984). Human intelligence isn't what we think it is. *U.S. News and World Report* (19 March), pp. 75–76.

11. Hunter, K. (1990). Navigating the Nineties. *The GAO Journal* (U.S. General Accounting Office). (Winter-Spring) 8:12.

12. See, for example: Lemlich, J. E. (1984). *Curriculum and instructional methods for the elementary school*. New York: Macmillan.

13. That is, the art of folding paper decoratively.

14. Gehlbach, R. D. (1990). Art education: Issues in curriculum and research. *Educational Researcher 19*, 7:19–25.

15. *Ibid.*, p. 21.

16. Willis, S. (1990). Health education: A crisis-driven field seeks coherence. *Curriculum Update* (November) 1.

17. *Ibid.*, p. 2.

18. The national debt level by 1991 came to over $12,000 for each American citizen.

19. The increasing change in "mode images" of Americans, see: Cherlin, A. (1990). "The American family in the year 2000," in Edward Cornish, E. (ed.), *The 1990's and beyond*. Bethesda, MD: World Future Society, pp. 23–30.

20. For a useful and succinct review of probable and educationally significant changes in the future, see: Cetron, M. J. and Gayle, M. E. (1990). Educational Renaissance: 43 Trends for U.S. Schools. *The Futurist 24*, 5:33–40.

# 17

# Project Curriculum Design for the Future: Breaking Through

## Introduction

Ordinarily, designing a curriculum is a culturally encapsulated process hindered by an array of political wranglings based on concerns that range from conserving one's job to the scarcity of local and state funds. While teachers are often recognized as having a profound impact on the curriculum as it unfolds in the classroom, they are rarely involved in any extensive revision of the curriculum at the level of design, that is, at the level where they could determine the kinds of studies that would best support their philosophy and vision of the future. If teachers, or, for that matter, the public at large do have the opportunity to work on a curriculum revision, it is almost always in terms of the curriculum as it is currently structured.

The traditional subjects — mathematics, science, social studies, foreign language, and English — are the usual starting points. For the most part, the subjects are viewed as being pedagogical simplifications of such disciplines as chemistry, physics, economics, algebra, French, history, and the like. The extent of study is measured in terms of equal units or credit hours per academic semester.

Typically, this design can be represented by a matrix with the subjects forming the rows and the academic years of study forming the columns. The curriculum for the James Madison High School, proposed by former Secretary of Education, William Bennett, is an example of this standard model. Table 17.1 is based on Bennett's proposal and is representative of the model that is usually presented as the starting point for any revision.

Revision usually means tinkering with the sequencing of topics or the updating of materials. It is highly unlikely that any group of teachers placed on a curric-

**TABLE 17.1** *The "Standard Matrix" Approach to Curriculum Design*

| Subject | First Year | Second Year | Third Year | Fourth Year |
|---|---|---|---|---|
| English | Introductory Literature | American Literature | British Literature | Introductory World Literature |
| Social Studies | Western Civilization | American History | American Democracy | Electives |
| Mathematics | Three years from: Algebra I, Plane and Solid Geometry, Algebra II, Statistics, Pre-Calculus, Calculus | | | |
| Science | Three years from: Astronomy/Geology, Biology, Chemistry and Physics or Principles of Technology | | | |
| Foreign Language | Two Years in a Single Language | | Electives | |
| Physical Education/ Health | Physical Education/ Health 9 | Physical Education/ Health 10 | | |
| Fine Arts | Art History Music History | Electives | | |

ulum revision committee would eliminate foreign languages or algebra in favor of, say, ecology studies, especially since there is probably no one on the committee qualified to teach in that content area.

This chapter attempts to help educators experience designing the overall curriculum from its very beginnings. All the political, social, and economic difficulties of actually engaging in such an activity are, admittedly quite unrealistically, suspended in an effort to free the culturally encapsulated mind from a design that has dominated public education for all of the twentieth century. As the years have passed, this design has become increasingly incapable of meeting the exigencies of a society beleaguered by an extraordinary explosion of knowledge, swiftly changing social circumstances, and a level of future uncertainty never before known.

The reform movement of the 1980s and 1990s reflects the kind of encapsulation that Americans typically exhibit whenever they approach the challenge of improving education. We do not, for example, discuss reconceptualizing the way mathematics is included in the curriculum; rather, suggestions are made for increasing the number of years that the mathematical disciplines are studied or for initiating the study of algebra or geometry earlier in the elementary program. In practice, reform rarely moves beyond the design of the traditional curriculum. There are many available routes for change. For example, we could decide to integrate the study of mathematics into all of the other studies at the junior high level as a way of exciting interest in the subject so that advanced mathematics might be pursued in high school by an increased number of students. In history, we might examine the beginnings of several mathematical disciplines and their historical impact. Students could thus learn introductory mathematics while studying history. In science, mathematics could be studied in terms of its usefulness for understanding the world around us, and in the fine arts it could be pursued as a tool for achieving perspective in drawing or for analyzing the nature of sound in music. Math specialists could work together with the teachers of these other areas to ensure conceptual correctness and real learning in mathematics. If such an overhauling of the math curriculum were authoritatively proposed, the resistance among math educators and even among the public at large would in all likelihood be immediate and insurmountable. While the probability of encountering such resistance is quite high, we also suspect that there would not be much public reflection about what mathematical knowledge is most worthwhile for the young to learn or why mathematics should be studied beyond basic arithmetic.

We are not suggesting that this particular idea be pursued. We are merely offering an example of how we might reconceptualize the curricular design of American education. It is only an incomplete example, for an adequate proposal would need to establish the philosophical bases underlying decisions about what is to be studied; it would state its perspective on how children learn; it would clarify those aspects of our current state of affairs that are addressed by the curriculum; and it would put forth a conception of our children's future and what they are likely to need from education to live well decades hence. Above all, it would take a holistic view of the school's overall curriculum, suggesting the scope and nature of what is to be studied and, when appropriate, the sequence. This chapter engages the reader in the process of curriculum design.

# The Macro and the Micro: Levels of Curriculum Design

## The Macro Level

The macro level of curriculum design is the development or selection of those broad categories of study that are believed to best reflect the aims of education established by society. Taken together, the categories form the macro design of the curriculum. It is rare for educators to actually work at this level of design. This is curriculum planning that goes well beyond a course of study or a subject area; this is curriculum planning at the broadest level of human knowledge where the very structures of school studies are formed and related to each other. The Spencerian question concerning what knowledge is of most worth must necessarily be confronted.

The temptation is to think of macro-level curriculum design as a national, or even international, undertaking. In actuality, even a local school district—or a teacher on his or her own—could engage in macro-level curriculum design because the most pertinent characteristic involves working with the totality of school experiences planned. While this is more likely to occur at a state or national level, even the individual can conceptualize a holistic model of the curriculum. That the teacher or school district is not likely to do so has more to do with social, political, and economic constraints than with an inability to analyze and redesign the macro curriculum.

### The Micro Level

It is not unusual for the curriculum supervisor or the teacher to work on improving a course or even developing a new course within the constraints of the dominant, macro curriculum design. This we call the *micro* level of curriculum design. Even at this level, we hardly move beyond tinkering. Certainly, the study of American history is not likely to be redesigned by excluding chronology or the romanticizing of our traditional heros. Still, it is conceivable that a curriculum committee might try to revise the emphasis of study, which is typically on major American wars, to major American inventions and their influence on subsequent historical events. Our cultural mindsets are so deeply embedded, even this micro-level revision may appear revolutionary. Concentrating on household inventions and their historical impact on the life of Americans is hardly the kind of study we currently associate with a course in American history.

### The Vertical Macro

There is another way of viewing the macro curriculum. Instead of working holistically with all areas of study, only one section is analyzed but for all grade levels. This longitudinal section of the curriculum is called a vertical macro. The comprehensive redesign of a vertical macro such as the K–12 English language arts curriculum can be of great significance for the quality of education. However, without the reconceptualization of the overall macro design, vertical macros tend to be limited to parameters established by the traditional curriculum.

In the very imaginative reforms of the 1960s, a number of vertical macros were objects of redesign. Among these were the "New Math," the "New English," and "Man: A Course of Study." Each of these vertical macros was to fit the school's traditional, macro curriculum across several grade levels. The reasons for failure were numerous. Certainly, one of the problems was the lack of consistency between the redesigned vertical macro and the other vertical macros of the curriculum. While, for example, in "Man: A Course of Study" important and controversial cultural values were to be discussed with scientific objectivity, in the traditional science and history programs students were still memorizing extensively and had little controversial discussion. With the traditional curriculum largely unchanged, the revised vertical macro almost always became the object of negative criticism — it was the part of the curriculum that was seemingly out of step with reality.

In 1991, Civitas, a project to improve civic education in kindergarten through twelfth grade, was undertaken by the Center for Civic Education in California and the Washington-based Council for the Advancement of Citizenship.[1] This three-year collaborative effort is clearly a vertical macro undertaking. The proponents believe that "young people do not know much about their democratic institutions and do not participate in them."[2] The developers have a keen awareness that civic education appears to be low among our national education priorities while history continues its dominance of the social studies. Notwithstanding some very sound preliminary development, we are concerned that the circumstances that undermined past vertical macro revisions are still present and threaten the success of Civitas. However, limited revisions of the school's curriculum may be all that are possible at this time.

### Regaining Control

This chapter establishes a process for originating a broad, macro-level curriculum design without the political and cultural constraints ordinarily present during the revision effort. In a sense, we try to help the reader escape the realities of daily school life and to enter a kind of curricular "cyberspace," an imaginary dimension based on rational analyses and independence from cultural mindsets.

An immensely complex and uncertain future requires the unencapsulation of the school's curriculum design. Revising the vertical macro is a valid undertaking, but it gives only limited support to our goal of viewing the total or macro curriculum with new eyes. We believe that reconceptualizing the curriculum in a holistic fashion, is a necessary experience in our efforts to regain control over the curriculum. Although we realize that the mere development of a differently conceived macro design will not alone undo the current hold that the traditional design has on school study, we believe it is an important first step, especially for professional educators, in the quest for a curriculum that can help us face a future full of conundrums.

## Basic Design Concepts

In undertaking the design of the macro curriculum, certain basic concepts are useful to refer to when ascertaining the completeness and sufficiency of the design for school purposes. This is not to say that every design must meet these concepts in the same way or to the same extent, or that one or more of the concepts could not be ignored if that suited the nature of the design. Rather, these basic concepts should be viewed as useful tools to put together the syntax of a broad but implementable curriculum.

### Scope

The term "scope" refers to the range as well as depth of studies planned. The questions imbedded in this concept are: (1) Does the content chosen refer adequately to the major topics or concerns for this area of study? (2) Are there provisions for a reasonable depth of treatment? Though the questions are posed in an objective fashion, their responses involve a set of value judgments that need to be resolved within the context of one's basic educational philosophy and one's view of learning, learners, and their future.

The concept of scope may be validly applied at the vertical macro and micro levels as well. That is, a set of courses, a single course, or even a brief workshop will typically have a range and depth of content to be studied. Of course, in a truly open curriculum, the range and depth may not be known beforehand but must be allowed to develop as the curriculum unfolds.

## Sequence

The term "sequence" refers to the order of studies encountered by students. Implicit in the concept of sequence is *continuity*. That is, there is a logical ordering of studies so that one topic or activity leads to the next. Sequence also implies *completeness*, that is, a study, once initiated, is not left at a point where more is expected or what has been learned is too little to form a basis for future study.

The questions imbedded in the concept of sequence are: (1) Are the components of study linked together in such a way that the order contributes to learning and understanding? (2) Is an identifiable rationale associated with the order of content? (3) Is the study sufficiently complete to be productive for the student? Again, the questions are more objective than the responses can be. For example, the very nature of a "desirable" order is debatable. Should order follow the interests of individual youngsters or should it reflect the structure of knowledge, say, of a discipline as it functions in the world beyond schooling? Or should it be based on how youngsters learn, moving, say, from what is simple and familiar to what is more difficult and foreign? While it is true that these are not necessarily mutually exclusive conditions, it is equally true that the debates are philosophically grounded, and their resolutions are often eclectic compromises of the kind typically found in American education.

At the macro level, sequencing is most often viewed from the vertical perspective.[3] That is, the term refers to the flow of content from one grade to the next. To the degree that articulation between content areas is planned, there is horizontal sequencing at the macro level as well. There is also horizontal sequencing at the micro level, usually within a single course. Hilda Taba, the well-known curricular theorist, argued that horizontal sequencing is really a question of relating activities, materials, and in-class experiences in one unitary and logical whole, which she called *integration*.[4]

We feel obliged to note here that some curriculum experts, including Taba, would take the position that change is best achieved through revisions at the micro level. In the real world of politics, economic realities, and cultural mindsets, micro curriculum design appears to offer a viable, grass-roots way to achieve change. Experience of the past few decades does not, however, support this view; while there have been numerous efforts to achieve significant curricular change, most at the micro level, successes have been so few that we are hardly aware of them. We are therefore trying to lead the reader into reconceptualizing the broad model. Sequnce, then, needs to be viewed vertically and across all categories of study. The content and activities of each course would be briefly explained with one or two concrete examples. First and foremost is the goal of reconceptualizing the macro framework of the curriculum.

## Articulation

The term "articulation" refers to the planned relationships between different content areas that are simultaneous rather than sequential.[5] Macro curriculum designs based on the articulation of studies in two or more subject areas are called *correlational*. For example, the study of Shakespeare in English is planned to coincide with historical studies of the Elizabethan period as well as with art and music studies of the same period, even though each of the components is being taught separately by different teachers.

The questions inherent in the concept of articulation are: (1) Are opportunities to support the content in one area of the curriculum through the content of another area of the curriculum being pursued? (2) Should such opportunities be pursued? Again, the responses are debatable. For instance, if we articulate the studies of physics and history, do we risk distracting students from a fuller understanding of the true nature of the discipline of physics?

## Balance

As Ronald Doll notes, balance is difficult to attain because what is considered balance in one period is not necessarily accepted as such in another period.[6] Balance involves achieving a satisfactory relationship among competing demands placed on the curriculum. For example, the school is asked to meet students' individual differences as well as to support core studies considered necessary for the society as a whole. The school's curriculum needs to achieve a balance between these two competing demands.

Implicit in the idea of balance are two questions: (1) What are the most important and valid demands being placed on the school's curriculum? (2) Has sufficient attention been paid in the curriculum to all of these demands? Of course, adjectives such as "important," "sufficient," and "valid" are prone to subjectivity and, in this context, are largely dependent on the curriculum worker's educational philosophy. Furthermore, the response to sufficient attention needs to be couched in such conditions as "time allocation" for a given activity, "frequency" of a given item, "centrality" of the item, and so forth.

## Consistency

In our earlier discussion of vertical macros, we referred to the lack of consistency that has sometimes occurred between different subject areas of the curriculum. The expectations for academic behavior built into one segment of the curriculum is incongruous with expectations built into another area of the curriculum, and thus the curriculum is inconsistent. The term "consistency," as it is being used for curriculum design, refers to congruency in the expectations set forth for student performance and in the educational philosophies underlying the different components of the macro curriculum.

Let's use a concrete example. Suppose we require students to read a group of great literary works, say, in a high school English class. We preselect the list of readings, present teacher lectures and written critiques of the works to students, and lead discussions about the most important ideas, giving students an opportunity to express their own views of what they have read. However, instruction usually culminates with an essay-type exam in which students summarize in their own words the analyses and views of others. This same group of students then attends an innovative course in social studies that deals with major current events of the day. The curriculum plan involves having students select those events they consider most important; it requires them to research the events, to exchange their materials with other students, to present critiques of their own, and then, for a final grade, they must produce a fifteen-minute news analysis of the year's major events for broadcast over the local public channel. Certainly, the social studies course sounds exciting, but its view of what comprises important knowledge is fundamentally different from the one underlying the English course, which would have students study works widely accepted as "great" rather than their becoming involved themselves in determining what works merits their attention. The English course requires students who are active listeners but otherwise passive participants; the social studies course requires students who are actively involved in all aspects of the course.

Without some provisions for the kinds of bridges that need to be made if both courses are to coexist in the same macro curriculum, most students would be unprepared for the inconsistencies in the demands made on them. Even if the curriculum is based on an eclectic combining of philosophies, the design must provide ways for students to understand clearly the kinds of shifts that are being expected. The questions embedded in the concept of consistency are: (1) Is there a clear educational philosophy built into the expectations of the curriculum? (2) What provisions are made to develop congruency among expectations that would not otherwise be congruent?

## Basic Design Concepts as Construction Tools

As one engages in making a macro curriculum design, the basic design concepts — scope, sequence, articulation, balance, and consistency — need to be thought of as a set of tools that can be used to help form and tighten the design. As tools, they are not themselves representative of a particular educational philosophy, nor do they represent judgments about the most pressing social problems. They are, rather, open-ended guidelines that help the developer examine certain aspects of the curriculum in a broad and consistent fashion. Each concept, used as a tool, has a set of questions, which we have tried to approximate in our preceding discussion without knowing the specific nature of the curriculum. Presumedly, the designer will make his or her own adaptations. In any case, the following is the set of questions that we have associated with the basic concepts and that we believe need to be used as construction tools during the development phase of the design:

1. Does the content chosen refer adequately to the major topics or concerns for this area of study?
2. Are there provisions for a reasonable depth of treatment?
3. Are the components of study linked together in such a way that the order contributes to learning and understanding?
4. Is an identifiable rationale associated with the order of content?
5. Is the study sufficiently complete to be productive for the student?
6. Are opportunities to support the content in one area of the curriculum through the content of another area of the curriculum being pursued?
7. Should such opportunities be pursued?
8. What are the most important and valid demands being placed on the school's curriculum?
9. Has sufficient attention been paid in the curriculum to all of these demands?
10. Is there a clear educational philosophy built into the expectations of the curriculum?
11. What provisions are made to develop congruency among expectations that would not otherwise be congruent?

## Constructing the Foundations for a New Curriculum Design

### Building a Philosophy

In the latter half of the twentieth century, there has been growing confusion about what we as a society expect from public education and a diminishing sense of confidence that we can redirect our educational efforts toward the requirements and needs of a new millennium. Our inability to reconceptualize the macro design underlying all our curricular efforts has been a crucial factor in our growing discouragement. The basic design concepts described above are useful guidelines only if and when we have first set forth our basic educational philosophy.

As we have discussed throughout this work, the reasons for our failure are numerous and complex. Significant among these has been an unwillingness to view education from a philosophical perspective, that is, to analyze logically and, to the extent possible, objectively, what it is we expect from education. We need to explore first our basic premises about the nature of humankind, its society, and its childhood; about the nature of important knowledge and of the "good" life; and about not only how we learn, but also the most "desirable" ways for knowledge to be acquired.

The taxonomy of educational philosophies that we presented in Chapter 6 and then returned to several times in Part 3 can serve as a starting point for the reader to come to grips with his or her own educational philosophy. Are children primarily social beings who, in paying attention to their own interests, will ultimately support the interests of society, as the progressives would have us believe? Is there a finite quantity of great knowledge that we must strain to discover and teach, as the perennialists would have us believe? Do you find yourself not quite agreeing with any of the philosophical positions described? Do you find your views straddling several positions and call yourself an eclectic, or possibly an "original"?

Developing a new macro curriculum design—as we hope you will do—requires you to come clearly to grips with your own educational philosphy. Only then does it make sense to decide what is appropriate to expect from the schools and what the basic nature of the curriculum ought to be.

### Envisioning the Future

As a society, we have also been reluctant to view our likely futures and to take steps educationally that would help meet, reinforce, or even modify the directions we foresee. But then, having a futures vision without a clear understanding of our philosophical belief system is of little use to educational decision making or the establishment of a new curriculum design. Without a philosophical position, we are reduced to reacting to our short- and long-term future predictions in a haphazard or "gut-level" fashion. Sometimes, we may come out ahead. But in the long run, we will be mostly confused and unable to take control of our schools and education.

In viewing the future, we need to look closely at the present. How well have schools responded to the circumstances of change already a part of our lives? Have they reacted at all to such phenomena as intragenerational disjunctures, experience compression, a rising murder rate that shows no signs of abating, or a family unit that is disintegrating? Should they react and, if so, how?

What are the signs of the future that we can see in the present? What can we predict or forecast about the future that would be of significance to our educational planning? A futures study such as we described in Chapter 9 and pursued somewhat in Chapter 10 would be a useful undertaking even if we ultimately decide that some aspects of the future cannot be profitably dealt with by the schools. Even if a futures study cannot be pursued in depth but only tentatively explored, it offers some basis for examining one's philosophical position in terms of significant new circumstances. For instance, how important, in terms of education, was knowledge of the universe at the turn of the twentieth century? Has that changed significantly a century later? What is its likely importance in the year 2010?

## Selecting the Core Elements

### The Creative Leap

As the reader has surely discerned, we put a great deal of stock in rational analyses. We do, however, acknowledge the limitations of rationality. We can force ourselves to state our positions clearly, to set forth our premises, and to base our generalizations about life and education on them. We can research the future, devise scenarios, undertake Delphi studies, and the like and achieve as well developed a view of the future as is possible — and, still, we do not have the elements of a new curriculum design.

When we have gathered our information and analyzed it carefully, we must then decide the structural elements of the curriculum that most closely correspond to our view of what education ought to be doing. To some extent, this is a form of educated guessing. Would subjects based on the structure of the disciplines comprise core elements of the curriculum best suited to our view of humankind, its society, and its most worthwhile knowledge? Certainly, if we think of the learning of disciplined knowledge as being centrally important to the continued success of American society through science and industry and if we hold this to be part of the "good" life. Disciplines, modified for pedagogical purposes, which is what school subjects today tend to be, are the chief core elements of our current curriculum design. Still, we cannot be sure that applied studies and activities placed in real world settings — let's call these "applications" — would not comprise more effective structural components for the curriculum design, given our philosophical perspective, than do the disciplines. As with subjects based on disciplines, we would need to select the categories of applications to be pursued. In an effort to achieve an adequate range of experiences, we might settle on governmental, commercial, cultural, and communication applications. Under communications, we might include experiences in news broadcasting and public relations.

Viewing the curriculum from different philosophical perspectives, social problems or characteristics of the child might well be adopted as core design elements. If the continued organization of society as a democracy is placed among our foremost "goods" and the active participation of individual members of society in their own governance is viewed as necessary for the survival of democracy, then the social problem is a likely choice. As with applications and disciplines, selecting the kinds of social problems to be pursued is an important aspect of developing the design.

A good deal of imaginative thinking goes into determining the core elements of a curriculum design. For instance, let us say we are developing a child-centered curriculum. We might decide that activities spontaneously pursued by children comprise the *real* core elements of the curriculum and our work is to see that what unfolds during a semester covers an adequate range of experiences. On the other hand, the needs of children everywhere as well as across time could be viewed as a legitimate basis for the core elements of a child-centered curriculum design. A selected ranged of generalized needs could be consistently related to each child's needs. As children grow older, the needs and the comparisons would become more complex and sophisticated as well as more cognizant of future needs. Trying to represent one's philosophical views as well as one's vision of the future through the curriculum design is an imaginative as well as analytical enterprise.

### Modeling the Interrelationships of Core Elements

Not all core elements of the curriculum are of equal importance or treated in the same way. The matrix model based on William Bennett's proposed high school curriculum described above implies an equality in the treatment of subjects that differs primarily in the amount of time assigned to each subject. On the other hand, the generalized needs of the child-centered curriculum would be absolutely misrepresented by a matrix model. The general needs are each related to the individual child's needs. A model showing this relationship would probably be circular, with the child's needs at the center and the general needs represented by a set of arrows all directed toward the center (Figure 17-1).

Models such as the one shown in Figure 17-1 serve as a kind of curriculum shorthand for representing the intended relationships among core elements. If the reader should undertake the project proposed in this chapter, that is, developing a curriculum design at the macro level free of traditional constraints, then a graphical representation of how core elements interrelate will be a useful descriptive tool.

## Putting It All Together

### Step by Step

The following is a summary of the steps we have discussed throughout this chapter. Although we started with an overview of basic design concepts, we recommend their use as guidelines only after an initial selection of the core elements along with their further subdivision into specific areas of study has been made. The development of full-fledged courses is a micro-curricular undertaking and is not necessary in this effort. It would be useful, however, to give examples of the kinds of studies that might be pursued.

We have greatly simplified our undertaking by avoiding significant political

**FIGURE 17-1**  *Circular Model Representing Child-Needs Curricular Design*

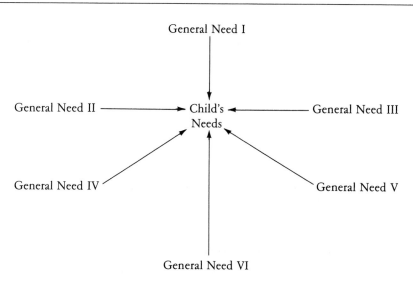

considerations. We start with the development of our educational philosophy. We then engage in an analysis of significant changes in our current way of living and their implications for the curriculum. The next step involves a futures study, possibly, though not necessarily, predicting several alternative futures. We are now at the step of integrating our educational philosophy with our scenarios of present and future conditions. The selection of core design elements would be our heuristic representation of this integration in the structure of our curriculum design. Each core element represents a category for educational pursuit. These categories are general and would need to be further sub-divided into subject areas, a process that is, in this context, our way of approaching scope and sequence.

Having reached this point, the basic design concepts and their eleven associated questions need to be employed not only to assess the work that has been done, but also to extend it so that each question has some form of response possible. Consistency, for example, would need to be addressed not in terms of a set of full-fledged courses, an undertaking well beyond this project, but as a set of intentions built into the relationship of the core elements. Balance and articulation are to be treated similarly. Scope and sequence, of course, are closely allied with the selection and arrangement of the core elements of the design.

Finally, we need to determine in general terms how the curriculum and its results are to be evaluated. There is no denying that the kind of evaluation pursued will have an impact on the ultimate nature of the curriculum. Chapter 8 explores the importance of evaluation for the curriculum and several innovative ways of pursuing evaluation.

*Designing a Course.* We have not yet discussed designing a specific course. Courses intended to become a part of the public school's macro curriculum need to fit the scope and sequence planned for the macro. They also need to relate well to the other components of their vertical macro "family" (e.g., science, social studies) and be appropriately balanced and articulated. Above all, they need to be consistent with the curriculum's underlying philosophy and with the overall design established for the school's curriculum. In sum, the basic design tools need to be employed as the course is being developed. In a "purely rational" world, courses at the micro level would not be designed for the macro curriculum without the macro curriculum being well understood.

In developing a course sequence and selecting activities, how children learn best is an inevitable consideration. If one were to pursue a Piagetian view of cognitive development, it would be important not to introduce activities beyond each child's stage of readiness. There would also be a good deal of emphasis on children's active involvement in the thinking processes as opposed to rote learning of basic facts. On the other hand, a behaviorist's approach to learning would emphasize teacher-based instruction of very small segments or "building blocks" of learning that would establish for children the foundations of some precisely delineated area of knowledge.

Learning theories are particularly important when one sets about putting into practice the broad outline of the curriculum design. The underlying philosophy associated with whatever learning theory is pursued needs to be consistent with the philosophy embedded in the design. A course that selects and arranges its activities in a manner inconsistent with the goals of the broad curriculum is likely to contribute to the failure of the school's efforts.

There is, however, no one way better than any other for applying the various learning theories or, for that matter, the basic design concepts. The selection and sequencing of content within a course or the sequencing of courses within a macro curriculum may be approached quite differently without any one approach being distinctly superior. Articulation, balance, and consistency may be based on rationales that range from those that pursue societal needs to those that set children's developmental needs as a basis for curricular decision making. However, without a clear understanding of the conceptual organization intended for the overall curriculum, decisions about how a course should be organized would be little more than haphazard, albeit "educated," guesses.

### A Final Word

What is to be gained if the project we propose is actually carried out by the reader? We cannot be sure that anything will be gained. But we do believe that engaging in this experience will help liberate the participant from those cultural mindsets that currently dominate our curricular thinking. Once able to think about new macro and vertical macro designs, we can begin to move toward implementing truly effective curriculum change. We may even be ready to face the future of a new millennium.

### QUESTIONS FOR DISCUSSION AND REFLECTION

1. Would a person who claims not to have a set of beliefs about the nature of humankind necessarily be without a philosophy? Please explore your answer in depth.

2. Are people who claim to be of a practical bent and not at all interested in educational philosophy really without an educational philosophy? What philosophical positions might they be expressing without being aware of their positions? What is the importance of being aware of one's philosophical position?

3. Describe each of the basic design concepts and how they may be used in developing a new curriculum design.

4. Discuss at least two significant changes in the present that you think could have a major impact on our future lives. Is there something education could do about or in support of these? Should education do anything?

5. Develop a scenario of probable future school settings. What do you think the impact of these settings are likely to be on the curriculum?

6. Given your own values and background, develop your own ideal scenario of the future.

7. What are your visions for an innovative macro-curricular design? What are the kinds of courses that would fit into your visions?

## NOTES

1. Viadero, D. (1991). 2 groups unveil detailed plan for civic education. *Education Week*, XI: 5, pp. 1, 13.
2. *Ibid.*, p. 13.
3. Taba, H. (1962). *Curriculum development: Theory and practice*. New York: Harcourt Brace Jovanovich.
4. *Ibid.*, pp. 428–429.
5. Oliva, A. (1977). *Curriculum improvement* (2nd ed.). New York: Harper & Row.
6. Doll, R. C. (1990). *Curriculum improvement: Decision making and process*. Boston: Allyn and Bacon.

# BIBLIOGRAPHY

Adler, M.J. (1981). *Six great ideas*. New York: Macmillan Publishing.

Adler, M.J. (1982). *The paideia proposal*. New York: Macmillan Publishing.

Adler, M.J. (1983). *How to speak, how to listen,* New York: MacMillan Publishing.

Adler, M.J. (1983). *Paideia problems and possibilities*. New York: MacMillan Publishing.

Aldridge, B.G. (1988). *Essential changes in secondary science: Scope, sequence and coordination*. Washington, DC: National Science Teachers Association.

Alkin, M.C., Daillak, R.H., and White, P. (1979). *Using evaluations: Does evaluation make a difference?* Beverly Hills, CA: Sage.

Allport, G. (1961). *Patterns and growth in personality*. New York: Holt, Rinehart and Winston.

Altbach, Philip G. et al. (1985). *Excellence in education: Perspectives on policy and practice*. Buffalo: Prometheus Brooks.

American Association for the Advancement of Science (no date, first issued 1990). *Project 2061: Educating for a changing future*. Washington, DC: American Association for the Advancement of Science.

American Council of Learned Societies and the National Council for the Social Studies (1962). *The social studies and the social sciences*. New York: Harcourt, Brace and World.

Applegate, M. (1954). *Helping children write*. Evanston, IL: Row, Peterson and Company.

Arbuthnot, M.H. (1957). *Children and books* (rev. ed.). Chicago: Scott, Foresman.

Arms, C. (ed.) (1990). *Campus strategies for libraries and electronic information*. Bedford, MA: Digital Press.

Babbie, E.R. (1979). *The practice of social research* (2nd ed.). Belmont, CA: Wadsworth.

Barker, P. (ed.) (1988). *Multi-media computer assisted learning*. New York: Nichols Publishing.

Barr, R., Barth, J.L., and Shermis, S.S. (1977). *The nature of the social studies*. Palm Springs, CA: ETC Publications.

Barth, J.L. and Shermis, S. S. (1970). Defining the social studies: An exploration of three traditions. *Social Education, 34*, 2:743–751.

Barth, R.S. (1990). *Improving schools from within*. San Francisco: Jossey-Bass.

Barton, B. and Booth, D. (1990). *Stories in the classroom*. Portsmouth, NH: Heinemann.

Beard, C.A. (1932). *A charter for the social sciences in the schools*. Report of the Commission on the Social Studies, Part I. New York: Charles Scribner's Sons.

Beard, C.A. (1934). *The nature of the social sciences*. New York: Charles Scribner's Sons.

Beauchamp, G.A. (1981). *Curriculum theory.* Itasca, IL: F.E. Peacock. (Revised edition: previous editions published in 1961, 1968, and 1975 by Kagg Press, Wilmette, Illinois.)

Becker, J.M. (1979). The world and the school: A case for world-centered education. *Schooling for a global age* (J.M. Becker, ed.). New York: McGraw–Hill.

Bell, D. (1972). *The coming of the post-industrial society: A venture in social forecasting.* New York: Basic Books.

Bell, D. (1989). The third technological revolution: And its possible socioeconomic consequences. *Dissent, 36,* 2:164–176.

*Benet's reader's encyclopedia* (1987, 3rd ed.), New York: Harper and Brothers.

Bennett, W.J. (1987). *James Madison High School.* Washington, DC: U.S. Department of Education.

Bennett, W.J. (1988). American education: Making it work. Reprinted in *The Chronicle of Higher Education* (May 4):A29–A41.

Bering-Jensen, H. (1990). Teaching all things to all people. *Insight, 6,* 14:49–51.

Bering-Jensen, H. (1990). Tongue tied by foreign languages. *Insight, 6,* 5:46f.

Berman, L.M. (1968). *New priorities in the curriculum.* Columbus, OH: Charles E. Merrill Publishing.

Bernier, N.R. and Williams, J.E. (1973). *Beyond beliefs: Ideological foundations of American education.* Englewood Cliffs, NJ: Prentice-Hall.

Berryman, S.E. (1983). *Who will do science?* New York: Rockefeller Foundation.

Bestor, A. (1953). *Educational wastelands.* Urbana, IL: University of Illinois Press.

Bestor, A. (1956). *The restoration of learning.* New York: Alfred A. Knopf.

Besvinick, S.L. (1988). Twenty years later: Reviving the reforms of the '60s. *Educational Leadership, 46:* (September) 52.

Bettman, O.L. (1987). *The delights of reading.* Boston: David R. Godine, Publisher.

Bhola, H.S. (1989). International literacy year: A summons to action for universal literacy by the year 2000. *Educational Horizons, 67,* 3:52–67.

Biklen, D. et al. (1989). *Schooling and disability.* Chicago: University of Chicago Press (88th *Yearbook* of the NSSE).

Birdwhistell, R.L. (1970). *Kinesics and context.* Philadelphia: University of Pennsylvania Press.

Bishop, A.J. (1990). Mathematical power to the people. *Harvard Educational Review, 60,* 3:357–369.

Bloom, A. (1987). *The closing of the American mind.* New York: Simon and Schuster.

Bobbitt, F. (1912). Elimination of waste in education. *The Elementary School Teacher, 12* (February):268–310.

Bobbitt, F. (1913). The supervision of city schools: Some general principles of management applied to the problems of city school systems. Twelfth Yearbook (NSSE), Part 1.

Bobbitt, F. (1918). *The curriculum.* Boston: Houghton Mifflin.

Bobbitt, F. (1924). *How to make a curriculum.* Boston: Houghton, Mifflin.

Bode, B.H. (1938). *Progressive education at the crossroads.* New York: Newson and Company.

Boorstein, D.G. (1988). The shadow of democracy. *U.S. News and World Report*, (November 14):61.

Borg, W.R. and Gall, M.D. (1989). *Educational research: An introduction.* New York: Longman.

Boulding, K.E. (1966). Nobel Conference Lecture, "The prospects of economic abundance," presented at Gustavus Adolphus College.

Boulding, K.E. (1985). *Human betterment*. Beverly Hills, CA: Sage Publishing.

Bowman, B.T. (1989). Educating language—minority children: Challenges and opportunities. *Phi Delta Kappan, 71*, 2:118–120.

Boyer, E. (1983). *High school*. New York: Harper.

Braddock, R., et al. (1963). *Research in written composition*. Champaign, IL: Nationl Council of Teachers of English.

Brameld, T. (1950). *Patterns of educational philosophy*. Yonkers, NY: World Book.

Brameld, T. (1956). *Toward a reconstructed philosophy of education*. New York: Holt, Rinehart and Winston.

Brandt, R.S. (1989). Preparing today's students for tomorrow's world. *Educational Leadership,* Arlington, VA: The ASCD, (September) 47:1.

Brandt, R.S. (1989). *Conversations with leading educators*. Alexandria, VA: The Association for Supervision and Curriculum Development.

Brandt, R.S. (1990). On learning styles: A conservation with Pat Guild. *Educational Leadership, 48*:2.

Braskamp L.A. and Brown, R.D. (1980). *Utilization of evaluative information*. San Francisco: Jossey-Bass.

Brentano, F. (1874). *Psychology from an empirical standpoint*.

Brewster, J.A., et al (1989). *World resources 1988–89: An assessment of the resource base that supports the global economy*. New York: Basic Books.

Briggs, J. and Peat, D.F. (1989). *Turbulent mirror*. New York: Harper and Row.

Bromley, K.D. (1988). *Language arts: Exploring connections*. Boston: Allyn and Bacon.

Broudy, H.S., Smith, B.O. and Burnett, J.R. (1964). *Democracy and excellence in American secondary education*. Chicago: Rand McNally.

Brown, A. and Weiner, E. (1985). *Supermanaging: How to harness change for personal and organizational success*. New York: Mentor.

Brown, L.R. (1973). *World without borders,* New York: Vintage Books (original copyright 1972).

Brown, L.R., et al, (1984). *The state of the world*. New York: W.W. Norton.

Brown, L.R., et al. (1991). *The state of the world, 1991*. New York: W.W. Norton (published annually).

Bruner, J.S. (1960). *The process of education*. New York: Vintage Books.

Bruner, J.S. (1966). *Toward a theory of instruction*. Cambridge, MA: Harvard University Press.

Bruner, J.S. (1974). "Man: A course of study." Social Studies Curriculum Project. Cambridge, MA: Educational Services Incorporated.

Bryson, B. (1990). *Mother tongue: English and how it got that way*. New York: William Morrow.

Buchler, J. (ed.). (1940). *The philosophy of Peirce—Selected writings*. London: Routledge and Kegan Paul.

Burress, L. (1989). *Battle of the books: Literary censorship in the public schools, 1950–1985*. Metuchen, NJ: Scarecrow Press.

Caffery, J.G. (1955). Auding. *The Review of Educational Research,* (April) *25*:121.

California Department of Education (1987). *History-social science framework*. Sacramento, CA: State Department of Education.

Wagner, C.G. and Fields, D.M. (Nov-Dec., 1989). Future view: The 1990's and beyond. *Futurist, 23*, 6:29–38.

Carnegie Council on Policy Studies in Higher Education (1980). *Three thousand years*. San Francisco: Josey–Bass.

Carrier, C.A. (1983). Note taking research: Implications for the classroom. *Journal of Instructional Development, 6,* 3:19–25.

Carroll, J.M. (1990). The Copernican plan: Restructuring the American high school. *Phi Delta Kappan, 71,* 5:358–365.

Caswell, H.L. and Campbell, D.S. (1935). *Curriculum development.* New York: American Book.

Cawelti, G. (1990). How will schools be different in the 21st century? *ASCD* Report, *10,* 1:4.

Cetron, M.J. (1988). Class of 2000, the good news and the bad news. *The Futurist, 22,* 6:9–15.

Cetron, M.J. and Gayle, M.E. (1990). Educational Renaissance: 43 Trends for U.S. Schools. *The Futurist, 24,* 5:33–40.

Champion, A.G. (1989). *Counterurbanization: The changing pace and nature of population deconcentration.* London: Edward Arnold Co. (Distributed in the U.S. by Routeledge, Chapman, and Hall, New York, NY).

Channing, E. and Hart, A.B. (1903). *Guide to the study of American history.* Boston: Ginn.

Chastain, K. (1989). The ACTFL proficiency guidelines: A selected sample of opinions. *ADFL Bulletin 20,* 2:47–51.

Cheek, E.H. (1989). *Reading for success in elementary schools.* New York: Holt, Rinehart, and Winston.

Chomsky, N. (1965). *Aspects of the theory of syntax.* Cambridge, MA: M.I.T. Press.

Chomsky, N. (1969). *The acquisition of syntax in children from 5 to 10.* Cambridge, MA: M.I.T. Press.

Commission on Excellence in Education (1983). *A nation at risk: The imperatives of educational reform.* Washington, DC: U.S. Government Printing Office.

Commission on Reading (1988). *Becoming a nation of readers: The report of the Commission on Reading.* Champaign, IL: ERIC.

Commission on the Reorganization of Secondary Education (1918). *Cardinal principles of secondary education.* Washington, DC: U.S. Printing Office.

Commission on Standards for School Mathematics (1989). *Curriculum and evaluation standards for school mathematics.* Reston, VA: National Council of Teachers of Mathematics.

Connecticut ASCD. *Supervision and curriculum for the new millennium: Trends shaping our schools.* Arlington, VA: The Association for Supervision and Curriculum Development.

Connolly, P. (ed.). (1989). *Writing to learn mathematics and science.* New York: Teachers College Press.

Corbitt, M.K. (1985). The impact of computing technology on school mathematics: Report of an MCTM conference. *Mathematics Teacher, 77,* 380–381.

Cordes, C. (1990). Big science and technology projects near important milestones in face of federal budget crunch and mounting criticism." *The Chronicle of Higher Education, XXXVII,* 2:23, 28.

Cornett, J.D. and Beckner, W. (1972). *The secondary school curriculum: Content and structure.* Scranton, PA: Intext Educational Publishers.

Cortes, C.E. (1981). The societal curriculum: Implications for multiethnic education. *Education in the 80's: Multiethnic education,* Banks, J.A. (ed.). Washington, DC: National Education Association.

Counts, G.S. (1932). *Dare the schools build a new social order?* New York: John Day.

Cropley, A.J. and Kahl, T.N. (1983). Distance education and distance learning: Some psychological considerations. *Distance Education, 4*, 1:27–39.

Cubberley, E.P. (1947). *Public education in the United States* (rev. ed.). Boston: Houghton Mifflin.

Cubberley, E.P. (1920). *The history of education.* Boston: Houghton Mifflin.

Dale, E. (1969). Things to come. *The News Letter, 34*:4, 1–4.

Dale, E. (1967). What can literature do? *The News Letter,* (November) 32:3, 1–4.

Dalkey, N. and Helmer, O. (1963). An experimental application of the Delphi method to the use of experts. *Management Science, 9*:3.

Darling-Hammond, L. and Hudson, L. (1990). Precollege science and mathematics teachers: Supply, demand, and quality. *Review of research in education, 16* (Courtney B. Cazden, ed.). Washington, DC: American Educational Research Association.

Dawson, M.A. and Zollinger, M. (1957). *Guiding language learning.* Tarrytown-on-Hudson, NY: World Book.

De Garmo, C. (1895). Most pressing problems concerning the elementary course of study. In: *First year book of the National Herbart Society for the Scientific Study of Teaching.* McMurry, C.A. (ed.). 2nd ed., published 1907. Chicago: University of Chicago Press.

de Jouvenel, B. (1967). *The art of conjecture.* New York: Basic Books.

Dede, C. (1989). The evolution of distance learning. Prepared as a Congressional Office of Technology report.

Dede, C. (1989). *The evolution of distance learning: Technology mediated interactive learning.* Houston TX: University of Houston—Clear Lake.

Dewey, J. (1897). My pedagogic creed. *The School Journal, 54*: 3.

Dewey, J. (1900). *The school and society.* Chicago: University of Chicago Press.

Dewey, J. (1902). *The child and the curriculum.* Chicago: University of Chicago Press.

Dewey, J. (1903). *Logical conditions of a scientific treatment of morality.* First published as a pamphlet; this version appears in *John Dewey on education,* Archambault, R.D. (ed.), 1974. Chicago: University of Chicago Press.

Dewey, J. (1916). *Democracy and education.* New York: Macmillan.

Dewey, J. (1917). *Essays in experimental logic.* Chicago: University of Chicago Press.

Dewey, J. (1922). *Human nature and conduct.* New York: Henry Holt.

Dewey, J. (1931). *The way out of educational confusion.* Cambridge, Massachussetts: Harvard University Press.

Dewey, J. (1938). *Experience and education.* The Kappa Delta Pi Lecture Series. New York: Collier Books.

Dewey, J. (1957). *Reconstruction in philosophy,* New York: Beacon Press.

Dickens, C. (1868, correlated edition). *Nicholas Nickleby.* London: Hazell, Watson, and Viney.

Didsburg, H.F., Jr. (1990). Beyond mere survival: A report in a poll of Nobel laureates. *Futures Research Quarterly, 6,* 2:7–25.

DiSilvestro, F.R. (1989). Effective listening in the classroom. *Teaching and learning at Indiana University.* Bloomington, IN: Indiana University Press.

Dodge, S. (1990). Average score on verbal section of 89–90 SAT drops to lowest level since 1980. *The Chronicle of Higher Education*, (September 5):A33–134.

Doll, R.C. (1990). *Curriculum improvement: Decision making and process.* Boston: Allyn and Bacon.

Doll, W.E., Jr. (1989). Complexity in the classroom. *Educational Leadership, 47,* 1:65–70.

Drucker, P. (1969). *The age of discontinuity.* New York: Harper and Row.

Druva, C.A. and Anderson, R.D. (1983). Science teacher characteristics by teacher behavior and student outcome: A meta-analysis of research." *Journal of Research in Science Teaching, 20*, 5:467–479.

Duckworth, E. (1964). The element of surprise in education. In: *Piaget Rediscovered,* R. Ripple and O. Rockcastle (eds.). Ithaca, NY: Cornell University Press, pp. 1–25.

Dunn, A.W., compiler, (1916). *The social studies in secondary education.* Washington, DC: U.S. Government Printing Office.

Early, M.J. (1983). A common curriculum for language and literature. In: *Individual differences and the common curriculum,* Fenster, G.D. and Goodlad, J.L. (eds.). 82nd Yearbook, Part I, National Society for the Study of Education. Chicago: University of Chicago.

Eichinger, J. (1990). Science education in the United States: Are things as bad as the recent IEA report suggests? *School Science and Mathematics, 90*: 1:33–39.

Eisner, E.W. (1979). The use of qualitative forms of evaluation for improving educational practice. *Educational Evaluation and Policy Analysis, 1*, 6:11–19.

Eisner, E.W. (1970). Using professional judgment. In: *Applied strategies for curriculum evaluation,* R. Brandt (ed.). Alexandria, VA: Association for Supervision and Curriculum Development.

Eisner, E.W. (1979). *The educational imagination: On the design and evaluation of school programs.* New York: Macmillan.

Eliot, C.W. (December, 1892). Wherein popular education has failed. *The Forum, 14*:423–424.

Engle, S.H. and Ochoa, A.S. (1988). *Education for democratic citizenship: Decision-making in the social studies.* New York: Teachers College Press.

Engle, S.H. (1963). Thoughts in regard to revision. *Social Education, 27* (April):182–184, 196.

Engle, S.H. (1965). Objectives of the social studies. In: *New challenges in the social studies* (Massialas, B.G. and Smith, F.R., eds.). Belmont, CA: Wadsworth.

Engle, S.H. (1982). "Alan Griffin 1907–1964. " *Journal of Thought, 17*, 3:45–54.

Engle, S.H. and Longstreet, W.S. (1972). *A design for social education in the open classroom.* New York: Harper and Row.

Engle, S.H. and Longstreet, W.S. (1978). Education for a changing society. In: *Improving the human condition: A curricular response to critical realities,* Jelinek, J.J. (ed.). Washington DC: Association for Supervision and Curriculum Development.

Evans, R.W. (1990). "Reconceptualizing social studies for a new millenium," *Louisiana Social Studies Journal XV*, 1:30–33.

Faunce, R. and Bossing, N. (1951). *Developing the core curriculum.* New York: Prentice-Hall.

Feigenbaum, E.A. (1989). Toward the library of the future. *Long range planning,* (February):118–123.

Fey, J.T. (1989). Technology and mathematics education: A survey of recent developments and important problems. *Educational Studies in Mathematics,* (August):233–272.

Fisher, C.J. and Terry, C.A. (1974). *Children's language and the language arts.* New York: McGraw-Hill.

Flesch, R. (1955). *Why Johnny can't read.* New York: Harper and Brothers.

Fort, D.C. (1990). From gifts to talents in science. *Phi Delta Kappan, 71*, 9:664–671.

Fraenkel, J.R. (1973). *Helping students think and value: Strategies for teaching the social studies.* Englewood Cliffs, NJ: Prentice-Hall.

Freire, P. (1970). *Pedagogy of the oppressed.* New York: Herder and Herder.

Frymier, J. (ed.) (1984). *One hundred good schools.* West Lafayette, IN: Kappa Delta Pi.

Frymier, J. (1989). *Programs and services for at-risk students.* Bloomington, IN: Phi Delta Kappa.

Gagne, R.M. (1966). Elementary science: A new scheme of instruction. *Science, 151,* 3708:49–53.

Gagne, R.M. (1970). *The conditions of learning.* New York: Holt, Rinehart and Winston.

Gay, G. (1990). Achieving educational equality through curriculum desegregation. *Phi Delta Kappan, 72*:1.

Gehlbach, R.D. (1990). Art education: Issues in curriculum and research. *Educational Researcher 19,* 7:19–25.

George, C. (1986). 'Success'ful reading and instruction. *Educational Leadership 44,* 3:62–63.

Giese, J.R. and Glade, M.E. under the direction of the original authors, Oliver, D.W. and Newmann, F.M. (1988). *Public issues series.* Boulder, CO: Social Science Education Consortium.

Giltrow, D. (1989). *Distance education.* Washington, DC: Association for Educational Communication and Technology.

Giroux, H.A. (1983). *Ideology, culture, and the process of schooling.* Philadelphia: Temple University Press.

Glasman, N.S. (1984). Student achievement and the school principal. *Educational Evaluation and Policy Analysis, 6,* 3:283–296.

Glatthorn, A.A. (1987). *Curriculum leadership.* Glenview, IL: Scott, Foresman.

Gleick, J. (1987). *Chaos: Making a new science.* New York: Penguin Books.

Goodlad, J.I. (1983). Individuality, commonality, and curricular practice. *Individual differences and the common curriculum,* Fenstermacher, G.D. and Goodlad, J.L. (eds.). Eighty-second Yearbook of the National Society for the Study of Education. Chicago: University of Chicago Press.

Goodlad, J.I. (1984). *A place called school.* New York:McGraw-Hill.

Goodlad, J.I., et al. (1990). *The moral dimensions of teaching.* San Francisco: Jossey-Bass.

Goodlad, J.I. (1990). Studying the education of educators: From conception to findings. *Phi Delta Kappan, 71,* 9:698–701.

Goodman, P. (1964). *Compulsory mis-education.* New York: Horizon Press.

Goodman, P. (1970). *New reformation.* New York: Random House.

Gordon, T. and Helmer, O. (1966). Report on a long-range forecasting study. In: *Social technology* by O. Helmer. New York: Basic Books, 1966, Appendix I.

Gorman, C. et al. (1988). The literary gap. *Time, 132,* 25:56–57.

Grobman, A.B. (1969). *The changing classroom: The role of the Biological Sciences Curriculum Study.* Garden City, NY: Doubleday.

Gross, B. and Gross, R. (eds.). (1985). *The great school debate: Which way for American education?* New York: Simon and Schuster.

Grunwald, P. (October 1990). The new generation of information systems. *Phi Delta Kappan, 72*:113–114..

Haas, J.D. (1988). *Future studies in the K–12 curriculum* (2nd ed.). Denver, CO: Social Science Educational Consortium.

Haas, J.D. (1977). *The era of the new social studies.* Boulder, CO: ERIC Clearinghouse for Social Studies/Social Science Education.

Haber-Schaim, U. (1967, March). The physics course. *Physics Today,* pp. 26–31.

Hall, E.T. (1959). *The silent languagage.* New York: Doubleday.

Hall, E.T. (1966). *The hidden dimension.* New York: Doubleday.

Hall, G.S. (1904). *Adolescence,* New York: D. Appleton.

Hall, G.S. (1904). The contents of children's minds on entering school. *Pedagogical Seminary, 1,* pp. 139–173.

Hamburg, D.A. (1989). *Early adolescence: A critical time for interventions in education and health.* New York: Carnegie Corporation.

Hanna, P.R. (1957). Generalizations and universal values: Their implications for the social studies program. *Social studies in the elementary school,* 56th Yearbook of the National Society for the Study of Education (Part II). Chicago: University of Chicago Press, pp. 27–47.

Harding, L.W. (1953). Influence of commission, committees, and organizations. In: *The American elementary school.* New York: Harper and Brothers, (*XIIIth Yearbook,* The John Dewey Society).

Hardison, O.B., Jr. (1989). *Disappearing through the skylight: Culture and technology in the twentieth century.* New York: Viking.

Harris, P.E. (1937). *The curriculum and cultural change.* New York: D. Appleton-Century.

Hart, E.W. (1985). Is discrete mathematics the new mathematics of the eighties? *Mathematics Teacher,* (May):334–337.

Hatfield, W.W. (1935). *An experience curriculum in English.* Urbana, IL: National Council of Teachers of English.

Heidegger, M. (1949). *Existence and being.* Chicago: Regnery.

Helmer, O. (1966). *Social Technology.* New York: Basic Books.

Henry, N.B. (1960). Introduction. *Rethinking science education* (59th Yearbook, National Society for the Study of Education). Chicago: National Society for the Study of Education.

Herbart, J.F. (1895). *The science of education: Its general principles deduced from its aims* (trans. Felkin, H.M. and Felkin, E.). Boston: D.C. Heath.

Herbart, J.F. (1904). *An introduction to Herbart's science and practice of education* (trans. Feldman, H.M. and Feldman, E.). Boston: D.C. Heath.

Herrick, V.E., Jacobs, L.B. (1955). et al. *Children and the language arts.* Englewood Cliffs, NJ: Prentice-Hall.

Hildreth, G. (1955). *Teaching spelling.* New York: Henry Holt.

Hill, W.F. (1985). *Learning: A survey of psychological interpretations* (4th ed.). New York: Harper and Row.

Hirsch, E.D., Jr. (1987). *Cultural literacy: What every American needs to know.* Boston: Houghton Mifflin.

Holt, J. (1964). *How children fail.* New York: Pitman Publishing.

Holt, J. (1969). *The underachieving school.* New York: Pitman Publishing.

Holt, J. (1970). *What do I do Monday?* New York: E.P. Dutton.

Holt, J. (1972). *Freedom and beyond.* New York: Delta.

Holt, J. (1981). *Teach your own.* New York: Dell.

Hopkins, L.T. (1941). *Interaction: The democratic process.* Boston: D.C. Heath.

Horn, J. (1989). *Supervisor's factomatic,* Englewood Cliffs, NJ: Prentice Hall.

House, E.R. (1979). The objectivity, fairness, and justice of federal evaluation policy as reflected in the follow through evaluation. *Educational Evaluation and Policy Analysis, 1,* 6:28–42.

Gardner, H. (1983). *Frames of mind: The theory of multiple intelligences.* New York: Basic Books.

Huck, C.S., Hopoler, S. and Hickman, J. (1987). *Children's literature in the elementary school* (4th ed.). New York: Holt, Rinehart, and Winston.

(1984). Human intelligence isn't what we think it is. *U.S. News and World Report* (19 March):75–76.

Hunkins, F.P. (1980). *Curriculum development program improvement.* Columbus, OH: Merrill.

Hunter, K. (1990). Navigating the nineties." *The GAO Journal* (U.S. General Accounting Office), (Winter–Spring), 8:12.

Hurd, P.D. (1969). *New directions in teaching secondary school science.* Chicago: Rand McNally.

Husserl, E. (1931). Ideas: General introduction to pure phenomenology (trans.: W.R. Boyce Gibson). New York: Macmillan (first published 1913).

Hutchins, R.M. (1936). *The higher learning in America.* New Haven: Yale University Press.

Inhelder, B. and Piaget, J. (1958). *The growth of logical thinking from childhood to adolescence.* New York: Basic Books.

International Assessment of Educational Progress (1989). *A world of differences: An international assessment of mathematics and science.* Cited in: Baker, C.O. and Ogle, L.T. (1989). *The condition of education,* vol. I. Washington, DC: National Center for Education Statistics.

Jackson, P.W. and Haroutunian-Gordon, S. (1989). *From Socrates to software: The teacher as text and the text as teacher.* The NSSE 89th Yearbook, Part I. Chicago: IL: University of Chicago Press.

James, W. (1907). *Pragmatism: A new name for some old ways of thinking.* Boston: Longmans, Green.

Jarolimek, J. (1984). In search of a scope and sequence for social studies: Report of the National Council for the Social Studies. *Social Education, 48,* 4:250–261.

Jaspers, K. (1951). *Way to wisdom,* (Manheim, R., translator). New Haven, CN: Yale University Press.

Johnson, Julie, et al. (1990). Shameful bequests to the next generation. *Time, 136,* 15:42–46.

Kahn, H. and Weiner, A. (1967). *The year 2000.* New York: Macmillan.

Karplus, R. (1962). The science curriculum—One approach. *Elementary School Journal, 62,* 5:243–252.

Keating, S.K. (1989). A lesson in year-round schools. *Insight, 5,* 26.

Kierkegaard, S. (1940). *Stages on life's way.* Princeton, NJ: Princeton University Press.

Kierkegaard, S. (1941). *Fear and trembling.* Princeton, NJ: Princeton University Press.

Kierkegaard, S. (1944). *Concluding unscientific postscript* (Swenson, P., trans.). Princeton, NJ: Princeton University Press.

Kilpatrick, W.H. (1918). *The project method.* Bulletin, 10th Series, No.3. New York: Teachers College Press.

King, J.A. and Pechman, E.M. (1982). *The process of evaluation use in local school settings* (Final Report, NIE grant 81-0900), ERIC Document No. ED 233 037.

Kliebard, H.M. (1968). The curriculum field in retrospect. *Technology and the curriculum,* Witt, P.F. (ed.). New York: Teachers College Press.

Kliebard, H.M. (1987). *The struggles of the American curriculum: 1893–1958.* New York: Routledge and Kegan Paul.

Kline, M. (1973). *Why Johnny can't add.* New York: St. Martin's Press.

Kohler, W. (1925). *The mentality of apes* (trans.E. Winter). New York: Harcourt Brace Jovanovich.

Kolstad, A. (1989). *Changes in course-taking patterns from 1982–1987.* Washington, DC: Department of Education.

Koul, B.N., (ed.). (1988). *Studies in distance education.* New Delhi: Association of Indian Universities.

Krug, E. (1950). *Curriculum planning.* New York: Harper and Row.

Kubey, R. and Csikszentmihalyi, M. (1990). *Television and the quality of life: How viewing shapes everyday experience.* Hillsdale, NJ: L. Erlbaum Associates, 1990.

Kuhn, T.S. (1970). *The structure of scientific revolutions* (2nd ed., enlarged). Chicago: University of Chicago Press.

Kyle, W.C. (1984). What became of the curriculum development projects of the 1960s? How effective were they? What did we learn from them that will help teachers in today's classroom?" *Research within reach: Science education* (Holdkom, D. and Lutz, P.B., eds.). Washington, DC: National Institute of Education.

Lado, R. (1989). *Teaching English across cultures.* New York: McGraw–Hill.

Lamm, R.D. (1988). Post-crash institutions. *The Futurist, 22,* 4:8–12.

Lampert, M. (1986). Knowing, doing and teaching mathematics. *Cognition and Instruction, 3,* 4:305–342.

Lamy, S.L. (1987). "The definition of a discipline: The objects and methods of analysis in global education." Occasional paper. New York: Global Perspectives in Education.

Langer, J. (1969). *Theories of development.* New York: Holt, Rinehart and Winston.

Langer, S. (1964). *Philosophical sketches.* New York: Mentor Book (original copyright 1962).

Lapham, L.H. (1989). "Notebook: Multiple choice," *Harper's Magazine, 218,* 166:12–16.

Larick, K.T., Jr. and Fisher, J. (1986). Classrooms of the Future: Introducing technology to the schools. *The Futurist,* 10:3.

Lauer, R.M. (1990). Self-knowledge, critical thinking, and community should be the main objectives of general education. *The Chronicle of Higher Education, XXXVI,* 20:B1, B3.

LeCompte, M.D. and Goetz, J.P. (1984). Ethnographic data collection in evaluation research. In: *Ethnography in educational evaluation,* D.M. Fetterman, ed. Beverly Hills, CA: Sage.

Lee, J.M. and Lee, D.W. (1940). *The child and his curriculum.* New York: Appelton-Century.

Lemlich, J.E. (1984). *Curriculum and instructional methods for the elementary school.* New York: Macmillan.

Levy, M.R. (ed.). (1989). The VCR age. In: *Home video and mass communication.* Newbury Park, CA: Sage Publications.

Perelman, L. The learning revolution. In: *Chalkboard.* Bloomington, Indiana University Alumni Association, Fall/Winter, 1989.

Lewis, A.C. (1990). Getting unstuck: Curriculum as a tool of reform. *Phi Delta Kappan, 71,* 7:534–538.

(1988). The literacy gap. *Time, 132,* 25:56–57.

Livingston, D.W. (1983). *Class ideologies and educational futures.* Sussex, England: Falmer Press.

Illich, I. (1971). *Deschooling society.* New York: Harper and Row.

Locke, J. (1690). *An essay concerning human understanding.* New York: Dover Publications, edition published in 1959.

Longstreet, W.S. (1979). Open education—A coming to terms with uncertainty. In: *Lifelong learning: A human agenda,* Overly, N.V. (ed.). Alexandria, VA: Association for Supervision and Curriculum Development.

Longstreet, W.S. (1982). Action research: A paradigm. *Educational Forum, XLVI,* 2:135–158.

Longstreet, W.S. and Shane, H.G. (1979). Educating for the 80's: A transdisciplinary approach. Bloomington, IN: The School of Education, Indiana University. 10 pp. (mimeographed).

Loraine, J. (1980). *Global signposts to the 21st century.* Seattle: University of Washington Press.

MacDonald, J.B. (1971). Curriculum development in relation to social and intellectual systems. In: *The curriculum: Retrospect and prospect,* XVII NSSE Yearbook.

Marland, S.P., Jr. (1972). *The Educational significance of the future,* a mimeographed report prepared for the U.S. Commissioner of Education. Washington, DC: USOE Contract No. OEC-072-0354. Later published by the Phi Delta Kappa Foundation: Bloomington, IN, 1973.

Maslow, A.H. (1962). *Toward a psychology of being.* New York: Van Nostrand.

Mason, R. and Kaye, A. (1989). *Mindweave.* Oxford, England: Pergammon Press.

Maxim, G.W. (1987). *Social studies and the elementary school child,* 3rd ed. Columbus, OH: Merrill Publishing.

Mayhew, K.C. and Edwards, A.C. (1936). *The Dewey school: The laboratory school of the University of Chicago, 1896–1903.* New York: Appleton–Century.

McClure, R.M. (1991) (ed.). *The Curriculum: Retrospect and Prospect.* 70th Yearbook, Pt I, National Society for the Study of Education. Chicago: University of Chicago Press.

McKenna, B. (1989). The new "new math." *On Campus* (April):8, 12.

McLuhan, M. (1964). *Understanding media.* New York: Bantam.

McNeil, J.D. (1990). *Curriculum: A comprehensive introduction.* Glenview, IL: Scott, Foresman/Little, Brown Higher Education.

Meadows, D.H., et al. *The limits to growth.* New York: Universe.

Mecklenburger, J.A. (1990). Educational technology is not enough. *Phi Delta Kappan, 72,* 2.

Mehitens, H. and Bos, H. (1981). *Social history of nineteenth century mathematics.* Boston: Schneider.

Met, M. (1988). Tomorrow's emphasis in foreign language: Proficiency. *Content of the curriculum* (1988 ASCD Yearbook). Alexandria, VA: Association for Supervision and Curriculum Development.

Milofsky, C. (1989). *Testers and testing: The sociology of school psychology.* New Brunswick, NJ: Rutgers University Press.

Mitchell, L.S. (1934). *Young geographers.* New York: John Day.

Mitsakos, C.L. (ed.). (1971). *The family of man: A social studies program.* Newton, MA: Selective Educational Equipment.

Moffett, J. and Wagner, B.J. (1983). *Student-centered language arts and reading, K–13.* Boston: Houghton Mifflin.

Monroe, P. (1940). *Founding of the American public school system.* New York: Macmillan.

Moreland, J. (1987). *Renaissance: 1300–1600 A.D.: Man the measure of all things.* Tucson, AZ: Zepher Press.

Morris, V.C. (1961). *Philosophy and the American school.* Boston: Houghton Mifflin.

Morrison, H.C. (1940). *The curriculum of the common school.* Chicago: University of Chicago Press.

Morrison, J.L. (1986). "Environmental scanning activities in higher education." Unpublished paper presented at the 1986 joint annual meetings of AAHE, AIR, SCUP.

Morrison, J.L. and Held, W.G. (1988). "Developing environmental scanning/forecasting systems to augment community college planning" (proceedings). Paper presented at the Annual Meeting of the Virginia Community Colleges Association, Williamsburg, VA.

Murnane, R.J. (1985, June). "Do effective teachers have common characteristics: Interpreting the quantitative research effort." Paper presented at the National Research Council Conference on Teacher Quality in Science and Mathematics, Washington, DC.

Naisbitt, J. (1982). *Megatrends*. New York: Warner Books.

Naisbitt, J. and Aburdene, P. (1990). *Megatrends 2000*. NewYork: William Morrow.

National Commission on Social Studies in the Schools (1989). *Charting a course: Social studies for the 21st century*. Washington, DC: National Council for the Social Studies.

National Council of Teachers of Mathematics (1989). *Curriculum and evaluation standards for school mathematics*. Reston, VA: Author.

National Education Association (1894). *Report of the Committee of Ten on Secondary School Studies*. Chicago: The American Company.

National Education Association Committee of Fifteen Report (1895). *Addresses and proceedings*. Washington, DC: The Association.

National Education Association Committee of Ten on Secondary School Studies (1893). *Report*. Washington, DC: U.S. Printing Office.

National Research Council (1989). *Everybody counts: A report to the nation on the future of mathematics education*. Washington, DC: National Academy Press.

Neill, A.S. (1960). *Sumerhill*. New York: Hart Publishing.

Newark, T. (1989). *More than stories: The range of children's writing*. Portsmith, NH: Heinemann.

O'Neil, J. (1990). Foreign languages: A new focus on 'proficiency'. *Curriculum Update*. Alexandria, VA: The Association for Supervision and Curriculum Development (January) pp. 1–8.

O'Neil, J. (1990). Music education: Experts take new look at performance, general music. *Curriculum Update*. Alexandria, VA: The Association for Supervision and Curriculum Development (June), p.2.

Oliva, P.F. (1982). *Developing the curriculum*. Boston: Little, Brown.

Oliver, A.I. (1977). *Curriculum improvement* (2nd ed.). New York: Harper and Row.

Ornstein, A.C. (1990). *Strategies for effective teaching*. New York: Harper and Row.

Ornstein, A.C. (1989). The growing nonpublic school movement. *Educational Horizons*, 67, 1:71–74.

Ornstein, A.C. and Hunkins, F.P. (1988). *Curriculum: Foundations, principles, and issues*. Englewood Cliffs, NJ: Prentice Hall.

Parke, B.N. (1989). Educating the gifted and talented: An agenda for the future. *Educational Leadership*, 46, 6:4–5.

Parker, F.W. (1894). *Talks on pedagogics*. New York: John Day (1937 original publication date).

Parker, J.C. and Rubin, L.J. (1966). *Process as content: Curriculum design and the application of knowledge*. Chicago: Rand McNally.

Parker, J.P. (1989). *Instructional strategies for teaching the gifted*. Boston: Allyn and Bacon.

Penick, J.E. and Yaeger, R.W. (1983). The search for excellence in science education. *Phi Delta Kappan* 64:621–623.

Perry, N.J. (1990). Computers come of age in class. *Fortune*, (August):72–78.

Perry, W. (1990). Bernal lecture: Science and education. *School Public Affairs*, 4:65–82.

Petty, W.T. et al. (1989). *Experiences in language*. (5th ed.), Boston: Allyn and Bacon.

Phenix, P.H. (1962). The disciplines as curriculum content. In: Passow, A.H. (ed.). *Curriculum crossroads*. New York: Teachers College Press.

Phenix, P.H. (1962). The uses of the disciplines of curriculum content. *Educational Forum, 26*, 3:273–280.

Piaget, J. (1926). *The language and thought of the child.* Trans. by M. Worden. New York: Harcourt Brace Jovanovich.

Piaget, J. (1968). *The psychology of intelligence.* Trans. by M. Piercy and D.E. Berlyne. Totowa, NJ: Littlefield, Adams. (First published in English by Routledge and Kegan Paul, 1950.)

Platt, J. (1981). The acceleration of evolution. *The Futurist, 15*, 1:20–23.

Plummer, J.T. (1989). Changing values. *The Futurist, 13*, 1:8–13.

Pogrow, S. (1990). A Socratic approach to using computers with at-risk student. *Educational Leadership, 47*, 5:61–66.

Popham, W.J. (1988). *Educational evaluation* (2nd ed.). Englewood Cliffs, NJ: Prentice Hall.

Porter, A. (1989). A curriculum out of balance: The case of elementary school mathematics. *Educational Researcher 18*, 5:9–15.

Postman, N. (1970). The politics of reading. *Harvard Educational Review,* (May):244–252.

Postman, N. (1981). The day our children disappear: Predictions of a media ecologist. *Phi Delta Kappan,* (January):382–386.

Potter, R.L. (1990). *Using reading in the middle school.* Bloomington, IN: Phi Delta Kappa (Fastback).

*Preliminary statements by chairmen of committees of the Commission of the National Education Association on the Reorganization of Secondary Education* (1916). Bulletin 28. Washington, DC: Bureau of Education.

Price, R.A., Hickman, W., and Smith, G. (1965). *Major concepts for the social studies.* Syracuse, NY: Syracuse University Press.

Purves, A.C. (1981). *Reading and literature: American achievement in international perspective.* Urbana, IL: National Council of Teachers of English.

Renner, J.W., Stafford, D.G., and Ragan, W.B. (1979). *Teaching science in the elementary school.* New York: Harper and Row.

Rickover, H. (1963). *American education—A national failure.* New York: E.P. Dutton.

Roberts, P. (1964–66). *The Roberts English series for grades 1 to 12.* New York: Harcourt Brace Jovanovich.

Roberts, D.M. (1980). The impact of electronic calculators on educational performance. *Review of Educational Research, 50*, 71–98.

Robinson, S.R. (1990). *Bringing words to life.* New York: Teachers and Writers Collaborative.

Romberg, T.A. (1983). A common curriculum for mathematics. *Individual differences and the common curriculum,* 82 Yearbook, National Society for the Study of Education. Chicago: University of Chicago Press.

Rosenblatt, L. (1976). *Literature as exploration* (3rd ed.). New York: Noble and Noble (first published 1938).

Rotberg, R.C. (1990). Resources and reality: The participation of minorities in science and engineering education. *Phi Delta Kappan, 71*, 9:672–679.

Rothman, R.C. (1988). Student proficiency in math is 'dismal,' NAEP indicates. *Education Week, VII*, 38:1, 23.

Rothman, R.C. (1989). Social-studies panel shuns call for radical changes. *Education Week* (Sept. 6):9.

Rothman, R.C. (1989). States turn to student performance as new measure of school quality. *Education Week, IX*, 10:1, 12–13.

Rothman, R.C. (1990). Energy Secretary unveils science-education projects. *Education Week, IX*, 36:17.

Rousseau, J.J. (1762). *Emile*. This edition 1979 (trans. Bloom, A.). New York: Basic Books.

Rugg, H.O. (ed.), (1926). The School Curriculum and the Drama of American Life. *Curriculum making: Past and present* (26th NSSE Yearbook, Part I), Bloominton, IL: Public School Publishing.

Rugg, H.O. (ed.), (1927). *The foundations of curriculum making.* Twenty–sixth Yearbook of the National Society for the Study of Education (Part II). Bloomington, IL: Public School Publishing.

Rugg, H.O. (ed.), (1927). *Curriculum making: Past and present.* Twenty–sixth Yearbook of the National Society for the Study of Education (Part I). Bloomington, IL: Public School Publishing.

Rugg, H.O. and Shumaker, A. (1928) *The child-centered school.* New York: World Book.

Sagan, C. (1989). Why we need to understand science. *Parade Magazine* (September 10):6–12.

Saphier, J. et al. (1989). *How to make decisions that stay made.* Alexandria, VA: Association for Supervision and Curriculum Development.

Saylor, J.G. and Alexander, W.M. (1966). *Curriculum planning for better teaching and learning.* New York: Holt, Rinehart and Winston.

Saylor, J.G. and Alexander, W.M. (1974). *Planning curriculum for schools.* New York: Holt, Rinehart and Winston.

Schubert, W.T. (1986). *Curriculum: Perspective, paradigm and possibility,* New York: MacMillan.

Schwab, J.J. (1962). The concept of the structure of a discipline. *The Educational Record, 43*, (July).

Schwab, J.J. (1970). *The practical: A language for curriculum.* Washington, DC: National Education Association.

Scriven, M. (1978). The methodology of evaluation. In: *Curriculum: An introduction to the field,* J.R. Gress and D.E. Purpel, (eds.). Berkeley, CA: McCutchan.

Selsky, J.W. and McCann, J.E. (1984). Social triage: An emergent response to hyperturbulence. *World Future Society Bulletin, 18* (May-June).

Senesch, L. (1965). *Our working world.* Chicago: Science Research Associates.

Shane, H.G. (1967). *Linguistics and the classroom teacher.* Washington, DC: The Association for Supervision and Curriculum Development.

Shane, H.G. (1973). *The educational significance of the future.* Bloomington, IN: Phi Delta Kappa Foundation.

Shane, H.G. (1986). Educated foresight. *Computerworld.* (Special 1000th issue of the publication).

Shane, H.G. (1987). *Teaching and learning in a microelectronic age.* Bloomington, IN: Phi Delta Kappa Foundation.

Shane, H.G. (1989). Educated foresight for the 1990's. *Educational Leadership, 42*, 1:4–6.

Shane, H.G. with Tabler, M.B. (1981). *Educating for a new millennium.* Bloomington, IN: Phi Delta Kappa Educational Foundation.

Shane, H.G. and Yauch, W.A. (1957). *Creative school administration.* New York: Henry Holt.

Shanker, A. (1990). A proposal for using incentives to restructure our public schools. *Phi Delta Kappan, 71*, 5.

Shannon, T.A. (1990). New ideas proposed for educating work force. *School Board News* (October 9).

Shavelson, R.J., Carey, N.B., and Webb, N.M. (1990). Indicators of science achievement: Options for a powerful policy instrument. *Phi Delta Kappan, 71*, 9:692–697.

Shaver, J.P. (1990). Defining (conceptualizing) social studies. *Louisiana Social Studies Journal, XV*, 1:20–24.

Shaver, J.P. and Knight, R.S. (1986). Civics and government in citizenship education. In: *Social studies and social science: A fifty-year perspective*, Wronski, S.P. and Bragaw, D.H. (eds.). Washington, DC: National Council for the Social Studies, Bulletin 78.

Shepherd, G.D. and Ragan, W.B. (1982). *Modern elementary curriculum* (6th ed.). New York: Holt, Rinehart and Winston.

Sherman, H. (1987). A historical perspective in teaching mathematics: Numeration. *WCCI Forum, 1*, 2:38.

Shymansky, J.A., Kyle, W.C., and Alport, J.M. (1982). Research synthesis on the science curriculum projects of the sixties. *Educational Leadership, 40*, 1:63–66.

Skinner, B.F. (1938). *The behavior of organisms: An experimental analysis*. New York: Appleton–Century–Crofts.

Skinner, B.F. (1953). *Science and human behavior.* New York: Macmillan.

Skinner, B.F. (1974). *About behaviorism.* New York: Vintage Books.

Sleeter, C.E. (1990). Staff development for desegregated schooling. *Phi Delta Kappan, 72*, 1:33–40.

Smith, B.O., Stanley, W.O., and Shores, J.H. (1950). *Fundamentals of curriculum development.* New York: Harcourt, Brace and World.

Smith, B.O., Stanley, W.O., and Shores, J.H. (1957). *Fundamentals of curriculum development.* (rev. ed.). New York: Harcourt, Brace and World.

Snow, C.P. (1959). *The two cultures and the scientific revolution.* New York: Cambridge University Press.

Sojka G.A. and Shane, H.G. (1982). John Elfreth Watkins, Jr.: Forgotten genius of forecasting. *The Futurist, 16.*

Sorohan, M.G. (1989). Corporal punishment under fire. *School Board News, 9*, 21:1, 8.

Spencer, H. (1860). *Education: Intellectual, moral, and physical.* New York: D. Appleton.

Spillman, C. and Lutz J. (1986). A writing to read philosophy. *Childhood Education, 62*, 265–267.

Spring, J. (1978). *American education: An introduction to social and political aspects.* New York: Longman.

Steen, L.A. (1989). Teaching mathematics for tomorrow's world. *Educational Leadership, 47*, 1:18–22.

Steen, L.A. (1988). A 'new agenda' for mathematics education. *Education Week, VII*, 3:28, 21.

Stone, L.J. and Church, J. (1957). *Childhood and adolescence.* New York:Random House.

Strickland, D.S. (1990). Emergent literacy: How young children learn to read and write. *Educational Leadership, 47*, 6:18–23.

Strickland, R. (1957). *Language arts in the elementary school* (rev. ed.). Boston: D.C. Heath.

Strong, Richard W., et al. (1990). Thoughtful education: Staff development for the 1990's. *Educational Leadership, 47*, 5:25–29.

Suhor, C. (1988). Content and process in the English curriculum. In: *Content of the curriculum*, Brandt, R.S. (ed.). Washington, DC: Association of Supervision and Curriculum Development.

Suleiman, S. and Crosman, I. (eds.). (1980). *The reader and the text: Essays on audience and interpretation.* Princeton, NJ: Princeton University Press.

Summers, H.G., Jr. (1989). A Bankrupt Military Strategy. *The Atlantic, 263,* 6:33–40.

Suydam, M.N. (1981). *The use of calculators in pre-*college education: Fifth annual state-of-the-art review. Columbus, OH: Calculator Information Center.

Taba, H. (1967). Implementing thinking as an objective in the social studies. In: *Effective thinking in the social studies,* Fair, J. and Shaftel, F. (eds.). 37th Yearbook. Washington, DC: National Council for the Social Studies, pp. 25–50.

Taba, H. (1962). *Curriculum development: Theory and practice.* New York: Harcourt Brace Jovanovich.

The New York Times (1990). Biology teaching under fire by panel. *The Times Picayune* (September 7, 1990), p. A–9.

Thorndike, E.L. (1924). Mental discipline in high school studies. *Journal of Educational Psychology, 15,* 98.

Thorndike, E.L. (1913). *Psychology of learning* (3 vols.). New York: Teachers College Press.

Thorndike, E.L. (1924). Mental discipline in high school studies. *Journal of Educational Psychology, 15* (February).

Tierney, R.J. (1990). Redefining reading comprehension. *Educational Leadership, 47,* 6:37–42.

Tifft, S. (1989). How to tackle school reform. *Time,* (August 14), pp. 46–47.

Tifft, S. (1990). Of, by and for—whom?" (Education Essay). *Time, 136,* 13:95.

Tifft, S. (1990). Reading, writing and rhetoric: Education goals by the year 2000. *Time, 125,* 7.

Toffler, A. (1970). *Future shock.* New York: Random House.

Travers, K.J. and McKnight, C.C. (1985). Mathematics achievement in U.S. schools: Preliminary findings from the second IEA mathematics study. *Phi Delta Kappan, 66:*407–413.

Tryon, R.M. (1935). *The social sciences as school subjects.* Report of the Commission on the Social Studies, Part XI. New York: Charles Scribner's Sons.

Tuckman, B.W. (1979). *Evaluating instructional programs.* Boston: Allyn and Bacon.

Tyler, Ralph W. (1990). *Education: Curriculum development and evaluation.* Berkeley, CA: University of California.

Tyler, R.W. (1971). Curriculum development in the twenties and thirties. In: *The curriculum: Retrospect and prospect,* McClure, R.M. (ed). 70th Yearbook, Part I, National Society for the Study of Education. Chicago: University of Chicago Press, pp. 26–44.

Tyler, R. (1949). *Basic principles of curriculum and instruction.* Chicago: University of Chicago Press.

Tyman, W. (1990). Is TV ruining our children? *Time, 134,* 75:75–76.

U.S. Office of Education (1962). *What high school pupils study.* Washington, DC: U.S. Government Printing Office.

U.S. Department of Education (July 1990). *National goals for education.* Washington, DC: U.S. Department of Education.

U.S. Office of Education (1972). *The educational significance of the future,* Washington, DC: United States Office of Education.

United Way of America (1988). *The future world of work: Looking toward the year 2000.* Alexandria, VA: United Way Mission.

Vandergrift, K.E. (1990). *Children's literature.* Englewood, CO: Libraries Unlimited.

Viadero, D. (1991). 2 groups unveil detailed plan for civic education. *Education Week, XI,* 5:1, 13.

Viadero, D. (1990). Notions of 'literary canon' in schools not valid, report says. *Education Week, X,* 14:5.

W. Wager (1971). *Building the city of man,* New York: Grossman.

Wadsworth, B.J. (1978). *Piaget for the classroom teacher.* New York: Longman.

Wallis, C. (1987). The child-care dilemma. *Time, 129,* 25:54–60.

Watson, J.B. (1913). "Psychology as the behaviorist views it. *Psychological Review,* 20:158–177.

Watson, J.B. (1919). *Psychology from the standpoint of the behaviorist.* Philadelphia: J.B. Lippincott.

Watson, J.B. (1925). *Behaviorism.* New York: Norton.

Watson, J.B. and Raynor, R. (1920). Conditioned emotional reactions. *Journal of Experimental Psychology, 3:*1–14.

Watson, B. (1990). The wired classroom: American education goes on-line," *Phi Delta Kappan, 72,* 2:109–112.

Weber, L. (1971). *The English infant school and informal education.* Englewood Cliffs, NJ: Prentice-Hall, p. 169.

Weinstein, G., and Fantini, M.D. (1970). *Toward humanistic education: A curriculum of affect.* New York: Praeger Publishers.

Weiss, I.R. (1978). *National survey of science, mathematics, and social studies education.* Washington, DC: U.S. Government Printing Office.

Weiss, I.R. (1987). *Report of the 1985–86 National Survey of Science and /mathematics Education.* Research Triangle Park, NC: Research Triangle Institute.

Wesley, E.B. and Wronski, S.P. (1958). *Teaching the social studies: Theory and Practice.* Boston: D.C. Heath.

Wesley, E.B. (1978). Foreword to *The nature of the social studies* (Barr, R., Barth, J.L., and Shermis, S.S., authors). Palm Springs, CA: ETC Publications.

West, E.G. (1984). Are American schools working? Disturbing cost and quality trends. *American Education* (January-February).

West, P. (1990). Academic calls for a panel to oversee efforts to reform science education. *Education Week, X,* 2:5.

West, W. (1990). English secures the melting pot. *Insight,* (May 21), 6:21.

Whaley, C.E. and Whaley, H.F. (1986). *Future images: Futures studies for grades 4 to 12.* Trillium Press, 1986.

Wheatley, G.H., Shumway, R.J., Coburn, T.G., et al. (1979). Calculators in elementary schools. *Arithmetic Teacher, 27,* 18–21.

Whitehead, A.N. (1967). *The aims of education and other essays.* New York: The Free Press (original copyright 1929).

Wiener, A.J. (1967). *The year 2000: A framework for speculation.* New York: MacMillan.

Wild, J. (1959). *The challenge of existentialism.* Bloomington, IN: Indiana University Press.

Willis, S. (1990). Health education: A crisis-driven field seeks coherence. *Curriculum Update,* (November), 1.

Wirszup, I. in testimony before The Task Force on Women, Minorities, and the Handicapped in Science and Technology, Chicago, IL, October 29, 1987.

Witty, P.A., (1949). *Reading in Modern Education.* Boston: D.C. Heath.

Woodward, A. (1986). Taking the teacher out of teaching reading. *The Education Digest, 52,* 4:50–53.

Yaffe, Stephen H. (1989). Drama as a teaching tool. *Educational Leadership, 46,* 6:29–32.

Zais, R.S. (1976). *Curriculum: Principle and foundations.* New York: Thomas Y. Cromwell.

Zinsmeister, K. Growing up scared. *The Atlantic Monthly, 265,* 6:49–66.

# INDEX

*The abbreviations f and t stand for figure and table, respectively.*